Broadcast Journalism

This seventh edition of *Broadcast Journalism* continues its long tradition of covering the basics of broadcasting from gathering news sources, interviewing, putting together a programme, news writing, reporting, editing, working in the studio, conducting live reports and more. The authors have brought the material further up to date with the integration of social media, uses of mobile technology, the emergence of user-generated content and updated examples, illustrations and case studies throughout. End-of-chapter exercises are also included.

New for this edition:

- Updated with new examples, quotes and pictures.

- Restructured with end-of-chapter summaries, exercises for students, notes for tutors, links for further reading and references to invaluable websites and smartphone apps.

- Extended chapters on ethics, responsibilities, interviewing, mobile newsgathering and filming.

- New additional information on coping with reporting traumatic stories, and how news organisations use Twitter and Periscope.

Peter Stewart is an award-winning broadcaster, radio consultant and author with twenty years' experience in media, and works in the BBC's regional news centre in Surrey. His book *Essential Radio Skills* (2006 & 2010) has been widely praised by BBC and commercial radio presenters and managers as being the book on how to present and produce a radio show. He's also updated *Essential Radio Journalism* (formerly *Basic Radio Journalism*) and wrote a weekly column in *The Radio Magazine* from 2001–10. He produced a monthly training newsletter for broadcast journalists from July 2004–7. 'Useful Stuff' had 7,000 subscribers among media professionals around the world.

Ray Alexander has more than 25 years' experience in media management, broadcast journalism, production and presentation, as well as training more than 3,000 journalists and presenters at the BBC and at 15 other broadcasting organisations. He is a specialist in coaching sport professionals and corporate/public sector clients in how to use broadcast techniques in presentations, speeches, interviews and communication in social, live and recorded media.

Broadcast Journalism: Techniques of Radio and Television News
Seventh edition

Peter Stewart and Ray Alexander

Routledge
Taylor & Francis Group

NEW YORK AND LONDON

First published 1988
This edition published 2016 by Routledge
711 Third Avenue, New York, NY 10017

Simultaneously published in the UK
by Routledge
2 Park Square, Milton Park, Abingdon, Oxon OX14 4RN

Routledge is an imprint of the Taylor & Francis Group, an informa business

Library of Congress Cataloging in Publication Data
Names: Stewart, Peter, 1967– | Alexander, Ray, 1954–
Title: Broadcast journalism : techniques of radio and television news /
by Peter Stewart and Ray Alexander.
Description: New York : Routledge, 2016. | Includes bibliographical
references.
Identifiers: LCCN 2015031412
Subjects: LCSH: Broadcast journalism. | Television broadcasting of news. |
Radio broadcasting of news.
Classification: LCC PN4784.B75 S84 2016 | DDC 070.1/9—dc23
LC record available at http://lccn.loc.gov/2015031412

ISBN: 978-1-138-88602-5 (hbk)
ISBN: 978-1-138-88603-2 (pbk)
ISBN: 978-1-315-71512-4 (ebk)

Typeset in ITC Giovanni Std
by Keystroke, Station Road, Codsall, Wolverhampton

Printed and bound in Great Britain by CPI Group (UK) Ltd, Croydon, CR0 4YY
on sustainably sourced paper.

Contents

Part 2   Radio

Part 3   Television

Preface

WHAT THIS BOOK IS ABOUT

By the time a broadcast journalist has written and then said the words 'and as a consequence of fiscal restrictions there is a negative equity situation at this point in time and this will impose impacted difficulties upon consumer habitation choices', the person who hears those words is wondering if it's getting harder to get a place to live. Your audience is gone. Too much to do. So little time. So many choices. Good broadcast journalism – apart from being live at whatever is happening – is also supposed to explain complex subjects rather than leave an audience bored or puzzled.

We know people can construct their own media experiences, seek out desired information instead of waiting for it, participate in chat and get analysis and information about their interests. Or anything they didn't know they didn't know and should be interested in. Live-streaming mobile applications can let anyone broadcast from a phone – but users may act on impulse and can make up their own 'news' out of stolen work, gossip, chatter and rumour. A broadcast journalist would pause and work out the risks and implications.

Even the boundaries between print, broadcasting and internet are so unclear that consumers cannot be sure which medium started out on which legacy. Many newspaper sites are full of video and sound from their own broadcast journalists. Broadcast sites are full of text and stills and comment.

This means the decision-making agenda of broadcast news now fills with on-demand, convergence, digital workflows, user content, interactive data, audience 'engagement', blogging, vlogs and social media.

In general, technology is something you buy – broadcast journalism is something you do.

If you could transport William Caxton, the fifteenth century printer, into a modern newsroom he might say: 'I also love new technology. What do you do with it and what do you put into it?'

This book is about things you do: scripting, finding, judging and processing broadcast news, being in a production or newsroom team, reporting, presenting, interviewing, planning and more. These are not natural or simple skills. As well as the fundamental and traditional skills, editors want to hire potential staff with considerable digital and online literacy and judgement, especially with any specialism on offer.

This new seventh edition is divided into sections on core skills and needs, radio and television. Each chapter also has extra information sources.

This is not a sociological or academic study. The aim has been to produce a comprehensive manual for students, teachers, trainers, lecturers and anyone who wants to learn more about broadcast journalism.

Peter Stewart
Ray Alexander

Acknowledgements

Sincere and grateful thanks to all who have helped with this updated edition, provided wisdom, offered advice, put themselves out, supplied pictures and information. Without that help this book would not have been possible.

Richard Sambrook; Alex Thomson, Channel 4 News; Annick Goerens; Sean McGuire; Caroline Scott; Jamie Angus, Adrian Bhargava and all on the Today programme on BBC Radio 4; Jonna Petterson, The Nobel Foundation; Sarah El-Hadidy, Sky News; Iain Webster, Network Media (NI); Peter Burdin; Peter Davidson; Sarah Fuller; Richard Jarrett; Kevin Steele; Richard Porter, Jeremy Vine, Andrew Harding, Sarah Montague, Fergal Keane and Nick Tarry at BBC; Han Chuan Quee, Faith Yang and Debra Soon, Channel NewsAsia; Richard Satchell, Autocue; Roger Thornton, Quantel; Dalet Digital Media Systems; Kate Ford, Manor Marketing; Neena Dhaun; Bashar Sharaf; Robin Thwaites, Tiffen Europe; Chyronhego; Janet Trewin; Eric May, European Broadcasting Union, Geneva; Peter Berry, Edge Hill University, England; Laura Brander, ITN; Paul Clarke, UTV; Katherine Adams; all at 107.8 Radio Jackie; all at BBC Radio Kent; all at BBC South East Today; Nahed Abou-Zeid and colleagues; Stephanie John at CBS 5 San Francisco; Vin Ray; Neil Everton; Mike Dodd; Judith Melby, CBC; Harry Adcliffe, CBS; Freda Morris, NBC; Malcolm Downing, Pepita Conlon, Paul Cleveland and Ian Henderson, ABC; John Rodman and Annette Bosworth, WEEI; Broadcast News, Canada; Federation of Australian Broadcasters; National Union Of Journalists, UK; Canadian Bureau for International Education; RTNDA Communicator magazine; Sony Broadcast Ltd; Avid; Lucy Pogson at Scope; Valerie Geller; Martina Purdy; Graeme Newell; Julia Paul; Mervin Block; Linda Wray; all at CBS 5 San Francisco; Poynter.org; Dartcenter. org; Jenni Mills; The London Assembly; Andrew Boyd; Ryan Phillips (www.ryan-phillipsphotography.co.uk); Bitly, Inc.

The Seven Habits Of Highly Effective Storytellers is by Deborah Potter and Annie Lang.

Whilst every effort has been made to contact copyright holders, the publisher would like to hear from anyone whose copyright has unwittingly been infringed.

PART

1

The Principles of Broadcast Journalism

CHAPTER 1

Do You Want the Job?

> They made it clear that while you may not become rich doing the work, your life would be exciting.

That is how a school student summed it up for every hopeful broadcast journalist when she wrote about what her tutors told her.

> The adrenalin rush keeps me going. No two days have ever been the same.

. . . and that is what a veteran learned.

Ask yourself these questions. Am I a curious person? Do I ask about people, processes, events and how things happen? Am I sceptical sometimes? Do I like the sound and images of life and human activity: action, conflict, harmony, delight, emotion, surprise or shock? Can I write words that are to be spoken and understood immediately? Can I write in sentences that offer one thought at a time? Words that fit with sound or moving pictures? If not, can I learn to do that? If you start by ticking Yes to these, then you do go for it.

Forget nine to five or the comfort of routines. Then the stress, flogging to meet constant deadlines because the broadcasting world never sleeps, and spending time on dubious blogs and social media trying to work out what's real and what is not and who is real and who is a hoaxer or downright liar. Add some disrupted family life, or your social life is disturbed because you leave the party when you hear that a helicopter has crashed into the Town Hall. Sometimes you spend your time waiting, in case something . . . happens!

But you might think: I can make money in banking, or in a new social media start-up. You could have your own news website from your bedroom – but who wants to see it and why? Can you make money from it? Do you know what to write anyway?

Many wannabe broadcast journalists are aware only of reporters and presenters. But those are not the only jobs.

Your career route could start out with a job with the word 'assistant' or 'trainee' in the title but then later jobs might variously be described as: newsroom producer/script-editor/field producer/multimedia producer/video-journalist/website editor/bureau producer/social media content producer or output producer.

Many broadcast journalists soon decide they prefer production to reporting and take a route which eventually leads to an editor position with people management responsibilities and control over the entire direction and style of a programme, station, channel or network.

Nor should you think it's only the national channels or networks that matter.

Local is often the best place to start a career and some broadcast journalists stay in their home county or region for their entire career – they know everything and everyone in town is a contact. People can get more passionate about local issues than anything that goes on in global affairs.

You need to have:

- curiosity about everything from your town to the entire world – an information-scout. Combined with a good sense of pictures and sound – understanding how they can show or tell a story in a way that words alone may not.

- digital literacy. A sceptical attitude that includes double or triple checking information. You understand the abilities or limitations of mobile devices for news gathering, user-generated content (material the public sends) and, for TV and websites, big data graphics, visuals and maps.

- an understanding that Google or Wikipedia are not faultless research tools but can be used only as a guide to look further and deeper.

- an ability to generate and develop ideas and to check that you have the facts to back them.

- an ability to communicate quickly and clearly in a team, especially with fast-moving online and social media working methods in a newsroom.

- knowledge of media law: defamation, copyright, court reporting, intellectual property. You know that rumour is not news.

Personal qualities include:

- initiative, commitment, self-motivation and energy;
- drive and resilience under pressure;
- flexibility and adaptability to cope with changing priorities;
- ability to be a good editorial all-rounder.

Underpinning all of these are two abilities wired into the minds of everyone in the news operation: writing skills and an understanding of the needs of the audience no matter what technology is used.

Broadcast news is about showing and hearing people and events, or processes that affect people. The best storytelling takes the audience on a journey. It says – come with me and look or listen to this.

For radio and TV they hear it or see it or both, so make sure you get it into their heads first time. If they have to go to the bother of hearing/seeing it two or three times then the words and the content have failed.

You must have sound and picture awareness. The team at BBC's Radio One's news service, Newsbeat, can write, present, report, shoot and edit their own films – that is as well as their regular radio slots.

You must have an ear for sounds that help a story. Not just people talking but the sound of protest or joy, or birds and bells in the distance. You have to have an eye for an image that explains a story – that could be just a few seconds that crystallise a moment, like a kite flying in a clear blue sky in a place where kite-flying was once banned.

Writing for broadcasting is not a natural process in which you just write sentences in your usual way. For The Job you will obviously have done a lot of writing and enjoy the power of words. You read lots of news, books, maybe poetry. Sometimes you read something and you can think: I love that sentence and I wish I'd written a sentence like that. And one day, you will.

FIGURE 1.1

'We don't focus simply on what we do – we also care how we do it' is a typical message for applicants. Demanded skills include: finding stories, crisp, concise fast writing, packaging together scripts, sound, interviews, pictures, maps or graphics, reporting live, reading news, multimedia skills, understanding media law and social media hazards, versioning text to be seen on mobile devices, knowing the names of people in the news, people about to be news, people who once were news, getting wet, hot, cold, being alert at three in the morning or standing outside a building for hours waiting for a moment that will last seconds. The good news? You will never be bored.

AN INTEREST IN WORDS

It should be known to sensible people, if not our pedants, that the language we used a century ago will not be that in common use a century from now. Neither was the language of Chaucer the language of Shakespeare.

The Observer, London, 1899

A nineteenth-century time-traveller would probably understand most of what is said today, but might think a website is a place where spiders are kept as pets. For a job in broadcasting you should have an interest in words to be spoken and their precise meaning. In any language.

To be a broadcast journalist you will start with this interest and over several years you will begin to have discussions with colleagues about single words in a script. It is not uncommon in newsrooms to hear someone say, 'what's another word for . . .?' and hear if anyone replies with either a useful response, or says 'look it up' or just offers some quotation from Ernest Hemingway or George Orwell.

Indeed there can be quite lively discussions among broadcast journalists about the use or meaning of a single word. Someone starts it off and then everyone else joins in a prolonged debate about whether 'that word is unacceptable' or 'what a terrible cliché he used in that report . . .' and another expression once heard was 'any noun can be verbed . . .' as the discussion gets louder. The public get involved as well.

Audience Complaints

Presenter said the priest got fulsome praise for his work with the homeless. I'm sure she means plenty of praise or a lot of praise. This word fulsome means fawning and is often misused.

A cheese cannot be almost unique. Nothing can be. Unique means only one.

Did your reporter just say the team manager was decimated? I mean did he really, really say that?

FIRST PUSH

Being a brilliant world-beater is not enough. You have to prove how good you are: market yourself, persuade them they will miss out if they don't agree to see you. To succeed you need wit, charm, subtlety, persistence – and heaps of talent.

Broadcasting is an industry of many villages. By the time a job is advertised an editor might already have a candidate lined up, so you should make your play before the job ads appear. The candidate-lined-up has to be . . . you.

FIGURE 1.2
Although this is about words to be read rather than spoken, this quotation was printed, framed and placed in a local radio and TV newsroom by the editor. John Ruskin was a nineteenth-century critic and writer. Any new journalist who did not know was told that Mr Ruskin was the man who owned the sandwich shop across the road.

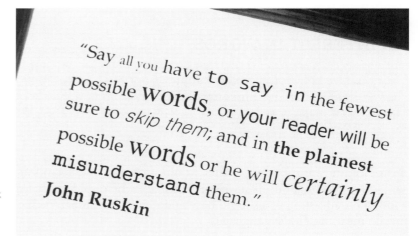

"Say all you have to say in the fewest possible words, or your reader will be sure to skip them; and in the plainest possible words or he will certainly misunderstand them."
John Ruskin

Plan your campaign. Make sure you are easy for potential employers to find. You could send a link to a demonstration recording of your work and curriculum vitae (CV) or resume. A demo could include a three-minute radio bulletin followed by a topical interview of no longer than two and a half minutes and a sparkling news report of the same length. It should be professionally presented and labelled. If you do a television demo make sure it is well lit.

If you send a traditional written and printed CV/resume this should be no more than two pages.

A simple format is best – a kaleidoscope of colours is irritating to read. It should give your name and email, relevant broadcast experience (including any freelance work), broadcast training, educational qualifications, any language skills, brief relevant details of previous employment, whether you hold a driving licence, a note of personal interests, achievements and the names and addresses of two referees.

- Use a clear classic font such as Arial, Times New Roman or Garamond and tailor it to suit each application. So have:
    - at least ten point size and one-inch margins;
    - black on white;
    - consistent spacing;
    - name and contact details on every page.
- Research organisations. Tailor your application or approach whether it is internship, work experience, freelance work or a contract.
- Connect with potential employers who you've met, perhaps at a school careers event, on campus or social networking sites.
- Be aware of what you are putting online that potential employers could see. You need to have what some professionals call a hygienic background, which means a professional and clean social media presence. Be cautious about what you post, including pictures.
- Small and large broadcasters have a culture – find out about that. Some say they have 'values' – find out. Even find out how people dress, or what they talk about. Where do they go nearby outside their buildings for coffee breaks? Go and watch and listen. Sit there as if you are doing something on your laptop. Do not behave like a creepy spy – even though that is what you are doing. This is reasonable job research.

We don't focus simply on what we do – we also care how we do it. Our values and the way we behave are very important to us. Please make sure you've read about our values and behaviours in the document attached below. You'll be asked questions relating to them as part of your application for this role.

Extract from a radio station job description

Presenter of the Radio 4 Today programme, Sarah Montague says:

> Go to your local newspaper, television or radio station and ask if you can make the coffee unpaid, or else generally make yourself useful.
>
> I went to Channel Television and offered to make the coffee for two weeks, and that's how I got into journalism. I can't remember ever making a single cup though, because as soon as I got my foot in the door, I got to go out and cover stories.

The novelist and writer, Robert Harris, went into the profession at 21:

> If you haven't got the nous to talk your way into journalism, then you probably haven't got the nous to be a journalist. To that extent, the profession is self-selecting. Persistence pays. There isn't a conspiracy to keep good people down. And, contrary to popular myth, people are very generous in journalism. Once you've got your foot in the door, you get a lot of help from old lags.

Television and radio presenter Jeremy Vine says you should never take no for an answer and never stop knocking on doors:

> Be very aware of what you want to do – people come into my studio and say they want to work there and it transpires they've never even heard the programme. Volunteer for everything; don't just work for the rota – come in on your days off. We get students who come in to watch the programme, and they're thinking: 'Should I offer to do something?' and we're looking at them, thinking: 'Why haven't they offered?' But it's up to them to force their way on to the programme.

Richard Porter started on a local newspaper and eventually was responsible for the BBC World News channel:

> I started at my local newspaper, the Newbury Weekly News. I answered an advert for a trainee after an unspectacular set of A-level results. That was in 1981 and I spent three years being indentured, and going on block release for my NCTJ proficiency qualification. By 1989 I was working on the Western Daily Press in Bristol.
>
> Then I joined the BBC in Bristol, working on its evening regional Points West programme as a producer. I then worked my way around the BBC in Newcastle, Leeds and Manchester, before joining News 24 when it launched in 1997. In 2001 I became editor of Breakfast News – horrible hours but I've barely ever worked nine to five. Three years later I moved over to BBC World News, and I've spent the past decade working in various roles in the BBC's international news division. I now have responsibility for the BBC World News channel and bbc.com/news (the digital services outside the UK).
>
> My advice now would be to go to do the very best you can academically, but combine that with experience and commitment which you can demonstrate to any employer.

You have to stand out from the crowd, and showing your experience writing for a student newspaper or creating your own website is highly relevant. And it might sound obvious, but make sure you've watched or read or listened to as much output as possible of the organisation you are writing to/applying for. I still remember the interviewer for my first ever BBC job telling me how impressed he was that I had obviously done my homework on them.

A plausible manner, some literary skill and rat-like cunning were the qualities the journalist Nicholas Tomalin identified as the requirements for being a reporter. I copied them down in my application to the BBC. The example Tomalin gave of rat-like cunning was that he had stolen this particular phrase from another journalist, who was also trying to identify the vital qualities. You should not be squeamish, he argued, about pinching other people's ideas, and it is difficult to imagine a journalist who does not do that as a matter of course. It is not simply laziness, it's a matter of practicality: you often have to work at great speed, and waiting for the perfect word, or the brilliant original thought, may not be possible. You have to deliver, and you have to do so quickly.

John Sergeant. From his autobiography *Give Me Ten Seconds*

Everything so far applies whether you are seeking a place on a training scheme, a first job, studying for a broadcast journalism degree, working in print or online journalism but want to go into broadcasting or want to work freelance. For freelance exposure do not limit yourself to Facebook or LinkedIn, although you could set up your own website. Get business cards. Go to networking events about broadcast journalism. Target the right people when you pitch ideas. It should be obvious what specialist programmes about food, cars, travel or science are interested in hearing about.

The work market is crowded but is always getting bigger. Never restrict your aims to familiar broadcasters. There is a lot of cross-media journalism in newspapers and there are journalism-based sites like Digital Spy. There can be paid broadcasting work in the many offices of global organisations, public/press relations agencies, government departments and the bigger charities.

If you already know some freelance journalists ask them for their insight and experience. It is an undeniable truth that getting work also often depends on luck, and on who you know. Tell everyone. Tell your friends. You never know who knows who.

FIGURE 1.3
Neena Dhaun had experience as a reporter and TV presenter at the BBC and GMTV and then joined the Press Association in London as a Video Journalist. 'I don't think I would have done anything differently, because now in my later thirties I see that every stage of my career taught me something.' Courtesy Peter Crane Professional Photography.

Get as much work experience or shadowing as possible. See if internships or graduate schemes are running in the place you want to work and see if you can get onto them. They can be very lucrative once over, for short term contracts or freelance work. I was a Reuters intern very early on and it opened many doors for me and gave me great experience.

The freelance world is saturated – especially in journalism – and even though it can be very lucrative, there is a constant stress of earning enough for a rainy day. I freelanced a lot in my late twenties and always told myself: 'I'm as good as my last shift' so work hard and impress all the time. Enjoy it – it's the only time you get to pick or manage your own time.

Networking helps hugely – places like the Frontline Club and lectures and seminars not only inform your news sense but are a great avenue to meet people in the industry. They're a great night out too if you like that sort of thing.

Believe in yourself. If you don't, no-one will. There's a fine line between realism, arrogance and self-belief, but if you get it right then it will radiate and you will be the sort of person people want to hire and have in their team. Accept there will be a lot of rejection and that you will be working for little or no money to get experience in the beginning. I met so many peers in my early years who moaned about how little journalists earned and the hours we had to do. Of course if you have financial support it helps, but the hours never bothered me. I lived and breathed stories I covered and would never change that. Yes, night shifts and 4 AM starts and weekend working are tough but if you don't do it in your twenties when are you going to do it?

If the unknown excites you, then journalism is for you.

News is a 24 hour, seven day a week beast so if you are a reporter or producer then unsociable hours are what you sign up for. From personal experience the one difference or indeed problem I faced was that I didn't want to work nights, weekends or evenings when I had my children, so I made a conscious choice to do a career shift from journalism into PR. I personally think that when you have children you can't work the way you used to, so pre-empting or accepting that you will be torn between work and home is realistic. That means not covering stories or working in a way that you used to – some might say not getting senior roles because you won't put the unsociable hours in. Some may see that as a problem – I just see it as another life choice.

Neena Dhaun

MULTITASKING

Carrying out multiple tasks are part of all broadcast operations. Everyone new to the business is expected to be able to deliver material on all platforms.

As far as a career is concerned, any separation between radio, television and social media or online news has vanished. Multimedia delivery used to be a trend. Now it is entrenched into all broadcast media. When the newcomer is not expected to work as a part of a team, she's expected to also work independently. It's not a contradiction. Breaking news means all hands to the task, and yet minutes later she has a specific job to do, such as getting maps or graphics into the system without any spelling errors on place names. Channels damage their credibility with even small errors.

That does not mean that a career decision must be based on courses or training with the title 'multimedia' because the reality is that if you study radio or go immediately into television you will find yourself writing for the website anyway and providing video, audio and graphics. Many television news services also provide radio, and vice-versa, so the old silos have broken down.

Look at any broadcast journalism job advertisement anywhere in the world and the description will be very generic, containing sentences which will mention that the job will ask you to work 'flexibly' across the full range of accepted journalistic work, including cross-platform and multimedia.

You will be asked: 'Do you have any story ideas?'

For a story idea for broadcasting you can ask yourself:

- Why is this idea important?
- What's stopping me?
- Is it original, or a new way to look at a traditional subject?
- What would it sound like?
- What would it look like for television – what is there to point a camera at?
- Would my audience be interested in this? Is it something people will talk about?

Ideas that combine sound, pictures, graphics and words must be practical, achievable and original. It means ideas for coverage. Ideas for stories, angles, interviews. It is useful to know what the German writer and scientist Goethe said: 'Everything has been thought of before. The challenge is to rethink it.'

You will be asked for 'story ideas' or how you would fill a news programme on a day when not much seems to be happening. You will be asked this at an initial job interview, but if you do get the trainee position and eventually a fulltime job this will continue.

The editorial meeting, where decisions are made at various times in the day, is the place for original debate and what is often called creative tension. The newcomer may find that modest silence is fine for a few days – but soon will be expected to take part in what is essentially a democratic process where the newcomer can have as good an idea as the veteran. These meetings also aim to test accuracy, impartiality and balance of coverage.

All large news organisations hold a daily meeting of senior news staff and probably a second meeting later in the day. Smaller programme meetings are also held and everyone can contribute. Special meetings may also be held each week to look forward to planned coverage. This is also a chance to get a snapshot of audience feedback from the website.

One weekly planning meeting at a British TV channel was discussing how to do a story about research into the development of a contraceptive pill for men. The usual ideas came along: interview the scientists in Zurich, get pictures of the laboratories, graphics on how they might work.

This went on for five minutes until the editor pointed out that there were six males and four females in the room. He went around all the men and asked each one of them if they would take this pill? It was a simple question, and therefore unavoidable.

Some of the men said they would 'rather' not. That, he told the meeting, could be the story. Will men take it? Nobody had mentioned it. Everyone seemed wired into their technology and conventional methods.

The fact is that what make a good broadcast story is all around you.

One potential trainee travelling to an interview saw some skateboarders and thought nothing more about it. Of course she had a pile of story ideas already researched anyway. When those were exhausted over about 20 minutes she was asked for more – the experienced journalist doing the selection kept pressing onwards and upwards – more, more, more? More ideas please?

'I just saw some skateboarders in a park.'

'So what about skateboarders?'

Then she was thinking fast.

Yet there is a basic technique.

Curiosity again.

You are being asked a question at the assessment or interview – so, you ask yourself the questions.

Why do they enjoy skateboarding? What makes a good location or track? Do they get shouted at by drivers? How much is a skateboard anyway? What are skateboards made from? Is there such a thing as skateboard culture or lifestyle? Do they have their own websites? What sound can I get? What pictures can I get? Could I tape a small camera onto a skateboard to get shots of it moving across the concrete?

And then, you might need a reason to do a report about this. Something that makes it current, new or of present interest. Perhaps the local council wants to ban them, or provide them with a facility, or perhaps there is a big skateboard event coming up. Any of these things are enough to give the audience a reason to be interested.

Just talk and think like this and you can come across as bold and interesting, which is what the editor wants. Which bring us to . . .

INTERVIEWS

Preparation is everything, whether you are applying for a job or work experience. Know your local radio and TV station and study their websites in detail. Be familiar with the output and the style. Know about the area – its industry, people, politics and stories. Be familiar with the news the station is running that day and have constructive comments to make about its output and ideas on how to develop those stories. Just be well briefed in current affairs.

- Be prepared to face news writing or voice tests.

- Be early.

- Obviously, be smartly dressed.

- Be prepared for standard interview questions:

  - Why do you want to work here?

  - What can you offer us – give us examples of what you've done?

  - How much do you use social media? What social media do you use? How would you find someone? Tell me how to find a circus clown?

  - What do you think of the website/channel/station output?

  - What do you see yourself doing in five years?

  - Do you work well in a team? Give an example?

  - What three people anywhere in the world would you love to talk to and what would you ask them?

Be positive, lively, interesting and above all, enthusiastic. Sit up straight. Do not mumble. Do not talk in the Interrogative – raising your voice at the end of sentences as if life is a question.

Factual Interview Questions and Initiative Testing

There can also be direct factual questions that the candidate cannot possibly know the exact answer to but has to demonstrate a journalistic ability to think in a positive or intuitive way.

Sometimes these questions can seem very unusual but they have a point. When this happens you would not be asked – how would you find out how many surgeons there are in Germany? You might be asked, quite bluntly – How many surgeons are there in Germany? Or Glasgow. Or New York. Or Smallville.

You do not whip out your phone and try to access Wikipedia. You do not say, 'I have no idea' or 'How am I supposed to know that?' and you do not sit in silent panic.

The person asking the question probably has no idea how many surgeons there are in Germany. Here the rule about never guessing or making assumptions takes on a new direction.

So you could say, 'I will find out if there is a professional body for surgeons in Germany and ask them' or you could say that you think on average there is probably one surgeon for every 10,000 people and the population of Germany is about

80 million. That may be wrong of course but if you get that far the editor might be happy with your demonstration of initiative.

Simple factual questions for vacancies or trainee posts on local TV/radio stations might be about local issues, politicians, sport teams or club managers, prominent buildings, people or places or recent news events.

One local radio editor in the UK was in the habit of asking a few quick-fire questions like this and then ending with, 'Fine OK. Who is the President of France?' You might have thought you would not be asked that question for work at a small-town local station. Either you know, or if not then a reasonable response would be, 'I don't know, but I can find out very quickly.'

Assessments and Tests

You should be told in advance if there is to be any kind of test, but that does not always happen. Larger broadcasters can have an entire assessment day for many applicants for trainee schemes.

A group task is usual, often about pitching different multiplatform content ideas around a single news event. It means having ideas for television and radio news and the website and social media. There might also be a deadline for all this.

You could be given a pile of statements, figures and quotations. Then a time period – and a word limit – to write a news story and a headline based on that information. To make it just like reality, the assessment people will then start giving you more information which changes the direction of the story you had started writing.

FORMAL AND PRACTICAL TRAINING FOR BROADCAST JOURNALISM

Good training means a chance to do practical things and to make your mistakes before you get anywhere near real airtime.

There is no single or simple route into broadcast journalism. There are many different types of journalism and ways in which journalism skills can be applied but doing a journalism course in higher education can open the first door. This should provide a broad, if not a full, range of journalism skills and the technical skills which are so important in multiplatform journalism and fit into different media organisations.

Courses which are devoted specifically to broadcast journalism are likely to include plenty of writing, radio and TV production, putting programmes together, reporting, video-journalism and IT skills, media law, regulatory and ethical issues.

Undergraduate courses now teach across print, broadcasting and online journalism to match the converged nature of the industry.

In the UK, the Broadcast Journalism Training Council (BJTC) accredits journalism courses and has a multimedia and multiplatform approach across television, radio, online and print.

The website www.bjtc.org.uk includes college courses.

Many large broadcasting organisations – national and regional – have training courses, sponsorship schemes and placement opportunities, but these are constantly changing so check their websites.

Colleges and media organisations often go into schools to give students a chance to make small news items, present news, learn about doing broadcast interviews and offer tips on ways to enter the business.

In the meantime there are some things you could do:

- Enter student journalism awards, at school, college, university or some that are organised by broadcasters. Whether you actually win an award or not, just entering will help you stand out from the crowd.

- Learn shorthand – that is how words can be represented as symbols so they can be written as fast as they are spoken. Many broadcast journalists did not bother with shorthand because they felt they did not need it. It is not essential, but could give you an advantage.

- Consider your Unique Selling Point – your USP. Do you have an unusual talent? Have you done something unusual? What's special about you? It could be something that shows practical skills. Or unusual experiences either in work or just personal. This can make you an interesting candidate and show potential.

- Note phrases you should avoid: 'I am good with people . . . I am enthusiastic . . . people say I'd look good on TV . . .' These are phrases they have heard over and over again. You would probably be better off saying, '. . . people say I'm nosy . . .' Write down your reasons for wanting to go into broadcast journalism, memorise them and consider what follow-up questions you could be asked.

- Make it simple for people to find any work you have done, such as a link to your CV and also any items you have written, or anything you have recorded and/or filmed. You could also have a well-maintained blog. It can be very simple but should have a professional look and with good writing skills on show.

- Be a news junkie. Read, listen and watch. All the time. From local news to global.

- Read poetry. It has an economy with words and an almost musical application to word use. This is useful for broadcast journalists who will use the spoken word in scripting.

FIGURE 1.4

There is no strict rule about needing a university degree to be a broadcast journalist. Editors and those who interview and hire vary in their opinions. Much also depends on the job market at a particular time. Not all top broadcast journalists have a university education. Others have experience or qualifications which are regarded as just as important, as well as an ability to show enthusiasm, flair, imagination, curiosity and a reluctance to accept things at face value. An editor might hire someone who left school at 18 and worked her way up through print and/or local stations or has a popular blog and stories and references to prove it. He might also hire someone with little practical experience but who got a degree in Mandarin and has the right attitude. But both of these people must be literate and numerate and committed.

Never be afraid of rejection. Do not give up. It can take many applications before you find the work to suit you and that matches your skills and experience. Learn from your mistakes. Some broadcasters may never reply. But you cannot be sure that one day, one of them will.

THE HEADLINES

- Be curious and enquiring. About everything: local, national and global.

- Broadcast news is about showing and hearing people and events. You need to write words to be spoken and heard for broadcast, but also to be read for websites.

- Go to networking events about broadcast journalism. Target the right people when you pitch ideas. It's useful to also know what specialist programmes (e.g. food, cars, travel, science, politics, business) are interested in hearing about.

- Good training means a chance to do practical things and to make your mistakes before you get anywhere near real airtime.

QUESTIONS FOR YOU

1. Can you prepare a short demo with a link – can you make it easy for employers to find? That is, not just a written CV but include a three-minute spoken news bulletin, a short interview with someone about a topical subject and a short news report.

2. Get something ready for the question – do you have any story ideas? Ideas that combine sound, pictures, graphics and words must be practical, achievable and original.

3. Do you know your local radio and TV station/channel and websites in detail? If they ask to meet you, be familiar with the news the station is running that day and have constructive comments to make about its output and ideas on how to develop those stories.

4. Have you checked your CV/resume? Try checking your CV by reading it backwards – you are more likely to see writing problems.

OTHER RESOURCES

- From covering letters and applications to coming up with story ideas, industry experts share advice on work experience. Show you've done some research on a broadcaster and know the type of stories they cover and their target audience (http://bit.ly/1CLRNWt).

- Put http://www.poynter.org in your favourites – multiple resources for broadcast journalists on industry and career news, training, discussion and general wisdom.

- Creative Skillset (http://creativeskillset.org) – skills body for the creative industries also working across film, television and radio.

- The website called http://wannabehacks.co.uk says: 'Our mission is to offer an insight into the different routes into journalism.'

- 'Journograds' has job and career links to Sky News, BBC, ITV News, Al Jazeera and others (http://journograds.com/finding-a-job/).

TUTOR NOTES

Try an assessment day exercise and explain why it's useful. Create some raw copy on a story, anything. Get them to re-write it for radio/television. Pen and paper in groups is fine as it gets them active and talking. Then give them new copy that puts a totally new twist on the story and make them re-write it in ten minutes. At ten minutes tell them they are 'on air' and then also ask them what they will do to cover the story, as well as what they will write. Tell them what a job assessor watching groups might think about their responses.

To get into the mood for future job interviews, give them 15 minutes to look at some newspaper (not broadcast news) websites for the main stories of the moment – local, national, global. Then get them away from the screens into small groups to pitch broadcasting ideas for today. Get them all together again and concentrate on what their ideas will look like and sound like. Where do the cameras and microphones go on each idea? What is there to see or hear?

CHAPTER 2

Ethics, Responsibilities and Law

Louis Bloom found a place where he fitted in. An ethically challenged world of broadcast news. He was up all night monitoring police messages, racing to incidents in time to get the chaos. He was part of an old and traditional maxim – *If It Bleeds, It Leads*. An ambulance-chaser immoral freelance who knew that blood and carnage made money, who would even pose bodies at the scene of a car crash to get a better shot. He did worse much later to help his career. He got the ratings material the station needed in a media-obsessed society. The audience knew that what they saw or heard on the news was not a computer game or fantasy.

'I want something that people can't turn away from,' his new boss told him.

The film *Nightcrawler* (2014) is a dark satire on broadcast news and 'Louis' (Jake Gyllenhaal) plays out the situations that some people outside the business believe actually do happen. Broadcast journalists talking about it said it was just another black-humour implausible poke at the business, but a moment later would ponder – of course could things like that *possibly* go on? Somewhere? But broadcasting has always been a ripe mother-ship for satirical fiction. Louis is just a cheaper version of 'Richard Thornburg' (William Atherton), the TV reporter character in *Die Hard* who thinks every story is there just to promote himself, even if it endangers lives.

Broadcast journalists are being held to high standards of ethics by their editors and owners or regulators. Ethics are now heavily considered in the reporting of news. Newsrooms do think carefully about suspicious websites, bad taste, offending the audience, upsetting the bereaved, the vulnerable or children, victims of crime or disaster, showing how a scam or crime can be carried out, showing the moment of death in accidents or war and terrorist executions.

There used to be a consensus that if you see it or hear it happening, then it must carry more authority than the written word alone. That is a version of twentieth-century expressions like: The Camera Never Lies, or A Picture Tells A Thousand Words. This did not prepare us for a world of image and media software which – in dishonest hands – will allow a picture or sound to confuse, tinker with truth, or be just another fiction.

The primary rules of honesty in broadcast journalism are simple, but simple does not always makes everything obvious:

- Do not misrepresent people or events with editing.

- Do not fake pictures or distort sound or use sound effects that can deceive or mislead.

- Do not get hoaxed but if you do, then just admit it.

But even before that, the first things most journalists learn on a college degree or on the job are:

Facts Are Sacred, Comment Is Free and *When In Doubt, Leave Out.*

Information, facts and comment come at the broadcast journalist from many directions – social media, emergency services, on video, audio and online news releases, on global wire services and above all from people just telling you and/or sending in their pictures from their phones. Then various websites, vlogs and blogs, which should be treated with the same caution as other sources.

If the broadcast journalist is also using social media on behalf of his employer to ask questions, find people or tell the audience something, he should first ask: 'Is it OK for 50,000 strangers to read this?'

We have done training in social media and I have commissioned one of the best social media trainers I know to come in again in the new year to do a few new sessions. The field is constantly changing and we take it extremely seriously. I personally monitor many of the tweets by our people in news and current affairs to satisfy myself that they are not putting anything out there which in any way questions the impartiality of what they do.

Kevin Bakhurst. Managing Director, News and Current Affairs, RTE

It is a difficult issue. We are putting in place new guidelines and we are adamant that people cannot tweet opinions and should display impartiality in what they do in social media. We are clear with our people about that.

Noel Curran. Director-General, RTE
(Giving evidence to a committee of the Irish Parliament; http://bit.ly/1MKo44X)

Honesty in broadcasting is not just broadcasting what is known to be true, but legally and provably true and impartial. What is ethical is more complicated and this chapter can do no more than explain, for practical reasons, why it is important to understand the role of the broadcast journalist in any society and at any point in time.

Ethics comes up more and more in editorial decisions now, whether they are decision-making meetings, or just conversations among journalists. This is often driven by the changing ways in which people can get information.

News is everywhere and the increasing speed of news and comment means an understanding of the demands of the law, of regulators and in compliance.

Leveson Report (UK) extract

Compliance at ITN is the responsibility of the Head of Compliance, John Battle. Mr Battle is author of the Compliance Manual, first published in July 2004. The Compliance Manual sets out 'the industry regulations that affect news reporting, the main areas of laws affecting journalism such as libel, copyright, privacy and contempt of court and internal ITN standards and procedures'.

This manual is the centrepiece guidance issued to staff at ITN and forms the basis of ITN staff training.

ITN recently reviewed its Compliance Manual in light of allegations of phone hacking, as well as allegations of payments to public officials by journalists and others working at the NoTW.* Although Jim Gray, Editor of Channel 4 News, told the Inquiry that the review of the Compliance Manual was regular procedure, he explained that additionally 'as part of the process triggered by this Inquiry, we have held an independent external Inquiry into ITN's journalistic practices and some the [sic] findings of that will feature in the new Compliance Manual.'

Mr Battle also gave evidence to this effect, stating that: 'It's fair to say that as a grown-up and professional organisation, we'd have to have on board the Inquiry and what's been discussed here and within the news. There have been some tightening up procedures, tilting, as you said this morning, sir, towards better regulation. I don't think there's been substantive changes as a result of this Inquiry but it also includes a lot of updates on other issues, such as Twittering in court or online posting, so it's an update.'

An Inquiry into the Culture, Practices and Ethics of the Press. Lord Justice Leveson. November 2012. Volume I. Pages 162/163 (http://bit.ly/1GRH0d2)

* News of the World

REGULATION AND AUDIENCE ATTITUDES

Most regulation aims to ensure decency, fairness and impartiality and to support the basic democratic concept of freedom of expression. Other aims are to prevent harm to viewers and listeners and protect children.

Because as social attitudes change, regulations can change. What might have been acceptable just 20 years ago may be less so now.

Sometimes news channels put a warning in the introduction of a story. Editors might consider a particular story to be unsuitable for young children, or the story or interview that is still worth telling or showing might be distressing. The script that says 'some viewers/listeners may find parts of this report upsetting . . .' can also mean that editors and journalists have spent a long time considering whether to carry the story at all.

Suicides were once rarely covered. But the BBC's Editorial Guidelines for example state:

> The sensitive use of language is also important. Suicide was decriminalised in 1961 and since then the use of the term 'commit' is considered offensive

by some people. 'Take one's life' or 'kill oneself' are preferable alternatives. We should consider whether a helpline or support material should be provided, or linked to, when our output deals with such issues. The Samaritans are usually willing to be consulted by programme makers and other content producers about the portrayal of suicide and have published their own guidance for broadcasters.

The Poynter Institute has a line-by-line study of a television news item about a ten-year old boy at: https://vimeo.com/23456945 (http://aimfortheheart.com/ethics-guidelines-written-by-al/).

As a general guide many broadcast journalists should understand that perceptions of taste and decency fit into the moral climate of the times in which we live. It also matters what country the broadcaster is based in. There is a Where and When principle with matters of taste and decency.

These days a news item in Britain showing extreme cruelty to animals would probably dominate social media. Such an item may have less interest in other countries.

Centuries ago it was considered an interesting day out to go and watch a hanging. At London's dockside you could see the bodies of convicted pirates lying in cages by the river. In Belfast in the 1970s a series of bombs left many people maimed or injured. Local TV sometimes showed body parts being put into bags, although not usually in a close-up shot. It is unlikely that broadcasters would show such shots today, although it is not possible to predict that they never would.

A former editor of ITN, Sir David Nicholas, put it like this: 'You've got to tread this fine line of not bowdlerizing it to the extent that it's all so pleasant. It's a matter of degree, suggestion and hint. Don't dwell. The difference between getting it right and getting it wrong may be about a second.'

SOME LEGAL HEADLINES. BROADCASTING ISSUES – TALKING ON AIR IS PUBLISHING

Every journalist has to be part lawyer now and in this text we can only highlight the main issues. Detailed study of media law is needed.

But above all remember – never say something on air that you would never dare to write in print.

The biggest legal trap facing many broadcast journalists around the world is the law of defamation. Defamation is divided into libel and slander. Slander is a spoken statement and libel is a published statement. If something is spoken on air then it is a published statement and is therefore categorised as libel. This differs in detail from country to country but is quite universal in its purpose, which is to protect reputations.

Everyone – not just the rich and famous – has a reputation and could suffer harm or loss if it is damaged. In Britain, a libel traditionally is defined as the publishing of anything that would:

Expose a person to hatred, ridicule or contempt, cause him to be shunned and avoided, lower him in the estimation of right thinking members of society generally, or disparage him in his office, profession or trade.

British libel laws also hold a journalist responsible for broadcasting a libellous statement made by somebody else. So if a business owner gave you some dirt on the owner of a competitor, you could be sued for libel for putting those words on air. Can you prove that what that businessman told you was true? Never mind that 'he told me . . . I only quoted him' – can *you prove* it is true?

Yet without some protection investigative and public interest journalism and court reporting would be impossible. In Britain, the main defences are complex and provide a lucrative field for lawyers. In essence they are that the report was true, or offered a reasonable opinion based on facts that were true, or that it was protected in law by Privilege, which covers reporting of parliament, courts and public meetings and in most cases those meetings include news conferences.

The other defence is Fair Comment, which enables journalists to write about films, books, plays or even a new model of car. But for a comment to enjoy this defence, the view must be honestly held. Legally this means absence of Malice. In law, Malice means an improper motive, rather than being plain nasty in a review. If you've been bribed by a theatre owner to go on air and criticise a new play at a different theatre then your opinion may not be honestly held, and you could lose that defence.

The defence of truth – Justification is the legal word – means that the allegation is true, and you were justified in publishing it.

There is also some defence for live broadcasting – when somebody says something that maybe he or she should not have, and a libel writ arrives. The broadcaster needs to have taken all reasonable care and must not be the author of the remarks. Lawyers urge the immediate distancing from the remarks and then move on swiftly.

Media trainer Sarah Fuller says: 'The reasonable care bit means the person involved doesn't have a propensity for uttering libellous remarks in that subject area – or any other really – and that we could not have predicted the libel.'

In addition to the traps of libel there are laws governing court reporting, confidentiality, copyright, race relations, official secrets and other areas, which make reporting a minefield for the ignorant. Safe and successful reporting requires a thorough working knowledge of the law that allows journalists to push reporting to the brink of legality without falling into the chasm.

Broadcast journalists working on potentially contentious stories must keep detailed and organised notes. Do not delete emails. Keep them in a file/folder with names and dates and copy them to backup memory. Keep written, audio or video material that you might need to support what you broadcast.

46% of 18- to 24-year-olds are unaware they can be sued for defamation if they tweet an unsubstantiated rumour about someone, according to research for law firm Wiggin. That compares to 17% of over-65s.

BBC News Magazine (http://bbc.in/189dCQM)

Many people still think that statements on social media are safe simply because large numbers of people are involved – the 'everyone is saying it' myth. They think they can say whatever they like about someone because the public figure could not possibly sue everybody. The news broadcast journalist knows better and must never think or behave like the angry mob:

> She had it coming . . .

> Trending everywhere – always knew he was a . . .

> So, they finally got him . . .!

Simply not naming someone in a report does not help. The issue is – can the person be identified? If you use an interview in which someone says that all the bakers in Britain are using contaminated flour then it is very hard for one baker to claim that it was him being accused. But if the report says that all the bakers in Smallville Main Street are doing it, then if there are only two bakers on that street then you have identified them.

A BBC Newsnight report wrongly claimed a leading politician (unnamed) from the Margaret Thatcher years had abused boys living in care. Sally Bercow drew attention to internet speculation that this person was Lord McAlpine. Mrs Bercow was the wife of the Speaker of the House of Commons and had thousands of followers. Lord McAlpine sued her for damages. He could have sued hundreds more people who posted messages.

Copyright

Intellectual property is the oil of the 21st century.

Mark Getty, Getty Images

You must never use someone else's material without attribution and pass it off as your own work. Plagiarism has been a rising problem for broadcast newsrooms because the web makes it seem easy to think you can use whatever you want. The law says you cannot lift video, images, sound or music off the internet or anywhere else and use it just because it is there.

Intellectual property is also a big business. Specific problems arise with what images are used and/or what is heard or spoken, for example an extract from an historical speech such as Martin Luther King's 'I Have A Dream'.

Just because a clip is online does not mean it is a free-for-all.

Big broadcasting companies often have specialists to check all this for you. But you should know to watch out for a copyright icon © and ask permission. You can put the name of the speech or image into a search engine and add the word 'copyright' or 'permission' or 'estate of' and see who to contact. Explain exactly who you are and why you want to use it. Get your permission in writing. Email is fine. Then file the permission away, keep it and send a copy to your editor and/or the company lawyer.

In many cases you will find that you do get permission, especially if you are a small local radio or TV station and the purpose is just to explain or illustrate a story that does not damage the owner of the intellectual property. But you do still need permission.

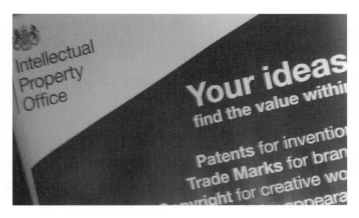

FIGURE 2.1

Broadcast journalists need to know that the kinds of works covered by copyright include: literary works such as novels, poems, plays, reference works, newspapers and computer programs; databases; films, musical compositions and choreography; artistic works such as paintings, drawings, photographs and sculpture; architecture; and advertisements, maps and technical drawings. Courtesy IPO.

Another problem for broadcast journalism is that film companies often send out clips of new films that can be used in the news. Obviously, they want the publicity. But those clips can linger in a database for years and long after the permission to use has expired. So do not just lift a film clip for your report just because it is there and available and fits your story. Check.

In most countries an exception called fair dealing allows the copying of extracts of works for non-commercial research or study. You must be genuinely studying, for example as a student, teacher, lecturer. But do not use an entire work as this would not be regarded as fair dealing.

Criticism, review and reporting current events

Fair dealing for criticism, review or quotation is allowed for any type of copyright work. Fair dealing with a work for the purpose of reporting current events is allowed for any type of copyright work other than a photograph. In each of these cases, a sufficient acknowledgment will be required.

As stated, a photograph cannot be reproduced for the purpose of reporting current events. The intention of the law is to prevent newspapers or magazines reproducing photographs for reporting current events which have appeared in competitor's [sic] publications.

Intellectual Property Office, UK (www.gov.uk/intellectual-property)

Also remember:

- *Hamlet* may be out of copyright, but a famous Hamlet performance or recording by a modern actor will not be.

- A seventeenth-century painting may be out of copyright, but a photograph of it may not be.

- Material online – particularly images – often carries a digital fingerprint to detect when material is pirated.

- Computer and console games are covered by copyright.

- The copyright to *Peter Pan* (and the characters) is owned by the Great Ormond Street Hospital in London, forever.

Script and Image Together

What meaning could an ordinary person attach to certain words and images together? A sentence that combines with pictures of a building may be harmless, or may be dangerous and contain a reference to illegal activity. Remember that a building can identify a company and the people inside it.

Also be careful when using shots of a social media website. What names or faces do we see and what are you saying at the moment that particular shot is in view? Could you be writing a script about crime or illegal activity online – and do we see a face and a name in a shot? (Also see Chapter 20.)

Sexuality

There is a myth that it is legally safe in the times in which we live to say someone is homosexual. It is not. If a person says he or she is homosexual then that's fine. But do not suggest that a person is gay because people are saying he or she is, or because of rumour. Rumour is not news.

Media Lawyers

If you are new and find yourself talking to the media lawyer and/or your editor about a story which may have legal implications, first of all do not feel anxious. It is quite normal to talk it through.

Also, tell the lawyer everything. Do not hide or hold back some little thing because you are worried the lawyer might suggest dropping the whole story. In fact the lawyer is trying to find a way of getting the story on air, but in a form that is legally safe. Do not get into a situation in which the lawyer much later says to you – 'Why didn't you tell me it was your sister/brother/ex-wife/ex-husband?' Sometimes even a simple change can avoid trouble – one single word, or a few seconds of pictures or a clip of sound.

Email

Do not make or forward derogatory or potentially defamatory remarks about any person or organisation by email. Email is not a secure way of sending information and accidental breaches of confidentiality can happen by entering a wrong address or forwarding a message to inappropriate recipients on a distribution list.

An email sent from a newsroom is usually sent in the name of the broadcaster and so it then represents your channel, station or website.

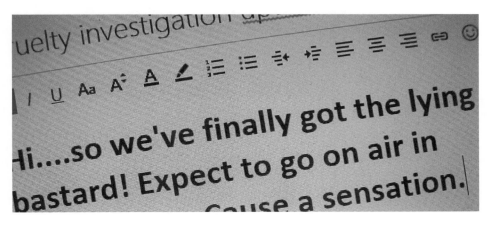

FIGURE 2.2
During any work on an investigative programme do not send anyone an email which says '. . . got the (lying/thieving/bent/corrupt) creep/bitch/bastard . . .' or similar. It may be true of course, but then again much later there could be reasons why it is not helpful to have this read out in a court. If your story is being challenged, this fails to show impartiality and would appear to a judge or jury to be unprofessional and/or malicious.

Reporting From Court

You will be with other journalists in the courtroom and the broadcast journalist's specific role is to report in sound and/or vision, usually standing outside court.

Never get a quotation from a judge wrong. For live TV it is best to use a traditional notebook – you can look at your notes when quoting a judge (see live reporting).

Never take a picture inside a courtroom.

Never attempt to interview someone on a jury. Do not even *talk* to anyone on the jury.

In many countries it is permitted for a reporter to use social media in a courtroom.

In England and Wales and some other countries broadcast journalists are allowed to tweet in a silent and unobtrusive way from the courtroom during a trial.

They do not have to ask permission, but members of the public do.

FIGURE 2.3

The main issue for the judge in deciding whether to allow tweeting is whether it may interfere with the administration of justice. For example, where witnesses who are out of court may be informed of what has already happened in court and so coached or briefed before they then give evidence. Or when legal discussions when a jury is sent out then appear online and can be seen by jury members. The Royal Courts, Strand, London, UK.

However – it is up to the judge.

There have been occasions when a judge has said that in a particular trial he will not allow it. There have also been cases where a journalist has tweeted something he should not and the judge has then banned it.

(In tweeting . . .) . . . be concise, informal, conversational. I enjoy conjuring a short phrase to keep people following, and a limit of 140 characters concentrates the mind under pressure.

With the usual warnings of not going over the top, live-tweeting is a case of saying: Here I am; here is what's happening; here is my opinion of what's really happening or likely to happen.

Brace yourselves, judge about to return . . .

Will she take tea break before asking #OscarPistorius to stand for final verdicts? Wouldn't bet against it . . .

I knew that a lot of people were following me and even using my tweets as their sole way into the story of the trial – so I needed to differentiate between the high drama, which I covered blow by blow, and just filling people's timelines with boring legal process.

Only tweet when you have something to say. That goes for an average news day as much as a sensational murder trial.

Andrew Harding, BBC Africa correspondent

Being Web Wise

There are men nowadays who cannot distinguish between the truth and the last thing they happen to have read.

Oscar Wilde

That could have be written by Oscar Wilde yesterday and still be valid. As every journalist must know – the web might contain useful facts, comments and contacts, but it is also the home of every conspiracy theorist, polemicist, liar, fraud, hoaxer and double-dealer imaginable. It's not just people who want to steal your credit card number – it's the people who want you to put their *opinions* into your news reports as *fact*.

It's very easy for people to create a fake online profile or a Twitter account with the aim of impersonating an individual or a company. Some can be convincing enough to appear genuine even to an experienced journalist.

So ask:

- Would she really say that?
- Does this fit in with opinions he usually expresses?
- Does she usually make errors like that?
- Do previous postings have any credibility?

Being sceptical means cross-checking information and looking at an address in the upper thread. If we imagine a person called Mr Fan Tassie and look for quotes from him on Google then you should not accept those as a *final* result. Check those with a site that *might* be called www.fantassie.com and then it might have more substance as this appears to be a primary source simply because of the name of the website. But it doesn't end there. That depends if Mr Fan Tassie actually owns that website name. Or he could be lying.

Among the websites that can be used to check website ownership are www.cool whois.com or www domaintools.com. Put the domain name you want to check into the box and it will give you the owner's registration details.

People who used to consume media a generation ago now create it, publish it and comment on it.

UGC (User Generated Content) also called Citizen Journalism are labels that many TV and radio journalists either accept, or hate. This is simply members of the public sending broadcasters their own sound and/or video or images. This is also included in other parts of the book. There's nothing new about eye-witnesses or the public tipping off newsrooms. What has changed is that everyone with a phone has a camera, the quality has improved, and so has the speed at which images can get on air or onto websites.

If a picture looks too good to be true (and nobody else seems to have it) then either it's an amazing scoop, or it's not true at all. In these circumstances there are two kinds of people in the world – those who believe in the Loch Ness Monster and those who do not. In general, journalists are safer being in the second category.

Another concern, particularly for local channels, is that the public will send newsrooms images that may not be justified on grounds of taste or decency. If such an image slips through the moderation, then others will think they too can take similar pictures with the intention of trying to get them on television. Police now put screens around the more serious road accidents, not only to stop drivers slowing down to have a look but to stop people taking pictures.

There are also cases of people sitting at home watching any major breaking story on live TV or online then sending postings about it which give a broadcast journalist the *impression* that they are there and therefore a potential eye-witness. Some people do this quite innocently – after all they are allowed to comment on an incident; after all, he didn't tell the radio station he was *not actually there*, they just *assumed* he was there. *They contacted him*, called him, put him on air and asked him: 'Tell us what's happening at the moment?'

Some people at home even film the screen and then post the video.

One way to check that material sent to you is to have a name and number for the sender and ask some direct questions, such as: were you there and did you actually get the pictures/sound yourself?

Ask him to spell his name when you start, and then ask him at the end if he could spell it again.

Impartiality

Whatever channel you ever work for, in any country, a small radio station or a global network, either you, or your entire news operation, will be accused one day of lacking impartiality. You will be told you are biased. They may even protest outside.

A senior broadcast editor would tell new journalists at an induction: 'We have editorial guidelines and they are public. But there are people who think our editors, and so you, are controlled by some mysterious all-powerful secret society, by the military-industrial complex or a network or clan that dominates the world. In fact, we just do news. And for all the detail in the guidelines we are the same as anyone in judgement – that killing people is bad, that cruelty to animals or children are bad, that stealing or corrupt use of power are bad. But that might not be written down anywhere.'

Complete impartiality is like perfection; an ideal for which many will strive but none will wholly attain. Even the most respected journalist can only be the sum of his or her beliefs, experience and attitudes, the product of society, culture and upbringing. No one can be free from bias, however hard they may try to compensate by applying professional standards of objectivity; for objectivity itself, subjectively appraised, must by nature be an unreliable yardstick.

The journalist's responsibility is to recognise bias and compensate for it. The BBC World Service claims to deal with the problem of personal bias through a combination of professional integrity and an exhaustive system of checks and balances.

'People do have their politics, but they are very good at keeping them out of the news,' says a former BBC World Service assistant editor. 'They'd never get through anyway, because there are too many people asking questions. There is a dual personality that says, "I'm an observer, this is not me talking politics, just me talking about things from both sides. I'm not directly involved, I'm merely telling you what is happening".'

The journalist must stand back and view the argument from all sides, before scrupulously drawing out the key points to produce as full, balanced and impartial a picture as possible in the time available.

Police and Emergency Services

What many civilians do not know is that broadcasters and all the emergency services frequently carry out training scenarios for emergencies, together. Senior police and fire officers have media training, although not usually from the broadcasting organisations.

Editors and police regularly talk to each other about security and safety in broadcast coverage.

Police also accept that radio and TV reporters and camera crews have a job to do and try to find an accommodation in emergency situations. It is a form of unwritten professional contract. You can do interviews and film and record and be told what is going on – but if you are asked not to film something (you *may* be told why) or to move back, then do so.

Anything broadcast can be heard or seen by people carrying out kidnapping, hijacking, sieges, hostage taking or planning bomb attacks. Occasionally police or security services may ask editors to withhold information and there can be agreed news black-outs on kidnappings.

The real danger is that you report something or do something that makes a situation worse. Typically this is a problem when those who took hostages or were under siege could find out from broadcasters what was going on.

Because of mobile technology and social media the situation is more complex. The attacks in Mumbai a few years ago were covered live on television. The people planning the attack watched this and gave instructions via mobile phones to the terrorists who were holding hostages.

Six people who hid in a supermarket cold-room during a hostage attack at Hyper Cacher in eastern Paris took legal action against some French media for broadcasting their location live during the siege.

Chris Webb, Scotland Yard's head of news in 2005 when London was hit by two terrorist attacks, said a voluntary agreement was hammered out with broadcasters.

When those behind the failed bomb attacks on 21 July 2005 were holed up days later and cornered in a west London flat, surrounded by armed officers, broadcasters were permitted to film but agreed not to transmit images live.

Webb said: 'It is a difficult balancing act for the authorities. They have to look at how to protect life, especially if taking executive action (sending armed police or special forces in to end a siege). Images giving the bad guys prior warning can impact on the fate of the hostages inside, and get hostages or officers killed.'

Webb warned that the massive growth of social media as well as the increase in the number of news channels makes avoiding coverage that tips off the terrorists much harder: 'You can ask broadcasters to use discretion, you can't do the same with social media.'

The Guardian (extract), 29 January 2015

Children

Broadcasters should normally seek the consent of parents or legal guardians (which can include teachers if filming or recording at a school) before interviewing children or young people, or otherwise involving them in a news story.

Most broadcasting organisations have guidelines about involving children and the overall aim to make sure they are treated fairly, are not misrepresented and are not exposed to ridicule or bullying or other damage as a result of appearing in a broadcast. Bribing children either to say things, or do things for the camera, is unacceptable and any accusations about this will be taken very seriously by broadcasters and the regulators.

Interviewing children – assuming consent has been obtained – demands that the reporter doesn't go into areas that may be beyond the child's understanding. Apart from that, you can interview children in much the same way you would interview an adult. That means you do not patronise them.

You should also try to be at the same eye-level, which means sitting down rather than stooping over them in a poise of superiority. In general, children under ten are more compliant and may give answers they think they need to give rather than their genuine opinions.

Be honest and clear about why you are talking to them. And finally, tell them when you expect it to be on air.

THE HEADLINES

- Ethics are now heavily considered in the broadcasting of news.
- Facts Are Sacred, Comment Is Free. When In Doubt, Leave Out.

- The law says you cannot lift material off the internet or anywhere else and use it just because it is there. Specific problems arise with what images are used and/or what is heard or spoken. Get permission.

- In siege or hostage situations – do no harm. Always assume that the hostage takers can see and hear what you are broadcasting.

QUESTIONS FOR YOU

1. You are filming in a street with a cameraman – just routine general view shots for a story about shopping. But you look like a professional news team rather than just a member of the public. A woman walks up to you and says she thinks she is in your filming and asks if you would not use shots of her because her ex-boyfriend is violent, has threatened her and he thinks she has moved to another town. What will you do?

2. You are at a news conference being given by a reclusive but famous person about an important issue. After this, he agrees to one interview with all the reporters at the same time, so multiple microphones are pointing at him. Then he leaves and will not talk any more. Everyone has the same recording. Another reporter – from a competing radio station – tells you that his recording device was broken and he asks you if he can have a copy of your recording. What will you do?

OTHER RESOURCES

- The Society of Professional Journalists has some ethical case studies (www.spj.org/ethicscasestudies.asp).

- Former ITN editor Stewart Purvis has a paper presented to a seminar on 'Ethical Spaces: What Leveson Missed' (http://profpurvis.com/2013/11/19/why-the-parable-of-the-canoe-man-is-important-for-media-freedom/).

TUTOR NOTES

'If it bleeds; it leads' (traditional). Discuss. What if a victim or someone hurt is in a foreign country of which we know little? What if the victim is a national of your country? What if the victim lives in your hometown? But what if the victim is the son or daughter of your next-door neighbour?

Set a 30-minute online research task – what are the chances of/statistics for . . .? Examples: Being struck by lightning? Being in a coach crash, a train crash, a plane crash or a car crash? Being the victim of a shark attack? Being hurt doing DIY/home improvements? Should broadcast news carry health warnings? Discuss.

Tell your group a cameraman has sent back some horrific shots of victims of a terrorist bomb attack on a crowded train – some of them are close-up shots. It's up to them to make a decision on what to show. Are they going to give the audience a warning? Are they going to broadcast a terrorist making a statement? Why? What time of day is this broadcast – are children likely to be watching? It's all on social media anyway – are they censoring the news?

CHAPTER 3

What Makes Broadcast News?

No people are uninteresting.

Yevgeny Yevtushenko, Russian poet. From the poem 'People'

News judgement and content is about knowing your audience, knowing how to get to them and knowing how to keep them. The broadcast journalist has to be universal in consulting a wider range of media from newspapers to specialist websites. That includes your social habits, because you are never really off-duty.

Apart from a lot of reading text and social media searching, the broadcast journalist is endlessly curious and understands a variety of ways and styles in which news events are reported and what stories sound and look like. One moment she tunes into Fox News and then a local radio station. She is looking at CNN and then Sky News or the BBC and then perhaps a channel in India if something has happened there. If there is a big story in Australia, then she might quickly go to the ABC to see what coverage there is and what sound and pictures are around.

But the audience might have different ideas and each person in that audience may have a news service that is used regularly and gets the content in different ways. The people who run news channels know that, and they, as much as the newcomer to the newsroom, need to know that person and what he expects, what he needs and also what he wants.

When asked which topics they considered to be news, six in ten UK adults (61%) nominated the weather.

This was followed by crime (53%), worldwide current affairs (53%), UK-wide current affairs (51%) and UK-wide politics (49%).

When asked which types of news were of personal interest, the weather was again most popular, with half (49%) of people saying they were personally interested.

Other types of news were much less likely to be rated as being of personal interest, with UK and worldwide current affairs being of interest to 37% of UK adults, sports to 36%, local events 35% and crime 35%.

News Consumption. Ofcom (UK) 2014 (http://bit.ly/1x1dwms)

Let us imagine a live breaking story, which is what broadcasting does best.

If the liner *Titanic* sank in the North Atlantic today rather than in 1912 then what is it the audience need?

Perhaps many are dead, or perhaps, because it is a century later and rescue services are faster, nobody is dead. Both situations are unusual events and therefore they are news.

All broadcasters throughout the world want to know, and quickly:

> The name of the ship and what happened? How many aboard? Where did it sink? Number dead? Number rescued? Where are they from? Do we know yet why it sank? Was this a terror attack? Was it an act of nature, such as an iceberg? Who screwed up?

Unlike 1912, when news took many hours or even days to emerge, the live 24-hour coverage has started. It's all over social media – and that includes the rumours and nonsense mixed with genuine messages from emergency services and the ship's owners or the cruise company.

In the big broadcast newsrooms there will (hopefully) be an editor who takes control to create order from the chaos of journalists running about. This is when journalism goes military. There is already a team that takes care of user content – and that includes the pictures coming from aboard the ship. Other tasks are assigned: material from the rescue, what comes in from the USA or the ship's home port, making sure presenters have what they need.

Others get guests for the presenters to talk to. There was an incident about an airline expert who was just leaving the building having been interviewed about airliner exports, when airliners hit the World Trade Center in New York. He was grabbed back from the exit door and put into a studio chair again.

The audiences are turning away from sport and movies to news. It's as if nothing else is happening in the world. In addition to any pictures and witness accounts they can get, the studios will fill with shipping experts, people who know the ship and have been aboard it, representatives of the owners, anyone who can add either information or context to the event.

Soon the stories of human action will come in – stories that the audience can relate to: tragedy, courage, heroism.

There are also specific audience needs.

Who? In Britain, the audience will want to know if British people are involved, whether dead, hurt or surviving. If the reporting is from America, Australia, Canada or Japan then the same questions will be asked about their nationals. If the report is on a radio station in Aberdeen then the news that an Aberdeen man was aboard is news there – but probably nowhere else.

Where? The website and TV services will show an animated and detailed map of where the ship went down. The map is a first visual, what we get as soon as the story breaks. It will probably show the port of departure, where the ship was heading and where it sank.

Why? This is likely to come later because we do not know yet. News may come in quickly that it hit an iceberg. What is an iceberg anyway? Where are they? How can an iceberg sink a ship? Was there human error and is there anyone to blame for this?

The Human Factor. Ultimately the most important way of explaining the story. People tell their stories. We soon hear from passengers and their survival stories – stories of heroism and courage, of endurance, or tragedy or joy or claims of cowardice, incompetence or neglect. A short clip of a man who 'slept through it all' will become famous. All broadcasters will prefer stories from their own nationals, but will not exclude stories from others if they are moving or informative, or both.

The Specialists. These include people who work in the travel or transport business, or in shipping or engineering or the risk and insurance sector. They will be asking very specific questions – didn't they see the iceberg and, if not, then why? How thin was the hull? What went wrong with procedure? What are the implications for sea travel? Risk assessors may also ask – is travelling by sea still relatively safer than flying?

All these things are audience needs and that is a priority in assessing what news is.

Added to all this – the competition. Broadcasting organisations compete like hungry beasts and for the journalist Beating The Others is a motivation. However morbid it seems in the middle of a tragic event, newsrooms want to stuff the competition, whether that's the BBC, Sky News, commercial radio, CNN or online news services.

So let's look at the elements of news judgements.

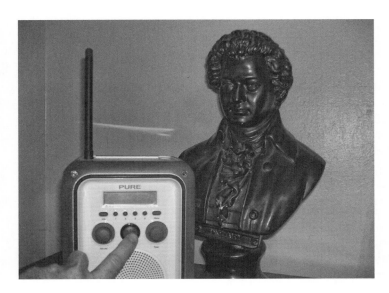

FIGURE 3.1

Tuned in but turned off? Audience needs come first. If it's not relevant to the audience you get switched off and the ratings go down as he finds more time for Mozart. Good writing means the reader forgets that he's reading; good radio journalism means she stays in the car when she reaches her destination; good television journalism makes your channel his chosen appointment to view on mobile or TV.

WHERE?

SMALL EARTHQUAKE IN CHILE – NOT MANY DEAD was an entry in a completion by a group of journalists to come up with the most boring headline. It was intended to be everything news is not: undramatic and remote, though the irony would have been lost on anyone living in Chile. Or anyone from Chile who lives anywhere else. Yet this has something to say about the nature of news. For a story to have impact, it has to be relevant. For news to be relevant, it has to have proximity.

RELEVANCE

Even when the proximity gap is narrowed, a news item may fail to interest different groups within the same country. New regulations for banks may stir the finance community in the City of London or Wall Street but fail to excite the tourism workers of Devon and Disneyland. But if the decision affects business loans or banking rules much later, then the item would come home to everyone in the whole country.

But even when a story contains both touchstones of proximity and relevance, the reaction it provokes in you will depend on your upbringing, environment, education, background, beliefs, and morality. In other words, news values are subjective.

Despite that, every editor would agree that the greater the effect of a story on the lives of an audience or website visitors, their lifestyle, income and emotions, the more important that item will be. Every editor knows that if a news service is to win and hold an audience, the bulk of its stories must have impact on most of the people at a particular point in time.

IMMEDIACY

News is about what is happening now – or the first inkling of something that happened earlier. 'Now more on that live and breaking news' is the common catchphrase in broadcast media and however tiresome it might become it does carry a boast that the printed word can never match. To the broadcast journalist, what happened yesterday is dead and buried. There has to be something new to say, some fresh angle. And with a 24-hour news service even what went on at eleven will have to be updated for noon. To put it another way: news is only news while it is new.

INTEREST

'Worthy, but dull' is one of the most damning indictments you could make about a news report. News should make you stop, exclaim, sit up, take notice and listen. News is what people talk about. Broadcast news is often criticised for pandering to the popular taste, but by its very nature, broadcasting caters for the mass interest rather than that of a minority. Stories must have a wide appeal or most of the audience will switch. The skill of the news writer comes in drawing out the relevance of a story and presenting it clearly and factually while making the most of every scrap of interest. This way the news writer can give the audience what it needs to know – as well as what it wants to know.

The most interesting element in news is often people, not just famous people but people in general and what they do or what happens to them or as witnesses. With broadcast news you can hear their voices and/or see their emotions. People give the news some feeling.

DRAMA AND IMPACT

Dramatic events of the stranger-than-fiction variety make striking headlines. Gun sieges, violent crimes, car chases, precarious rescues – the greater the drama, the greater its prominence in conversation. Excitement, danger, adventure, conflict have as great an appeal to the news writer as the novelist or movie-maker.

TV is about dramatic pictures so it's entirely possible for a story to earn a place in the TV news simply because it looks so amazing. Now, in all broadcast organisations, getting the storytelling right is a constant quest which goes alongside integrity and credibility. It is something the characters in a novel or film will be aware of.

> Billy: It's finding the centre of your story, the beating heart of it, that's what makes a reporter. You have to start by making up some headlines. You know: short, punchy, dramatic headlines. Now, have a look, what do you see?
>
> (Billy points at dark clouds on the horizon)
>
> Billy: Tell me the headline?
> Quoyle: Horizon Fills With Dark Clouds?
> Billy: Imminent Storm Threatens Village.
> Quoyle: But what if no storm comes?
> Billy: Village Spared From Deadly Storm.
> Film The Shipping News based on the novel by E. Annie Proulx

NEW, TRUE AND INTERESTING

> The two most engaging powers of a writer are to make new things familiar and familiar things new.
> Samuel Johnson

This traditional and very old journalism maxim says it all and still combines all the elements that decide what goes into a news channel.

Joe Black is 25 years old.

So what? It might be information, but it is not news.

> Half his short life has been spent in prisons and other institutions.

Well, that may be of some interest to somebody because it is unusual to have spent half your life in some form of custody when you are now 25. But it is still not news. Yet.

> Joe Black is coming out today . . . a free man.

It is information, it has some interest and it is new because he is coming out today, but it is still not news. Yet.

> Three months ago, Black was sentenced to life for the murder of his parents.

Now this is more interesting. How can a man who was jailed for murdering his parents be let out of prison after only three months?

> New evidence has come to light to show conclusively that Black did not commit the murders and that the killer is still on the loose – and has already struck again.

The information is new, interesting, and important, but for it to be newsworthy, it would have to be also relevant to you, the audience. If the murders were committed in your home town that is big news – and local radio and TV in that town would almost certainly run it as their lead item. A story like this would also be national and so unusual it could be of interest in countries where similar cases have happened.

DIFFERENT TYPES OF NEWS

Broadcast journalism news stories seek out sound and pictures. Whether a news story is local, national or international, it will usually fall into one or more of the following categories.

Emergencies

The emergency services deal with the high points of human drama – fires, sea or mountain rescues. Whenever human life is at risk there is a story, although the very word 'dramatic' has become an unfashionable cliché and many news writers will let the drama of a rescue speak for itself. After all, most rescues are dramatic.

Accidents are also a steady source of news, but the larger the area covered by the news service the more serious these will have to be to warrant coverage, otherwise the bulletins would be full of little else. So reporting of accidents is usually confined to death, serious injury or an unusual element such as the overturn of a lorry full of poisonous snakes. All the rest becomes traffic news.

Crime

Violent crime rates are actually falling in many countries. Online fraud and scams are increasing. Broadcast journalists are perfectly aware of anxiety caused by *fear of crime* in society, even if their critics complain that they seem oblivious and enjoy scaring people.

The larger the area, the more crime there will be, so only more serious or unusual offences are likely to be reported simply because they are interesting. Crime is not confined to cities. There is plenty of crime in rural areas and farms are frequent targets for thieves. Crime stories have many phases, from the actual incident, to the police raid, arrest and eventual appearance in court.

In television interesting crimes are often reconstructed using actors. TV news

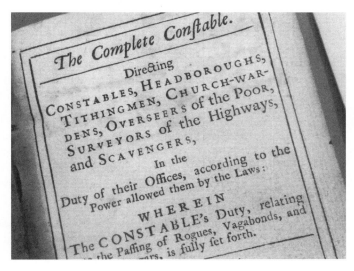

FIGURE 3.2
The 'Rogues' in *The Complete Constable* (1724) obviously get into the news in new ways. In America helicopter shots of cops-chasing-villains-in-cars can form a staple part of local broadcast news coverage. Courtesy Northamptonshire Police, UK.

broadcasters need to do the reconstruction based entirely upon known evidence and are not supposed to let any kind of fiction creep in to make a true incident more dramatic. News programmes also report crime reconstructions staged by the police to gather evidence. Background reports are often prepared during a trial but they should not be used until the trial has ended.

A BBC internal study on reporting crime aimed to ensure its journalists understood the realities: most crimes are never reported to the police, violent crime is a small proportion of all recorded crime and most victims of homicide are children under the age of one.

Government and Politics

Every action of government – locally or nationally – has a bearing on a potential audience, and whatever affects an audience is news. To prevent bulletins becoming swamped with items from city hall, news policy is usually to report the stories that have the greatest effect on the largest number of people *at a particular moment in time.*

So most stories which start at government level are reported from the point of view of people affected. A new motorway or high-speed rail project may cut through a community – some people will oppose it, but some may welcome it. Hearing from the people affected is more interesting than hearing from a planner or a politician.

When we do need to hear from the politician the other aspect of coverage of government is conflict or challenge. Broadcasters need to question the information they receive from government, but in a firm and testing way. There is a kind of broadcast tension which varies greatly between democratic systems and those countries where the media is controlled, or even owned by government. One way in which broadcast journalism does this is with the interview, where the politician can be heard, or heard and seen. Polite but firm challenging of political claims, statements or assumptions can help inform the audience.

Political interviews in broadcasting can be a mixture of Heat and Light. Too much Heat – lively or even bad-tempered exchanges – can be exciting but not very useful. Too much Light – long questions and answers littered with complex statistics – can be informative but very dull. A mixture of both makes good broadcasting and is more likely to be informative and interesting. *(See the chapters on broadcast interviews.)*

Another specific aspect of broadcast journalism is The Shout. This is when the journalist shouts some short question at the politician – in a public place – usually with no hope whatsoever of an answer.

This happens in several countries but in the UK this mostly happens from across the road opposite the door of No 10 Downing Street when the viewer watches politicians walk in and out, or the PM getting out of a car or posing with citizens: 'Are you going to Moscow Prime Minister?' bellows someone across the street who just happens to be a radio or TV reporter. Or, 'what are you going to tell the President?' or, 'are you going to apologise to . . .'

The shouter knows there is little possibility of a reply. The reason they do it is to have some sound to stick to the report and have a shot of a reaction – even the *I'm Ignoring That* reaction is good enough. Of course there are also countries where such behaviour is unacceptable, or end up with the reporter arrested, or worse.

Planning and Developments

Building developments are news which is emerging before your eyes. Big projects like an Olympic Stadium make big news. Leisure complexes, shopping malls and housing schemes which impact on an area are certain to be given the big news treatment in any local newsroom. Nationally, the difference is one of scale.

Newsworthy developments would include major road or house building schemes and other large projects. But the concept of developments as news expands beyond public works to mean any form of major change that is happening or is about to happen that will affect a given audience.

Conflict and Controversy

News is about change – events that shape our society and alter the way we live. Conflict is the essence of drama, and anything that is both true and dramatic makes news. This can be physical clashes in the streets, such as the London looting and riots of 2011, or a conflict of ideals – a row at the local council or in a national government or a political party.

Where actions or ideas mean upheavals in society, then that conflict is news. Every issue in the public eye has those who are for it, and those who are against it. Broadcast journalism can cover what is happening, stimulate debate and bring important issues into sharper focus.

The possibility of trouble at an event can sometimes be anticipated. For broadcasters this can be planned for, which means knowing the area, the streets and, above all, how to get out of there fast if necessary.

The most important bit of safety equipment is simple – what is on your feet? Good footwear is vital because you could end up surrounded by broken glass, debris and bricks. You may also have to run fast.

Industry and Business

Employment and the state of business is a major factor in most people's lives. These can affect jobs, pensions, savings, prosperity and welfare so developments in industry make big news. There is a generalisation that people who go into journalism do not do it to make money and so journalists have always been accused of failing to understand industry and business, or even displaying suspicion about people who do make money.

In large news organisations there will be a Business Editor or an Economics Editor or both and their expertise about what developments mean to the audience have pushed business stories up the agenda. The ups and downs of national economies, currency rates and fuel costs have become more newsworthy in recent years.

Health. Medicine. Science

Health makes news: rationing of drugs, new drugs and the cost of drugs, a new transplant, an epidemic, diet studies or a new kind of life-saving operation. One expression to be wary of is 'medical breakthrough' – often new products are not a breakthrough at all. Some consumer products marketed as a 'breakthrough' are only the re-packaging of existing drugs or treatments.

Broadcast news likes things that are impressive and mysterious for the camera and preferably make a noise. It likes the Large Hadron Collider, the Jet Propulsion Laboratory, images from NASA, probe pictures of Pluto, an eclipse, meteor showers, shots of a unique medical operation or from a micro-cam inside the human body, new images of a black hole and rocket launches with a countdown commentary.

Scientists and doctors worked out years ago that when being interviewed, or showing off clinical results, they need to explain their complex messages in a broadcasting style that is both accurate and clear for the audience.

The award of a Nobel Prize in science is usually always mentioned, briefly. One recent science prize got more coverage than many – and the reason is probably because it was about something in familiar use. The news judgement about the 2014 prize for physics was that this is science that touches you every day and for

FIGURE 3.3
Professors Isamu Akasaki, Shuji Nakamura and Hiroshi Amano enabled a new generation of energy-efficient white lamps and colour LED screens. Courtesy © Nobel Media AB. Photographer: Alexander Mahmoud.

television news there was something to show. This went to three scientists in Japan and the US for the invention of blue light emitting diodes (LEDs) that enabled a new generation of bright, energy-efficient white lamps, as well as colour LED screens.

A news meeting would be told that this provided LED-based computer and TV screens. The technology is in the lights and screens of mobile devices and smartphones.

Soft Human Interest

A soft human interest story may be defined as an extraordinary thing that has happened to an ordinary person. Or it could be an ordinary thing that happens to a famous person. Soft news is lightweight material which people like to gossip about, such as who has won a lottery or discovered a long lost Rembrandt in a garden shed. It is the unusual, ironic or offbeat.

> Coming up later – triumph over adversity . . . and: 'I'm giving away my lottery win millions' . . . 'I lost my brother but found him again after 30 years just by using Google Earth'. Our graphics will show you how it happened. We talk to the man who ate the most Bhut Jolokia chilli peppers in two minutes.

> Oscar winner goes into a fish'n'chip shop in Knotty Ash and your local station was there too. Coming up – that cat that walked 100 miles to return home. Man crosses channel in a bathtub and we glued a camera to him. Exclusive pictures. Woman told by three doctors she could never have kids gives birth to triplets and she wants them to be doctors!! Exclusive interview and pictures. Coming up. More later in the programme.

Sport

Sport is not just about action. It is also lifestyle, local interests, national and inter-national politics, marketing, big business and big money. The sport agenda is as likely to be about a special feature on a small-town snowboarding club as a spon-sorship deal for big league football. Many in the audience tolerate the news only because they know if they stay tuned they will get the pictures of a top golfer missing a hole from 12 inches because a spectator sneezed loudly.

Local teams and clubs obviously must feature strongly in local news, especially if they are doing well or badly in their leagues, and this is reflected at a national level, when news usually focuses on the promotion battles and relegation struggles that mark the changing fortunes of the top and bottom contenders. Broadcast journal-ists will have to deal with a lot of on-demand content, such as dramatic stills and short commentary or video clips from a live or pre-recorded event.

Most broadcast newsrooms have arrangements in place for news 'access' to the best sporting moments or commentary each day. Even the smallest newsrooms will have their own sports reporter and it is a myth to think that that all you need to be a sports reporter is to be an expert on many types of sport. Most sports reporters have wide broadcast journalism experience and training already and then they start to specialise in sport.

In broadcast writing, teams are usually plural – *Arsenal have beaten Real Madrid by . . .*

Clubs are usually singular – *Arsenal football club has revealed its plans for a new . . .*

FIGURE 3.4

When sport escapes from the 'sports news' and into the main news it can become a business story with a news graphic of big numbers, banknotes and balls. Formula One, Premiership football, test cricket, the World Cup and the World Series are studied for costs, value, sponsors, transfers and deals. But a small and poor local sports club that wins an international tournament can be inspiring and what its members say can make great broadcasting.

FIGURE 3.5

Weather, if extreme, is always a source of engaging live news. Taking to the skies during floods is a worthwhile investment for broadcasters if it provides views that both inform and interest the audience. To ensure his voice can be heard over the roar of the helicopter the reporter uses a lip-mike which isolates his voice and reduces interference from other sounds. Courtesy ITN.

Seasonal or Unseasonal Weather

In places where weather is usually benign this is when it moves from its regular slot called 'and now the weather, with . . .' and moves into the main headlines. Satellite pictures are often combined with graphics which take the viewer flying across the landscape of clouds, rainfall or drought.

Local radio comes into its own when there are flash floods, droughts or serious snowfalls. Stations can pick up both big audiences and local goodwill by running special information services live or on social media during extreme weather emergencies. Few things can touch local radio for its immediacy in times of crisis. The station and its website can provide a first-rate emergency information service.

Television news likes to send its forecasters to the weather on-site sometimes. The forecaster – having become familiar with standing in a comfortable studio with animated charts – is sent out to present on location. This can mean either sunshine with the apple blossom in the background, or a storm with the news team being hammered with wind, ice or rain.

FIGURE 3.6

A television crew has found an incident in a street that tells the story. A partly submerged car is an image that most of the audience can identify with. An ordinary part of life in extraordinary circumstances. Courtesy Channel NewsAsia.

Travel

Next to the weather, the first thing many people want to know quickly is whether the roads will be clear or if the trains are running. It may be on a phone app, but radio is the only medium motorists can safely or legally take in while driving.

In car-orientated societies where large numbers commute to work, traffic and travel news can pick up big audiences. Radio stations can give up-to-the-minute information on which roads are blocked and where there are traffic jams.

Car radios can automatically scan channels and seek out the latest traffic reports. Some larger stations have their own aircraft scanning the roads for traffic snarl-ups, with a reporter on board who can send back live updates.

Local and National Special Interest

London and New York are busy cities, so travel and transport have a place in a local agenda. Liverpool and Boston are long-established ports and the news often turns to the sea, ships and maritime festivals. Mountainous regions have local TV and radio journalists who have become experienced at covering rescues. Agricultural or industrial regions may have a specialist reporter. Local radio and TV wants news that is *of interest* to their local people – a much wider remit that just doing news about local people. A story from a national parliament about tourism becomes local news in tourist areas. A development at a big software company in California will be local news in a small town in another country where the company has an outpost.

When a small town story goes global, the local freelances can make a lot of money before the networks pour in, set up their equipment all over the place and provide business for local hotels. The arrival of network broadcasting correspondents is described in newsrooms as Big-Footing – as in the big beasts are taking over the local newsrooms.

Animals

Few items prompt greater reaction from the legions of pet lovers than anything to do with animals and wildlife. People may suffer in conflict or because of their environment, but if there is local news about a serial poisoner of kittens it will give a new reason for Going Viral.

For TV journalists the same sensitivity demonstrated for people suffering can apply to animals. It can be shown, but in the context of the report. Your script should explain the reason animal suffering is being broadcast.

Several years ago British broadcasters had regular stories about BSE (Bovine spongiform encephalopathy) also known as mad cow disease. But they kept showing library pictures of the *same cow*, suffering and staggering, until a local MP complained in Parliament about That Cow being shown over and over again.

When local stations start carrying stories about dog attacks (more than one that is) there is an increase in the number of people contacting the stations to report dogs on the street corners. Suddenly – there are bad or mad dogs everywhere.

Cultural and Religious Periods

Broadcast planning journalists must always note religious dates. They can affect the time you approach certain people, as much for story ideas with sound and pictures.

Beware of referring to any religious day as 'the public holiday' or 'a bank holiday' because that can be offensive. Never film or record in a place of worship without permission. Many larger religious places have a media contact.

Entertainment and Celebs

For entertainment and culture industry stories, the big news channels and stations usually define all this as the territory of a person called a Culture Correspondent, Entertainment Reporter or Arts Reporter. Small stations don't tend to have such titles. But usually the story now has to earn its place as being socially relevant. A new arts centre for a deprived area may have more social impact than a 1990s rock band reforming for a new tour – but that does not mean that both can earn a place in the news.

There is – in most channels – a distinction between an arts reporter and an art critic. The reporter who specialises in the arts might interview a critic about a new public work of art or architecture without the reporter being a 'critic' himself. Some channels might allow the arts reporter to express an opinion – although that might be in a programme that is separate from the main news.

Visiting personalities, royalty or film stars are usually good for a local news item, especially if their visit is linked to a local event although for much of the time the person is visiting to promote something. Nationally, the bigger the name, the more likely it is to make news.

These kinds of stories can cause plenty of conflict in newsrooms because many journalists hate doing stories about people who are just 'famous' for being famous. The usual refrain across the room is: What's he doing? What's she here for? Why should we bother with her?

MSNBC presenter Mika Brzezinski refused to read out a story about Paris Hilton (who had just been released from jail) before items on Iraq and developments at

FIGURE 3.7
The BBC noticed that more people visited its website via mobile devices than desktop and laptop PCs at a particular moment in time. This was recorded on a weekend – with news of the death of the actor Cory Monteith from the TV series *Glee*. Considering the age/lifestyle of the target audience for *Glee* – a musical drama set in a school – it is probably typical that a mobile is the device of choice, at weekends in particular. A four-line paragraph on a desktop story will appear as eight or nine on a mobile. Paragraphs need to be concise and simple.

FIGURE 3.8

Broadcasters may be thinking constantly about content formats for handheld technology – but it goes big and public as well. Screens with sound systems are in prominent locations throughout the world as a platform for continuous news, local information and cultural and sporting events.

the White House. She argued with her co-presenters about its place as the lead item and set fire to a script.

THE HEADLINES

- You need to know your audience to make news judgements and adapt writing styles. The audience can be local, national, global, or general or specialist.

- Good radio journalism means she stays in the car when she reaches her destination; good television journalism makes your channel his chosen appointment to view on mobile or TV.

- Broadcast news can be placed into types or groups such as crime, business, weather, politics, culture, arts and entertainment, sport or science.

QUESTIONS FOR YOU

1. An ocean liner is sinking and you are told it has about 50 people from your area among those aboard – you are on air live in ten minutes. Social media is full of messages. What are your priorities in your 30-second quick live report?
2. Places have special local interests and priorities. Can you list the special interests in your area? Find out what affects people where you live or study or both.
3. Can you recall three or four big news events? Where were you when you heard? If you found out on radio or television how did they do the story?
4. Have any newspapers this week moved sport news from the back pages to the front pages? If so, is that sport story also in the main radio and TV bulletins or channels and in the top headlines? Decide why – why isn't it just sports news rather than main news in the top headlines?

OTHER RESOURCES

- To develop an understanding of the structure of news bulletins and the ways news is broadcast – BBC school report (www.bbc.co.uk/schoolreport/27699415).

- 'Looking at what makes news stories go viral, researchers from Wharton Business School at the University of Pennsylvania found that stories that are highly emotionally arousing get shared more. Stories evoking sadness are the least likely to be shared and positive stories inducing awe were shared far more than stories that evoked fear or anger.' *The Guardian* (www.theguardian.com/media-network/2014/oct/24/constructive-journalism-de-correspondent).

- Learning how to make video work for online platforms has never been so important. In a 60-second video, Sabina Smitham explain the basics (http://bit.ly/1z61Uyx).

TUTOR NOTES

Get the top line or summary of ten news stories in a day – any day in the past few weeks – and list them in alphabetical order. Print copies for everyone including yourself. Put the team into six groups and tell them they are the editor (together) of six different broadcast bulletins. For example in the UK: BBC or ITN 1300 national news; Classic FM radio; BBC Radio Scotland; Sky News 1300; Newsround – plus the local commercial radio station in your area.

Give them about 30 minutes in their groups. Ask them to list the top three stories out of the ten for each channel/station. Get them to discuss and explain why their three are top, why not the others and what will the stories look/sound like? Who will they interview? What questions? Discuss the differences between the broadcasters in their criteria, approach and presentation of the same story.

Ted Turner, the founder of CNN, hoped that world news would help people understand each other and make the world seem smaller, but safer. But is the world any safer now because of global 24-hour news? Discuss.

CHAPTER 4

News Channels, Programmes and Streams

> Plenty more to come, none of it news. But that won't stop us.
> Simon McCoy, BBC News correspondent (http://bit.ly/BJMcCoy)

The 1990 edition of this book talked about how 'the ultimate news programme is the 24 hour news channel (which is) gaining popularity on satellite and cable TV'. Twenty-five years later such channels seem to be in decline (http://bit.ly/BJChannelStats). As people consume more content online, choosing their own stories and when they want to see them, are broadcasters playing catch up?

24-HOUR NEWS

Ted Turner's Cable News Network (CNN) was the first in 1980, earning respect for its outstanding coverage of the massacre in Tiananmen Square and the Gulf War, when it was the only news network to cover the start of Operation Desert Storm.

> See, we're gonna take the news and put it on the satellite, and then we're gonna beam it down to Russia and we're gonna bring world peace and we're all going to get rich in the process! Thank you very much.
> CNN launch speech, 1980

FIGURE 4.1
Outside CNN's world headquarters in Atlanta, USA.

The success of CNN prompted similar all-news channels around the world. In the UK are BBC News (and the international version BBC World), Sky News and, elsewhere, stations such as France 24 and Al Jazeera.

But 24-hour news was on radio years before television jumped on the bandwagon. All-news radio is credited with making its professional debut in Mexico in 1961, when the station XTRA in Tijuana began broadcasting a rip-and-read format that was later to spread to Chicago and be adopted and adapted by other networks.

The 24-hour news format has since developed a number of distinct styles: the magazine approach, which presents a variety of programmes and personalities throughout the day; and the news cycle, which repeats and updates an extended news bulletin, and lasts usually between 20 minutes and an hour (such as CNN's headline news service HLN, http://bit.ly/BJNewsFormat).

The US Westinghouse format adopted a news cycle, with a constantly updated sequence of hard news repeated throughout the day. Repetition was not thought to matter, because Westinghouse stations catered for an audience that tuned in for the latest news and then tuned out.

Give us 22 minutes, we'll give you the world.

One-time slogan of New York Radio Station 1010WINS

CBS stations extended that cycle to an hour to try to hold an audience for longer. National news could be taken on the hour, followed by local news, with traffic, sport, weather reports and other items programmed into the cycle, moving away from the extended bulletin feel to become a news programme. Programmes became double-headed for variety, and the style aimed to be warm and relaxed.

The other approach has been the magazine style which builds programmes, such as phone-ins and discussions, on to a backbone of regular bulletins and summaries which run at intervals throughout.

As news programmes get longer, and become more consumer oriented in the quest to cling to rating share in an ever fragmenting market, the distinction between news and entertainment becomes more blurred. Showbiz, technology updates, film reviews and viewers' and listeners' emails, texts and tweets now juggle for position amid the more usual news fare. The 'pre-records' of shows-within-a-show can be used as fillers in off-peak hours when there's not much news (such as overnights or weekends) and may run dozens of times a week. The appeal for 'user generated content' or 'eye-witness news' (such as the ubiquitous photos and videos of storms and snow) gives viewers the impression they are involved, and provides free and easy content for the broadcaster.

The network's programming focused around the idea that a viewer could tune in at any time and, in just 30 minutes, receive the most popular national and international stories, in addition to feature reports. The format, known as the Headline News Wheel, featured 'Dollars and Sense' personal finance reports at 15 and 45 minutes past each hour, Headline Sports at 19 and 49 minutes, lifestyle reports at 24 and 54 minutes past each hour, and general news during the top and bottom of the hour. Another regular feature was the 'Hollywood Minute' which was often fitted in after the Headline Sports segment. In the network's early years, a two minute recap of the hour's top stories, the CNN Headlines, would run after the sports segment.

Wikipedia entry on CNN Headline News

One advantage to a broadcaster of a dedicated news channel is it can be the 'on air' version of the stream of non-stop news that comes into the building. A new story from a court reporter or agency can be read as soon as it is received. The satellite feed from a news conference can go 'straight to air'.

Some of these live elements can then be used as the 'produced' version of that story: the best clip of the court reporter explaining the murder trial and the best clip of the distraught family on the courtroom steps are linked with archive shots of the appeal for witnesses, and a pre-produced backgrounder of the hunt for the killer.

The finished report can then be played several times on the news channel as well as in the scheduled news *programmes* (probably on the broadcaster's more mainstream channel).

THE BULLETIN

In the UK, the brief news summary is known as a *bulletin*. In the USA, bulletin may refer to a one-item snap of breaking news, while in UK parlance that would be known as a *newsflash* or *breaking news*. The UK definitions apply here, although even in that country there are various terms for the same thing.

The bulletin is a snapshot of the day's news at a point in time and may be on air from one to five minutes. Individual items are kept deliberately short – between

FIGURE 4.2

Editing the lunchtime news report for the interactive website. Credit: BBC South East Today.

FIGURE 4.3

With 24-hour news you have to be ready to broadcast from any location at any time. Here BBC World is at a polling station in Algiers during voting for the presidential elections. (Courtesy Nahed Abou-Zeid).

ten and 30 seconds – so a good number of stories can be packed in. TV bulletins are illustrated with video clips and stills, while radio bulletins use voice reports and extracts of interviews (*actualities*).

NEWS PROGRAMMES

News *programmes* aim to provide a broader view of the day's news, summarising the best stories of the day instead of the hour. Length usually ranges from 20 to 60 minutes. Items are generally longer and more detailed than those in a bulletin and more sophisticated, with features (or *packages*) using actualities or film footage, stills, graphics and explanatory links from a reporter which put the development into context. Some shorter stories may also be included to increase the breadth of coverage. If a programme is to gain audience loyalty, it will have to establish a clear identity and have a greater balance and variety of material than a bulletin.

DOCUMENTARY

The *documentary* or *feature* deals with a topical issue or subject in greater depth, and is less dependent on a *news peg* – some immediate and newsworthy occurrence taking place before that subject can be aired. Features can be as short as four or five minutes, while documentaries usually last between 30 minutes and an hour and will cover a single theme or a small number of issues.

Documentary styles vary from straightforward reportage to dramatised documentary and *vérite* techniques (also known as *direct* or *actuality* reporting). The *drama documentary* makes use of actors to reconstruct events and conversations. The use of reconstruction inevitably requires a degree of speculation and is a further smudging of the margins between fact and fiction, producing what is sometimes disparagingly referred to as *faction*.

Vérite

Vérite techniques try to get as close to the untainted truth as possible, by doing away with the narrator, chopping out all the questions and linking the various interviews and actualities so it seems as though no reporter was present. The intention is to produce a purer piece of journalism, closer to reality for being untainted by the presence and preconceptions of the reporter. But this is, of course, an illusion.

The reporter's influence, though unseen or unheard, is perhaps greater than ever, for a good deal of skilful setting-up and manipulation is required to get the interviewees to tell the story so it appears to be telling itself, without requiring linking narrative. Interviewees have to be primed to provide answers that effectively encapsulate the unheard questions so listeners can follow the drift.

WHO DOES WHAT?

The bigger the news organisation, the more specialists it is likely to employ. Job titles and descriptions vary across organisations and countries, but the news process in radio and TV is basically one of getting the stories in, and putting them out. These two jobs are called *input* and *output*.

On the *input* side, stories come in from news agencies, with reports from international news services and material from freelances. Each is *copytasted* (or scrutinised) by the relevant desk editor (to make an initial judgement on whether there is a potential story) and possible items are passed to the input (or intake) editor who will decide whether the station will commission them from correspondents or cover them itself. Assignments editors will detail reporters, correspondents and crews to those stories and the operations organiser will handle technical matters such as satellite booking and outside broadcast facilities.

Output is concerned with producing programmes from the material gathered. Editors and producers choose the items to go into their programmes. Journalists, writers or sub-editors write the stories and the presenters tailor them to suit their style of delivery. Reports are enhanced with graphics and archive shots, and put on air by studio production staff, led by the director, while engineers monitor the technical quality.

This is a simplification, and in most organisations there is a degree of overlap between input and output.

A local radio newsroom may rely on a national news feed from its parent company and regional news from a 'hub': a few reporters who can customise stories for several local stations from one location. They may also get audio from their sister TV station. That leaves a skeleton staff at the station itself, with a few people doing several jobs.

There may be a news editor who decides on stories, priorities and deployment, and a sports editor who works in a similar way. The roles of programme producers and reporters may be interchangeable, organising particular programmes, commissioning items, overseeing their presentation on air, operating the studios, newsreading, presenting and reporting.

TABLE 4.1
Input and output

Input	Output
Input editor	Programme editors/producers
Home/foreign editors	Anchors/presenters/newsreaders
Reporters and correspondents	Journalists/writers
Camera crews	Film/cutting archivists
Home/foreign assignments editors	Graphic artists
Operations organiser	Studio production staff
Engineering staff	

FIGURE 4.4

The headquarters of BBC News in central London. On the front facade of the original building to the left is a 1933 statue of Ariel and Prospero from Shakespeare's play, *The Tempest*. Ariel as a spirit of the air was felt to be an appropriate personification of broadcasting.

THE FUTURE

The internet is bypassing the professional reporter. Computers can do what journalists used to, namely compile the football results, produce travel news bulletins and write up company results stories. The services that used to be essential parts of the news are increasingly automated and available separately online.

And people in power are finding they can speak directly to the public without bothering with a reporter's pesky questions. The journalist's competitor is no longer another journalist. . . . Political parties, celebrities, corporations communicate directly with the public. An era of greater connectivity is not necessarily leading to more accountability.

It is an age of growing information inequality. Millions of people are online, millions are not. The world is dividing into those who seek the news and a growing number who skim it. . . . At the same time, people feel misinformed.

There is ever more data, more opinion, more freedom of expression, but it's harder to know what's really going on. Even though people say it's easier to get the news, they are increasingly unsure of the facts and unclear what they mean.

James Harding, Director of BBC News and Current Affairs,
'The Future of News' Report, January 2015

Rolling news on broadcast TV has been called 'the future' – but is it?

Keeping a news channel on air is expensive. Most news is not news at all: it's dull, repetitive or slow to materialise. Is the arrival of a man-in-a-suit at another conference really 'breaking news'? What about the speculation by an 'expert' of what the man-in-a-suit might say, or later, the analysis of what he *did* say . . . and speculation of what he meant by it. How can a correspondent on location find stories and sources if they are obliged to appear on camera every twenty minutes with 'the latest'? What amount of 'news' is waffle and padding: waiting for a news conference to start, or a sound bite to come out of it. Or as Simon McCoy suggested at the start of the chapter, are you are simply covering the event because everyone else is?

And all the while, the channel has to stay on air. The fire still has to be stoked. And the team of reporters and producers, guest-getters and graphic-designers still have to be available. And they still have to be paid.

> We should close BBC Three as a broadcast or linear channel and . . . reinvent it as a channel online and on the iPlayer. It will save the BBC over £50 million a year.
>
> Tony Hall, BBC Director-General, March 2014

From the viewer's perspective, with TV there's an inevitable delay before you actually get the news. And then what you see has been decided by someone else.

The internet is fast, delivers instant depth and unrivalled interactivity.

Platforms used for news 'nowadays': 16–24s and 55+

Those aged 16–24 are more likely than those aged 55+ to use the internet or apps to access news (60% v 21%) and they are less likely to use the television (56% v 90%). Use of a mobile for news shows the biggest difference between the age groups.

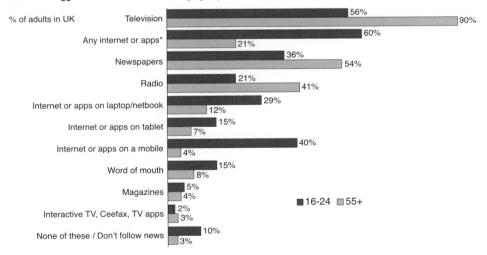

Q3a) Which of the following do you use for news nowadays?
Base: All adults 16+ (2731).
*Any internet or apps; aggregate of all internet devices.

FIGURE 4.5

The different platforms from which we consume news is evolving. Source: *News Consumption in the UK*: research report – 25 June 2014 © Ofcom (http://bit.ly/BJConsumption)

FIGURE 4.6

Top 20 news sources: reach among all adults

The top two news sources in terms of reach among UK adults are both TV channels, with BBC One being the most used (53%). The BBC websites or app is now the third most-used news source.

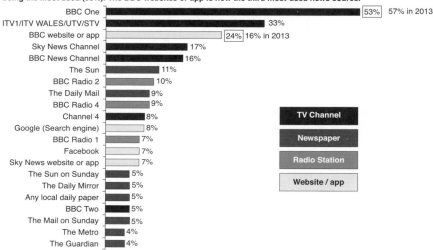

Q5a-e) Thinking specifically about <Source> which of the following do you use for news nowadays?
Base: All adults 16+ (2731)
Note: 2013 figures only shown where there are statistically significant differences between 2013 and 2014

Attributes for television news sources among those who use each source

Among users of the most-used TV news outlets, around one half rate them highly across the range of attributes. The perceived importance of Channel 4 and Channel 5 is lower than for other TV channels. TV news outlets are generally rated more highly for accuracy and trustworthiness than for impartiality by their users.

Proportion of users who rated the source highly (7–10) (%)

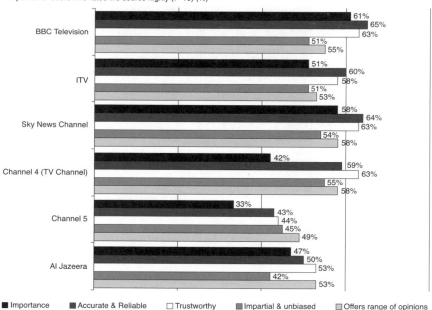

■ Importance ■ Accurate & Reliable ☐ Trustworthy ▨ Impartial & unbiased ☐ Offers range of opinions

FIGURE 4.7

Base: Those who use platform to access the news 'nowadays' on each type (varies) – Only includes bases over 50.
Note: News sources are ordered by consumption levels.

The industry remains wedded to the idea of a single, linear channel. Audiences have never been convinced. Viewing figures for news channels have always been low – spiking when a big event happens. The justification for broadcasters was to have a rolling spine of coverage that could be turned to at moments of need. Increasingly, however, we turn to the internet.

Richard Sambrook, Professor of Journalism at Cardiff University and former Director of BBC Global News; Sean McGuire, Managing Director of media consultants Oliver & Ohlbaum and former BBC News Head of Strategy. *The Guardian*, February 2014 (http://bit.ly/BJ24HourNews)

The future is in fact 'convergence'. With video and audio on demand on the internet, TV and radio stations already link from their online reports to text, archive, live camera positions and longer analytical packages.

It is leading to broadband 'smart' TVs streaming extra content linking the user to background material which can be played and paused, saved and shared and even edited with other material to create your own personalised newscast, like this video news aggregator http://watchup.com/.

Add to that the use of social media to gather and distribute material: clips or full reports go on Twitter and Facebook, reporters in the field broadcast live on Periscope and Meerkat (perhaps while they are waiting for their slot on traditional TV) and similarly eyewitness news comes in from the public via such platforms.

Traditional broadcast TV and radio can give immediacy but no depth. Their online presence gives both and saves their consumer time, and saves themselves huge transmission costs.

And as technology changes so do the roles of the staff within a newsroom (or perhaps more correctly 'news team' as they may not be all gathered in one location but working from home and dispatched to a story and feed items back from the field).

The role of the fact-checker and storyteller will surely remain, albeit in different forms and on different platforms. So in this sense the skills of knowing how to write to a deadline, questioning skills and understanding the role of images will remain important. The key will be to have transferrable and updated skills underpinned by the bedrock of core knowledge.

Return newsgathering to what it says on the tin – a service that goes out to speak to people, investigates, considers and then files packages as needed, with updates and commentary, freed of the need to fill empty space. When something happens, or new information comes to light, a new story can be generated. A package can be updated and be ready to go as soon as the consumer needs it. It's not two bodies in a studio waiting, hoping for something, anything to happen, or a miserable guy under an umbrella filling empty time.

Ibid.

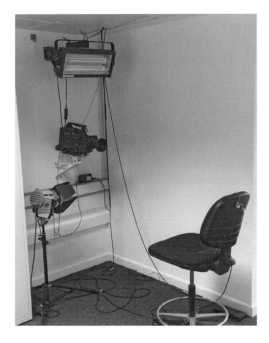

FIGURE 4.8
A remote-controlled TV camera at a regional BBC radio station. Guests can conveniently contribute to the national news channel via this camera, saving them and the Corporation time and money.

THE HEADLINES

- As news programmes become more consumer-oriented in the quest to cling to rating share in an ever fragmenting market, the distinction between news and entertainment becomes more blurred.

- The news process in radio and TV is basically one of getting the stories in, and putting them out. These two jobs are called *input* and *output*.

- With TV there's an inevitable delay before you actually get the news. And then what you see has been decided by someone else.

- The future is 'convergence'. With video and audio on demand on the internet, TV and radio stations already link from their online reports to text, archive, live camera positions and longer analytical packages.

QUESTIONS FOR YOU

1. Compare two radio bulletins – one a straight read, the other using illustrations. Which was the most interesting? Which told the news more succinctly? Did the actuality add to the story or could the newsreader have said the same things better? Which bulletin was the most memorable? Which did you prefer?
2. If you were given the opportunity to make a 30-minute fly-on-the-wall documentary, what subject would you choose, and why? Draw up a rough plan of coverage and think in detail how you would produce the first three minutes of the programme.

OTHER RESOURCES

- The BBC's 'The Future of News' is explained more on this BBC website, http://bit.ly/BJFutureVideos, which includes several embedded video discussions.

- This article in the *Guardian* newspaper discusses it in more detail: http://bit.ly/BJFutureGuardian.

- 'How Millennials Get News: Inside the habits of America's first digital generation': http://bit.ly/BJMillennials.

- 'Storytelling in the Age of Social News Consumption' is a short article on how 'social media is having a dramatic, perhaps outsized impact on how digital news is produced, distributed, consumed and ultimately monetized' (http://bit.ly/BJStorytelling).

- The future of news. It's not just print, or video or audio, it's all of these. And more. Here's the views of Katharine Viner, the editor-in-chief of *The Guardian* newspaper, which has the third most popular news website in the English-speaking world: http://bit.ly/BJViner1 and http://bit.ly/BJViner2 (includes a video of the lecture, which could be played to a tutor group for discussion).

- How news organisations are using SnapChat to report and distribute news: http://bit.ly/BJSnapchat.

- Here are some great podcasts on the future of broadcast and print journalism, including the use of mobile/cellphones (mobile journalism: MoJo), investigative reporting, social and local news . . . http://itsall journalism.com/.

- *The Newsroom* is an American television political drama series 2012–2014, chronicling the behind-the-scenes events at the fictional Atlantis Cable News channel. Here's its page on IMDB: http://bit.ly/BJIMDBNewsroom. Compare it with this series *E.N.G.*, a Canadian drama series of the lives of the staff at the fictional Channel 10 News room in Toronto (1989–1994) (http://bit.ly/BJIMDBENG), and what happens today.

- More general journalism websites to take a look at: The Reynolds Journalism Institute (http://rjionline.org/); Reportedly has lots of useful journalism articles and reports from practicing reporters (https://medium. com/reportedly/).

TUTOR NOTES

'Dramatised documentaries cheapen the news by mixing fact with fiction and information with entertainment.' Discuss.

Play the group a radio documentary and a shorter radio feature. Discuss how, apart from the length, what is the difference in the way they are constructed and the methods used to explain a story.

CHAPTER 5

Where the News Comes From

> Journalism – an ability to meet the challenge of filling the space.
>
> Rebecca West, *New York Herald Tribune*

There are some days when news just seems to fall into your lap. Everywhere you turn another story is breaking. Days like these are a journalist's dream.

The nightmare begins in the holiday season when nothing seems to happen. Most times the newsperson's lot is somewhere between these extremes. What stories there are have to be dug for. Graft is required to turn a tip-off into hard facts.

FIGURE 5.1

The main newsroom at the BBC.

A news story is usually:

Unpredictable – such as a house fire, resignation or factory closure

Predictable – a court case, a sports event, an election or anniversary

Universal – when all the media have been sent the same news release about a recent crime, product launch or survey

Unique – stories that have been generated by a reporter or listener/viewer.

THE REPORTERS

The biggest source of news for any radio or TV station should be its reporting staff.

What They've Seen and Heard

Many local stations rightly insist that their journalists live in the community to which they are broadcasting. Through everyday contact with people in the area, from their observations as they shop or drive to work, will come ideas for stories.

From the car window the reporter notices that the construction of a new factory seems to be behind time. There has been little progress for almost a month; so the reporter pulls in at the roadside and asks the foreman why. Closer to the station, rows of publicly owned houses on an inner city site seem to be rotting away; what can the authorities do to make them habitable? Squatters are moving in; are the neighbours concerned? Would the squatters resist attempts to evict them? Reporters need to keep their eyes and ears open.

Often great stories spring from the basic questions 'I wonder . . .?'As in 'I wonder why that circus poster has "cancelled" written across it . . . perhaps they didn't get a licence to perform, or animal rights' protestors are trying to cut attendance' and then following it up with a Who? What? When? Where? Why? How?

Maybe a story comes from a reporter 'joining the dots' on two separate incidents: two independent butcher's shops open in neighbouring towns? Why is there an increased interest in non-supermarket meat?

Or it may be asking themselves the question, 'if x has happened, is it likely that y will follow?': has the closure of a factory led to an increase in the number of people at a local food bank? Or having the same thought in reverse: is the increased expenditure on school places because of more people moving to the area? If so, why are they coming? And what other changes are likely to come as a result?

Reporters should get out into their community as often as possible, overhear snatches of conversation and get a feel of what real people are talking about, not just those in air-conditioned newsrooms.

Our problem is 'air conditioned journalism'. Andrew Marr (BBC news presenter), as I recall, described the cult personality as a product of news driven by press release and the personal computer. I think the heritage of a chap in a Mac walking the streets finding out what is going on and recording it, the wealth of colourful news and incidents and events, has diminished. The story content in all news across the United Kingdom and across Europe has been changed by technology and not necessarily enhanced.

Pat Loughrey, BBC Director of Nations and Regions, speaking to the
Select Committee on the BBC Charter Review, November 2005

Although many journalists may not have time to do this during working hours, most if not all can eavesdrop in their own time. Some stations have 'district reporters' or 'field reporters' whose job it is to get into the community and get to know the people and events that are there.

Wealthier stations are able to employ *specialists* – reporters who are experts in certain areas, with experience behind them and a key set of contacts. Chief fields are local government and industry, and increasingly crime and the environment.

The job of the *investigative journalist* is to find something wrong and expose it. He or she is a positive force for change, a professional with the ability to penetrate the closed ranks of vested interests and free imprisoned information from behind enemy lines. Investigative reporters may also work in teams on projects such as documentaries.

Not every station can spare the time or has the scope to permit an ordinary reporter to develop into an investigative journalist, but all reporters have to be investigators at heart.

Perhaps the best stories are the ones which are original, not the ones which have been gathered from press releases. If you've got an original story it's automatically an exclusive, and if it's targeted well and told well, it should help increase your audience numbers.

Contacts and Sources

A reporter is only as good as their sources.

Traditional journalism saying

When the big story breaks, the first thing a reporter reaches for is their contacts – whether a book or on a computer, always her most valuable resource. It contains the names, phone numbers and social-media contacts of everyone in the area who regularly makes or comments on the news, plus national figures whose sphere of influence may include the reporter's own 'beat'.

The relationship between the reporter and her contact is double-edged. The newswriter needs a story, the newsmaker needs publicity.

Clearly, a line has to be drawn, and the place to draw it is well before the point where editorial freedom and integrity begin to be compromised.

After a while, reporters may find some of their regular contacts become friends. That may be fine when there is good news involving that contact, but if the news is bad, it still has to be reported. It would be unethical to drop a story because you knew one of the people involved. It may be that you can ask another reporter to do the story, or at the very least call your contact and give them the opportunity to disagree with you and to be heard. Listen to what they have to say and explain yourself but don't get into an argument with them. Let them know you care what they have to say. In the end, the reporter must maintain her independence. She can never afford to owe anyone favours.

Remember that everyone is a potential source for information, maybe not immediately but over time. You have to be in it for the long haul. Details of almost everyone you speak with professionally or personally should be given your business card and go into your contacts book. You never know when they may be just the right person to lead you to a story.

But sources have to be maintained. Don't just call them when you want something from them. Make contact every few months or even weeks and have a chat: what's happening, is there anything that they think you may be interested in, what is the update on the story you last spoke with them about?

Obviously you will always let people know you are looking for stories and you would welcome tips or suggestions. It may be that they call with information which will never make a story, but always accept these calls and be patient. You will of course get better stories from them if you explain how the industry works and the kind of information you want from them. Reassure them with an explanation of what you mean by 'off the record', it can only help them trust you more.

There is no 'official' definition of 'off the record'. As every journalist will have a slightly different interpretation of what they mean by it, and to be fair to your contributor, you should always explain to them what you understand by the phrase.

Having said that, here is a guide to help you come to your own conclusion:

On the record: that everything that is said or recorded in the meeting or conversation can be used, and the speaker can be identified by name. Attributing a comment or fact to someone else strengthens the story by giving it a foundation, and distances you from what has been said. Indeed, you are *reporting* it.

Off the record: This could mean that the information cannot be used at all. Or it may mean that it can be used, but not attributed to the source (sometimes you may be able to use their position and not their name, other times they may ask you use neither). Or it may mean that it can't be used in a broadcast report, but that the reporter can use the information without saying where it came from, to help in their background to the story or to persuade someone else to speak *on* the record.

Always try to persuade a source speaking in their professional role to speak to you *on the record*. Background briefings are becoming increasingly common especially in government, and even though that is perhaps less of a concern for print media, broadcasters need pictures and sound.

Anonymous sources can be extremely useful. They may be a 'whistleblower' who can give you the inside scoop on what's really going on inside the hospital or council. But if they are identified they may be threatened verbally or physically by colleagues or neighbours, or lose their job. They may be sued for breaking the terms of their contract of employment.

Also consider that an anonymous source may not want to be named, because they don't want to stand by the accusation they are making. People are more likely to exaggerate if no one knows who they are. They may want to deliberately spread misinformation, or take revenge on a boss who recently sacked them. So if you have a great story, but can't attribute it to someone, always verify the information with several other sources. That may be several more anonymous sources who tell you the same thing, or a single *named* individual who can confirm it.

Networking with sources is important: tell them what topics you are interested in even if it's not in their area. Maybe they know someone who knows someone else who can help you, especially if you admit you're not an expert. (Of course if you become an expert in their topic, the more sources will respect you and give you more time.)

The more sources your story has, the more views and greater veracity it has. Different views from different people give the story context and perspective. And those different views help you check the accuracy of what each is saying, which you can use to explain the situation to the wider audience.

Politicians

Local politicians are a prime source of news for the regional newsroom. Usually they are happy to oblige as this raises their profile and may win votes. A reporter should be wise to that and make sure legitimate news, rather than vote-catching rhetoric, gets on air.

Every journalist should know the names of the area's representatives in both local and national government, and should have contact numbers for them at work and at home as well as their mobile phone numbers and those of their representatives.

When politicians are not making news themselves, they are usually good for a comment or reaction to stories that affect their constituencies. Political comment is cheap and readily available and this type of reaction can be overdone, lead to accusations of political bias, and leave a bulletin sounding as dull as a party political broadcast. Use sparingly.

Freedom of Information Requests

Several countries (notably Sweden and France) have similar Acts to the one in the UK, which give people right of access to information held by around 100,000 public bodies. It means that journalists can get information that was previously hidden – although there are still a lot of exemptions that can thwart their endeavours. Where you are not given the information, the authority approached has to give a reason.

Exemptions to the UK Freedom of Information Act include:

- Matters of national security or defence
- International relations
- The economy
- Law enforcement
- Communications with the royal family
- Personal information
- Information of commercial interest.

Ministry of Justice website (http://bit.ly/BJFoI)

It obviously takes authorities time to collate the information that is requested (up to 30 days), and then for you to interpret the figures provided (and perhaps compare them with those of other authorities, or identify a trend over several years). Therefore using an FoI request is much more appropriate for long-term investigations and background research.

YOUR NETWORK

Cross-platform Material

A growing number of BBC TV and radio newsrooms now share the same building, so there is a crossover of ideas, information and expertise. The BBC increasingly requires material to be made available on more than one platform, so reporters have to be aware that a report may be on television, its audio used on radio and then as an 'on-demand' service on the website.

Sharing resources requires a lot of planning, but saves time (and money) in the long run, and is made easier by the 'digital workflow'.

TV and radio producers in the same region may share the same computerised newsgathering diary and have access to potential stories that have been sent to, or picked up by, one or other of the teams. Planning meetings may involve a representative from another platform (such as online or social media), so while the producers discuss how a story can be covered for the visual and audio media they can start planning their pages, including links to archive material or other appropriate websites or apps ('platforms').

A TV reporter will record a report where both the interviewee and interviewer are wearing microphones (not always necessary if only a clip is needed for their bulletins, but imperative if radio want to run questions as well as

FIGURE 5.2
Stories flow into the central BBC newsroom and staff are alerted via screens such as this.

answers). The video and audio can be fed back to the station and *ingested* (fed into) into the digital system so that TV and radio staff can be editing it at the same time.

Clips that a TV reporter edits from the interview for their video package may be used as bulletin clips on radio. Alternatively they may rework their TV package (to include introductions to speakers, where a strapline would otherwise have been used) for radio playout. Or the TV reporter might present a clip-link sequence on radio. And all or some of this will make it to the website cross-promoting both platforms. Additionally, the reporter may have live-streamed the whole sequence on the smartphone, or tweeted pictures and video updates.

The advantages are that material gathered once, is used many times . . . and that there's cross-promotion to different parts of the output. The radio presenter promotes the television output ('and you can see that full report on *South East Today* on BBC1 tonight at 6.30 . . .'), which in turn promotes the website coverage ('if you've missed any of today's top news stories you can see them at bbc.co.uk/southeasttoday . . .').

Radio's part in this process is admittedly more of a consumer than provider: where TV reporters naturally gather sound and pictures, radio reporters only gather sound (unless they are 'bi-' or 'tri-media reporters'). But there are other ways radio can help provide material for the greater good: TV stations may make use of radio reporters to supply phone reports on breaking stories; they may make appeals for interviewees or case studies for their reports on the radio; and radio reporters may take short video of a news event on their mobile phone and send that back to the online desk.

At an international level, news services frequently exchange reports with one another to enhance their worldwide coverage. A number of broadcasting unions act as clearing houses.

The Network

Networking can take place in a formalised system where all the stations are owned and regulated by a single body, such as the BBC, or in a looser federation, such as Independent Radio in the UK, who use a service from Sky News Radio, which itself takes much material from its TV news service. Many radio stations are clustered into groups such as Global Radio, whose staff at their London-based news hub rewrite national and international agency copy which is sent to their local newsrooms around the UK.

Canada and Australia both have their equivalents of the BBC – the Canadian Broadcasting Corporation and the Australian Broadcasting Corporation. In many developing countries the state retains a high degree of control over TV and radio.

The first US national network came into operation in 1928, with 56 stations under the control of the National Broadcasting Company (NBC). Others followed, including ABC (American Broadcasting Company); CBS (Colombia Broadcasting System); MBS (Mutual Broadcasting System) and NPR (National Public Radio).

As trade barriers come down and satellites go up broadcasting has gone increasingly global. Moguls like the Italian Silvio Berlusconi and Australian-turned-US citizen Rupert Murdoch have vied for greater control of an increasingly volatile marketplace.

Many networks feed their string of local stations with national news from a centralised newsroom, and those stations in turn send back reports of major stories to the network.

Sky News Radio in London is Britain's main commercial radio news agency, providing news bulletins on the hour, as well as copy and audio to most of the nearly 300 stations in the independent network. Distribution is via satellite. Stations can take the national news live, or assemble and read their own versions of the bulletin. (Read more at http://news.sky.com/info/radio.)

Some stations in remote regions such as Scotland prefer to compile their own national bulletins which can be angled to suit their Scottish audiences, rather than settle for news with a real or perceived London bias.

The BBC's network 'rip and read' service operates differently, providing copy and audio which are distributed electronically, but no live bulletins.

In the USA, regional networks range from groups of stations who exchange reports on a regular basis, to scaled-down national networks with a centrally produced bulletin transmitted every hour.

When a station switches over to take the network news, this is called *opting-in* to the network. The process of switching back is called *opting-out*. Where opt-outs are used, bulletins will end with a readily identifiable *outcue* such as a timecheck, which is the presenter's cue for switching back to local programming. Some of the outcues contain tones or signals (inaudible to the human ear) within a jingle, which can automatically fire commercials or a pre-recorded programme at the 'home' radio station.

Some radio stations follow the national news with a local bulletin, although in the UK most prefer to combine the two in a single bulletin, known as a *news-mix*. On television in the UK, national news is followed or preceded by a local bulletin; in the USA it's usually a national/local mix.

Local TV and radio stations will also be expected to contribute to the pool of news stories available to the network. So in the UK, Global's network of Heart radio stations will get a service of national news from their London HQ, while reporters at each station produce local material. In return if a major event happens in their area, a Heart reporter will file audio to London for redistribution to the network (which includes Capital FM and Smooth radio stations, and the national station Classic FM), and may also report live on the company's speech service, LBC.

Audio can be emailed to a central newsroom, or (as is the case with video) dropped into a central server direct from the reporter's desktop. This material can then be retrieved by any other reporter in the network.

Wire Services and News Agencies

The major external source of news is the international news agencies. Among the largest is Reuters, with 2,600 journalists at 200 locations, supplying news by satellite to hundreds of broadcasters across the world (www.about.reuters.com). Other global giants include the US-based Associated Press (AP – www.ap.org), which

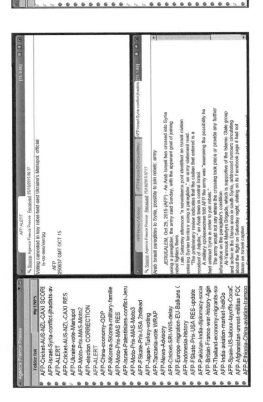

FIGURE 5.3

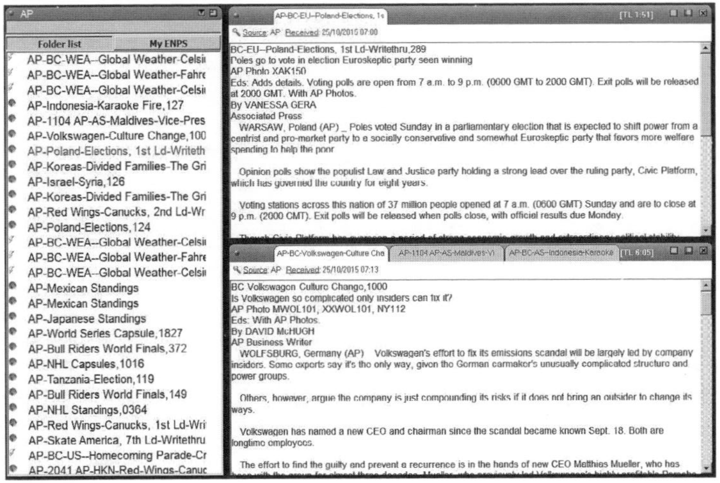

FIGURE 5.4

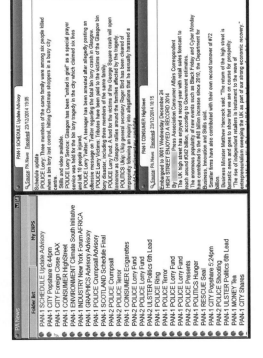

FIGURE 5.5

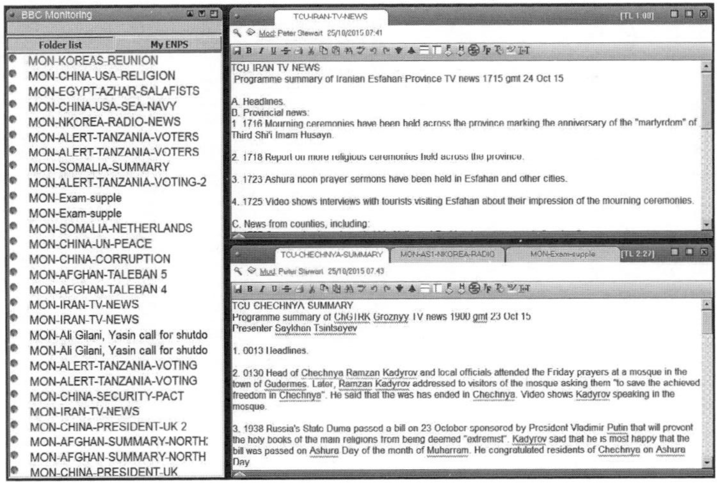

FIGURE 5.6

Breaking news from various news agencies flow into the newsroom where they are read and rated for their significance by editorial staff

has 4,000 employees and delivers news to more than 130 countries and 1 billion readers, listeners and viewers through its AP Television News.

Britain's domestic news agency is the Press Association (PA – www.thepagroup.com), whose legion of journalists and stringers provide thousands of stories a day to most British newsrooms. Equivalents include the Australian Associated Press (AAP) and Canadian Press.

Agencies employ correspondents whose reports are relayed directly into newsroom computers. Audio and video reports are beamed to newsrooms by satellite where they are re-recorded for later use.

Agency correspondents can effectively boost even the smallest station's coverage to incorporate national or international news, multiplying by many times the number of reporters at that station's disposal and leaving local journalists free to concentrate on their patch.

As well as news, some agencies offer specialised wires, covering fields of interest such as weather, sport or business news.

Freelances and Stringers

Most newsrooms supplement their own material by buying news tip-offs and stories from freelances. Non-staff members who contribute regularly are known as *stringers* or correspondents; working journalists who add considerably to the eyes and ears of a station. Freelances may also be employed to fill for absent members.

Stringers are often local newspaper reporters boosting their incomes by selling copy to other media in the area – with or without the blessing of their editors. Some will make their living this way.

The most organised may band together to form a local news agency. These often specialise in fields such as court, council or sports reporting – assignments that would often take too much time to make it worth an editor's while to cover. Instead, a stringer will be commissioned to cover the event, and will usually file for a number of outlets.

Stringers will either be specially commissioned to report a story, or will offer their copy 'on spec.', in the hope that the station will buy it.

Advantages and Disadvantages of Using Stringers

Advantages:

- Stringers are cost-effective because they are often paid only for work that gets used on air.
- They enhance a station's 'ground cover', by using local specialist knowledge to get stories that might not be available to staff reporters.
- They can be commissioned to cover stories that would be too time-consuming to warrant staff coverage.
- Experienced broadcast freelances can fill for staff members who are sick or on holiday.

Disadvantages:

- Stringer copy is seldom exclusive as their living depends on supplying news to as many outlets as possible.

- Copy may not be in broadcast style, as many stringers are newspaper journalists more familiar with writing for print.

- Stringers have to sell their copy to make a living, so stories may be dressed up to make them more marketable.

- Stringers are less accountable than staffers who can be more readily disciplined for their mistakes.

Syndicated Recordings

Among the daily plethora of unsolicited material that arrives in the newsroom may be a number of recorded items sent in by public relations companies. These are often available free of charge and usually have some advertising tie-up.

The video version is known as the *video news release* (VNR). This and its radio equivalent are more sophisticated variations of the news release which appeal to producers who are slothful or overstretched and who may be grateful to receive something for nothing. But as the saying goes, there is no such thing as a free lunch. The PR company hopes stations will find a slot for the item and play it on air unedited. Used in this way, syndicated recordings are simply free, unadulterated, publicity.

They may be interviews with airline bosses talking about new or cheaper flights; company directors explaining plans for a superstore in the area or even agricultural hints and tips from a government agency.

At best, syndicated items are harmless, even useful, fillers. At worst they can be scarcely disguised adverts or propaganda. No unsolicited recordings should be used without checking for violations of the advertising code, and that journalistically and technically the piece is up to standard and relevant to the audience. Handle with care and include an on-air credit mentioning the material's source.

OTHER NEWS MEDIA

Monitoring

Journalists take a professional pride in beating other media to a story. Most news editors monitor their 'rivals' to make sure they are ahead with the news and to see if there is anything they have missed.

This is what we said in the previous edition:

> One of the news editor's first tasks each day is usually to go through the national and local papers to see if there are any stories referring to the area which need to be followed up.

Now more than ever 'the news never sleeps'. Although looking through newspapers is a valuable exercise, it is very likely that the stories you see will have been reported hours ago on other platforms. That could be the newspaper's own online edition, on tweets from their reporters, or by a local community or residents' blog. It is hugely likely that the emergency services have used social media to warn about a crash or a crime, or that residents have tweeted to their followers about a house fire. It is simply not enough nowadays to wait for someone else's news to be distilled, collated, edited, printed and distributed and for you to follow up *hours* later.

Set up lists on Twitter to better monitor what is going on in your area.

News sources:

- Councils and politicians
- Emergency services
- Other local/national news media
- Other lists for schools, faith groups, residents' associations and blogs, sport clubs, business, tourist locations . . .
- Specialists in your 'beat' – perhaps science, health or the environment.

Local place names:

- Mentioned by your followers and non-followers (listen-in to their conversations to discover what's going on in your TSA)

Essential Tweeting Skills for Radio Stations: http://bit.ly/BJTweets.

Chasing and Checking

Following-up a news item means checking and developing it to find a new angle. This means much more than just taking a story from a newspaper and rewriting it for broadcast. That would be plagiarism – stealing somebody's work. Facts may also be wrong and errors repeated.

So you need to go back to the original source of the story and confirm that what has been reported so far is correct. Then you can develop it and perhaps find another or a better angle.

There is no copyright on ideas and journalists often feed on one another for their leads and inspiration, as in this actual example.

'Get the father . . .'

Two rival TV news programmes went on air close to one another in the evening: *Coast to Coast*, the independent programme, between 6 and 6.30; *South Today*, the BBC service, from 6.35 to 7.

Coast to Coast picks up a breaking news story. A local businessman is to be released from Libya. He had been jailed because his boss's company had run into debt there and he was being held responsible. He is to be set free and is flying home tonight. *Coast to Coast* has carried the item as a copy story.

South Today is monitoring the programme and immediately gets a reporter to phone Gatwick airport to try to interview the father, who is waiting for his son's flight.

Meanwhile *Coast to Coast* has just finished and the opening sequences of *South Today* are going out on air. The presenters are told to stand by for late breaking news.

Minutes later copy comes in saying the businessman is due to arrive within the hour, and a presenter breaks from the script to read the story unrehearsed.

At the airport, public relations staff are busily trying to find the father.

Twenty minutes into the programme and all that remains is the weather and the headlines. The father has not been found and time is running out. The producer takes over the story. He gets through to the father even as the closing headlines are being read.

The director quickly tells one of the presenters through his earpiece that the father is on the phone waiting to be interviewed. The presenter has 45 seconds to ad-lib the interview before the programme ends and transmission returns to the network. It is not possible to overrun by even a second.

The businessman's father says he is delighted his son is returning home. The Foreign Office confirmed the news yesterday. As alcohol was forbidden in Libya, they will crack open some bottles of his son's favourite beer.

The director counts down the closing seconds while the presenter thanks the father for talking to him and wishes the viewers a calm good evening. The programme ends bang on time and as coolly as if it had all been planned from the start. Independent television led the way, but the BBC got the better story.

Developing and Knocking

Checking a story from another media and running it yourself is all well and good. But when does 'following up' on a story actually mean you are simply 'following': reporting the same facts, just hours later?

You need to get your own angle and develop the story, telling it in your own way. That may be a different angle or different speakers. It may be that you knock the original information and tell the *opposite* story. The other station has an interview with the local council about their increased lighting of a park and subway. Your story could ask why the equipment wasn't put in sooner, or report on similar schemes in the area where the equipment has been left to vandals. Or ask why the pathway that nurses use to get to the local hospital hasn't been fitted out in a similar way . . .

The other media gave you a 'tip off' on one story, but that's led you to find a new story yourself, which has trumped theirs.

Citizen Reporters

Many stories coming to broadcasters from the public are now more than just tip-offs (or complaints) and can include audiovisual material leading this information to be classified as 'user generated content' or 'citizen journalism'.

The term user-generated content (UGC) . . . has been a contentious phrase for quite a few years now, with a definition so broad and awkward that it cannot accurately describe the phenomenon that we are focused on. It feels impersonal, ignoring the fact that a person, an individual, has borne witness to an event. That event may be mundane (a sunrise used in a weather report); it may be spectacular (meteorites falling out of the sky in Russia); it may be traumatic (Paris). Whatever it is, the evidence has been captured by an eyewitness – hence we say let's leave UGC behind and use the term 'eyewitness media'.

Sam Dubberley, Eyewitness Media Hub

People who send in stories or pictures are not journalists per se, they gather information maybe, but they don't necessarily gather *facts*, or check them, or look for second sources.

After the explosion of the oil depot at Buncefield, UK in 2005, the BBC received 6,500 emails with video clips and still pictures attached. That was perhaps the first major example in the UK, at least, of such reporting contributing to the newsgathering process.

It may be 'amateur photography' but it's also 'eyewitness video', real events and real reaction to them. And with all mobile phones having good quality still and video cameras, a 'citizen reporter' is rarely far away from any unfolding event.

The problem though is verifying authenticity, accuracy and legality, and asking other questions of the listener/viewer. Did they get into danger to film something? Did they create an incident in order to film it? Did they film it with a view to getting a fee?

Certainly a picture, text or email is a good tip-off (in the same way as a phone call from an eyewitness always was), but it always needs to be followed up and checked out.

Every station has its time wasters and hangers-on who phone in or call round out of sheer self-importance. Worst of all, the tipster may be malicious, and the information a hoax. (See more on hoaxes and how to guard against them, later in this chapter.)

Pressure Groups

A similar warning applies to using pressure groups for reaction and comment: beware of vested interests. Big pressure groups include trade unions and employers' organisations. Smaller groups and many charities also act as pressure groups; test the views of each one vigorously.

Although you should beware of unrepresentative groups with only a handful of members, bona fide pressure groups do have an important contribution to make to public debate.

HOAXES

BBC World broadcast an interview on 3 December (2004) in which a bogus Dow Chemical official – Jude Finisterra – admitted responsibility for the Bhopal disaster in 1984 and offered $12 billion in compensation. That interview was then used on BBC News 24 and domestic radio stations Radio 2, Radio 4 and Radio Five Live. However, Mr Finisterra turned out to be a hoaxer from a group called the Yes Men, online activists who create fake but well-crafted web parodies to make political statements.
http://bit.ly/BJDow

Broadcast news, with its quick-fire deadlines and lack of time for checks and balances, sometimes falls prey to the most elaborate of hoaxes. People ring up claiming to be contacts who are known by the station, such as police inspectors, and offer phoney information.

If in doubt, check it out. The only sure protection against the hoaxer is a set of sharp wits and the common sense to check the information.

Always ask yourself:

- How does this person know what they are telling me?

- What is my knowledge of their previous accuracy?

- Why might they be exaggerating, lying or omitting some facts? What is their self-interest?

- How can I check what I am being told?

If someone rings up claiming to be a regular contact and does not ring true for some reason, get her number and check it against the known contact's number. Even if it matches, ring her back to make sure she had not simply looked up the number and quoted it. If the caller is genuine, she should not object to the care with which her information is being checked.

Occasionally, a tip-off will yield some useful information, but for safety's sake *all* tip-offs, whether they appear genuine or not, must be checked before running

– even if it does mean missing the deadline. In the end, accuracy counts for more than speed – *if it doesn't check out, chuck it out.*

Or in the mantra of the BBC – 'it's better to be second and right, than first and wrong'.

In an age of more airtime to fill, more desire for speed, and more 'amateur correspondents', there's also more likelihood that you too will one day become a victim.

- Photoshop and other digital manipulation. The camera *does* lie.

- People lie too: they say the picture was taken in a certain place. Is the image geo-located? Does the location look authentic to an expert in that area, or from basic checks on maps and other pictures from that place?

- Look at the background of the picture for other clues. The weather for that location on that day. Any writing on signs, car number plates or the vehicles themselves. Do all the clues add up to this picture being of where it is claimed it is of? If you have video, is the language or accent used authentic for that area?

- Can the sender of a picture or video be contacted? Are they using a 'proper name' rather than a social media name? Is their job or role a 'trustworthy' one? Can they send you another picture right now or prove that they are where they claim to be?

- Does the information or picture clarify or give added weight to other images you are getting in? *Is it too good to be true . . .?*

- The video may be authenticated but it may be from a source which you are wary of using: perhaps a political pressure group or terrorist organisation. That may change the context of the item.

PLANNED EVENTS

The Newsroom Diary

This electronic diary provides the 'bread and butter' of the daily output. All staff may be expected to contribute to it, putting in details of embargoed news releases, staged events and conferences, meetings, openings and anniversaries of previous news events. Alongside these may be court appearances (together with copy relating to earlier hearings), diary notes and follow-ups ('check whether the Jones family flooded out of their home on Christmas ever got compensation from the water company . . .'), or scheduled features ('the start of our week-long series on the impact a new road through Ambridge will have on different communities living in the village . . .').

From the diary of potential stories the news editor will pick the 'best' ones which will be covered by her team, and create a shorter list of 'prospects'.

This will give details of stories the newsroom will cover, the times of events and the reporters allotted to them. It is the day's plan of action; the newsroom route map, so everyone is aware of what each one of them is expected to contribute.

Added to this mix will be new stories as they emerge during the day, as well as of course 'breaking news'.

What are the 'best' stories?

Each of your viewers or listeners will have a different view of what is news. That is why news aggregator apps are so successful: you choose the topics you want to know more about, and those stories are presented to you without the 'clutter' of, say politics or sport or financial news.

And each news editor will have a different view of what is news, or more specifically, what is news for their output, on that day, with these stories available, and these reporters on shift, and the time available. And a thousand other criteria.

A better story further away from the TV station may not be covered because of the logistics of getting there. Or maybe a story from that town *is* covered, largely because that place is rarely mentioned.

A good story may not be told because there are no good pictures available and 'it wouldn't make good TV'. Or the story is barely news at all, but there is action, lights, a celebrity and a troupe of dancers . . .

A complicated story that should go today may not be told at all because of the time and expertise needed to plough through pages of a report, and interpret data for the audience and present it all in a 90 second report.

Two mediocre stories may get into the programme because they are quicker and easier to set up and tell on the day that several members of staff call in sick.

It's a good story, but it's ignored because the station told a similar one last week.

It's a good story, and despite telling a similar one last week, it's covered because this could be the start of a trend.

It's a good story but, on a day where we already have several 'heavy and serious' items, we need something lighter to give shade and balance. Or it's from the same town that several of our other stories are from today. Or it was filmed yesterday by the same reporter who's on another story today and they can't be on two reports in the same programme. Or the speaker is a 'grey man in a grey suit' . . . what we need is celebrity, children and animals!

On the same computer system, or possibly still in hard copy in a filing cabinet, is background information on major stories containing up-to-date cuttings and background information, contacts and archive audio/video. Bigger stations have libraries and news information services to help with more extensive research.

An electronic archive will also come as standard in desktop newsroom systems, filing all the copy used and the recordings of the output.

News Releases

Each morning, editors in broadcast newsrooms have a pile of emails in their inbox.

Yet most of the items dispatched to the media will end up in the 'deleted items' folder after scarcely a second glance. That is because so much is irrelevant and of little interest to the audience. Middle Eastern countries have been known to send regular bulletins on their economic progress and internal politics to small town radio stations in England.

To sift the wheat from the chaff, incoming news releases are *copytasted*. To scrutinise each item carefully could take hours, so the content of each is hastily scanned. Unless a news angle presents itself almost immediately the copy is binned.

Most of the material comprises public relations handouts – usually dressed-up advertising the writers hope will pass as news. They are usually disappointed.

If the handout is one of the small percentage that does contain a possible story, it will be checked and written up into copy or may make a live or recorded interview, feature or possibly a series.

STAGED EVENTS

Staging a news event is the pressure group's ultimate way of winning attention. These usually fall into one of three categories: the *protest*; *announcement* and *set-piece*.

The Protest

This is the pressure group trying to give its voice as wide a public hearing as possible. A three-lane highway is to be constructed across green fields to run alongside a housing estate. Residents, environmentalists and opposition politicians form an action group to stage a march on the town hall. To make sure the cameras are there they make the event as visual as possible, with people dressed in fancy costumes and carrying banners. To ensure radio coverage they chant and sing specially written protest songs.

The Announcement

This is more formal, and often takes the shape of a news conference (many people in the broadcast media detest the phrase '*press* conference'!). When the town planners announce their three-lane highway they do so with a lavish presentation. All the media is invited to a conference in the chandeliered opulence of the town hall banqueting room. Drinks are laid on and a buffet provided.

When reporters have been wined and dined and their journalistic sensibilities submerged beneath a stupor of alcohol, the mayor and other senior officials are ceremoniously invited to make their presentation.

The road scheme is flourished with neat and convincing rhetoric about better traffic flow, reduced accident figures and the positive effect on trade in the town. For the cameras, there are stylish mock-ups of the road and artists' impressions. For the media, press packs are provided with slickly written articles the organisers hope will be published unaltered. Key speakers are available immediately after the presentation for photocalls and interviews.

The Set-piece

This is usually staged simply for publicity. The new highway has been built, and a TV personality hired to open it by leading a cavalcade of vintage cars along its length – very visual and almost assured of TV coverage. At its best the set-piece provides a bright and appealing story for the bulletin, at its worst it can be news manipulation of the first order.

A prime example was the funeral of an IRA hunger striker that received widespread coverage on British television. This was largely thanks to the specially constructed grandstand provided by the terrorist organisation just for the cameras.

At the other extreme was the 'Great Auk Story'. Reporters from British newspapers and a TV journalist were lured to the remote Orkney Islands where a team of five eccentrics was believed to be embarking on an expedition to find the Great Auk, a seabird thought to have been extinct for 150 years. Hopes were fuelled by reported sightings by islanders. When the bird eventually did make an appearance it was not only extinct, it was stuffed. It turned out to be a stunt for a whisky company. It was not wholly successful. At least one reporter, peeved at being taken on a wild Auk chase, refused to name the distillery which had organised the stunt.

Where news events are a lavish attempt at news management by publicity seekers, journalists should be aware of this and not let it influence their news judgement. Money talks, but it is up to you whether you listen.

Stunts and Photo-opportunities

Since broadcast journalists started looking for things to point cameras and microphones at, publicists have been hunting for ways to satisfy that need – for their clients. It is their job. Somebody always does a stunt about strawberries and cream for Wimbledon tennis. For more serious issues, be cautious about using the words 'publicity stunt' in a script because the people involved may claim it is not a 'stunt' but of 'genuine public interest' and that such a claim damages their reputation. But the audience can usually work it out anyway and make their views known within seconds.

Stunts are however often admitted by the publicity people – but they describe these events as 'photo-opportunities' which generations ago included politicians kissing babies, which rarely happens now.

There are always plenty of 'photo-opportunities' in election campaigns, and plenty of opportunities for them to backfire, such as the politician on a street walk-about whose words were picked up by a radio reporter's microphone when he said to an assistant, *'what's the next crap town?'*

A broadcasting news publicity pioneer was Jim Moran in America in the early days of TV and radio news. To promote an appliance company he sold a fridge to an Eskimo. For the benefit of TV journalists he searched for a needle in a haystack to promote a property development. To promote a confection bar he planned to attach a small adult actor onto a kite in New York. When the police stopped this stunt he said, '*It's a sad day for American capitalism when a man can't fly a midget in a kite over Central Park.*' So he was an early adopter of great sound-bites as well.

Embargoes

Some news releases carry *embargoes*, which means they are not to be used before a certain release date. Public relations people use the embargo to try to control the flow of news, and prevent stories being run in what they would regard as a haphazard fashion. On the plus side, the embargo gives the newsroom time to prepare its report by giving advance warning of the event. (If there is no mention of an embargo, or if the phrase 'For Immediate Release' is used, it indicates that the information can be used as soon as it is received.)

The Queen's New Year Honours List is a good example of embargoed material. The list is sent out well before the official announcement. Local stations can then produce stories about people in their area that are ready to run the moment the embargo is lifted.

Some journalists like the embargo system, though it encourages lazy reporting and props up poor correspondents. We have many fine science reporters in the UK but there are some poor ones that do little else but reproduce press releases and embargoed copy. Scoops, what every journalist should want, are few and far between in science as the embargo process militates against them.

David Whitehouse, former BBC Science Correspondent,
The Independent, 23 July 2007 (http://bit.ly/BJScience)

Other information that may be embargoed:

- Financial information on interest rates, company profits warnings or national budget announcements whose early release may affect local or global stock markets.

- For security reasons, visits by politicians or heads of state to dangerous locations may be embargoed until they have left the area.

- An embargo (or 'news blackout') may be requested or ordered by authorities involved in say, a siege or negotiations to release a kidnap victim, or to temporarily restrict publicity after a murder so investigations can continue out of the public eye.

Pros of an embargo:

- All media are on a level playing field. They all have the information released to them at the same time and the opportunity to work on a story for several days.

- More time to produce a story should mean that it is told more accurately, with more opportunity to interview several people or gather background information. This may make a longer and more interesting feature.

Cons of an embargo:

- With around-the-clock news channels and websites, there are more outlets that want to be first or get 'the scoop'. At the very least they may be frustrated by an embargo, or at worst, go ahead and break it.

- Breaking an embargo gives that outlet an unfair advantage: they are first with the news and may find any 'punishment' for their actions (not getting other embargoed information for a certain period of time) acceptable.

- Ignoring an embargo means that editors are more concerned with first than with being best. Perhaps they consider 'breaking' a story more important (to them? Their career? Their audience? Their ratings?) than a considered, well-produced feature.

- If a reporter wants to interview other people who are not directly associated with the story, how can they be briefed or questioned without the embargo being broken?

NEW NEWS

Check Calls

A story that is happening right *now*, such as an armed robbery, fire or air crash, is known in Britain as *breaking news* and often in America as a *spot story*.

Prime sources of breaking news are of course the emergency services – fire, police, ambulance, coastguard, etc. The media offices of those organisations would be called so often by reporters doing 'a round of check calls', that information was recorded by the PR staff onto a tape which the reporters called instead. Such recordings were usually updated several times a day, often had little relation to a deadline and left a newsroom at the mercy of a non-journalist's news judgement. Now the whole process has sped up: neighbours' talk of a house fire is likely to be seen by a reporter on social media while the incident is happening. It's possible that they can be at the scene before the fire service and very likely before a media relations spokesperson. Very often reporters can phone the media office asking for information about a breaking event, possibly one tweeted about by their own officers, only to find that they know more about the incident than the PR person!

The problem is that in an area rich in news media, the overworked emergency services may be tempted to shake off callers by playing down an incident, saying nothing is happening even when it is, misunderstanding the news angle of a story . . . or not releasing information to the media at large but only when specifically asked by individual reporters.

From the other side of the situation, shift changes may also mean a reporter's call is made before the new duty officer has managed to catch up on her paperwork, so she is unaware of the events of the previous few hours and gives the reporter a false impression.

A common mistake is for the reporter to try to get information from the wrong person. In British police stations constables are rarely authorised to talk to the media, who should instead refer inquiries to duty inspectors or station sergeants. If a serious crime has been committed, a station sergeant may know little about it, so the best contact would be the detective from CID (Criminal Investigation Department) or equivalent, handling the case.

Press officers are distant from the scene of the crime, so information can take some time to get to them. To make matters worse, local police may not realise the news value of an incident – and therefore tell the press office - until several hours after it has happened, or they may not consider the value in making an immediate appeal for witnesses to an incident or to trace a getaway car. If they *do* know what is happening at the scene of a big story, they are often instructed in major crimes to redirect all inquiries to the press office. And of course it should always be remembered that the role of the emergency services is to help those in immediate need, and that's more likely to be someone in a life-threatening situation than a reporter with a deadline.

Often the police need the media as much as the media needs the police, for making appeals for witnesses and help in tracing missing persons. Reporters are not obliged to co-operate, but goodwill is often the best way of ensuring a steady flow of information.

Emergency Services Radio

The surest way to keep in touch with major breaking news is to tune in to emergency services radio. By monitoring the transmissions of police and fire services you can hear the news as it is actually happening, instead of waiting for the official version to be collated and sanitised by a spokesperson.

In Britain it is illegal to listen to police radio and take action as a result of that information. The law is intended to deter criminals from listening to police activity. To make it harder, messages from base are given on one frequency and mobile units reply on another, so only half the conversation can be heard at one time.

In America it is common for reporters to turn up at an incident before the police, but British law means that writing a story from a police broadcast, or sending a reporter to the scene, could result in a prosecution. However, in practice it would be difficult to prove the reporter had been listening to police radio. A more likely outcome would be the straining of relationships between the newsroom and the police, which could result in a loss of goodwill and stem the flow of official information.

In places where listening in is legal, newsrooms commonly use radio *scanners*. These monitor the emergency airwaves for a transmission and home in on the conversation.

The 10 Code

In many countries the police talk to one another in a code designed to help them communicate clearly and rapidly over the air, while at the same time mystifying unauthorised eavesdroppers.

Frequently the code used is a variation of the 10 code. Instead of saying 'Fight in progress', for example, an officer might say '10–10', followed by the location. Each force may have its own version of the code where the numbers mean something different.

Some of the key messages in one variation of the 10 code are:

10–31 Crime in progress
10–32 Person with a gun
10–33 Emergency
10–34 Riot
10–35 Major crime alert
10–50 Accident

Whatever is heard over police radio *must* be checked before use. 'Emergencies' can turn out to be a storm in a teacup – or something else. People rushed to a field in Cheshire after police messages warned that a flying saucer had crash-landed. When they turned up they were promptly arrested by little *blue* men who charged them with listening illegally to police radio (source: *The Guardian*, 23 March 1993).

THE HEADLINES

- News is what someone, somewhere doesn't want reported.

- Don't fall into the trap of air-conditioned journalism. You have to build contacts and go out and find stories.

- Beware embargoes and don't break them without consideration.

QUESTIONS FOR YOU

1. Analyse the content of a news bulletin, newspaper or website. Look at every story and work out where the news originated. Was it a breaking news item? Was it a scheduled event or from a news release? Or do you think that they may have been prompted by an idea from a member of staff or viewer/listener/reader? What is the proportion of these? Do they change over time or in the course of a week?

2. A criminal investigation leads from a story that you produced, that was started by a conversation from an anonymous source. The judge orders you to name that person. Will you name them and break your word? Or would you protect your source and go to prison for disobeying the court?

3. A light plane has crashed in your local neighbourhood. What sources will you use for information and comment? You may want to consider those involved in the rescue, experts and eyewitnesses, as well as documents. How will you find these sources? What will you ask them and want them to say? How will the evidence you collect help you tell your story?

4. Your newsroom gets sent an audio or video release from the local council. In it, the leader is commenting about the new riverbank footpath that's opening tomorrow. Will you use it? If so, how will you write the cue to introduce the clip? What if instead she is talking about the following year's budget plans? Who do you think has conducted the interview? Will using this material have any long-term implications?

5. With non-stop breaking news from your area on social media platforms such as Twitter, papers no longer have the right to use the prefix 'news'. Discuss.

6. Get into pairs. One of you is the head of PR for a drugs company that is to release information on a breakthrough treatment for arthritis. It will relieve the pain felt by millions of people around the world. It is cheap and has few side effects. You have prepared a news release that will go out in 24 hours, and is embargoed until 24 hours after that. The other one of you is a reporter who last week got a hot lead about the drug from a trusted contact. You have done some investigations and realise you have an exclusive which is to run in the bulletins tomorrow morning. After putting most of the story together, the reporter calls the PR department to get a confirmation and a quote. Act out the conversation.

   - The PR person is furious their embargo is to be broken
   - The reporter has known nothing of this embargo until now. They have simply done some good journalism.
   - The PR person may threaten sanctions against the reporter's company if the story is broadcast ahead of other media. How might the reporter persuade them otherwise?
   - How can the PR person put their point about a controlled release of information?
   - Is there any negotiation that can be done, a middle ground that the two parties can meet on? What might that be?
   - How could the scenario be different if the reporter runs the (accurate) story without first contacting the drugs company?
   - This is a frustrating situation for the drugs company and for the reporter. Is anyone at fault? Could either side have played things differently?

- The development of the new drug is obviously good news for the company. How might the conversation have been different if the reporter had found evidence, ahead of an embargoed news release, that there'd been serious side-effects for patients taking an existing widely-used drug?

7. What would you do if as a reporter, you accidently break an embargo?
8. Give an example of when you may want to deliberately break an embargo. Write an email to your news editor trying to persuade them.
9. You have respected an embargo and prepared your story for broadcast, but you have just noticed a rival outlet has started running the story 24 hours ahead of time. What will you do? Who will you talk to? How will you phrase your part of the conversation?

OTHER RESOURCES

- The Eyewitness Media Hub 'supports the creation, discovery, verification and publication of eyewitness media' and has lots of useful reports and training: http://www.eyewitnessmediahub.com/.

- Five tips for verifying citizen footage that every journalist should know: http://bit.ly/BJVerify and more here: http://verificationjunkie.com/.

- The Global Investigative Journalism Network is a mine of useful information for those who want to dig a little deeper into stories: http://gijn.org/.

- If you use social media as part of your newsgathering, this site shows you geotagged tweets and other events in any area that you draw on the map. So, for example, draw a map near the scene of a fire for one-off story information, or have a permanent map of the area around a government building to see what's being tweeted near there (www.coeverywhere.com/trending).

- Search across multiple social networks with powerful filters that help pin-point valuable social media content, so you can see what people are saying about, for example, the fire across town (www.samdesk.io/).

- A pocket guide on verifying details of a video: https://storify.com/reportedly/a-pocket-guide-to, and a book with similar information: http://verificationhandbook.com/.

- Upload a picture to this website and it will trawl the internet in seconds to find every time that it was used before, so you can verify its authenticity: http://www.tineye.com/.

- Why do press releases get such bad press? http://bit.ly/BJReleases.

- Very rarely you almost literally fall over the news: This reporter spots a missing boy while reporting about his disappearance: http://bit.ly/BJBoy.

- The kind of topics that one police force accepts FoI requests for: http://bit.ly/BJFreedom.

- How social media is reshaping news: http://bit.ly/BJReshaping.

- How news outlets can cover the war on ISIS with social media: http://bit.ly/BJIsis.

- 'From Arab Street to Social Movements: Re-theorizing collective action *and* social media in the "Arab Spring"'– http://bit.ly/BJSpring.

- 'Coronary Calcium Screening and the American Heart Association News Embargo' — a detailed report on a news embargo on a Scientific Statement from the American Heart Association and the consequences of it being breached by journalists (http://bit.ly/BJCalcium).

TUTOR NOTES

Open up TweetDeck and search for 'can we use your photo' or similar and you'll see how dependent newsrooms have become on including eyewitness media in their output.

Lead a group discussion on the logistical, ethical and legal challenges surrounding eyewitness media – people who post pictures or video online and are asked whether a broadcaster can use it. Issues raised may relate to verification, ownership, consent, safety and critical consumption.

- How would your students approach someone to ask permission to use their material? What form of words would they use? Does it depend on the content (a snow-scene or a bomb-blast)? What should they say first? (Consider: 'are you OK?'). Should they mention giving credit? How can they not put added pressure on the member of the public, at what could be an emotional time for them? (Is someone able to make an informed decision about consent after just experiencing a traumatic event?)

- Consider how the eyewitness might feel if content they have shared for free then contributes to the increased traffic, readership and in some cases advertising revenue for news sites (for example, when commercials are placed at the start of a video on a website).

- If you are a journalist on your station's website, how will you use video taken at a news event? Is it ethical to brand it with your own logo? Does it matter you do this if you have paid for the video? Might doing this stop other broadcasters using it, or if it is shared on social-media would at least give your station some credit?

- Should you instead *link* to the original content?

There are several hypothetical stories used in this chapter to illustrate the points made: challenge your students to look for real-life examples from their local communities or from national news.

CHAPTER 6

Choosing and Chasing the Story

> The camaraderie of the newsroom; the mischief of asking questions; the fun of working outside the norm of 9–5; the special status of licensed voyeur, busybody; the envied status of being on the inside track.
>
> Kim Fletcher, *Media Guardian*, July 2006

News editors are to broadcast journalism what generals are to warfare. They set the objectives, weigh the resources and draw up the plan of campaign. Under their command are the officers and troops on the ground.

Some news editors prefer to be in the thick of battle, directing the action from the front line, while others favour a loftier perspective, set back from the heat of the action. These will oversee strategy, but delegate a number two to be responsible for tactics. In larger newsrooms, this may be the deputy news editor, senior producer or bulletin producer. Working to the news editor's plan of campaign he/she will keep in touch with the news as it develops and arrange coverage.

FIGURE 6.1

The main entrance to the BBC News headquarters in central London with giant 'ticker tape' updates.

Good afternoon from Westminster. Here's how it's looking:

:: HOAX: David Cameron has been speaking about the moment a hoax caller managed to get through to his mobile phone. Downing Street is reviewing its security procedures after the caller - who pretended to be the head of spy agency GCHQ - was put through to the Prime Minister. We're offering two-ways with our reporter Matt Cole 1600-1800.

:: FRACKING: Some MPs will attempt to bring in a moratorium on fracking for shale oil and gas, by tabling an amendment to a bill in the Commons today. The debate won't begin until 1530 at the very earliest. We'll dip into it and send clips - if they don't get to it until this evening, we'll file the clips overnight.

:: GREECE: UK politicians have been reacting to the far-left Syriza party's victory in Greece's general election. We've been sending clips.

:: ABUSE: The senior QC who advises the inquiry into historical allegations of child abuse, Ben Emmerson, will be questioned by MPs on the Home Affairs Select Cttee from 1530 approx.

:: SOLDIERS: Some of the last British soldiers to have served in Afghanistan will take part in a uniformed march to Parliament this afternoon, where a reception is being held for them. We're hoping to gather a few interviews before the march and will alert the relevant regions.

:: COMMONS: The Commons sits from 1430 with Work & Pensions questions, followed by a debate on the Infrastructure Bill.

FIGURE 6.2

The suggested stories to be covered by the BBC's parliamentary team

FIGURE 6.3

Sifting through story ideas at ITN to answer the perennial question – what to cover and what to leave out. Courtesy of Andrew Boyd.

COPYTASTING

Each newsroom will have someone in charge of the newsdesk at all times, keeping a close eye on agency material and breaking stories. As news comes in, a senior journalist will copytaste each item to see if it is worth running or pursuing or offers new information on an existing story.

When a good story breaks unexpectedly, the news editor, like the general, must be prepared to switch forces rapidly from one front to another to meet the new challenge.

Reporters may be asked to drop what they are doing and cover the new story instead; old running orders will be scrapped and new ones devised. This demand for sharp reflexes, total flexibility and all-stops-out performance puts the buzz into news reporting.

NEWSROOM CONFERENCE

In larger newsrooms the plan of campaign is drawn up at the morning conference. Producers and senior staff put their heads together with the news editor to map out the day's coverage.

Many stories will already be in the diary; some of yesterday's items may still be current and could be followed up to find new angles. The news wires or other news media may produce items, which can be used or pursued. Producers and reporters will be expected to come forward with their own ideas, and other leads may come in from viewers or listeners, or via social media.

Stories are then ranked in order of importance and in line with station policy and resources are allocated accordingly.

If more stories present themselves than staff reporters can cover, the news editor will bring in freelance support or put some stories 'on ice', to be followed only if others fall down.

On a thin day, the news editor may have to rely on back-up material to fill the programme. Most stations have a small collection of timeless features, which have been kept for such emergencies, called *fillers*, *padding* or *evergreen stories*. Where there is little hard news to cover, reporters and crews may be sent out to get more filler material to top up the reserves.

If the station is running news on the hour, the news editor will attempt to spread coverage throughout the day to provide an even balance, with the emphasis on peak-time listening (at breakfast time for radio, in the evening for television). For longer news programmes, producers arrange coverage to ensure reports are back in time to make those deadlines.

BALANCE OF NEWS

Chasing breaking news is only half the story. The news editor or producer also has the overall balance of the programme to consider.

In a 30-minute TV programme time will be set aside for regular slots or segments, such as sport, headlines and the weather, and material will have to be found to fill them.

In any audience some would prefer to unwind to light items at the end of a working day rather than endure heavyweight stories; others will prefer national news to local, and commercial stations may be expected to inject enough entertainment into the show to shore-up audience ratings. All these conflicting demands will be brought to bear in shaping the news priorities and arranging coverage at the start of the day.

VISUALS AND ACTUALITY

Getting the story in radio and TV means more than simply gathering the facts. How these facts are illustrated is also important. Like newspapers with their photographs, radio has its sounds, recorded at the scene. These are called *actuality*.

Radio brings a report to life by painting a picture in the imagination of the listener, while TV takes its audience to the scene through pictures and graphics. The cost of all this artistry is to make TV sometimes slower and less flexible than radio, but attractive visuals and interesting actuality breathe life into the coverage of news. Good illustrations can boost the position of a report in the programme, and poor actuality or footage may make a producer think twice about running it at all.

FIGURE 6.4
Where the chase begins . . . setting the news agenda at the editorial conference. Credit Katherine Adams.

THE BRIEF

The ideal brief is a printed note giving details of the story, saying who the interviewee is, the time and place of the interview, with the relevant background and a selection of suitable questions.

But reality usually falls short of the ideal. News editors are busy people who say the reason they have two ears is so they can perch a telephone under each. Most reporters will be all too familiar with the phrase that greets them when they arrive for work: 'Don't take your coat off . . .'

Sometimes 'brief' is the operative word . . . It may go something like this: 'The strike at the car plant – the MD's in his office, he'll see you in ten minutes. Give me holding for 11, a clip for 12 and I'll take 2 and a half for the 1 o'clock.'

No note and no background list of questions.

The reporter is already expected to know the strike has been called, the car plant it concerns, where it is, how to get there, who the managing director is, all the necessary background to produce three separate items, and to have the know-how to come up with a line of questioning that perfectly matches the unspoken ideas in the news editor's head. So what's unreasonable about that?

However frantic the news editor may be, the reporter will have to prise out the answers to three questions before setting out on the assignment:

- What do you want?

- When do you want it for?

- How long do you want it to run?

With the car workers' strike, the plant's managing director will be asked: 'What's your reaction to the stoppage? How damaging could it be for the company? Will jobs or orders be lost? How long can the company survive the action?' The union point of view will also be required for balance.

Knowing the time of transmission and the length of the item is vital. There would be no point in returning to the newsroom at 3 o'clock with enough material to make a half-hour documentary when what was wanted was a 20-second clip for the lunchtime news. No one will appreciate this masterpiece if it arrives too late or runs too long to go in the programme.

News reporters usually work to the next bulletin deadline. On some stations deadlines crop up every 15 minutes, so when reporters go out on a story, that story must not vanish with them. Hence the instruction to write *holding copy*. This is a short news item that can be run in the next bulletin or headlines to tide the newsroom over until the reporter returns with the interview.

If they are likely to be out for some time, say, at a conference, they may be expected to phone in regular reports from the venue to keep the bulletins topped up with the latest news. Recorded interviews can also be fed back from a satellite van.

The next directive is to provide a clip for noon: that would be the best 20 seconds or so from the interview to illustrate the story.

Lastly, the reporter here has been asked to produce an interview of 2 minutes 30 seconds for the 1 o'clock news programme. The questions above would satisfy that, with any leads picked up from the managing director which give a new slant on the story.

Many news editors would argue that an elaborate brief should not be necessary, as reporters are expected to have a good working knowledge of their area and keep abreast of breaking news. But things are not always so hectic. When reporters arrive on duty, they may be given time to catch up by reading through the output of the previous shift. *Reading-in* helps reporters familiarise themselves with what has already gone on air.

Where more background is required, reporters on small stations would be expected to research it themselves, while those on larger stations may be able to call upon a researcher or the station's news information service or library.

> What you need is a wide background knowledge, rather than narrow specialization, and you need to keep it up to date.
>
> BBC World Service Newsroom Guide

THE ANGLE

Think of a news story as a diamond. A diamond has many facets, and whichever way you hold it, it is impossible to look at them all at once. Some will always be hidden from view. Likewise, it may impossible to cover every aspect of a news story at once – there is seldom the time or space. The reporter will be forced to concentrate on a few of the story's facets.

Take a story about a big new contract at a steelworks: the fact of the contract is the story, but that may not be reason enough for running it. Information only becomes news when it affects a given audience. If the contract is big enough, it might make national news, but the editor in a local newsroom would run the story only if the steelworks were in his or her area. The story would then have a *local angle*. With national news, the main angle is often the importance or significance of the story to the nation. At a local level, the importance to the community comes first.

Once the news editor is satisfied the story is relevant to the audience, he or she may want to cover it a number of different ways. The angle will change according to viewpoint, and with the steelworks, the obvious viewpoints to go for would be those of the management and workforce.

An interview will be arranged with the company about the size of the contract, the effect on the company's prospects and the likelihood of more jobs. If the reporter discovers 500 new jobs will be offered over the coming 3 years, the follow-up angle would shift to the union viewpoint. The major union would be asked to comment.

So far, both interviews have been with spokespeople; one to establish the facts of the story and the other to react to them, and there is a constant danger in journalism of always talking to experts, or *talking heads*, and overlooking ordinary people with grassroots opinions and real-life experiences.

Another viewpoint, closer to the audience, would be that of the workers at the steelworks. The reporter would ask some for their reactions to the news and might follow that by talking to several unemployed people who now have their first chance for some time of finding a job.

Deciding what your angle is may depend on factors such as these:

- what your transmission area is – a local station may decide the angle is what the jobs boost will mean for the town; a national station may take a wider view such as the resurgence of steelmaking in the country

- the age of your audience – a commercial radio station with a younger audience may take the angle of new jobs; one with an older demographic may think that with more people moving to the area to take up the jobs, could there be a strain on social services?

- the time of the broadcast – business people are more likely to be early risers so the financial aspect of the deal could be an angle for early breakfast bulletins; a more general overview of the story could be in the early evening bulletin which is more generally consumed by a family audience.

Workers and unemployed alike are the people whose lives will be affected by the contract, and they and their dependants will probably make up a significant part of the station's audience. In the end, it is their reactions that matter the most.

Using extracts from all the interviews, a comprehensive and well-rounded report could be built up, with background material filled in by the reporter. In TV, radio and online this is universally known as a *package*.

A TV reporter will want to illustrate the item with good footage of the steelworks in action. Dramatic images of red hot molten steel and flying sparks would feature with shots of blue-collar workers with their protective facemasks, contrasting perhaps with images of a be-suited director in a plush office.

Radio will certainly go for the noise of the steelworks, the clashing of metal and the voices of people at work.

It is always worth remembering the basics of reporting: the Who What Where When Why and How. Asking yourself those questions will help you work out what angle of the story is the most impactful for your audience.

CHASING THE CONTACT

Once the reporter has been briefed and found out *what* is wanted and *when*, the process of getting the story begins with their own or the station's contacts.

Much precious time on a 60-minute deadline can be saved by going for the right person from the start. Go straight to the top. Don't waste time with minor officials who will only refer you upwards. If you are dealing with a company, go for the managing director. Only settle for the *media office* if the MD or secretary insists. A press officer is one step away from the person you want to interview and may have reasons for putting you off.

Some organisations will insist you use their media officers – that is what they pay them for – and it is possible to build up a good working relationship with the best of them, but remember that behind every plausible statement and off-the-record remark there lurks a vested interest.

Research by *Press Gazette* revealed that 20 central Government departments employ more than 1,500 communications staff. *Daily Mail* political sketch writer Quentin Letts described the figure as 'ludicrous overstaffing'.

'The citizen in me is outraged by the cost,' he told *Press Gazette*. 'The journo in me wonders how come, with so many press officers, it can still be impossible to get answers from the Whitehall machine until after deadline.'

Daily Mirror associate editor Kevin Maguire said: 'I never realised there was such a large army declining to answer questions and be unhelpful.'

Press Gazette, November 2014 (http://bit.ly/BJGazette)

Setting up the interview can be the dullest, most time-consuming chore in journalism. Sometimes the ringing round can seem interminable and more time can be spent waiting for people to phone you back than in reporting.

To save time, the best tip is never to rely on anyone to call you back. If a secretary tells you your contact is speaking on another line and will return your call, politely insist on holding on while he or she finishes the conversation. If you hang up, your name will be added to the list of callbacks, and that list could be a long one. Also, if the story might mean adverse publicity, you could find yourself waiting by the phone forever.

If your contact is out, ask for their mobile phone number. Failing that, leave a message stressing the urgency of your business, and ask if there is someone else who could handle your inquiry. If they try to put you off, be polite but persistent, and if that fails, go above their heads to someone more senior. If no one can talk to you, find out where your contact is and call him or her there. Don't be fobbed off. Remember, every minute wasted brings you closer to your deadline. The approach should be assertive rather than aggressive – but always polite.

If you have spoken to the person previously you may well still have their direct office, mobile or home phone number. Subject to data protection laws, and your own personal relationship with that person (would they welcome being called at home, at a time such as this, on a story such as this . . .?), you could by-pass their 'gatekeeper' and go straight to them. A message sent to their social media account is sometimes very effective. (Press officers have been known to say that someone is 'unavailable', when that person is totally willing to be interviewed.)

Contact details and background research are a vital journalistic resource, and you are likely to want to keep them for long periods or indefinitely, even if there is no specific story in mind at present. But you are 'processing' personal data just by keeping it, so you must comply with the DPA.
Data Protection and Journalism: A Guide for the Media (http://bit.ly/BJData)

If after that your interviewee is still playing hard to get, then put that angle 'on hold' and approach the story from another direction.

With the steelworks item, if management is being elusive, go instead for the union line. With a more controversial story, such as plans to build a prison in the area, if those behind the scheme won't talk, go directly to the opposition or the grassroots and interview residents who may be frightened about the prospect of prisoners escaping near their homes. Broadcasting their angle first may lure the other side out to speak to you as well.

It is very likely that you will be asked to 'put your request in an email'. This is a double-edged sword. It is undoubtedly a delaying tactic used by media staff: they hope that it will mean only important requests are made, and of course answering an email is more easily delayed than a ringing telephone (some offices have a policy that emails are only checked at certain times of the day).

Also, some enquiries especially at an initial stage are best dealt with on a one-to-one basis: if you have a rumour that local tax rates are to increase by 5%, that's what you want confirmed or denied before you decide where to go with the story. Putting that request in writing and the inevitable delay in getting a response slows down the whole process of (if the rumour is true) asking for an interview with the council leader. To get around this you may send an email asking for initial confirmation, and then listing different interview requests and questions depending on the various scenarios (for example, if the council tax is *dropping* by 5%, or rising by .5% . . .). Many staff in press offices have worked in media themselves and know what you are likely to want to know, who you want to talk to and when by. Their job is not always to help you.

On the other hand, putting requests in writing may be beneficial to the journalist. It gives a paper trail of what was asked and when. It means that you can go back to the media office later, politely pointing out that the time you put in the original request for information and that the delay seems unreasonable, or noting that the specific question asked was not actually answered. Although of course, it is easier for a press officer to claim 'that email never came through . . .'

You can as mentioned, get in contact with someone direct on social media, such as Twitter. That way you by-pass normal protocol and get straight to the person you want. However, consider that this may strain the relationship you have with the press office in the future.

All too often, despite your best endeavours, you will find yourself staring at the telephone or inbox, waiting for a response. At this stage, you are wasting time and should go back to your news editor. Say what steps you have taken, and seek further direction. Should you continue to wait by the phone, firing off still more messages, or should you cut your losses and try a different angle or abandon this and get on with another item?

STAGED NEWS CONFERENCES

News conferences can be a time-consuming way of getting a story. Having sat through a 40-minute presentation, when questions are invited from the floor the tendency is for reporters to talk over each other and fire their questions at once, often in pursuit of different angles. How do you 'mic up' several speakers at the 'top table'? Some may not even be in front of a mic at all. You could take a feed from the main mixing desk through which the signal from all those microphones go . . . but only if you arrive in time, have the right cables and no-one else got there first.

Alternatively you could hold your mic up to the loudspeaker in the room. But that could record a thin and tinny sound, and of course you would also have the background noise of reporters mixed in with the speaker's voice.

Questions from different reporters will inevitably not follow a theme, and the answers may ramble on irrelevantly, which makes for troublesome editing. Always then, have plenty of battery and space on your memory card and note when the interesting points are made.

Press conferences generally live up to their name. The format was devised for print journalism and is largely unsuited to the digital era. Some newsrooms refuse to give coverage unless the main speakers make themselves available for private interviews well in advance and provide copies of speeches so questions can be prepared.

The alternatives are to hang around for interviews until the conference is finished, or record them on location before the conference gets under way, but there may well be a queue of other reporters with the same idea.

Radio has an advantage. When TV moves in to do an interview, the crews usually take a little time to set up their lights and cameras, so radio reporters are advised to be assertive and to get in first, pleading that the interview will take only a few minutes. Cooling your heels while TV completes the cumbrous operation of lights, colour check, pre-chat, interview and cutaways will only push you closer to your deadline.

Tweeting Stories, Tip-offs and Updates

In 2012 reporters from Sky News were banned from reposting non-company tweets and told to check with the news desk before breaking news stories.

A staff email said that the guidelines were introduced 'to ensure that our journalism is joined up across platforms, there is sufficient editorial control of stories reported by Sky News journalists and that the news desks remain the central hub for information going out on all our stories'.

It would obviously be confusing if details of a story were broadcast on air, but contradictory information was tweeted by staff from their own personal accounts. And as the email continued 'always pass breaking news lines to the news desk before posting them on social media networks'.

A reporter's priority should usually be to get information back to the newsroom, so that it can be verified if necessary and combined with other detail that is coming in from other sources. Reporters filing stories to their own followers rather than to the newsdesk means that a news editor would have to monitor the personal accounts of all their reporters to gather information, and that rival media could get free tip-offs of stories.

The BBC has a similar policy.

[O]ur first priority remains ensuring that important information reaches BBC colleagues, and thus all our audiences, as quickly as possible – and certainly not after it reaches Twitter . . . we're asking them to prioritise telling the newsroom before sending their own tweet. We're talking a difference of a few seconds. In some situations.

Chris Hamilton, BBC Social Media Editor (http://bit.ly/BJSocial)

FIGURE 6.5

'Breaking news' sent from a correspondent into the main BBC news system using the internal Quickfire app.

BBC journalists have access on their desktops and mobile phones to an internal publishing system called Quickfire. It allows them to send a message, tip off, advisory or full story into the BBC system via text or email.

Financial Times columnist John Gapper said it makes sense for news outlets like the BBC to try and preserve some news for their existing readers and viewers, and added that it doesn't make sense to employ a journalist whose 'loyalty is to his Twitter feed' instead of his organization. In other words, news should be saved for the company in an attempt to maintain its brand (and revenue), rather than being given away on Twitter for nothing.

To me, this puts the emphasis in the wrong place. I think news outlets that encourage their employees to break news on Twitter — such as Reuters, where social-media editor Anthony De Rosa wrote a critical post about the Sky News move — see the value of having journalists who become sources of news for their followers, many of whom may already be readers of their journalism, and others of whom may be potential readers. Whether that news comes after it has hit the wire, or after it has appeared on a BBC website, or whether it is even a retweet of someone close to the events, doesn't really matter to most people.

Matthew Ingram, gigaom.com (http://bit.ly/BJGigaom)

BEATING THE CLOCK

The fastest way to get a report on air is via the telephone, and live pieces can be taken directly into news programmes and bulletins. But although they provide a certain excitement for the viewer/listener (enforcing the fact that the story is so new that there's been no time to set up a satellite feed), for TV they lack that essential visual element.

Stations with few reporters will often rely on interviewees to come to them. Alternatively, your interviewee could remain at the office and talk to you in studio quality along an ISDN digital phone line, Skype or Periscope. Either practice frees the journalist to remain in the newsroom and chase more stories, but both are better suited to radio than TV where the choice of location is often determined by the need for interesting visuals.

If time is short and the reporter has to travel to the interview, precious minutes can be clawed back by knowing where you are going, where you are going to park and the likely delays en route. Another option is to travel by cab and put a taxi driver's expert knowledge at your disposal. This also gives you time to plan your interview on the way there and check your material on the way back.

If the station has a radio car or outside broadcast vehicle, live reports can be sent back which save time and add considerably to the sense of urgency and occasion.

WORK TO SEQUENCE

Another way to claw back precious minutes is to plan your story before you arrive at a location.

- Arrange to do your interviews in the order in which they will appear on air.

- Maybe have all your interviewees in the same place.

- Decide what questions you will ask each of them so they can best explain the story for you in a logical way.

- Bridge the different interviews with a link recorded on location – so in effect the whole story is packaged up in one 'as live' recording.

- Decide what the main angle is, or the best quote is, and record that interview again afterwards: one guest, one question, one answer. That short response will then be easy to find and will need minimal editing before it can be used as a standalone news bulletin clip.

- Rehearse your guests. Obviously you don't want to tell them what to say, or to have their answers off by rote, but if you explain what you will be doing, what you will ask each of them, and that you want short answers, then it will help you (and them) save time.

DON'T PANIC

Back at their desk, many inexperienced journalists, sweating against the clock, let circumstances panic them. There is always the hope that you *will* be able to turn round that three-minute package in the last moments before the programme, and an experienced hand will have little trouble in doing just that. But the old adage about more haste less speed is especially true in broadcasting.

Be realistic. If you doubt your ability to get the piece on air by the deadline, then warn the producer or news editor that it may not be coming. Give them time to prepare a standby. Whatever you do, don't leave them without that safety net. If they are banking on your item and it fails to turn up, at best you will try the patience of your colleagues, and at worst you will leave a hole in the programme that could prove impossible to fill, throw the presentation team into confusion and lead to a disaster on air.

Similarly, by rushing your piece you could easily make a mistake and the first time you realise your blunder may be when you see or hear it going on air. When a deadline is rapidly approaching, the temptation to run the piece without checking it through can be almost irresistible.

If mistakes do appear, the station's credibility takes a nosedive, and the authority of that bulletin is knocked. The audience and your colleagues will judge you, not by the amount of well-intentioned effort that went into your work, but by the results as they appear on air. In the end, that is all that really matters.

Challenges of working at a small TV station

Working at a small television station can be a rewarding and thrilling part of your career, but the environment brings its own challenges.

The luxury of honing your skills in one specific part of news production is left behind at larger news organisations; the ability to source, shoot, write and edit your own stories to tight deadlines is essential for the journalist working as part of a tight knit team of sometimes only three or four people.

You take on multiple roles in and out of the studio: you may find you are both the programme editor and sound technician of the lunchtime news, and a reporter on location and camera operator for the evening bulletin. As the producer one day and the runner the next, you'll quickly learn to lose your ego.

The 2013 general election in the Falklands Islands, a group of islands in the South Atlantic, marked the first live broadcast from local TV station, Falkland Islands Television (FITV – www.fitv.co.fk/) which broadcasts to approximately 2,000 people in the capital, Stanley. We had a team of five people on the night responsible for the entire coverage which lasted for four hours – we had two reporters on location, I anchored the programme from the studio, and two of us ran the desk and controlled the running order.

Team work and trust within small TV stations is essential: with a limited number of journalists and resources, decisions must be taken quickly and effectively in order to ensure broadcasting is of the highest quality. Investigative reporting and the production of longer projects (such as documentaries) can therefore suffer, unless members of the community come forward to expose wrong doings in the area.

Regardless of how big or small your news team is, as a journalist you should spend your time away from the newsroom asking the 'what, why, when, where and how' questions that can spark tip offs and original story ideas.

Broadcasting to a smaller area means that journalists from a small TV or radio station may know most of the audience. That may mean that residents are more likely to approach staff with a story, but it may also mean you have to report on a 'negative' story that affects a friend or neighbour, or criticises part of the community. That's when the ethics of objectivity and fairness are put to the test.

You are likely to face many challenges as a journalist in a small TV station – but the benefits are many, and you will almost certainly gain an appreciation for the different ways in which stories and situations should be approached to ensure fair reporting and a better quality of journalism.

Caroline Scott, presenter, Falklands TV (www.carolinescott.net/)

FIGURE 6.6
FITV VJ Caroline Scott with some rather unusual contributors.

THE HEADLINES

- Remember you are not merely looking for a guest 'to talk about the story'. You want someone who can explain what's happened, or has a personal involvement or perspective. Or maybe someone who can advance the understanding of the issue.

- Keep your colleagues in the know with what is happening. That's where you are and what you are doing (so they know how you are deployed) and also how the story you are working on is developing, or maybe changing to be a stronger (or less strong) one.

- Keep your audience in the know. With social media you can feed them nuggets of information during, say, a news conference or as a story you are working on unfolds. But remember to promote your main on-air coverage for the 'full report'.

QUESTIONS FOR YOU

1. Find out the names of the news editors at your nearest radio and TV stations and ask if you can visit their newsrooms for a day (longer if possible) to observe what goes on. Talk to the journalists about their jobs without getting in their way and ask if you can go with any of the reporters on a story. Watch how the news develops from an idea to a full-blown report.
2. Look back at the example of the steelworks used in the section on 'the angle'. Who would you talk to and what questions would you ask if your editor asked you to come up with a 'human interest' angle? What angle might you take if you were education reporter?

OTHER RESOURCES

- The BBC live-blogged their main editorial conferences one day in January 2015: http://bit.ly/BJDemocracy (scroll to 08.43 and 09.00).

- Want to get more out of Twitter at your TV or radio station? There's this useful book you can download: http://bit.ly/BJTwitterSkills.

- Or these *Five Ways for Journalists to Make Best Use of Twitter* during an election campaign: http://bit.ly/BJTwitterElex.

- BBC editorial guidelines: http://www.bbc.co.uk/editorialguidelines/.

- More on issues raised on reporting in the Falkland Islands here: http://bit.ly/BJFI1 and, more specifically, here: http://bit.ly/BJFI2.

TUTOR NOTES

View these cartoons from Daryl Cagle and discuss with your group what the artists is saying: http://bit.ly/BJCagle.

Use this suggested online scenario with your students to curate news stories: http://bit.ly/BJGeeks.

CHAPTER 7

Setting up the Interview

> The interview is an intimate conversation between journalist and politician wherein the journalist seeks to take advantage of the garrulity of the politician and the politician of the credulity of the journalist.
>
> Emery Kelen, US journalist (1896–1978)

News is often too immediate to allow detailed research, and news items are frequently too brief to warrant an in-depth approach. The average length of a bulletin clip on British independent radio is around 15 seconds – just enough for one or two succinct points. Even a 3-minute report (and even most speech-based stations keep interviews to nearer two) can support only four or five questions.

Longer interviews are more frequently the province of national speech-based stations and current affairs departments. Many regional TV newsrooms will produce a daily half-hour programme that takes items of nearer three minutes' duration.

A common criticism of broadcast news is that it is shallow, tending to polarise issues into black and white for the sake of simplicity by removing all shades of grey. While broadcasters deal with the *what* of the story, they seldom trouble to explain the *why* or the *how*.

Over this chapter and the next, we'll go through the various stages of the interview: before, during and after, so you get the best from your guest.

SETTING UP THE INTERVIEW

Know the Story

Why are you doing the story? What is its significance? What angle does the editor want? And how long do they want the finished item and when by? Make sure that you get this basic brief so you know what is expected of you. The most important question perhaps is 'what are you aiming to get from this interview?' in other words, what is the new line that you are anticipating will emerge?

What is the Background to the Story?

You should keep up to date with the stories your station is covering. Before beginning your shift, hear a number of bulletins including those on rival stations and read other local media, so you know what is happening and have a shrewd idea of the follow-ups you can expect to be given, or that you can suggest yourself. Be your own researcher, constantly topping up your reservoir of knowledge about local news.

Once you have been given a story to work on, do some specific research. Read the news release or old stories on the subject. When did you last see or hear a similar subject? What was said? Who said it? Why are you going back to it again now?

Consider who will be affected and is likely to have the strongest opinions. Do you need to talk to other people for an explanation or balance?

Carefully research the right people. Don't instinctively go for the chief, the deputy may be better. Is there a 'real person' who has been affected by the story, as well as a 'man in a suit' who may be responsible? Beware the person who is put forward as interviewee because of their position: 'You must talk to Doris – she's the boss' can present diplomatic problems. Doris may not be as good a performer as Elsie so perhaps persuade them that you need to talk to both of them, aware that you will in fact never use Doris' contribution

Before Calling

Rehearse what you want to say. How will you introduce yourself and explain the reason for the call. How did you get the story and their number? How do you think they may be able to help you? Write some notes to help you remember, if necessary. Be ready to suggest calling back later if the person is not available right now – and have your phone number to hand.

Avoid saying 'I read about you in the paper . . .' as that reinforces the perception that other media are our main sources of news. Just say that you heard about it, or 'I understand that . . .'

Audition Prospective Guests on the Phone

See whether they are a good talker and take the line you expect. Or maybe they take a dramatically different line that was not expected – and possibly changes the whole story! Be naive in your questions to help you get the information that you need. Do not commit yourself to doing the interview until you know that they are right. No one will thank you for filling a slot – but with a poor speaker!

How and where will you interview the guest? On the phone or face to face? If the latter, where? Consider the need for good pictures and sound.

Ask for an Interview

Describe what it is that you want and how they are the very best person to help you. Flatter and be persuasive . . . and always polite. In general people want to help other people, especially when things are explained to them. Remember that for most people, being approached by a reporter can be quite daunting. So too, can a phrase such as 'we'd like to come along with our *team* and *record* a *ten-minute interview* with you . . .'. Don't mislead, but you might get quicker agreement from a nervous potential interviewee if you said 'I'd love to come with a colleague to have a quick chat with you on tape about what we've just been talking about . . . we'll only use a minute or two. You've got such great experience and I know people would love to hear what you've just told me . . .'. Remember this call may be the only chance you have to ask this person for an interview . . .

Also explain to the guest the context of their contribution, the programme and the part they will play in it and whether anyone else has also been invited, particularly if they take an opposing view.

Explain that you want 'their side of the story', but if you are turned down for an interview be careful how you explain this on air. Did they 'refuse to comment' or was 'no one available' or did they 'decline the interview'? You may want to put such a statement in context. 'We approached them yesterday morning to come on tonight, but they said no one was available', if truthful, lets the audience read between the lines. Telling the potential interviewee that you'll be using one of these phrases may encourage them to be a little more open and reconsider the request.

'We'll Send Over a Statement'

The potential guest may decline an interview and say they'll send over a written statement instead. Politely point out that that doesn't work very well on TV and even less well on the radio! You are under no obligation to use their whole statement as long as you fairly represent them in the parts of the statement that you do read or paraphrase. After all, if they were coming on they'd be asked questions. Turning down that opportunity and having you read out an unchallenged statement without the chance to ask any follow-ups gives them the upper hand and is hardly 'journalism'.

The next step is to ask them to read their own statement (which you can then edit down). That way at least you have audio with them, and the listener can hear how they read the statement and what they look like when they do so (Confident? Shifty?) If they refuse to do that, then get the part of the statement you use voiced up by a colleague. Consider *not* using another news presenter, as that may give added credibility to the statement that may not be appropriate.

Discussing the Questions

Be careful. Some interviewees, particularly those who have been 'caught out' at some time, may want to take control of the interview. Don't let them. If they say they will only answer from a set list of questions, then politely but firmly tell them that you are happy to tell them the question *areas*, or the *kind* of thing you may ask.

Providing a list of questions beforehand:

- Means that you won't be able to ask any follow-up questions: 'so the pay increase is at 1% this year, rather than losing 10 members of staff.' If you can't follow up on an unexpected comment, or to seek clarity on an issue, then you won't be doing your job as an interviewer.

- Means that you won't be able to provide balance: this is achieved not just by interviewing two people with opposing views, but also by the interviewer asking difficult and demanding questions.

- Means that the guest has time to rehearse: you will want them prepared, but not to script their answers or to read them out loud.

There is a trend among politicians and celebrities to refuse to give interviews unless all the questions are agreed in advance. Only cave in to that kind of blackmail if there is absolutely no other way to get them to talk. But make sure you get your boss's approval before you do. If they request not to be asked a certain question, then try to steer around that without making any promises.

Think What a Presenter or Reporter Will Need to Know

If you are researching the story and setting up the interview for a colleague make sure that you write up a full briefing sheet: the guest's name, the background to the story and their connection with it (why are they being interviewed?) Include their correct title and description, what line they will take, and suggested line and style of questioning. Write enough questions – it's better to have too many than too few and you don't know how eloquent the person will turn out to be; just make sure

FIGURE 7.1

LIVE EX SKYPE

PRES Vets are prescribing dogs and other pets with sedative medicines like Prozac because they are stressed and suffering from anxiety.

Let's speak to behavioural therapist for dogs and dog owner herself KENDAL SHEPHERD

Q Why are pets, particularly dogs, suffering from these kinds of mental health issues?
Q Are drugs the answer?
Q What traits to stressed pets display? What can owners look out for?
Q And what can they do to ease their stresses?

WHY ARE WE DOING THIS GUEST

She is a behavioural therapist for dogs and has three herself, one Jack Russell and two Lurchers

WHAT DOES GUEST SAY ABOUT STORY
 * in a lot of cases dogs become scared of something that happens when they're left alone such as a rain storm, so then associate that with being left alone. Not wanting the dog to leave
 * dogs aren't designed to be left alone
 * if you work you can afford all the things that dogs need so working and having a dog isn't necessarily a bad thing
 * if you have a dog who is happy to be left on its own. Not as needy as human attention
 * dogs possibly get more stressed out if you give them too much attention
 * leaving your dogs is such a recent thing in dogs evolution, dogs just wander about, don't have to be excluded, in western culture we see this as not responsible,
 * social evolution
 * it's a tangled webb we weave, wexpect too much of dogs
 * it's expecting a single dog
 * aloof dogs, don't like people - the dogs we don't want

* can't possibly pick a breed, the calmest one in the litter. not the one that rushes up to you
* depends on why putting it on medication
* symptoms of true anxiety?
* they are potent drugs, we can't jus sedate the dogs and think it's ok for convenience
* i very rarely recommend drugs. if people are not pepared or cna't offer tehir do g the right relationship, i don't beleive any dogs have any mental problem, they'e stresed out by the lfie we impose on them that is not the same as having a mental health

BACKGROUND
(Telegraph)
With a growing number pets being left alone all day while their busy owners are out working, veterinary surgeons have reported that more and more of them are suffering from 'separation anxiety'.
They fear it has become common for some to give their animals tranquillising and antidepressant drugs to treat symptoms such as bad behaviour and aggression.
The trend has prompted vets to warn that such use of drugs is masking the real problem and makes a mockery of Britain's claim to be a nation of animal lovers.

the really important ones are first! You could also put down what the anticipated answers will be, or a quote or two from what the guest said in your initial chat, so the reporter can ask questions to get them to tell that anecdote or quote that statistic again.

FIGURE 7.2
A script, cue, questions and background in a briefing sheet.

> Interviewees should understand why they are being interviewed, what subjects they are being asked about, and what part they are playing in a programme.
>
> BBC Guidelines

PREPARING FOR THE INTERVIEW

Do More Research

'Research' is not 'information you gather during the course of a live interview'! You need to establish early on with the guest that you know what you are talking about. They won't expect you to be an expert, but they will expect you to have a basic understanding of what it is that you have come to talk to them about and that you have had the courtesy to take an interest in their line of work and are not just using them to fulfil your own ends.

The more you know about the subject, the better your questions will be. You don't want to waste their time, or time in the interview asking for the basics. You can put that kind of information in the cue or introduction to the story. The interview is to get insight, opinions and emotion of experience.

Before leaving the newsroom, make sure you have your facts right. There is nothing more embarrassing or more likely to undermine the reporter's reputation and that of the station than an ignorant and ill-informed line of questioning:

Reporter: Mr Smith, as hospital administrator, just how seriously do you view this typhoid epidemic?

Mr Smith: Hmmm. I'm actually the deputy administrator, and two isolated cases hardly constitute an epidemic. Oh yes . . . and the name is Smythe. Now what was the question?

What chance of a successful interview?

The Questions

If you are going out for a 20-second clip, there is no point coming back with 12 minutes of material. You would simply be laying up trouble for yourself; there will be 12 minutes to review and 10 different answers to choose from. That takes time, and with hourly deadlines, time is one commodity the reporter never has to spare. Five minutes beforehand spent thinking out the questions is worth an hour's editing back at the station.

Working to your brief, set up a chain of thought – a plan of campaign – by jotting down a few questions and arranging them in logical order.

The first actual question (you will probably start off by asking them to say their name and title on the 'tape', so it's there for reference) needs to be clear and straightforward. It'll be a question that will be easy for the guest to answer and so will put them at their ease. It may be something general such as 'tell me a little about your role here in the hospital kitchen . . .'

Then come the core three or four questions that focus on the angle of the story. Each of these may have a follow-up question which clarifies or elaborates on a previous answer, but of course you won't be able to prepare for these in advance.

Also consider a question that may be a little unexpected, but the answer to which may make the entire interview. 'You're in charge of education, what is it that you enjoy most about your favourite Shakespeare play?', 'What you do is hard work, long hours and low pay . . . why do you do it?', 'Have you ever been made redundant? What was it like? How did you explain it to your kids?'

And also think through how you will end the interview. If it's a pre-recorded interview it may not need anything specific as you can just leave the last answer hanging, or put in a closing comment in the script. But if you are preparing a live interview you will need to know how you will summarise what they have said, and hand back to the studio, handover to another presenter or move on to the next topic.

Questions such as 'what's your message to . . .' or 'how can people get in touch if they want some more information?' should not be overused. In a live interview, don't leave the audience suspended and frustrated in mid argument, or irritated by references to running out of time. The good interview will come to an orderly conclusion.

And finally, as mentioned earlier, a supplementary question whose short answer will summarise the main thrust of the story and can be used in bulletin clips without the need for editing.

FIGURE 7.3

The news room at Free Radio in the UK. Credit Kris Askey/David Lloyd – Free Radio/Orion Media.

Before You Set Off

Check your equipment – ensure that the batteries are full and the memory card empty. Check it out before you take it out.

Check directions – If time is of the essence, then no reporter can afford to waste it by heading the wrong way down a motorway or arriving at the wrong address. Arriving late for an interview only raises everybody's blood pressure. Check the arrangement before leaving and allow plenty of time to get there.

Dress appropriately – Each reporter is an ambassador for his or her radio or TV station. How you look and conduct yourself can make or break a station's reputation.

Stations have different approaches to dress. Some permit an informal, even sloppy style, others insist on staff being suit-smart. First impressions matter. What your clothes and manner say about you in the first two seconds may affect the whole interview. A business suit might lose some interviews in a downtown area, where a casual style would be more credible, but if your news trade is with business people and politicians, then dress to suit . . . in a suit.

It's important to treat your guests well because:

- It's good to be polite and friendly.
- They will help you make great TV or radio.
- They will get their message across and have a positive experience and be more likely to help you again.
- Your behaviour reflects on your company.

On Arrival

A pleasant greeting, a firm handshake and a good deal of *eye contact* is the best way to begin, with a clear statement about who you are and which radio or TV station you represent. Beware also of putting up barriers from the start. Even if you intend your interview to be adversarial, don't size up to your guest like a hungry lion to an antelope. To put it another way, every boxer knows the best punches are delivered when his opponent's guard is down.

Then:

The pre-chat – Almost as important as the interview itself is the pre-chat. This is when you establish rapport, and explain again what is going to happen and how the interviewee can help. (It's also advisable to say at this stage how much time you have before you have to leave, so you are not thought rude when you have to.)

If the interview is non-controversial and there are no conflicts of interest you can save editing time by outlining your questions and discussing the answers you are looking for. As one news editor puts it: 'What I need is ninety seconds, so I will ask you these four questions, and I expect your reply will be something like this . . . Yes?'

This 'stage-managed' approach will only work where all the key facts of the story are evident beforehand and both parties agree on the angle. The biggest dangers here are the reporter showing her aces before the interview begins or putting words into the interviewee's mouth.

If you are unsure about the subject it can help to let your interviewee chat about it beforehand so you can be clear you are heading in the right direction. But beware of letting the pre-chat drag on for so long that the adrenalin dies and the conversation gets stale. It should continue just long enough to explore the topic, establish a direction and relax the interviewee, and set up your equipment (and listen for extraneous noises which may interfere with the recording) while you are doing so.

Even if your deadline is only 15 minutes away, your manner must be calm and relaxed, polite yet assertive but never aggressive. Approach is all-important. If the interviewee is inexperienced and nervous he or she will need to be relaxed and put at ease (show them the equipment and, briefly, how it works – and don't thrust a microphone in their face). Conversely, nothing is more unsettling than a nervous interviewer.

Location, location, location – Go for the natural habitat – the doctor in his surgery, the farmer in the farmyard. The background sound may not be obvious to you at the scene but will help lift the piece. It also means that you will be able to write 'Our reporter Peter Porter talked to the new Managing Director of GoSlow Trains, on the platform of Blankstown station . . .'

The background sound is important: it should tell us something about the interviewee, but it shouldn't intrude. It shouldn't give conflicting messages or be so busy as to be distracting.

Sometimes a desk is not appropriate at all. The chairman of a water authority was not being well-served by his PR people who would not let him leave his desk to be interviewed about severe water shortages. Everyone else in the report was interviewed outside – at dry reservoirs, street pipes, emergency centres. The man in charge was at a desk and sounded complacent – no matter what he had to say! If you do have to interview in an office, look for a small one with carpets and curtains and don't interview across a desk. Sit side by side. Support your microphone arm.

If a guest comes to you for an interview, consider taking them outside and away from the 'antiseptic' location of a studio. There will be more colour and movement, there will be some background hubbub and you give the impression that you went to see them!

Never rehearse an interview, just discuss it – Repeats of interviews are like second-hand cars – they lose their pace and their sparkle. Even nervous interviewees usually perform better when the adrenalin is flowing. Agree to a run-through only if you think there is no other way to calm your interviewee's nerves, but make sure your recorder or camera is rolling. Then, if the 'rehearsal' goes well, you can ask the first few questions again when you sense they are into their stride and suggest dispensing with the retake. An alternative is to warm them up with some minor questions before getting down to the nitty-gritty.

When the interviewee gets out their script – Less media-savvy interviewees may want to answer from notes or a script. Don't let them. It will sound 'read' and artificial. Reassure them they will come across better without notes and that any mistakes can always be retaken. Discussing your first question may help to relax your guest and if the interview is more probing, that first question can be a dummy that you can edit out later.

> If they're frightened it's a matter of just talking to them beforehand, joking with them and putting them at their ease. Usually I say how I keep making mistakes as well, and then I fluff a question, and say, 'I'm sorry about that!' Although you go in as a professional, you can't be too aloof, because people won't talk to you. It's got to be a conversation, and you have to start it.
>
> Rod Mckenzie, former News Editor Radio 1 Newsbeat

Are you sitting comfortably? – Body language is also important. The way we sit, how we cross our legs and arms, reveals a lot about how we feel. If your interviewee is sitting legs crossed and arms folded, then you know he or she is on the defensive and needs to be relaxed. If the reporter is cowering in the corner, while the interviewee is leaning back exuding confidence, then something has gone badly wrong indeed! An old saying goes 'sit them down for honesty, stand them up for energy': in other words if the guest is sitting they are more likely to be comfortable themselves and with you and potentially let something slip. If standing up they are more alert, and you can walk and talk with them to add movement to your piece.

Try to ensure that your eye-level is the same as the interviewee. If the interviewee is six-foot-six and you are five-two it all works much better if you are both on chairs – but not swivel ones!

THE HEADLINES

- You may find yourself booking or recording half a dozen interviews a day and have the process of what you say almost automated. But remember that for your guest it may be the first or only time they will ever be asked for an interview. So take time to be courteous and explain what will happen and why. It is not only polite, but it reflects well on your employer and makes it more likely that they will 'give good interview' and be prepared to help you again.

QUESTIONS FOR YOU

1. Open a file marked 'interviewing'. Keep one page for each of the twelve categories of interview above and others for notes. Watch a variety of different TV news, current affairs and magazine programmes and see if you can identify all twelve types of interview in action.
2. See if you can come up with some new categories. Watch and listen to interviews critically. Each time ask yourself whether it worked or failed, whether it was good or bad, and why. File any tips on technique you pick up.
3. Log every interview you do in your file in the appropriate category. Over a period of time attempt to cover all twelve categories of interview. Make notes of any difficulties you experienced doing those interviews and any helpful tips. Share your problems and advice with others and pool your knowledge.

OTHER RESOURCES

- BBC on looking for on-air experts from ethnic minorities: http://bit.ly/ BJMinorities.

- Working as a producer on a national radio news/phone-in show: http://bit. ly/BJVine.

- If you have all your contacts in your phone, consider use of the Humin app which lets you search through terms such as 'works at city hall' or 'ex-police' or 'lives in Richmond': www.humin.com.

- Copy several sections of text and images on your phone in an easier way with CopyBubble: http://copybubble.com/.

TUTOR NOTES

Ask your students to break into pairs, preferably with someone they do not know too well, and without any preparation conduct personality interviews with one another. They should attempt to discover what makes their partner tick and find out something new about him/her. Aim to spend between ten and fifteen minutes on each interview. Afterwards, they should sum up in a couple of paragraphs to the class what they have discovered about their partner.

That interview was conducted off the top of the student's head. Ask them to discuss with their partner how they could best prepare themselves and their interviewee for similar interviews in future.

CHAPTER 8

The Interview

He puts his blunt, loaded questions with the air of a prosecuting counsel at a murder trial. As he swings back to face the camera, metaphorically blowing on his knuckles, one detects the muffled disturbance as his shaken victim is led away.

Sir Robin Day, *Through the Eyes of a Critic*

It's marvellous! I have the opportunity to be impertinent to people I'd never normally meet and I can say what would be considered rude things and they have to answer. It's a position of great responsibility and I'm privileged to do it.

Richard Bestic, Parliamentary Correspondent

Every scrap of information that reaches the airwaves stems from an interview of some sort – a chat at a bar to get some background, an informal phone call to clear up some details or a recording for transmission.

Broadcasting's great appeal is that the audience can hear the facts straight from the horse's mouth. The speaker's own words lend greater authority to a report than any number of quotes in next day's newspaper. Listeners can follow events as they happen – live.

THE INTERVIEWER'S SKILL

Interviewers are brokers of information. Their skill lies in matching the goods on offer with the needs of their customers. Their art is to tease out the story in the teller's own words, while making sure every word will be clearly understood by the audience.

Listeners can then make up their own minds about whether to believe what is being said. The function of exposing the viewpoints of the powerful and influential to public debate and criticism is one of the major planks in the argument that a free news media is essential to democracy.

To the best of their ability, reporters must lay aside their own interests, points of view and prejudices. Reporters are watchdogs for their audience, and it is with them that their loyalties must lie.

Reporters' skills, their knowledge of the subject and their access to the interviewee give them the means and the responsibility to ask the sort of 'Yes, but . . .' questions their audience would love to ask in their place. The reporter is the bridge between the layperson and the expert, the person in the street and the official, and a good interview will often test the validity of an argument by exploring its points of tension or controversy.

DURING THE INTERVIEW

- *Who are they?* – get the basic information at the start of the recording, for example their name and title and any spellings (for TV graphics and the website). Getting this is also useful if you want the guest to introduce themselves in the final package: edit their name and title to flow into their first answer. You may also want to consider recording an 'as live' introduction to the interview. Again this gives you and your colleagues another editing option back at the studio. So

I'm walking on the famous slopes of Box Hill, the scene of 2012 Olympic road races of course, but a few steps away from that course, in amongst the trees, are some juniper bushes. And these are the only ones in England that process berries good enough to make gin from. With me is Andy Wright from the National Trust who manage this land. Andy what are the conditions like here that make it such an ideal place for juniper to grow . . .?

- *Start with the easy questions* – as we mentioned before, a straightforward first question will help get you and the guest into their stride and feel confident. You may never have any intention of using it, but it's good to use to reassure.

- *Relax* – be friendly and curious. It's not quite a normal conversation (because there is a third person involved: the listener, on whose behalf we are asking the questions) but try and keep up the 'pretence' of one. Don't go in 'all guns blazing': as we mentioned before very often the best answers come from a question that was unexpected, or phrased in a careful, considered and pleasant way.

- *You are the expert* – OK you are interviewing the expert in that particular topic, but you are the expert in interviewing. Don't be put off by bullying tactics from your guest. If they don't answer the question, ask it again. If they still don't you can rephrase it: 'I'm so sorry I must be missing something . . . tell me again if you would, why the sluice gate wasn't operated at the right time . . .'

- *Colour, even for radio* – or *especially* for radio! For TV people, movement and pictures are their staples, but radio reporters often forget this. Listen out for the smallest sound that will help illustrate the story. Is there something tangible that can be described, held or turned on? The 'juniper' interview above was partly recorded as the interviewer and interviewee made their way through the trees to the site of the bushes. Even what could be the most boring story can be illustrated with a description from you, and may even prompt a question: 'Well, talking to you Mr Huxley in your oak-panelled board room, pictures of past directors looking down at you from the walls, and peacocks strutting in the expanse of parkland through the window, I wonder how easy it is for you to relate to those losing their jobs today . . .?'

FIGURE 8.1

Maintaining eye-contact and microphone distance during a location interview. Credit: *107.8 Radio Jackie.*

- *Nod and smile* – use body language and other 'non-verbal communication' to coax and reassure your guest. Make eye contact, give a nod of understanding (but be careful not to seem to be agreeing with them), and use other facial expressions to make them feel at ease. Face the speaker and if sitting, lean forward. Of course, you don't want to have on the recording, your verbal agreements: 'yes, I see, uh-huh . . .' If you are short for time, faster nodding, raised eyebrows and the occasional glance away will indicate that you would like them to finish.

- *Interviewing children* – treat them as you would an adult, with respect. Remember that you should get permission from their parent or guardian before you ask them anything and have another adult (not one of your colleagues) there with you at all times. Get the children's trust: show them the equipment and let them have a go at recording and seeing/hearing themselves back. And ask open questions.

- *Watch the time* – there's no point going back to the studio with so much material that it takes you hours to edit and you miss the deadline, so keep a focus on the point of the story. If you start by saying that you only have ten minutes, then the guest will naturally sharpen their questions to help you.

DIFFERENT TYPES OF INTERVIEW

The BBC tells its trainees that there are three basic types of interview:

1. The *hard exposure* interview which investigates a subject.

2. The *informational* interview which puts the audience in the picture.

3. The *emotional* interview which aims to reveal an interviewee's state of mind.

These three paint a broad picture of the art of the interview, which we can develop further into 12 different types, all with special functions:

- Hard news
- Interpretative
- Entertainment
- Information
- Vox pop ('man on the street') and multiple
- Actuality only
- Investigation
- Personal
- Telephone or remote
- Adversarial
- Emotional
- Grabbed

A disaster story?

The following extraordinary interview is something of a classic. It was broadcast on the British network news service IRN (Independent Radio News) during a long and bitter strike. The man facing the microphone was militant miners' leader Arthur Scargill, a Yorkshireman not known for his gentle touch with interviewers, or for giving any ground in an argument. But this reporter thought he could take him on and beat him at his own game – live on peak-time radio. Decide for yourself whether he succeeded and whether the result made good or bad radio.

The first major stumbling block came near the beginning when the interviewer asked the militant miners' leader to admit defeat:

Five weeks into the dispute the membership . . . is still divided over whether to follow your call. Would you concede that the strike is a bitter one and that like never before miner is pitched against miner?

Which prompted the swift response:

Scargill: . . . now I'm not going to correct you again, I hope . . . If people misinterpret what we're doing the way you're doing, then clearly it's little wonder the British people don't know the facts . . . (He then proceeded to reiterate a point he had made earlier.)
Interviewer: We'll deal with those points later . . .
Scargill: No, I'm sorry, you'll not . . .
Interviewer: Mr Scargill, could you please answer my question . . .
Scargill: No, I'm sorry, you'll not deal with those points later in the programme, you'll either listen to what I've got to say or not at all . . .
Interviewer: We'll come to those in a minute . . .
Scargill: No, I'm sorry, you can either listen to the answers that I'm giving, or alternatively, you can shut up . . .

Interviewer: We'll come to those figures later, Mr Scargill . . .

Scargill: No, I'm sorry, one thing you're going to learn is that on an interview of this kind, you're going to listen clearly to the things that I want to talk about . . . (this banter continued for some time, until)

Scargill: Now are you going to listen?

Interviewer: No, can you please . . . (but his voice is drowned out by that of his guest)

Scargill: Then as far as I'm concerned we might as well pack up this interview . . . Now it's obvious you're not going to listen, and if you're not going to listen, lad, than there's no point in me talking to you is there, eh? (They debated this moot point for a time, until)

Interviewer: (Exasperated) Mr Scargill, Mr Scargill, can you please answer the question?

Scargill: Now are you going to listen to my answers or not?

Interviewer: If you listen, if you listen to my questions and give answers to them, it's as simple as that!

Scargill: Quite frankly, either you're going to listen to my answers or not. And if you're not, then you're going to obviously make yourself look a complete fool . . .

Interviewer: (Pleadingly) Then why don't you give answers to the questions I'm giving, Mr Scargill . . .?

Scargill: You're either going to let me answer the questions in my way, or if you want, write the answers that you want on a board and tell people that you want me to answer those questions your way . . .

Interviewer: (Gathering about himself his last shreds of composure) Can you come to the point then, and answer the question?

Scargill: (Unrelenting) I can come to any point I want providing you'll shut up and let me answer, but if you won't shut up, then I can't . . . If you don't, then this interview is going to go on in this silly way as a result of your irresponsible attitude.

Interviewer: (Abandonedly) Let's move on to something else . . . (Sigh)

But that proved to be a vain hope, and, although the question had long since been forgotten, by the audience at least, interviewer and interviewee continued the same exasperating sparring match for some time, with Mr Scargill repeating the same point again and again, and punctuating his interviewee's unwelcome interruptions with observations that his would-be interrogator was:

- Speaking as a representative of the Coal Board or the Government.

- Trying to make himself a budding Robin Day (a veteran BBC interviewer), which he followed through with the stern rejoinder: *'well, tha's not doing it wi' me, lad!'*

- That his interviewer was an ignorant man who ought to have more sense.

- And that he ought to get out of the chair and let someone else sit there who *could* do the job.

Were his remarks justified? Judge for yourself. Full marks for persistence on the part of the interviewer, but perhaps that persistence could have been better placed in seeking answers to questions designed to elicit information rather than to invoke the other man's wrath. In the end it was a victory on points for Mr Scargill, but one which was unlikely to popularise either him or his cause or do much to enhance the reputation of live broadcasting.

Strangely though, however disastrous it may have sounded, it did make compelling radio . . .

Hard News

The *hard news interview* is usually short, to the point and to illustrate a bulletin or news item. It deals only with important facts, or comment and reaction to those facts.

Let's set up a scenario to see how this and other types of interview apply:

A cruise liner is in trouble 80 miles out to sea with a fire apparently out of control in the engine room. You have the coastguard on the phone and he is prepared to be interviewed. Once the name of the ship, the number on board, her destination, her point of departure and the name of her owners are established for the cue material, the questions to the coastguard would be:

- How bad is the fire?
- How did it start?
- How can the fire be prevented from spreading?
- How safe are the passengers?
- What about the crew?
- Are they likely to have to abandon ship?
- What steps are being taken to rescue them? etc.

The answer that will illustrate the news will be the strongest to emerge from these key questions. Important facts and background will be given in the cue, while more detail and explanation will go into the programme-length interview of between two and three minutes.

There is no reason to settle for interviewing the coastguard if there is a chance of raising the crew of the ship by radio telephone. A first-hand account from the people at the centre of a story is always preferable, though here the crew would almost certainly be too busy fighting the fire to talk.

Informational

The *informational interview* is similar to the hard news interview, but need not be restricted to major stories. An informational interview can be about an *event* – something that is happening or about to happen.

It can also provide *background*. Returning to the cruise liner story, an interview could be set up with the network's transport correspondent, who would probably be a freelance with specialist knowledge. He or she would be asked about the whole issue of accidents at sea, with questions such as:

- What is the normal procedure for abandoning ship?
- How safe is this?
- How long before the passengers could be picked up?
- Would they suffer from exposure in these weather conditions?

Broadening to:

- Just how safe is travelling by sea these days?

- How does it compare with air travel? etc.

Informational interviews go beyond the main point to seek an explanation of the *hows* and *whys* of the story. As such they tend to produce better extended features than short bulletin items.

Investigative

The *investigative interview* aims to get behind the facts to discover what *really* caused events and sometimes what could be done to prevent a recurrence.

This kind of interview can run and run and often forms the basis of a documentary.

Assuming with the above story you discover there has been a recent spate of accidents involving cruise liners, and this is the second vessel belonging to that shipping line to have caught fire within three months; then your next step would be to raise this with the owners.

With investigative interviews it is only sensible not to put your prey to flight by scaring them off with your first question, so the interview would be conducted something like this:

- How did the fire break out?

- How quickly was it discovered?

- Why wasn't the crew able to control it?

- When was the ship last checked for safety?

- What problems were discovered then?

- How would you describe your safety record?

- This is your second liner to have caught fire in three months . . . how do you account for that?

At this stage it is likely the interview will rapidly move from being investigative into the category below.

Adversarial

No one likes to be cross-examined or have their motives questioned, so frequently the *adversarial interview* turns into a war of words between the two parties as the interviewer tries to get the other to admit to things that he or she really does not want to say.

Jeremy Paxman:	Did you threaten to overrule him?
Home Secretary Michael Howard:	I was not entitled to instruct Derek Lewis and I did not instruct him. And the truth of it is . . .
Paxman:	Did you threaten to overrule him?
Howard:	And the truth of the matter is Mr Marriot was not suspended. I did not . . .
Paxman:	Did you threaten to overrule him?
Howard:	I did not overrule Derek Lewis.
Paxman:	Did you threaten to overrule him?
Howard:	I took advice on what I could and could not do . . .
Paxman:	Did you threaten to overrule him, Mr Howard?

And so it continued, with Paxman fixing the Home Secretary with the same question some 14 times, he later admitted, because his producer said the next item was not ready.

The Home Secretary later reflected: 'It's not uncommon for a politician not to answer a question directly. It's pretty uncommon for them to be asked the same question.'

Newsnight, BBC2, 1997 (http://bit.ly/BJPaxman)

Our disaster at sea interview might continue:

- Some people might see two fires in three months as negligence on your part. How would you answer that?

- Would you agree that your safety standards need looking into?

- What plans do you have for improving those safety standards? etc.

And if it turned out that the crew had been unable to control the fire because they had set sail five hands down owing to a severe outbreak of flu back in port, the right and proper questions to ask would be:

- Why was the ship permitted to sail with too few crew to deal with an emergency?

- Some would say this action put your ship and your passengers' lives in jeopardy. How would you answer that?

- What disciplinary action do you plan to take against the captain who authorised the sailing? etc.

But beware . . . The adversarial approach should never be seen to be a head-on clash between the interviewer and the interviewee. The reporter is representing the audience or speaking up on behalf of public opinion. Even the question above about risking the safety of passengers and ship begins: 'Some would say . . .' (although expect the retort 'Who? Who would say that . . .?')

A verbal assault on an interviewee might result in allegations of victimisation and bias (see the interview with Arthur Scargill earlier in this chapter). And if this happens it could shift public sympathy away from the reporter and towards the 'victim'.

Adversarial interviews run the greatest risk of a libel suit. This is where a person who has had something damaging said about them seeks compensation in the courts. As a journalist, opening your mouth before thinking could prove to be your costliest mistake.

By nature, the adversarial interview attempts to undermine or disprove an argument by direct and public confrontation. The atmosphere may get heated, but the professional should always resist getting hot under the collar. In the heat of the moment it is too easy to say something disparaging or harmful to an interviewee.

The adversarial approach comes and goes with fashion, but should only be used where appropriate. There is really no excuse for cross-examining a welfare organisation about plans for a new orphanage, unless the proposal really does smack of corruption.

Interpretative

There are two prongs to the *interpretative interview:* the first is the *reaction* story – a response either for or against what has happened; the second is an *explanation* of events.

Both approaches offer a perspective on what has taken place, and put the event into context. By bringing an issue into the light it is possible to examine it more closely.

Reaction is frequently stronger and more effective when it comes from someone who is personally involved.

Analysis, explanation or *interpretation* comes best from an expert eye far enough away from the story to remain objective.

Our shipping correspondent in the example above fits that bill exactly. He or she could ask:

- How will this accident affect public confidence in sea travel?

- Do the safety laws need tightening up? If so, how?

- What provision is there in maritime law for setting sail without an adequate or healthy crew?

- What cover does travel insurance offer passengers?

Personal

The *personal interview* might be a short interview with a celebrity about their favourite subject – themselves, or a longer, more inquisitive and intentionally revealing *personality profile*. Among the best of this breed was BBC Radio 4's *In the Psychiatrist's Chair*. Professor Anthony Clare (who was a psychiatrist) talked to well-known people from different walks of life, and attempted to get beneath their skins to find out not what they did, but why they did it, what drove and motivated them and what in their past had made them the people they were. In short, what made them tick?

The interview was intimate and penetrating. To lower a person's guard to the point where they become vulnerable and yet still secure enough with the interviewer to answer questions such as 'Do you believe in God?' and 'Have you ever wanted to take your own life?' requires the interviewer to combine the insight of a psychiatrist with the empathy of a priest at the confessional. It made fascinating listening.

Emotional

The *emotional interview* is an attempt to lay bare someone's feelings, to enable an audience to share in a personal tragedy or moving event. The emotional interview springs from the personal interview, above, and is perhaps the most sensitive area of reporting. It is dealing with a subject's inner self, an area into which the media too frequently trespasses uninvited.

Returning to our stricken cruise liner: time has passed, the fire has proved impossible to contain and the captain has been left with no option but to give the cry, '*Abandon ship*!' Fortunately, rescue vessels were already at the scene and the passengers, bedraggled and nearing exhaustion, are starting to come ashore.

The reporter is at the quayside with the instruction to get the *human angle*. Closing in on the first of the passengers, a woman who is weary but obviously greatly relieved to be setting foot on terra firma, he asks:

- How does it feel to be back on dry land?

- Were you able to save any of your possessions?

- When did you first realise the fire was out of control?

- How did the passengers react to the news? etc.

Mercifully, the reporter has remembered that the hackneyed and crass 'How do you feel?' should only be asked to let us share in someone's relief or happiness, never their tragedy or misfortune.

For emotional interviews the rule is to tread carefully when your foot is on somebody's heart, and then only walk where you have been given the right of way.

Journalists can help victims and survivors tell their stories in ways that are constructive, and in ways that make for great journalism.

- Sometimes you can't avoid intruding upon someone in grief. If you can't postpone your contact, remember to be sensitive and respectful in your approach. Try approaching neighbours first to gauge reaction.

- Be polite and apologise for the intrusion. 'I'm sorry for your loss,' and/or 'Would you like to talk about it now?' are good ways to start the conversation. Do they 'want to pay a tribute' to the person they have lost?

- Don't assume a victim or family member won't want to talk; often they are eager to share their story and memories with a journalist.

- If someone doesn't want to talk to you, be respectful and polite. And don't forget to leave your business card; at some point, the person may decide to talk to a reporter, and they will likely call the one that made the best impression.

- Make sure the person understands the terms of the interview. Remind them of the terms periodically. Give a sense of what you want: 'I'd like to talk to you for a few minutes', 'I'd like to ask you a few questions'. And give a sense of purpose for the interview 'I'm sure this must be really difficult for you to talk about, but I think it'd be good to share your story because . . .'

- Avoid unsympathetic questions such as 'how does it feel?' A less direct approach, which has the same ends, might be 'what do you want people to know about what happened?' Don't say 'I know how you feel . . .' You don't. Don't say 'You must have felt . . .' but instead help them articulate their own feelings. Avoid pat responses: 'It could have been worse' or 'You're lucky'.

- Respect silence. If they ask 'why did it happen?' don't try to give a direct answer. Instead echo back to them: 'yes, why did this terrible thing happen?' Speak slowly, softly and simply.

- Pay attention to your own emotions during the interview and let your reactions inform your reporting (while remaining professional). If you find something emotionally stirring, chances are others will, too.

- Your tone of voice and body language matter. Show empathy not detachment. Show openness, and don't be surprised if they don't hold your eye contact.

- Have a small pack of tissues with you, ready to offer one if the interviewee starts crying. Even if one is not taken, it's a nice gesture.

- End with a warm handshake, a thanks and perhaps a comforting word such as 'I wish you well'. If it was a long interview, consider calling them a week or so later: 'I just wanted to see how you are doing'. That way they won't feel 'used'.

- You can feel drained and guilty for asking people about their loss. They may show anger towards you – although they agree to continue with the interview. This can be a show of their emotion towards the situation rather than you. Examine your conscience. If it is clear move on and don't carry the emotions around with you.

Collated from Dart Center for Journalism and Trauma
(dartcenter.org) and the Columbia Journalism Review (cjr.org)

Emotion can also affect journalists. We witness trauma. We report it. We experience it.

Reporting about death is an almost weekly occurrence on a local station. It's likely to be an accident involving a stranger, but could be someone you have interviewed before. The victim could be a child . . . or several children. The death may be deliberate. It may be someone you know personally. You will know how the community you live and work in will feel the pain. And that pain can suddenly hit you as much as any of your audience.

Later in your career you may report on natural disasters, large-scale rail or plane crashes, riots, famine, war or mass murder.

Every such experience leaves a trace of trauma with us and can build up over time. Usually we can cope, but then it coincides with other pressures in the newsroom or at home and gets too much. Maybe months or years later. And then ripples out to colleagues, family and friends.

You may feel sad about a death, or guilty for not having done anything to help that person or because you survived. You may feel anger at a lack of explanation as to why it happened, or shame for reacting as you do . . . and fear that you may have the same emotions again.

These emotions can lead to loss of sleep, memory, concentration, appetite and sex drive. You may feel sick, or moody. You may turn to drink or drugs.

If you see such changes in yourself or a colleague, get help soon.

It is normal to feel distressed by trauma.

It is important to talk about it early.

It is OK to seek help.

Entertainment

The entertainment factor often plays a part in attracting and keeping an audience. The *entertainment interview* looks at the lighter side of life, the things that make us smile. If, on board the liner, a troupe of dancing girls had kept people's spirits up when the flames were spreading amidships by doing the can-can, then that is entertainment and the reporter who sneers at that angle is likely to get reprimanded when he or she returns.

Actuality Only

The *actuality interview* is where the reporter's voice is removed from the recording, leaving only that of the interviewee. The technique is occasionally used to good effect in documentary or feature making, but is harder to master than it sounds.

The skill lies in building up a clear storyline, which needs no narration to prop it up and in asking questions that prompt the interviewee to give all the information that would normally arise as background in the question.

Wrong approach:

> Interviewer: Where were you when the fire broke out?
> Passenger: At the bar.
> Interviewer: Who told you?
> Passenger: The steward.
> Interviewer: What was your reaction?
> Passenger: I didn't take it seriously. I thought they'd manage to put it out.

Better:

> Interviewer: Could you tell us where you were when the fire broke out, how you got to hear about it, and what your reaction was?
>
> Passenger: I was at the bar with half a dozen others, when the steward came in and told us fire had broken out in the engine room. We didn't think much of it. We were sure they'd put it out. But we didn't know how wrong we were.

With this technique multiple questions are often required to get a good flow of answers. The interview will usually have to be worked out in advance with the interviewee, and several retakes might be necessary to get the important background while still sounding conversational and natural.

Other examples of questions that may prompt longer answers for this kind of interview may start 'tell me more about . . .', 'take me back to what happened . . .', 'what was going through your mind when. . . .?'

Telephone or Remote

Interviews may be carried out on the phone (mobile, landline or satellite) or with a subject speaking from a remote studio. Remote studios are linked to the mother station by cables, microwave, ISDN (high-quality phone-line) or satellite or Skype, offering near-studio quality sound for radio, and combining sound with vision for TV.

Alternatives are going out to record the interview in person, or, even better, getting the interviewee to do the hard work and come into the studio.

Vox Pop and Multiple

Vox pop is an abbreviation of the Latin vox populi, or *'voice of the people'*. The vox is used in broadcasting to provide a cross-section of public opinion on a given subject. In the USA it is often known as the *'person in the street'* or *'streeter'* interview.

The technique is to get a broad mix of opinion and different voices and although it may be represented as a guide to what people think, should not be considered a 'scientific survey'. Try to alternate between male and female, young and old. Begin and end with strong comments and make good use of humorous remarks.

Vox pops work best where the reporter's voice is kept out as much as possible. A single question should be asked, which is introduced in the cue, and the reporter puts that question to people in turn with the recorder kept on pause during the questions.

Variations in background noise can make editing difficult, but recording and overlaying some of that background sound, known as *wildtrack*, can cover the edits.

Returning to our running seafaring story, if the holiday booking season is at its height, our reporter could catch people outside travel agents, and after making introductions, ask them:

There's been another fire on a cruise liner, and passengers have had to abandon ship, so how does that make you feel about travelling by sea?

The vox pop production:

- is pacey, and cut together rather than mixed

- is short – usually about 30 seconds

- has a variety of voices and ages.

- usually starts with a strong statement, and ends with a viewpoint that summarises the argument or is funny or shocking

- is a good scene-setter for a discussion.

The vox pop question:

- is 'open', so you don't just get yes/no answers.

- is something people have a definite and instant view about; you don't want to start a discussion.

- may be recorded at a location that fits with the topic being asked about (the price of beer, outside a pub for example).

- is asked somewhere busy, to get more people in less time.

The *multiple interview* differs from the vox by taking a smaller number of selected extracts, often drawn from longer interviews and having the reporter link them together. This is known as a *package*.

Our ship saga is ideal for such treatment. Excerpts from the coastguard and the ship's owners could be mixed with comment by the shipping correspondent and edited together with narrative by the reporter.

Grabbed

Our final category concerns interviews that people don't want to give but which reporters are determined to take.

These are usually short and may comprise a few brief comments or a terse 'No comment!' which is often comment enough.

Grabbed interviews are obtained by pushing a camera or microphone under the nose of a subject and firing off questions.

Our reporter has caught sight of a smoke-stained uniform. It is the captain coming ashore. He seems in no mood to answer questions. Rushing over, our reporter pushes the microphone towards him and asks:

How did the fire begin?

(The captain ignores him and quickens his pace. The reporter pursues and repeats his question.)

Captain: It began in the engine room . . . overheating we think.
Reporter: Why weren't you able to put it out?

(No answer)

Reporter: Could it be that there weren't enough crewmen on board?

(Silence)

Reporter: Why did you set sail without a full crew?
Captain: No comment!

The grabbed interview usually works best on camera, where, even if the subject says nothing, they can be watched by the audience and their reactions noted.

Frequently there are so many reporters that there is no chance to pursue a line of questioning. If you ask even one question at a free-for-all, you are doing well. Not that it matters a great deal; the melee and persistent refusals to answer add to the sense that here is Someone with Something to Hide.

Grabbed interviews are often intrusions of privacy, or could be regarded as harassment. It would be unwarranted to grab an interview with a widow after a funeral or with anyone who is grieving or suffering. Ethically, personal privacy should only be intruded upon where someone's understandable desire to be left alone runs counter to proper public interest. That could be argued to be true of our captain.

Sometimes grabbing interviews can do more harm than good. Royalty will understandably take umbrage – they will usually speak to the media by appointment only. Similar rules apply to heads of state or anyone to whom the station would rather not risk giving offence. And as with the adversarial interview, there is always the risk of saying something libellous. Bear in mind that your unwilling subject may be only too happy to find occasion to sue you.

Your interviews may be:

- *One interviewer, one interviewee*: a one-on-one or one-to-one interview. This is the case with most interviews with 'regular' people.

- *One interviewer, several interviewees*: for example with several prize-winners at an event. They will tend to talk over each other, and so much of what they say will be off-mic or off-camera. Try and politely organise them, so you ask each of them a different (or the same) question. If you want them all to chip in and create the sound of hubbub and excitement, then get them to crowd around the mic rather than stand in line.

- *Several interviewers, one interviewee*: the best example is at a formal news conference: the chief of police is there to explain why he is stepping down and after making a statement he takes 'questions from the floor'. Every reporter has a chance to chip in, and everyone can record and use the answers that are given. (Hint: sometimes you may have a chance to have a one-to-one interview with the speaker, after the main conference. If that is the case, hold fire on your best questions during the general melee so you don't give your best angle away to other media.)

- *Several interviewers, several interviewees:* this very often happens at a formal news conference too. Say there have been local riots, and on the top table may be representatives from the emergency services as well as a politician and a community leader.

During the interview:

- *Listen closely* – in other words 'active listening'. That means, don't let the interviewee get away with talking, but not actually answering. Listen between the lines – what are they *really* saying or more importantly what are they *not* saying or admitting? But also respect what they are saying: pick up on a nugget they have just mentioned.

- *Don't worry about asking the same question again* – in fact we have made this point before but it's worth repeating (like a question might be). If you haven't understood the answer or think the guest has been evasive, ask it again or rephrase it. You don't have to be rude, just firm and polite. Claim ignorance if needs be: 'sorry, I still don't get it . . .'. At all times beware of conflicts of interest and be assertive but always courteous. Remember, *you* are in charge. The BBC advises its fledgling reporters to adopt an attitude of 'informed naiveté' – in other words, be a wolf in sheep's clothing.

- If an answer is good but too long, at the end of your interview explain your predicament: 'that was really good when you explained about the transplosive widget generator, but y'know what, I've got to edit that down to about 20 seconds or my boss will shoot me! If I asked that question again, you couldn't just give me a really quick and basic answer could you . . .?' It is your job to work for clarity on behalf of your audience.

- *Ask for examples* – they are really useful as they add colour and context to a interview.

- *Don't be afraid to challenge* – 'Tell me more . . .' or simply raise your eyebrows, cock your head and stay silent. Silence is a great technique to use to make the other person feel uncomfortable and keep on talking. Or reflect their question back to them: 'more troops . . .?'

- *Listen for the sound-bites* – with experience you will be able to identify the best bits of the interview as you go along, as well as how long each potential clip will be, what edits will be needed in each answer and how it will fit into the overall story. You must never leave until you have the contribution that your news editor has asked you for.

■ *Don't just focus on the bad points* – we also want answers to problems. What is going to happen now? How can the situation be sorted or moved on? What will be the situation a year from now?

■ *Think ahead* – not only get what you went for, but go back with more! Is there anything else that the interviewee is involved with that you should know about or a follow-up angle that you can record while you are with them? Say you interview the MD of a building company about their plans to develop a run-down local hotel. She talks about the cost of the development, how the building and area will be transformed and the jobs that will be created. But what about getting a few answers 'in the can' for the day the planning committee meets? 'What would be your message to those making the decision . . .?'

THE QUESTIONS

Our thoughts so far have been confined to the preparations for the match, the warm-up and the strategy. Now on to the tactics for the match itself – the questions.

There is more to the art of interviewing than developing the ability to engage complete strangers in intelligent conversation. Good questions produce good answers. The secret is to think ahead to the answers you are likely to get before asking your questions.

Using Notes

Most interviewees would agree that preparing questions is constructive in planning the interview, but sticking closely to a list of written questions can be unhelpful during the course of the interview itself. The problems are:

■ Eye contact is lost.

■ When the interviewer is concentrating on the questions, he or she is unable to listen to the interviewee.

■ Fixed questions make for an inflexible interview.

If you intend to use notes, use them sparingly. Write out the first question *only if you have to* to get the interview off to a good start. Complex questions are seldom a good idea, but if the form of words is critical then write the question down. Write legibly. Preferably don't write at all – print. If you have to pause to decipher your handwriting you will lose the flow.

Perhaps the best compromise between maintaining rapport and keeping the interview on course is to make brief notes or headings of important points only. These should be sufficient to jog the memory without breaking concentration. You should always be prepared to follow up an answer that was unexpected, but you should have notes so you know how to get back on track. And when changing tack in the interview, from one of your 'headline topics' to another, it may help your guest and

FIGURE 8.2
The control room for the prestigious daily morning news programme 'Today' on BBC Radio 4, in whose studios many politicians have been grilled. Credit BBC Radio 4.

the audience if you signpost that in some way: 'On a different subject and away from the economy Mr President, let's turn to climate change . . .'

Ask the Questions That Will Get Answers

The *who, what, when, where, why* and *how* framework for writing copy applies equally to the news interview and the type of questions the interviewer should ask.

No reporter wants to be left with a series of monosyllabic grunts on the recording, so questions should be carefully structured to produce good useful quotes rather than single word comments.

- The question *who* calls for a name in response
- *What* asks for a description
- *When* pins down the timing of an event
- *Where* locates it
- *Why* asks for an interpretation, opinion or an explanation, and often gets a great answer: 'why did you decide to . . .?', 'why do you believe it's necessary to . . .?'
- *How* asks for an opinion or an interpretation.

Questions beginning with these words will propel the interview forward and yield solid facts:

- '*Who* was hurt in the crash?'
- '*What* caused the accident?'
- '*When* did it happen?'
- '*Where* did the accident occur?'
- '*Why* did it take so long to free the trapped passengers?'
- '*How* did you manage to get them out?'

Yes/No Questions

Inexperienced reporters often fall into the trap of asking 'closed questions' that produce *yes/no* answers. They may come away with some idea of the story, but will seldom have recorded anything worth using.

Sometimes though, a yes or a no answer is required to establish a fact that will open the way for a new line of questioning:

> Interviewer: In the light of today's street violence, do you plan to step up police patrols?
> Police chief: No, we think that would be unhelpful.
> Interviewer: Why?
> Police chief: It could be taken as provocation, etc.

Other examples to pin down a fact, might be questions that start 'what do you mean when you say . . .?', 'are you saying that . . .?', or 'will . . .?', 'Is . . .?', 'Did . . .?' or 'Have . . .?'

Less artful interviewers are sometimes tempted to ask a yes/no question in the hope that it will prompt their guest to do the work for them and develop a new line of argument:

> Interviewer: Critics would say the plan to put a factory on the green land site is ill conceived. Would you agree?
> Developer: No, of course not. The design is modern and attractive and will bring many much-needed jobs to the area.

That time the technique worked. More often than not, it doesn't:

> Interviewer: Critics would say the plan to put a factory on the green land site is ill conceived. Would you agree?
> Developer: No.
> Interviewer: Oh err . . . Why not?
> Developer: Well how could you expect me to agree to that . . . I'm the one who's building the darned thing!

Using the question this way encourages a non-answer, or worse still, permits the interviewee to pick on the 'yes' or 'no' in whatever way he or she wishes and head off on a tangent. The interviewer should always try to keep the whip hand.

So, asking a closed question may elicit a single word response . . . so be ready with a swift follow-up!

Avoid Questions That Call for Monologues

The opposite of the yes/no question, but which can have the same effect, is the 'open question' which is so wide its scope is almost unlimited:

> Interviewer: As a leading clean-up campaigner, what do you think is wrong with porn shops and peep shows anyway?

Leave your recorder running and come back in an hour when she's finished! Pin the question to one clearly defined point:

> What's the main reason you're opposed to these porn shops?

Or:

> Which peep shows in particular do you want cleaned up?

Question scope is important. Make it too narrow and your interview will keep on stalling. Open it up too wide and it can run away from you.

Interviewer: Now obviously, er, Reverend, you don't like the idea of, em, these prep schools being used as, em, fashionable schools for middle class parents, but, em, y. . .d-do you really think that i-i-it matters whether or not they believe – the parents themselves – in-in a Christian education as such. I mean, would you be happy if they particularly wanted and believed that the Christian, em, or th-the-the Anglic . . . the Anglican sort of education was right for their kids, would you like to see the church schools remain in that case, as long as you were convinced of their sincerity, rather than of the fact that they were doing it simply because it was a middle class fashionable thing to do?

Reverend: That's a very good question. I don't know.

UK Radio

Short, Single Idea Questions

If a question is to be understood by both the audience and the interviewee it has to be kept clear, simple and straightforward, unlike this example:

Interviewer: Coming back to your earlier point about owners who get rid of their pets, don't you think there should be some kind of sanction, I mean, some sort of measure or something, against owners who dump their unwanted pets, as happens so frequently after Christmas, when they get given them as presents and find they didn't really want a pet after all?

Animal welfare spokesman: Em, well, er, I'm not exactly sure what you've in mind . . .

Cotton wool, by the sounds of it. Try:

Interviewer: What penalty would you like to see against owners who dump their unwanted pets?

Keep the threads of the argument untangled and stick to one point at a time.

Progress From Point to Point

To maintain the logic of the interview each question should naturally succeed the previous one. If the interviewer needs to refer back to a point, this should be done neatly and followed through by another question that progresses the argument:

Interviewer: Going back to owners who dump their pets after Christmas, would you like to see some form of penalty imposed against them?
Animal welfare spokesman: We most certainly would.
Interviewer: What have you got in mind?

Building Bridges

Each question should arise naturally from the previous answer. If the two points are only distantly related the interviewer should use a bridge, as in the question above. Another example is this from interviewer Michael Parkinson, talking to Oscar-winning actor Ben Kingsley on BBC Radio 4:

Parkinson: Then I suppose after getting the Academy Award for best actor in *Gandhi* you must have been offered an enormous range of parts. What parts were you offered?

Avoid Double Questions

The interviewer should ask one question at a time, otherwise a wily subject would be able to choose which to answer, and which to ignore. Even the most willing of subjects may forget one half of the question.

Bad question:

What form will your demonstration take, and do you think County Hall will take any notice?

Better:

What kind of demonstration are you planning?

Following the answer with:

What effect do you think it'll have on the views of county councillors?

If you ask more than one question at a time, an experienced interviewee such as a politician, will choose which one they want and ignore the other!

Keep the Questions Relevant

The news interview is not some esoteric exercise in analysing abstractions. But the trouble with experts in any field is that they are liable to lapse into jargon. If you let them, you will lose your audience. And the interview is for their benefit, not yours.

So help your experts keep their feet on the ground. Keep them to the point. And the only point that matters is the point of relevance to your audience.

As with news writing, examples should be concrete and real. If you begin by asking how high inflation will rise, be sure to follow it up with a question about whether wages and salaries are likely to keep pace or what it will do to the price of bread.

If it is a question about inner city poverty, don't just talk about living standards, ask about the food these people eat or get a description of their homes.

Get away from the abstract and relate ideas to everyday realities.

Avoid Leading Questions

A leading question is one designed to lead interviewees into a corner and trap them there. More often it has the effect of boxing-in the reporter with allegations of malice, bias and unfair play:

- You've got to admit that . . .

- Isn't it a fact that . . .?

- Do you not think that . . .?

- You're not trying to suggest that . . .?

- I presume you are confident that you can do that . . .?

Take the example of an interview with an elderly farmer who was seriously burnt trying to save his photograph album from his blazing house:

Interviewer: Why did you attempt such a foolhardy and dangerous stunt over a worthless photograph album. Surely that's taking sentimentality too far?

This question, like most leading questions, was based on assumptions:

- Saving the album was stupid.

- It was dangerous.

- The album was worthless.

- The farmer's motive was sentimental.

- And that a sentimental reason was not a valid one.

But assumptions can prove to be false:

Farmer: My wife died three years ago. I kept all my most precious things together. The deeds to my house and all my land were inside that album with the only pictures I had of my wife. It was kept in the living room, which was away from the flames. I thought I had time to pull it out, but in my hurry I fell over and blacked out. Now I've lost everything.

The scorn of the audience would quickly shift from the farmer to the callous interviewer. If somebody is stupid or wrong or to blame, draw out the evidence through polite and sensitive interviewing and leave the audience to pass judgement.

Bad question:

> You knew the car's brakes were faulty when you rented it to George Brown, didn't you? The car crashed, he's in hospital and it's your fault. How do you feel about that?

Better:

1. When did you find out the car's brakes were faulty?

2. But later that morning, before the brakes could be repaired, didn't you rent it out to another customer?

3. Weren't you worried there could be an accident?

4. How do you feel now your car is written off and your customer, George Brown, is in hospital?

Expose the fallacy of an argument, not by putting words into a person's mouth, but by letting the evidence and his own words condemn him.

Leading questions are frowned on by the courts. The same should go for broadcasting.

Hypothetical Questions

These can be quite useful as long as they are based on a reasonable assumption. Asking someone how they might feel in a situation is one thing ('how do you think your staff made redundant are feeling today?') but asking them to gauge what someone else is *thinking*, or what someone else *might do*, especially when they are taking an opposite stance to your interviewee, is preposterous ('what do you think the union response might be to the redundancies?').

A hypothetical question may also ask about the guest's aspirations and provide a good final answer to your report: 'and after the quarry has been closed and returned to nature . . . what do you think this place will look like in a year from now?'

So, a hypothetical question may get someone to imagine a situation they may not have experienced, but it is poor to use it when that person lacks knowledge of the situation or subject to be able to give an informed answer.

Mixing Statements With Questions

Sometimes it is necessary to give some background information before coming to the question. The question and the information should be kept separate for the sake of clarity, and the question at the end should be brief:

First commentator: So, for the fourth time in a row the Lions have romped home with a clear victory, and are now standing an astonishing

> eleven points clear at the top of the table. Manager Bill Fruford, tell us, what's the secret?

Avoid statements posing as questions:

> Second commentator: With me here is manager John Turnbull whose team's performance crumpled completely in the last five minutes, with the Lions making all the running over a dispirited side.
>
> Turnbull: (silence)
> Commentator: Mr Turnbull?
> Turnbull: Sorry, you talking to me? What was the question?

In passing the ball to the manager the commentator lost possession, but letting it go, especially after such a disparaging account of the team's performance, has left the commentator's own defences wide open. The manager could have said anything he wanted as no direct question had been asked of him. As it was, because of the phrasing of the question, the manager was completely unaware the ball had been passed to him.

Beware of Questions That Would Be Out of Date

If the interview is being pre-recorded, remember to say nothing that would render the item out of date. If the piece is to go out next Wednesday, avoid:

> Well, Mrs Wilson, what's your reaction to today's events?

Similarly, watch the changeovers from morning to afternoon, afternoon to evening, evening to night, night to morning. The safest position is to drop any time reference from a story or an interview. Broadcast news is about immediacy. Even an only slightly out of date time reference can make the news sound stale.

Avoid Sounding Ignorant

Always check your facts before you launch into an interview. Clear up details like the following during the pre-chat:

> Interviewer: Mr Schaeffer, why have you decided to sack half your workforce?
> Mr Schaeffer: They have not been sacked.
> Interviewer: You deny it?
> Mr Schaeffer: What has happened is that their contracts have expired and have not been renewed. And it's not half the workforce; it's 125 staff out of a total of 400.
> Interviewer: (Sheepishly) Oh.

If you are not in the full picture, get filled in before the interview begins, but remember, as soon as you rely on your interviewees for background, you are putting them in a position where they can manipulate the interview to their advantage.

Play Devil's Advocate

You can, and often should, put the other side of an issue, but not as though it is your view. Say, for instance 'It could be said that . . .' or 'there is another view that maybe . . .'. Don't say 'Some people say . . .' as it can backfire:

Interviewer: Some people say that you should resign, Mr Carter.
Mr Carter: What people? Name them.

You need to be ready to justify your question with some evidence, preferably the names of specific people or publications . . .

Interviewer: Well, head of the company and the union leader . . . and The Daily Bugle has not been very supportive either . . .

Or, if necessary . . .

Interviewer: Are you saying nobody is suggesting you should resign . . .?

WINDING UP THE INTERVIEW

The words 'and finally' are best avoided during an interview, as a point may arise which may prompt a further question or clarification, and saying 'and finally' twice always sounds a little foolish.

A phrase such as 'Briefly . . .' may also serve as a wind up signal if necessary. Save your gestures and hand signals for experienced studio staff.

Finish Strongly

An interview should go out with a bang and never a whimper. It should end in a way that gives the whole performance a bold and emphatic full stop.

BBC Radio 4's evening news programme is called 'PM'. Here's an extract from a live interview in which the MP, Francis Maude (FM), appeals for people to do more volunteering in the 'Big Society'.

FM: Our obligations to each other and society don't end with just paying our taxes . . . when people do more, not just for themselves but more in communities . . . and that's what binds us together.

Q: Point made. What sort of volunteering do you do?

FM: Eh, I eh, Golly. Load of things . . . eh . . . involved with my local church. Gosh that's a really unfair question. Cold. Like that. I mean the real point is . . .

Q: Well given that you're telling us how important volunteering is, I thought you might be able to say, not least because it's in your manifesto which says 'It is our ambition for every adult in the country to be involved in an active neighbourhood group.' So, you?

FM: Well, I'm involved in things in my local . . . I mean MPs at times are involved in voluntary groups . . .

Q: Yes well that's part of your job. You get paid for that. What else do you do?

FM: We do it seven days a week, kind of thing. I do, eh, various things. That's eh, a great question to drop on me. Look my main point is that most people in their lives can be doing things you could define as volunteering, are doing things that support their neighbourhoods as part of being an active citizen in an active community

Ends: Thank you Francis Maude.

Recorded interviews should not end with 'Thank you very much Geraldine Smith'. Save your thank-yous for rounding off live interviews and handing back to a presenter.

If during a live interview a guest insists on going on over her time, then don't be afraid to butt in with a polite, 'Well, I'm afraid we must stop there', or 'That's all we've got time for, thank you very much'. And if she refuses to take the hint, it is the job of the producer to switch off the microphone and usher her out.

TOUGH TALKING

Beware of the trained interviewee. Powerful people pay money to learn how to use an interview as a platform, while avoiding its proper purpose. Expert tuition teaches them how to get across their key three or four points at all costs, so you must find several different ways of asking your key questions.

Interviewees expressing contentious views must be rigorously tested, but in a calm and even-handed manner. Evasion should be exposed. This can be done calmly and politely, if necessary by repeating the question and explaining to the interviewee why the previous answer didn't address it.

Interviews should be well mannered. Leave it to the interviewee to be aggressive, hectoring or rude if they feel so inclined. Audiences are quite capable of judging

FIGURE 8.3

A reporter and various cameras converge on a politician who's suddenly headline news.

the blusterer and the bully. In a well-conducted interview, viewers regard the interviewer as working on their behalf. Discourteous questions can make the audience hostile to the interviewer and sympathetic to the interviewee.

Any heat or emotion in an interview should come from the interviewee.

Professionals' Tactics

- Embarrass the interviewer.

- Ridicule their knowledge of the facts (or lack of them).

- Refuse to answer any questions.

- Evade the questions and stick to their own agenda by getting their point over instead. They do this by using phrases such as:

  - The key point here is . . .

  - What you must understand is . . .

  - What you've missed is . . .

  - The fact is that . . .

  - What I can tell you is . . .

- They re-work the question to one that they can answer. ('Can you guarantee that something will be done?'/'What I can guarantee is that a full investigation will be done . . .')

- They sidestep questions by claiming they're not the right person to ask ('Do you think the government's done enough?'/'I'd rather leave politics to the politicians')

- They answer questions with a question.

- They always ask the source of an interviewer's information – the interviewer rarely knows.

- They deliberately upset the programme schedule and arrive late . . .

- They flatter the interviewer – by using their first name a lot . . .

- They accuse the interviewer of putting forward their own opinion . . .

- They claim not to understand the questions . . .

- They criticise the company/media/journalists generally . . .

- They waffle, to use up time and so there are fewer questions . . .

- And they prepare a few 15-second soundbites of key messages in dynamic language that are more likely to get on news bulletins.

Interviews should be searching and to the point, well-mannered and challenging but not aggressive. When interviewing ordinary people, the tone should be appropriate . . . Interviewees should be given a fair chance to set out a full response to questions. Interruption needs to be well timed and not too frequent.

BBC Guidelines

BEING INTERVIEWED YOURSELF: THE Q & A

Sometimes the tables get turned on reporters and they find themselves having to answer the questions. If they have been covering a major breaking story, such as an air crash or a gas explosion, they will have the latest information and the advantage of being available.

It is right to interview BBC correspondents and ask them to express judgement based on their specialist knowledge. But be careful not to encourage speculation.

BBC Guidelines

'Q & A' stands for *question and answer*. The reporter, hot foot from the air crash, may be invited to break into normal programming to give the audience a first-hand account of events. If she has been covering the story live, the station can cross to her at the scene for description as well as background.

The reporter should script the questions. It would be pointless to leave the line of questioning to a music presenter who has little idea what has been going on. Worse still, the presenter might ask questions the reporter couldn't answer.

The *answers* should not be scripted, though. The conversation would sound almost as artificial as an interviewee who insists on reading from a statement.

With unscripted pieces there is always a danger of repetition or hesitation. Beware of this. Under nerves, people often say too much or too little. Keep a check on yourself and say just enough to fill the allocated time with solid details and interesting information without resorting to filler, bulk or repetition.

At the end of being interviewed by a colleague, the reporter should be wary of clichéd ways to end the report. Phrases such as 'whether the planned strike will have much effect . . . *only time will tell*', or '*we'll have to wait and see* whether by the time it is built it will still be the tallest residential property in the city . . .' are empty and usually meaningless ways to end an item.

Introducing Actuality

If the Q & A is with a radio reporter live at the scene, that reporter may want to introduce some actuality, such as an interview recorded earlier with a witness or an official. This should be edited and cued-up ready to go and introduced in the

FIGURE 8.4
Conducting a celebrity interview at Free Radio in the UK. Credit Kris Askey – Free Radio/Orion Media.

same way as any news interview. For a smooth production, it would be better to have that interviewee beside you when you go live.

Of course, one may record a twenty-minute interview, but only a short clip from it may ever make it to air. The facts may clarify or extend the knowledge the reporter already has, in which case a pertinent clip from the conversation may be used on air as a 'quote' or soundbite to illustrate their viewpoint.

But people don't always talk in soundbites when you want them to, or it may be that you are unable to record them (or the potential guest may be unwilling to be interviewed, issuing instead, a statement). In such situations you need to be able to paraphrase what was said; attribute it to the speaker and read it yourself.

Attribution is when you tell the audience the source of a quote or information used so it is clear that you are reporting what someone else has said, not saying it yourself. As it says in *Inside Reporting* (Tim Harrower, published by McGraw Hill) 'Make sure sources get proper credit (or blame) for what they say'. So gather information from various sides of an argument, explain them carefully and accurately, and attribute all the sources. But stay neutral and keep your own views to yourself.

That last point is a thread throughout reporting of course, but your own personal take on a story can creep in at the most unexpected times. It may never cross your mind to make an outright statement about your personal stand on a story, but what about when you write that 'the Mayor *stated* that he was not responsible'? Does using that word give a slightly different emphasis on the situation than if you had used '*said*' or '*denied*' or '*declared*'? It may be a subtle but important difference.

Incidentally, attribution of a quote that is read out in a broadcast stylistically happens at the start of the sentence. It's to make it immediately clear who said what. For example, if a presenter came on and said 'The world ends on Thursday', viewers would be rightly alarmed: the date of the apocalypse would be interpreted as fact. Instead the presenter says 'The leader of a small cult in south-east Asia has claimed that the world ends on Thursday . . .' – ensuring that the attribution at the start of the sentence puts what follows into immediate context.

On occasion it may be that none of the interview makes it to air: the conversation may be unusable (a boring guest, or some technical problem, or maybe they did not come out with the line that had been anticipated), or it may lead the reporter on to another angle of the story completely. Sometimes an interview may be conducted with no intention for it to be broadcast, but to have statements 'on the record' and act as a firm foundation for other interviews or other story investigations.

The disaster story continues

Having concluded our foray into the jungle of the interview, let us return to hear how Mr Scargill and his hapless interviewer are getting on. They are still at it . . .

Interviewer: Let's move on to something else . . . the meeting you're having tomorrow . . .

Scargill: No, I'm sorry, we're not moving on to anything until you let me put the point of view across on behalf of those that I represent.

Interviewer: I think you've put it over several times, Mr Scargill.

Scargill: . . . all I've done so far is to be interrupted by an ignorant man like you, who ought to have more sense . . .

Interviewer: Mr Scargill, we've . . . (sigh). Can we conduct this interview rather than having a slanging match?

Scargill: Well you started it, not me! . . . All that you're doing so far is to present a question and then conveniently ignore the point that I want to give by way of response

Interviewer: (Struggling to get a word in) Let's move on to another question . . .

Perhaps it is not surprising the interview has turned out the way it has. If you can remember back to where we came in, it was with the statement that the miners were divided over following Mr Scargill, and a request that the fiery miners' leader *concede* that the strike was bitter and that '*like never before miner is pitched against miner*'.

You could hope for more success arm wrestling a gorilla than in asking a determined and embattled interviewee whose reputation is on the line to *concede*.

Another moral of this tale might be that if you plan to fight fire with fire, then don't pitch a match against a flame-thrower. If there is ever an occasion when interviewer and interviewee should be evenly pitted it is against one another in an adversarial interview.

There are signs that this interview may be just about to shudder to its conclusion . . .

Interviewer: It seems you're incapable of answering any questions, Mr Scargill.

> Scargill: It seems as though you're the most ignorant person that I've ever discussed with on radio. Now either you're going to listen to answers even though you don't like them, or you're not. It's entirely up to you.
>
> Interviewer: Mr Scargill, thank you for joining us and I'm afraid not answering any of our questions here in Sheffield this afternoon. This live interview with the miners' leader Arthur Scargill . . .
>
> Scargill: This live interview has been absolutely appalling as a result of . . . (He is faded out.)
>
> Interviewer: Independent Radio News, it's 1.30!
>
> Reproduced by kind permission of Independent Radio News

After the interview:

- *Check your recording* – is it all there? How distracting was that slamming door in the first answer or do you need to do it again?

- *Record any wildtrack* – this may be effects that help tell the story (the interviewee answering the door to you, the schoolgirl entrepreneur doing her music practice) as well as 'constant' sounds that you can put underneath the entire interview to 'hide the edits'. (This technique is discussed later in the book.)

- *Dissuade the interviewee from hearing the interview back* – it will take too long, they will usually want to retake part of it, and it may reduce your independence.

- *Thank them* – for their time and contribution and remind them again when the item is likely to go out.

THE HEADLINES

Tips for interviewing:

- Choose a focus for the interview.

- Research – do lots.

- Choose the interviewee carefully.

- Prepare yourself.

- Prepare the interviewee.

- Put questions clearly, concisely and pertinently.

- Facts are good but very often ask questions that get a reaction, a feeling or opinion.

- Listen to the interviewee and react.

- Use body language.

- Don't record too much.
- Have an outline on paper or in your head.
- Avoid multiple questions.

Open questions:

- ask the respondent to think and reflect
- give you opinions and feelings
- hand control of the conversation to the interviewee.

Closed questions:

- give you the facts
- are easy to answer
- are quick to answer
- keep control of the conversation with the interviewer.

QUESTIONS FOR YOU

1. Listen to (and record if possible) a number of interviews on radio and TV and list the questions that were asked in each.
2. What proportion of the questions were of the *who, what, when, where, why* and *how* variety? Do all the questions follow on from one another? If not, why not? Does each interview follow a logical thread? Where do you think the interviewer has deviated from his/her planned list of questions to pick up on one of the interviewee's answers? Can you pick out any *bridging* questions or *double* questions? Are there any *leading* questions? If so, how do you react to them? Are there any badly phrased questions? How would you rephrase them? Do the interviews finish strongly? If not, how could they have been edited to give them a more definite conclusion?
3. Interview simulation: taking control.

   - This is a power game requiring two players. One plays the reporter and the other the interviewee. The story is about a landlord who has bought houses that are due for demolition and is letting them to tenants who he is keeping in squalor for profit.
   - The story concerns eight houses in Bridge Street split into single and double rooms, some are in need of repair and all are badly inadequate.
   - The landlord, Albert Smith, is leasing the houses cheaply from the local authority and charging high rents. The tenants are mainly poor immigrants. A shortage of rented accommodation means they have to stay there or become homeless. They have complained about the squalid conditions which they say are to blame for the constant ill-health of some of their children.

- The reporter's brief is to interview the landlord to expose what is happening and, in a manner that is both fair and reasonable, call him to account. The landlord's aim is to defend his reputation and show himself up in the best possible light. If the local authority accepts the case against him, he could lose his houses. The central plank of his defence is that the immigrants would be homeless without him, and he knows that if the local authority ruled his houses uninhabitable, they would then have the responsibility of housing the immigrants.

- The reporter has one constraint upon him – if the landlord disputes any facts that are not included in this brief, the reporter must not be dogmatic about them.

- Both parties should finish reading this brief and then re-read it. The reporter should then spend up to five minutes privately thinking up questions, in which time the interviewee should anticipate the questions that would be asked and prepare a defence.

- The exercise is one of control. Both parties want the interview to go ahead, though both are hoping for a different outcome. Each should try to take charge and to bend the interview to his own purposes – one to expose the facts, the other to gloss over them and turn them to his advantage by making them seem more acceptable.

- If you have recording equipment, record the interview. Conduct it preferably in front of a small audience of classmates who can later offer constructive criticism. You have fifteen minutes to conduct the pre-chat and the interview.

- Afterwards discuss the interview. Who came out on top and why? How did the reporter attempt to expose the facts and how did the landlord try to cover them up? How did each side feel about the attempts to manipulate him during the interview? Were the right questions asked? How did you resolve differences in opinion about the facts of the story? What did the audience think?

4. Interview simulation: Q & A.

- There has been a serious accident on a main highway from town. Several cars are involved and some people have died. You are at the scene of the crash and your station wants to conduct a live interview with you about what you have seen. Imagine the scene and work out a scenario, then draw up a list of questions for the presenter. You should have enough material to stay on air for three minutes. If you are in a class, find someone to be the presenter and go ahead with the Q & A.

5. Look back at the transcript of the Francis Maude interview. Was the interviewer fair? Should the guest have been warned about the question? Should the interviewer have pushed the politician further? Why do you think they concluded the interview where and how they did?

6. What do you think makes a good interview?

7. You telephone a government official to arrange an interview. He agrees on condition that you submit your questions in advance. What do you do?

8. You arrive at an interviewee's office to conduct an interview. His contribution is vital to your programme. He hands you a list of the four main questions, typed verbatim,

which he says you may ask. You had no hint of this arrangement before. What do you do?

9. You arrange to interview a prominent local businesswoman in her office one morning. She agrees but says she wants to hear the finished, edited interview before the broadcast at lunchtime. She wants to be sure that nothing she has said has been distorted. What do you say?

10. You record an interview with a woman who then calls you before transmission and asks you to drop it. She says that although the interview is factually accurate, it would embarrass her professionally. If you drop the interview it will leave a hole in your programme which will be difficult to fill at this late stage. What do you do?

OTHER RESOURCES

- You don't have to hector an interviewee: you can be polite and gentle and still be persistently probing. Hear Michael Gove's interview on BBC Radio 4 in which Eddie Mair politely asks the same, short and simple question several times: http://bit.ly/BJGove. And then from about 6:30, Mr Gove gets rather tongue-tied when asked to explain himself. From 9:00 the interviewer corners his guest (work out the phrasing of the previous questions that got Mr Gove to say what he did). At 10:00 Mr Gove turns the question on its head and uses one of the 'avoiding' techniques of politicians. From 10:15, hear how Eddie Mair sets up the next but one question.

- Here is a (one-hour!) BBC radio programme about vox-pop/man-on-the-street interviews including some from the US in 1935: http://bit.ly/BJVoxProg.

- What to expect when you're interviewed by AP. A useful guide that you could adapt for your station. It certainly helps you see the interview from another perspective: http://bit.ly/BJAPGuide.

- Some of the best advice about interviewing for journalists comes from Canadian author and journalist, John Sawatsky, who has been giving workshops to journalists in Canada and around the world for years; http://bit.ly/BJQuestionMan and http://bit.ly/BJQuestionMan2.

- CBC's index of great interviews: http://www.cbc.ca/archives/.

- The 'art of the interview' in this Poynter article: http://bit.ly/BJArtOfInterview.

- More ideas particularly for younger reporter wannabes, here: http://www.radiodiaries.org/trh/ and for the slightly more experienced in this 21-page pdf: http://bit.ly/BJSound.

- An interview with Jennifer Aniston goes wrong (although she was playing along with a stunt to make the reporter feel awkward!): http://bit.ly/BJAniston.

- And here's a BBC documentary of interviews that went disastrously wrong: http://bit.ly/BJAnger.

- When an interview goes right. (What are the chances of this happening?!): http://bit.ly/BJfootballer.

- Recording a whole meeting sounds great, until it's time to go back and listen to it. Since Cogi only records the important moments, by keeping audio buffered until you tell it that you want to keep it, you can review exactly what was said without wasting time on all the 'jibber-jabber': www.cogi.com.

TUTOR NOTES

In 2007, while investigating the Church of Scientology for BBC's Panorama, reporter John Sweeney had a dramatic on-camera confrontation with a church spokesman named Tommy Davis. The church was accusing the reporter of bias and it attempted to stop the documentary from being broadcast. Watch what happened: http://bit.ly/BJScientology1.

- Discuss the reporter's reaction. Do you think it was justified?

Now read this article and watch the embedded video, which gives the background to the flare-up: http://bit.ly/BJScientology2.

- Has your view changed?

The *In the Psychiatrist's Chair* programmes on BBC radio revealed the inner life of the famous and successful, as they were questioned by psychiatrist Dr Anthony Clare about their public and private lives. At the time of first broadcast this candid and often devastating approach was considered ground breaking. Take a listen to a complete episode.

- What do you learn from the guest?

- Do you think they revealed more than they usually did, or intended to?

- Listen to the questions, the order of them and how they are phrased.

- What do you think about the tone of the questions?

- Draw a spider-diagram or flow chart to show how Dr Clare introduces and then develops a theme, gently probing a little deeper.

Imagine that you have been sent to the scene of a warehouse fire and are the first reporter there. Who do you talk to? What do you ask them?

- You have been told that the warehouse contained valuable items of art. Who do you talk to now? What questions do you want answered?

- You have been led to believe that the lapse in security at the warehouse may have had a part to play in the fire starting. Who do you question and what do you ask?

- You have been told by a distressed woman at the scene that her daughter is missing following the fire. What do you ask her? What checks do you make on her story? What considerations do you have before you interview her live on air?

CHAPTER 9

Writing Basics

> Write like you talk. Tell me the story as though you were telling it to a friend. Remember to talk to only one person at a time and try using the word 'you'. Describe details visually for radio as though you were telling it to a blind person.
> Valerie Geller, author, *Creating Powerful Radio* (creatingpowerfulradio.com; gellermedia.com)

When writing for broadcast, you often need to forget your literary aspirations. Unless you are writing a script for a considered and perhaps lengthy feature piece, such as *From Our Own Correspondent* on BBC Radio 4 (www.bbc.co.uk/programmes/b006qjlq) you need to get the point of the story over quickly and crisply.

What may be clear and sparkling to the eye may be confused and baffling to the ear, and may also be difficult to read out aloud. And that's because writing (at least the way we were taught it at school) obeys the rules of the written, rather than the spoken word.

Writing for broadcast can mean throwing away literary conventions, including the rules of grammar, so the words make sense to the ear, rather than the eye. In print, shades of meaning are conveyed with choice adjectives and skilful prose, but the spoken word makes use of a medium which is altogether more subtle and powerful – the human voice.

FIGURE 9.1
Reading the news while keeping a straight back and a stiff sheet of paper. Courtesy Annie Edwards and 107.8 Radio Jackie.

TELLING THE STORY

My rule of thumb is, 'If it seems awkward and long when you say it aloud, it probably sounds that way to the listener.' Long sentences can be exhausting to read – and hear. I try to keep each sentence focused on a single thought, and keep it simple.

Peter King, CBS Radio (poynter.org)

For graduates, or print journalists starting out in radio or TV, the hardest adjustment can be breaking out of the literary mould imposed on us since our schooldays, writing essays and theses that are meant to be read to oneself, rather than out loud. Everything in broadcasting is written to be spoken, so it sounds natural to the ear and is easy to read out loud, without causing the reader to stumble over words and gasp for breath.

Picture yourself leaning on a bar telling a story to a friend. Without realising it, you'll translate the story into the spoken, conversational word, naturally dropping parts of the story that clutter it up.

For television, 'a picture is worth a thousand words': the images on the screen will often tell the story more effectively than any description in a script.

WRITING FOR A MASS AUDIENCE

If you can't figure out what the top line is on a complicated story, imagine you are calling your mother and you can only tell her one thing about the story. What would it be? Because that's nearly always the best line.

Martina Purdy, Politics Correspondent for BBC Northern Ireland

The secret of communicating with an audience, however large, is to write and speak as though you were talking to only one person. Visualising a single well-disposed listener warms up the approach, makes it more personal and avoids the trap of sounding patronising. Aim to talk *to* the audience and not *at* them.

And get a story *across* to them, don't talk *down* to them. You'll lose the interest of the listener or viewer if you talk over their heads. *Broadcasting* means just that: reaching out to a broad cross-section of the community, and the skill lies in pitching it so what you say satisfies every demographic, background and level of education.

Learn to *tell* a story rather than *write* it, and you're halfway there. The next stage is to realise that the broadcast audience has different needs to the newspaper reader, and that those needs differ again between radio and television.

NO SECOND CHANCE

Newspaper readers have one big advantage: without much effort they can glance back at a story and re-read it to make sense of it. But broadcasters have only got one chance to be understood. Despite 24-hour rolling news, and devices that can instantly play back live programmes, information is still fleeting. The listener or viewer *could* rewind the programme to listen again, but that requires effort. It's best to get it right, and easily understood, the first time.

The onus on making sense of the news lies always with the newswriter and newsreader, never with the audience. This means the broadcast story has to be crystal clear the first time it's heard. Cut the clutter and iron out convoluted writing. Sentences should be clear and straightforward, without clauses and sub-clauses.

Mark Twain described the way a good writer constructed a sentence:

> He will make sure there are no folds in it, no vaguenesses, no parenthetical interruptions of its view as a whole; when he has done with it, it won't be a sea-serpent, with half of its arches under the water; it will be a torch-light procession.

What do you think Mark Twain would have made of the following?

> The docks' dispute, which is now in its 17th day, as 300 members of the Freight and Transport, Britain's largest industrial union, take strike action, because of an overtime ban which has been in operation since February 9, as well as unsocial hours, shows no sign of letting up, despite warnings by the F&T that lorry drivers could be asked to block the port.

Chances are you would have to read it through twice to be clear about it, which means the story would have failed on radio or TV. Yet all it needs is a little unravelling:

> There's still no sign of a let-up in the docks' dispute, now in its 17th day. This is despite warnings by the Freight and Transport, Britain's biggest industrial union, that lorry drivers might be called on to blockade the port. 300 members of the F&T have walked out in protest at unsocial hours and a ban on overtime. The ban was imposed on February the 9th.

FIGURE 9.2
The other side of the autocue. An operator checks the script before the evening news programme. The writing style is conversational and the phraseology and pace match those of the presenter. Courtesy Katherine Adams/BBC.

In this written version, the one sentence of the original has become four. The tangle of subsidiary clauses has been unravelled and chopped into three short sentences. The story progresses logically and the only kink which remains is the brief subsidiary clause, *'Britain's biggest industrial union'*, which is too small to restrict the flow of the sentence. Notice too, that *'February 9'* which is standard newspaper style, has been changed to the slightly longer, but more conversational, *'February the 9th'*.

Sentences for broadcast need to be clear and declarative, containing a minimum of different ideas. 'Simplicity' and 'conciseness' are the watchwords.

One rule of thumb on the length of sentences is around 20–25 words with one thought per sentence. However, there's always a danger that several sentences of a similar length can produce a rhythmic effect.

The greatest writers use the shortest sentences. Plain and simple, readers are looking for value. They are too busy for you to waste their time. They want the most meaning in the fewest words. Far too many writers clutter up their message by using extra words. Get comfortable using sentence fragments. I know your grammar teacher will hate you, but remember that news copy is written for the ear, not the eye. Conversational English is its own language with its own set of rules. All of us use sentence fragments throughout our day.

'How about that game . . .?' 'Hungry?' 'Too tough for me.'
Graeme Newell, Television and Digital Media Training Company (602communications.com)

CONFUSING CLAUSES

An item that makes sense on paper where the punctuation is visible can have an altogether different meaning when read aloud:

Ethiopia said the Eritrean leader had started the conflict.

Just *who* has been found negligent and by *who* comes down to a little matter of punctuation, or lack of it, which can completely alter the sense of the story:

'Ethiopia,' said the Eritrean leader, 'had started the conflict.'

For broadcast, the copy style has to be unambiguous. Assuming the second version of this hypothetical story is the correct one, it should be re-written as follows:

The Eritrean leader said Ethiopia had started the conflict.

INVERTED SENTENCES

Because listeners have to hold in their memory what has been said, inverted sentences such as this one are to be avoided.

Inversions often demand that listeners hold on to information that has no meaning until it is put into context. By the time that context comes, listeners may have forgotten what they were supposed to remember or be terminally confused. This is how *not* to do it:

> Because of the fall in the mortgage rate, which has stimulated home buying, house prices are going up again.

> Rather: House prices are going up again. The fall in the mortgage rate has led to an increase in home buying.

State the point to begin with and then explain it, not the other way round, and avoid beginning a sentence with 'Because' or 'According to'. Listeners can never refer back.

PLAIN ENGLISH

> Journalism – a profession whose business is to explain to others what it personally doesn't understand.
> Lord Northcliffe, British newspaper and publishing magnate 1865–1922

Plain English should not be confused with dull language; the English tongue is too rich and varied for it ever to need to be boring. Plain English does away with woolliness, wordiness, officialese and circumlocution and replaces it with words and descriptions that are concrete and direct.

Plain English is about rat-catchers and road sweepers, never 'rodent operators' or 'highway sanitation operatives'. It is about straightforward writing using commonly understood words, rather than highfalutin phrases intended to impress. As journalist Harold Evans puts it, plain English is about calling a spade a spade and not a 'factor of production'.

The enemy of good writing is the official, the bureaucrat and the so-called expert who uses words as a barrier to understanding instead of as a means of communication. Their aim is to mystify rather than enlighten. A good deal of the journalist's time is spent translating their gobbledegook into plain English so people can make sense of it.

The danger is that some reporters, out of deadline pressure or laziness, may put something down on paper which they don't really understand in the hope that those who hear it *will*. They won't.

Never run anything on air that does not make complete sense to you. You will lose your audience.

> In the BBC we are very fond of acronyms – it's one of the first things newcomers to the corporation notice. But remember how stupid you felt having to ask a colleague what they meant when they asked you to go to TX and pick up a ROT? Don't do that to your audience. You may know what the CBI is, but not everyone else does. Make sure you spell out acronyms on the first mention.
> Julia Paul, BBC Northern Ireland reporter and journalism trainer

FAMILIAR WORDS

Speaking the layperson's language also means using familiar words. Prefer:

- Cut out   to   Excise
- Destroy   to   Obliterate
- Against   to   Antagonistic to
- Highest point   to   Zenith

If you use a word your listeners may not immediately understand, while they are puzzling over its meaning the information that follows will vanish into the ether. By the time they reach for a dictionary or more likely shrug and give up, they will have missed the rest of the story.

EASY LISTENING

American broadcaster Irving E. Fang researched what makes broadcast copy easy or difficult to understand. He devised the Easy Listening Formula, which is based on the length of words in a sentence. The idea is to add up all the syllables in a sentence, then subtract from that the number of words. If the final score is higher than 20, the sentence contains too many long and abstract words that would make it hard to understand, and it should be subbed down.

For example:

> The British-based human rights organisation, Christian Solidarity Worldwide, is accusing the Sudanese government of using outlawed chemical weapons and breaking the ceasefire in the long running civil war with the South in an offensive to clear civilians from oil fields where the first supplies of crude are beginning to flow. (Score 36)

> Rewrite: The Sudanese government has been accused of using banned chemical weapons and breaking the ceasefire in the long-running civil war with the South. (Score 13) The British human rights organisation, Christian Solidarity Worldwide, says Khartoum has launched an offensive to clear civilians from oilfields which are just beginning to produce oil. (Score 20)

As you can see from this, lengthy attributions stand in the way of easy listening.

ACCURATE ENGLISH

Taking shades of grey and turning them into black and white for the sake of simplifying an issue is often the mark of an inexperienced journalist. Some precision might have to be sacrificed for the sake of simplicity, but the final story should still give the facts accurately.

> Our job is to dejargonize, to declichefy, to make everything clear, simple and concise.
>
> BBC Newsroom Guide

How would you translate the following ghastly, but typical, example of officialese?

> The Chairman observed that the Government loan of one million dollars may serve to obviate the immediate necessity for the termination of the contracts in question among non-full time ancillary staff, but that this contingency could not be discounted at a later period in the financial year in the event that funds became exhausted.

The following version, distilled from the facts above, may look plausible, but would be completely misleading:

> The Chairman said the jobs of support staff had been spared for the time being thanks to a million dollar handout by the Government, but when the cash runs out later in the year, their jobs will have to go.

The above 'translation' makes the following fatal errors:

- First, the staff are part-time and on contract, which makes the stakes arguably less high than if they had been full-time employees, as the rewritten version implies by omission.

- Second, there is nothing definite about these contracts being spared; '*may* serve to obviate', were the Chairman's words.

- Third, the 'Government handout' is not a handout at all, but a loan, and loans unlike handouts need repaying.

- Fourth, it is not certain the cash will run out later in the year.

- Fifth, even if it does, it is by no means definite that those contracts will be cut.

Below is a more accurate translation:

> The Chairman said the jobs of part-time ancillary staff, whose contracts have been under threat, may be safe for the time being, thanks to a million dollar loan from the Government. But he added that job cuts could not be ruled out later if the money ran out.

If you really want to bewilder your listeners, try sprinkling in the odd word that means something other than most people imagine:

> When asked about the road building, Councillor Joe McFlagherty said he viewed the scheme with complete disinterest.

To translate that as '*Councillor Joe McFlagherty said he could not care less about the scheme*' would be to get the wrong end of the stick. *Disinterested* should not be confused with *uninterested* which suggests a lack of concern. 'Disinterested' means he had no personal or vested interest in the project.

'His alibi was that he had no reason to kill his own mother' does not make sense. Alibi means a plea that someone was somewhere else at the time. Alibi is not synonymous with excuse. Other terms that are often confused: assassinate and execute; injured and wounded; claim and say; imply and infer; and fewer and less.

KEEP IT CONCRETE

The fleeting nature of broadcasting means that information tends to be impressionistic, and radio in particular finds it difficult to convey technical details or abstract ideas. Precise instructions, complex ideas or statistics – anything, in fact, which is hard to picture in the mind – do not come across well. Television has the powerful advantage of being able to use graphic illustrations to bring home a point, but even then it is easy to overload the viewer with too much information. Compare this with hard copy, written at length in print where it can be pored over and digested.

The way to use the medium successfully is to keep statements simple, direct, concrete and to the point, and to express them in a way that everyone will readily understand.

Colloquialisms are acceptable for bringing home the meaning of a story, but in-words and slang that have grown stale through overuse will irritate listeners and should be avoided.

Metaphors and examples also help in putting over an idea. Radio paints a picture in someone's mind, but you cannot paint a picture of an idea, a concept or an abstraction. You have to relate that to things people are already familiar with, and that means using illustrations. For example:

> Not: The Chancellor is increasing taxation on spirits by imposing a 5 per cent increase in prices from midnight tonight.

> But: A bottle of whisky will cost around 60 pence more from midnight tonight. The Chancellor's putting 5 per cent on all spirits, which will push up the price of a shot by about x pence.

> Not: The Government's given the go-ahead for a massive new tower block in the centre of Wellington. Crane Towers is to be 297 metres high.

> But: . . . Crane Towers is to be almost 300 metres high . . . that's taller than the Eiffel Tower and almost three times the height of St Paul's Cathedral.

MAKE IT INTERESTING

The journalist has information. And the audience wants it as it's new, important and relevant. But however much they need this information; they will receive it only if it is presented in a way that is both interesting and entertaining.

At times, broadcasters will need to tell their audience not simply what they want to hear, but what they need to know. In newsroom parlance, not every story is 'sexy'

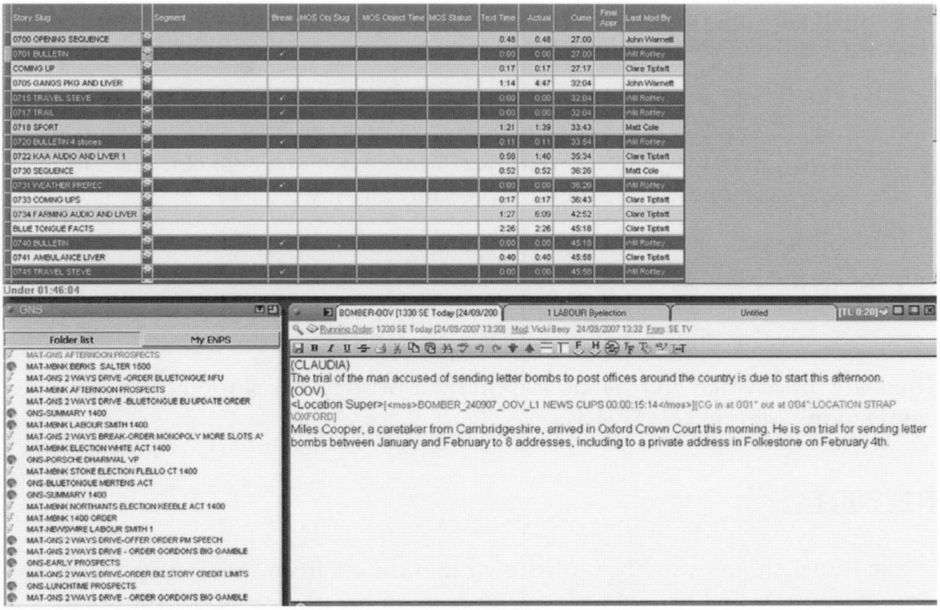

FIGURE 9.3
The split-screen
ENPS (Electronic
News Production
System) at the BBC
showing a running
order, script and
incoming stories.

with instant audience appeal. Some have to be worked at to draw out the point of interest.

The goings-on in the European Union, debates in the Commonwealth or Congress and the workings of local government are important areas, which traditionally turn off a mass audience. The challenge to the broadcaster is to demystify those issues by highlighting their relevance in specific terms that people can readily grasp and relate to. To get that far, you have to begin by capturing audience interest.

Turn people off, and they will simply turn *you* off. Hold their interest, and you will help bring issues home to people they affect, and, by raising public awareness, increase the accountability of those who make the decisions. And that's good journalism!

CONTRACTIONS

One of the most obvious differences between written and spoken English is the use of contractions. Words like *can't, couldn't, wouldn't, shouldn't, we'll, she'll, they'll, wasn't, didn't*; and even, *shouldn't've* and *can't've*, might look peculiar on paper, but are the substance of spoken English. In your next conversation, try to avoid contractions and see how difficult you find it and how stilted it sounds. Broadcasting is all about conversation, so contractions are a must.

> The Fire Chief said that they had tried everything but had not succeeded in rescuing the mother and her child from the upper window. 'We are giving it all that we have got, but we cannot do miracles. There has been no sign of them now for some time, and we are afraid that it is probably already too late.'

This might pass in print, but read out loud it becomes obvious the story would not work on radio or TV. All it takes is a few deletions and a smattering of apostrophes:

> The Fire Chief said they'd tried everything but hadn't succeeded in rescuing the mother and her child from the upper window. 'We're giving it all we've got, but we can't do miracles. There's been no sign of them now for some time, and we're afraid it's probably already too late.'

A little contraction can be a dangerous thing. The shortened form can confuse the ear and be misleading to the listener. 'He *couldn't* agree to the proposal', sounds very much like, 'He *could* agree to the proposal', and in some accents 'She said she *can't* remember' sounds like, 'She said she *can* remember.'

There are times when NOT is too important a word to risk skipping over it with a contraction. Put it in CAPITALS.

RHYTHM

Spoken English has a rhythm of its own that differs from the written word. The simple reason is that people have to come up for breath every now and again.

Sometimes sentences that look fine in print sound unfinished when read aloud, because they stray from the conventional rhythms of speech. Usually with spoken English sentences rise and fall and end with the voice turned down; unless that sentence is a question, when the voice will rise at the end.

While print journalists concentrate on cutting words out, broadcasters sometimes extend sentences to make them sound more natural.

'The trial resumes at one' may sound unfinished, while 'the trial is due to resume at one o'clock' is longer but more rhythmic with a more definite shape and more emphatic conclusion.

The only rule, which supersedes most rules of grammar, is if it *sounds* right, it probably *is* right. In the end the copy has to communicate, and if that means ignoring the traditional rules of written grammar, then so be it.

Another problem, which can often show up only when the copy is read out loud, is that of the unintentional rhyme:

> Defence Counsel Simon Crayle said the jury could not fail to set these men free on their not guilty plea, but the judge gave them three months in jail.

> One defendant, a stocky Croatian, yelled no justice was done in this nation. For disturbance in court, the judge said he ought to serve six further months on probation.

Jarring clashes of sound and potential tongue twisters should also be avoided:

> At election offices throughout Throstlebury today, each party is preparing to grind into gear for the great haul towards the imminent general election.

A little alliteration may occasionally be acceptable, but sometimes several similar sounds spoken aloud sound stupid, while a superfluity of hissing *s* and *c* sounds sound sibilant. Say these last few sentences yourself and see.

THE HEADLINES

- One sentence – one thought.
- Write straightforwardly.
- If you don't understand what you are writing, how will the audience?

QUESTIONS FOR YOU

1. Take two daily newspapers, one popular, the other serious, and read some of the stories out loud. Which newspaper style sounds more like conversational English – the popular style or the serious style? What makes the difference?

    Take the hardest story to read aloud and go through it using Fang's Easy Listening Formula and give a score for each sentence. Then rewrite the story using shorter sentences and words with fewer syllables until it satisfies the Easy Listening Formula. Now read it out loud and see how it sounds. Is it any better? Can it still be improved?

2. Find a better way to write this story and to bring the point home:

    The rate of inflation has continued to rise over the past 12 month period, according to today's figures, which show that the retail price of staple foodstuffs has increased by 10 per cent – 5 per cent higher than the average inflation rate.

3. Discuss the differences between:
    - Assassinate and Execute
    - Billion and Million
    - Injured and Wounded
    - Claim and Say
    - Imply and Infer
    - Fewer and Less

4. A new agricultural strategy for the country has been launched which requires increased productivity by farmers. How would you cover the story to make it sound interesting to a typical audience?

OTHER RESOURCES

- Lots of writing, and other resources for journalists, here: http://ijnet.org/en/news/520.

- George Orwell's Five Tips for Writing: http://bit.ly/BJOrwell.

- A Poynter article on 'how to write short': http://bit.ly/BJPoynter.

- What radio reporters can teach print reporters about writing: http://bit.ly/BJTeach.

- Online grammar quizzes: http://newsroom101.net/.

- Daily news writing tips: www.dailywritingtips.com/.

- Language rules and grammar tips from the Columbia Journalism Review: www.cjr.org/language_corner/.

- This is a little dated but interesting nonetheless. It's an examination of the differences in newswriting for print and broadcast journalists – *Newspaper, Radio, and Television News* (Irving Fang. University of Minnesota): http://bit.ly/BJFang.

- *Romps, Tots and Boffins: The Strange Language of News* by Robert Hutton is a book about 'phrases which started as shorthand to help readers have become a dialect that is often meaningless or vacuous to non-journalese speakers'. Available on Amazon etc.

- Advice on writing with numbers: http://www.robertniles.com/stats/.

TUTOR NOTES

There's lots of resources for tutors teaching broadcast writing skills (and other elements of broadcast news), here: http://bit.ly/BJSchoolReport.

Here's a maths test for journalists: http://bit.ly/BJMaths.

CHAPTER 10

Writing for News

When you've got a thing to say,
Say it! Don't take half a day . . .
Life is short – a fleeting vapour –
Don't you fill the whole blamed paper
With a tale, which at a pinch,
Could be covered in an inch!
Boil her down until she simmers,
Polish her until she glimmers.
Joel Chandler Harris, American journalist and fiction writer, 1848–1908

Hard news is new and important information about events of significance. *Soft news* and human interest items are stories run for their entertainment value first and their information second.

In the hard news story for broadcast there is no room for padding. The information must have the impact of an uppercut and connect with the audience in the first sentence.

THE NEWS ANGLE

There's a block of glass in one newsroom to remind staff that news must be clear, transparent, sharp and have a lot of angles.

Before writing a story, the journalist has to be clear about which angle to take on it. This will depend on where the story happened, what has been reported already and what is new about it.

Take the example of an air crash. All 329 people on board were killed when an Air India jumbo jet crashed off the west coast of Ireland. The disaster made headlines throughout the world, but had special significance in India and Canada. The Indian national airline was involved and the plane had taken off from Toronto, bound for Mumbai.

Apart from the international importance of the event, news media of both nations had major *local* stories on their hands. The local angle resurfaced time and again in India, Canada and around the world in the villages, towns and cities where the passengers and crew had lived.

A number of different angles would have to be pursued. The first is the fact of the crash, and the questions, '*When, where, why* and *how many dead?*'

That same day two people die when a bomb explodes in a suitcase unloaded from another Canadian flight, from Vancouver. The events are too similar to be a coincidence. So the next angle is *who planted the bomb?* Two militant groups claim responsibility – the Kashmir Liberation Army and the Sikh Dashmesh Regiment. A reporter is assigned to produce a background item about terrorism in the sub-continent, looking at the history of these groups and their possible motives.

As the names of local people on the passenger list filter back to newsrooms, stories would be prepared about the deceased, to be followed perhaps by interviews with relatives.

Meanwhile, a new angle comes into play when search teams set out to recover the wreckage. Eighteen days after the crash, the digital flight recorder is found, putting the story back in the headlines. Three months to the day after the plane went down, it makes big news again when the inquest takes place at Cork, in Ireland.

Developing stories, which constantly throw up new angles and call for different versions, are known as *running stories*. When a major running story breaks, it will often be more than a single reporter can do to keep up with it, so a team is usually assigned to cover every possible angle.

MULTI-ANGLED STORIES

Broadcast news can handle more complex stories by breaking the information down point by point and giving it out in a logical sequence. But a problem can arise when the story has two angles of near equal importance which both deserve a place in the introduction. This is known as the *multi-angled* or *umbrella* story.

The way to tackle this is with a double intro – which is not to say the intro should be double the length:

> Today's record crime figures reveal violence and sex attacks at an all-time high . . . Police chiefs say the streets are turning into no-go areas because of the shortage of trained officers.

Here we have two stories, the first the escalating crime figures and the second the equally dramatic police reaction to them – both would be developed in the rest of the report.

Multi-angled stories may arise from one good story leading to an equally good follow-up which beg to be combined. These can be refreshed and kept running by updating and emphasising different angles in subsequent bulletins. Sometimes two stories arise separately, which need to be run together under an umbrella:

> Sport . . . and it's been a tremendous day for New Zealand's athletes, with success in the hundred metres at home and a swimming triumph in Europe.

> Or: More bad news for industry . . . A smelting plant in Tema is to close with the loss of more than 130 jobs, and 50 workers are to be made redundant at a nearby steelworks.

Both examples begin with an umbrella statement, which covers the two stories in each and signposts what is to follow.

HARD NEWS FORMULA

There is a tried and tested hard news formula which is used in newspapers, radio and TV. It constructs the story by asking who, what, when, where, why and how questions. Answers to these should give most of the information required.

- What has happened?
- Where did it happen?
- When did it happen?
- Who was involved?
- How did it happen?
- Why did it happen?
- What does it mean?

Plus *extra information*, if there is time.

The news story begins with the most important facts, then backs those up with detail, background and interpretation, constructed to get the story across in a logical way that is clear and commands attention. Tell listeners all they need to know to understand the story and to stop there. No question should be raised that cannot be answered.

FIGURE 10.1

Writing the script isn't always done in front of a computer screen. Here the reporter handwrites the links for her TV news packaged on location in the editing van. Indeed the field reporter often has to write 'from scratch': piecing together interviews, observation and reaction and merging them with the sound and pictures already gathered. The writer in the newsroom is usually working from multiple texts: re-writing from agency or wire copy, and translating from print style to broadcast style. Credit: Andrew Boyd.

THE INTRO

The first sentence in a radio news story is all-important. It must have, partly, the character of a headline. It must instantly establish the subject in the listener's mind, show them why the story is worth hearing and signpost the direction it is going to take. But it should not try to say too much.

BBC Newsroom Guide

Once the angle is established, the writer has to work out the introduction (also known as *intro* or *lead* – UK, or headline sentence – US). This is the first sentence or paragraph of the story and also the most important. Its function is to:

- State the most significant point.
- Grab attention.
- Whet the appetite.
- Signpost the way into the rest of the story.

The first 20 or 30 words are the most important. It has to be bright, attractive, skilfully constructed and worthy of further investigation. Once listeners are interested and take the bait you can reel them in with the rest of the story.

The intro contains the most important point. If there has been an art auction at which a masterpiece by Rubens has fetched a record price, the main point will be the record sums paid for the painting.

To make it easier to select the main point, it can help to choose a key word or short phrase which sums up whatever is most important about the story.

The key word in the art auction story is 'record'. If the story concerned a car crash that had killed 16, the most important point would be the 16 deaths, not the crash. Car crashes happen all the time, but they seldom claim so many lives, so '*16 dead*' becomes the key phrase.

To build up the story, it may help to imagine a newspaper headline, which could be worked up into an introduction. So, '*Record price for masterpiece*' would be the starting place for the art auction story, and '*Car crash kills 16*' would do for the other.

Both stories would probably make national news, and would lead a local news bulletin if they happened in an area covered by a radio or TV station. The locality would become central to the story and the line would change to '*Record price for masterpiece at New York art auction*' and '*Car crash in Lagos kills 16*'.

Some stations also require the *today* angle to be pointed up in the intro to heighten the immediacy of the story.

Lastly, as it would scarcely do for broadcasters to speak in headlines, these stories need reworking to turn them into conversational speech, which is easily done.

> The highest price ever paid for a masterpiece has been reached at an art auction in New York.

A multiple car crash in downtown Lagos has this morning claimed the lives of 16 people.

The ideal hard news intro or headline sentence should be short – no longer than 20 to 30 words; uncluttered and without unnecessary detail; simple; direct and capable of grabbing and holding interest.

> The first line of a story is always the most important. This is where you prove that your story is worth watching. Great stories grab you by the throat right out of the gates and don't let go. Great first lines are the siren that lures you into the heart of the story.
> Graeme Newell, Television and Digital Media Training Company (602communications.com)

PLACING KEY WORDS

Looking more closely at the second example above, it might seem more direct to say '16 people were killed this morning in a multiple car crash in downtown Lagos'. This would get over the important information and communicate well enough in print, but for broadcast news, putting the main point right at the beginning of the story could create a problem.

The reader of a newspaper is led around the printed page by its layout. There's the position of the story on the page (those on the right-hand pages tend to be more significant), the size of the headline (and what it says) and the amount of space given to each story. They are clearly separated from the others and the reader can choose which items to look at and which to ignore at a glance. Television approaches this with its graphics and strong visual element, but in radio the layout is invisible and sometimes inaudible. Stories are separated by pauses and there is only the reader's voice and the writer's ability to help the listener tell where one story ends and the next begins.

With radio the problem is compounded because people tend to listen with half an ear while they do other things. Absolute attention is usually reserved for times of a major and/or breaking news story. So, under normal circumstances, the first few words of a news item may easily slip by unnoticed. If the main point does escape the audience, then by the time their attention is drawn back to the story, the whole meaning of the piece may be lost. So avoid putting key words right at the beginning.

FEATURES OPENERS

> Get straight to the point in the first sentence . . . Because if you don't you'll lose people's attention.
> Huw Edwards, BBC News Presenter

Not all opening sentences follow the hard news formula. The feature, human interest or soft news story is primarily for entertainment, so the order in which the information is given becomes less important. What matters most is that the story brings a moment of light relief to the audience, and this calls for a different writing technique:

> If you've got a thing about creepy crawlies and the thought of seeing a snake makes you sick, then spare a thought for Jeb Winston from Canberra.

> Jeb's going to be surrounded by snakes . . . many of them poisonous . . . for up to a fortnight. He's planning to sit cross legged in a tank with more than forty of them to keep him company, as he tries to break the world record for snake-sitting.

The hard news formula calls for the heart of the story in the first line, but the introductory paragraph here teases the audience into wanting to get to the bottom of the matter by beginning with a tantalizing appeal to the emotions. The style is conversational, even anecdotal, and contrasts with the brisk formality of hard news. The story is relaxed, and so is the style of its writing and delivery. This easy-going and informal approach is often used for cheerful end-of-bulletin items, often called an 'and finally' or 'kicker'.

Most bulletin stories will be written in the straight-backed, concise, hard news style. But the same story can undergo a revolution in style when written in greater detail for a longer programme. Where the presenter is given room to be a 'personality', the writing will often loosen up to take on a chattier, more relaxed and discursive approach:

Bulletin intro:

> Three counties in New Mexico have been declared disaster areas after a winter storm claimed the lives of five people.

Programme intro:

> The weather continues to make big news. Some places have more snow than they can handle and others, it seems, can't get enough of it. While St Paul in Minnesota is having to import 600 tons of snow before it can stage its Winter Carnival, elsewhere snowdrifts are paralysing whole areas and claiming lives. In New Mexico, three counties have been declared disaster areas, after being hit by savage winter storms which killed five people.

The feature style, which leads the audience into the story rather than presenting them with the facts in the first line, is used more freely wherever greater emphasis is placed on entertainment and a lighter touch than on straightforward and sometimes impersonal, hard news.

DEVELOPING THE STORY

Obey the two basic rules of broadcast newswriting. Rule Number 1: Write the way you talk. Rule Number 2: Never forget Rule Number 1.

Mervin Block, broadcast newswriting coach, author of *Writing Broadcast News – Shorter, Sharper, Stronger* (mervinblock.com)

Finding the intro is the hardest task in newswriting. Once that is settled the rest of the item will usually fall into place.

The next step is to list the points in their logical order, constructing a story that progresses from point to point without running back on itself or leaving the listener dangling for an explanation. The introduction is usually followed by the explanation, and after that comes more detail (beware of clutter), and the tying up of loose ends. This has been described as the *WHAT formula*.

The WHAT Formula

W   What has happened? The introduction tells the story in brief.

H   How did it happen? Explain the immediate background or context.

A   Amplify the introduction. Flesh out the main points in order of importance.

T   Tie up loose ends. Give additional background material.

The story as it is finally written should answer the questions, *who, what, when, where, why* and *how*, though not necessarily in that order.

The trickiest part is deciding which facts to include and which to leave out (every journalist's ethical dilemma). A 20-second story is only 60 words long (the formula of three-words-per-second reading speed is traditionally used), which leaves no room for superfluous detail. Frequently, important points have to give way if vital points are to remain. The test of non-essential information is, does the audience need it to make sense of the story, or will the story stand up without it?

In the case of our snake sitter above, his name and where he comes from are important, but his middle names, the name of his road and the number of his house are irrelevant. The details of how he and the snakes will be fed over the fortnight might be interesting, but could be dropped if space is short, while his chances of surviving unbitten and what would happen if a snake did sink its fangs into him would be well worth a mention.

Simply stated, the skill is to write up the information in order of importance until space runs out and then leave the rest.

Tell us why a story is significant, make the connections for us, don't use the language of the insider. Above all don't 'dumb down' . . . If people don't make the connections between their own lives and events in the world beyond, then it's partly because we are failing. Failing to understand what moves them, failing to explain the relevance of that issue or event.

Tony Hall, Director-General, BBC

SIGNPOSTING

Tell 'em you're gonna tell 'em; tell 'em you're tellin' 'em, and tell 'em you've told 'em.

Anon

The spoken word has an infuriating habit of going in one ear and out the other. Research has shown that people can only recall about two items in eight from the previous night's TV news.[1] So to beat these odds, the journalist has to work with the medium and write to create an impression – rather than trying to force-feed an audience with facts that are no sooner heard than forgotten. The art is to decide on the one lasting impression you want to leave your audience, which will usually be the main point of the story, and then to reinforce that by subtly pushing the point home throughout. This is called signposting, and it works like this:

> Murder charges are being drawn up after a prisoner accused of blasphemy was allegedly tortured to death in police custody in Pakistan.
>
> Under Pakistan's Sharia religious law the penalty for blasphemy is death. But Mukhtar Masih was killed before his case could come to court.
>
> Masih – a Christian – was charged with sending a blasphemous letter to the leader of a mosque.
>
> The note bore his name and address. If he had written it himself he would have been signing his own death warrant.
>
> Masih died within 24 hours of being taken into police custody. An autopsy showed he had been beaten with a blunt instrument.
>
> Lahore's High Court Prosecutor, Naeem Shakir, is filing a murder charge against two police officers.
>
> Opponents of the Sharia law say the case is another example of an individual being falsely accused of blasphemy to settle a grudge. They're calling for the law to be changed.

There are three key elements to this story: murder, blasphemy and their location – Pakistan. There is also a twist – the allegation that the police themselves committed the crime. All four points are combined in the intro, which sets the scene for the story.

The story is complicated and needs some explaining. So the second paragraph places the events in context. It takes care to explain that the Sharia is the religious law. Then it contrasts the legal death penalty with the unlawful killing.

The next two paragraphs explain why Masih was suspected of blasphemy – then raise an important question about the evidence.

The following paragraph returns to his death in police custody and explains why murder charges may be brought.

By creating contrasts these four paragraphs help us to understand the story more clearly.

Then we are brought up to date by returning to the main angle of the story, which was signposted in the intro: the charges against the police. That fact is amplified to tell us who is bringing the charge.

Finally the story is rounded off by placing the whole event in a wider context to illustrate its significance.

The aim is to make the message of the story inescapably clear. Signposting picks out the thread of the argument without requiring the audience to backtrack, which is impossible over the air. The skill lies in highlighting and restating the main points without making them *sound* like repetition.

LAST LINE

The last line should round off the story and point ahead to any next developments. This is the *'tell 'em you've told 'em'* part of the signposting. A story about trouble on the roads could end:

> . . . and difficult driving conditions are expected to continue until much later this evening.

A story about an unofficial bus strike could finish:

> Bus drivers will be meeting their union leaders this afternoon to try to persuade them to call a vote to make the strike official.

Both closings refer back to the events in question (conditions on the roads; the bus strike) and show the way ahead (difficult conditions continuing into the evening; the meeting with union leaders).

Another way to round off a story is for the presenter to pick up on the end of audio or film footage with a final comment. This is known as a *back announcement* (or *back anno, BA*). It is a useful device for giving out phone numbers, updating an item recorded earlier with new information and giving a short explanation of the preceding item for those who have turned on mid-way through:

> BA: And we've just heard that the road is now clear and traffic is starting to move. Tailbacks are still expected for the next half hour.

As well as reminding an audience who or what they have been listening to, back annos are commonly used in radio and as a bridge between items where some natural link can be found.

> BA: Mary Fernandez reporting on the growing numbers of teenagers who run away from home . . . Well, one of the biggest dangers to those children must come from the drug pushers, and there's worrying news of yet another kind of drug that is now being sold on the streets . . . etc.

LAST WORDS

The lasting impression of any programme or item is usually made by the first and last words, and as much care should be taken on ending the story as in writing the intro. As well as beginning strongly, the story should end on a positive note, and not be allowed to tail off weakly or to fizzle out: aim to create a pleasing rhythm.

News stories should end with a bang rather than a whimper. Strong, definite and emphatic last words are preferable to limp endings:

> Prefer: she said the investigation would be launched at once.
>
> To: . . . the investigation would be launched at once, she said.
>
> Weak: . . . the gunmen are threatening to shoot the hostages at midnight unless the Government gives in to them.
>
> Stronger: . . . the gunmen are threatening to shoot the hostages at midnight, unless the Government gives in to their demands.

The last words are the ones the audience will remember – so make them memorable.

ACCURACY

In the case of new we should always wait for the sacrament of confirmation.

Voltaire

FIGURE 10.2
Preparing to record a telephone interview in a local radio news studio.
Credit: Katherine Adams/BBC.

'Never let the facts get in the way of a good story' is a cynical quip which, unfortunately, sometimes contains more than a grain of truth. But nothing devalues a reporter's credibility faster than getting the facts wrong. Mispronouncing place names irritates listeners and slipping up over someone's name or job title can sour a valued contact. More seriously, an inaccurate court report could lead to a libel suit or an action for contempt. The best maxim for the journalist is 'If in doubt . . . check it out'.

The main points of the story should always be verified, so no contentious or uncertain points are left to chance. *If they can't be checked out, they should be chucked out.*

The example below illustrates how difficult it can be to get the facts right, especially on a breaking story. This snap arrived in the news room from a news agency:

86626 MYNEWS G

M AND Y NEWSAGENCY, PORTSMOUTH

OIL RIG

A 400 TON SUPPLY SHIP HAS COLLIDED WITH ONE OF THE LEGS OF THE PENROD THREE OIL RIG, 20 MILES SOUTH OF THE ISLE OF WIGHT AND IS TRAPPED IN THE OIL RIG AND SINKING, WITH EIGHT PEOPLE ON BOARD.

IT'S POSSIBLE THAT THE DAMAGE TO THE OILRIG WILL CAUSE IT TO COLLAPSE.

THE SAR HELICOPTER FROM LEE ON SOLENT HAS BEEN SCRAMBLED.

MORE FOLLOWS LATER.

86626 MYNEWS G

A battery of quick fire calls was made to the coastguard and the search and rescue (SAR) service among others. These threw up the following conflicting information:

Name of oil rig	Name of ship	Size of ship
Penrod 3	Spearfish	150 tons
Penrod No. 3	Spearship	400 tons
Penrod 83		500 tons
Penrod 85		
Penrose 85		

Number of crew	Damage to rig	State of ship
6	Slight	Sunk
7	In danger of collapse	Not sunk
8		Partially sunk
		Being towed ashore
		Scuttled

Method of scuttling	Number of helicopters at scene	Location
Blown up	1	10 miles south of island
Shot out of the water	2	15 miles south of island
		20 miles south of island

Fast moving events, inaccessible location and lack of official comment from experts too tied up in the operation to talk made the facts difficult to establish.

In the end, the story was that the 143-ton trawler *Spearfish* had become entangled in one of the legs of the *Penrod 85* oil rig when it was trying to land supplies. The six-man crew was winched to safety by *one* helicopter before the ship was towed clear by a frigate and sunk by *anti-aircraft fire*.

The best angle did not emerge until later, when an inspection of the helicopter rotors revealed they had flown so close to the rig that the blades had clipped the superstructure. A couple of centimetres closer and the helicopter would have crashed.

With news flashes and breaking news some reshuffling of the facts is expected as the story becomes clearer. But there are times when getting the facts wrong can have disastrous consequences.

Reports of accidents, air crashes and loss of life must be handled with utmost care. If a crowded passenger train has been derailed and passengers killed, there can be no excuses for confusing the time of the train with that of another. A slip of the eye or stumble on the keyboard can render numbers wildly out, which can have a dramatic effect on a story and create widespread alarm.

Unnecessary stress and panic can be prevented by giving specific and accurate details, and with an air crash, by broadcasting the flight number. When names of the dead are released, those names have to be got right, and if the name is a common one, like Smith, Brown or Patel, details of the address should be given to avoid needless worry.

THE HEADLINES

- Having a strong angle from the start, perhaps provided by your editor, will help you focus on the story that needs to be told and will help you choose your guests, the questions and your top line. It may also dictate your story's place in the bulletin or programme.

- A multi-angled story may provide enough content for a long-form report, a documentary or programme in its own right, or a series of shorter features across a week.

- Don't be put off by people who say that your station's stories or bulletins are short or 'tabloid': it is often harder to 'write short' and boil all the facts down to the most important ones, than it is to 'write long' and include everything.

- After being hard at the start of a story, don't go limp at the end of it.

QUESTIONS FOR YOU

1. Construct a hard news story from the following collection of facts:

- The Bantry Bay Company employs a workforce of 3,000.
- There are no plans to cut shopfloor workers.
- The company makes widgets.
- 10 per cent of the clerical workers are to lose their jobs.
- The company lost £2m in the first half of last year.
- The cuts are to try to improve efficiency and reduce costs.
- There are 1,000 white collar (clerical) workers.
- The company says that early retirement and voluntary redundancies should account for most of the job cuts.
- The last redundancies at the Bantry Bay Company took place five years ago.

2. Now put together a soft news feature from the following facts. Remember, the style needs to be less terse and more entertaining. You will need to think of livelier ways to present the facts than they are given here and should try to avoid repeating the word 'alligator' too often.

- The trapper's name was John Tanner.
- The alligator weighed 150 pounds.
- Mr Tanner took with him only a rope lasso and miner's lamp.
- The alligator tried to bite through the noose.
- With moments to spare, Mr Tanner managed to bind its jaws with electrical tape.
- The alligator was caught in the sewers beneath Orlando, in Florida.
- Alligator meat is a local delicacy. He could have sold it for its meat and its hide.
- He wrestled with the alligator and managed to slip the noose around its neck.
- He did not get any money for his efforts. 'It wasn't hurting anybody,' he said.
- He got the alligator to come to him by imitating the mating call of the female alligator.
- The authorities sent for Mr Tanner after state trappers had failed to catch the reptile, which had tried to bite four drainage inspectors.
- He took it to a remote part of the country and let it go.

3. Now turn that feature item into a hard news story of fewer than 100 words. Then go back over your stories and check they are well signposted, end strongly and are easy to read out loud. Finally, if you are in a class, swap your work with someone else, and sub-edit their versions, making any alterations you think are necessary.

OTHER RESOURCES

- Lots of examples of angles in a developing news story here: http://bit.ly/BJAngles.
- Five tips for news writing with mobile eyes in mind: http://bit.ly/BJMobile.

TUTOR NOTES

Training notes on story writing and angles: http://bit.ly/BJSlideshare.

Some exercises on finding news angles: http://bit.ly/BJAngleExercises.

NOTES

1 Laurie Taylor and Bob Mullen, *Uninvited Guests*, Chatto and Windus, 1986.

CHAPTER 11

Broadcast News Style Book

Each newsroom has its own style guide: a directory of FAQs about how that organisation's staff should spell certain words, write sentences and structure information. This is so the finished broadcast keeps a strong on-air identity or brand, so the audience is clear about what to expect and can easily interpret the information, so news anchors can be confident that one script is similar in style to another . . . and so editors aren't over-worked rewriting copy that could have been written 'correctly' originally.

Links to some Style Guides are listed at the end of this chapter, but many entries will be consistent between them.

> Good style:
>
> > If I had a donkey as wouldn't go,
> > do you think I'd wallop him? Oh no.
> > I'd give him some corn and cry out 'Whoa,
> > Gee up, Neddy.
>
> Bad style:
>
> > If I had an ass that refused to proceed,
> > Do you suppose that I should castigate him?
> > No indeed.
> > I should present him with some cereals and
> > observe proceed,
> > Continue, Edward.
>
> Harold Evans[1]

Most broadcast organisations have a view about good style, and though they differ in detail, most would agree that good style is usually whatever makes good sense. George Orwell wrote *Politics and the English Language* in 1946, but his advice still holds true today:

- Never use a metaphor, simile or other figure of speech which you are used to seeing in print.

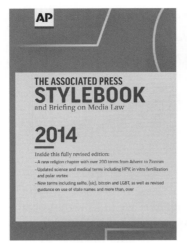

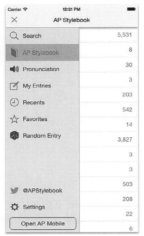

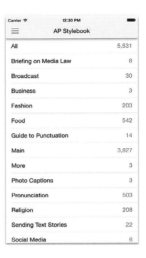

FIGURE 11.1   **FIGURE 11.2**   **FIGURE 11.2**

AP publish an annual style guide in print, online and as a downloadable app.

- Never use a long word where a short one will do.

- If it is possible to cut out a word, always cut it out.

- Never use the passive where you can use the active.

- Never use a foreign phrase, scientific word or a jargon word if you can think of an everyday English equivalent.

- Break any of these rules sooner than say anything outright barbarous.

CLICHÉS

Eric Partridge, in his *Dictionary of Clichés*, defines the cliché as 'a phrase so hackneyed as to be knock-kneed and spavined'. They not only fail to enliven dull copy, clichés make even the most significant item sound trite. If we accuse council tax payers of 'declaring war' against city hall whenever they write a letter of complaint, what will be left to say when war *is* declared?

Hyperbole and clichés are for hacks. This, then, is their dictionary:

acid test	headache	paid the penalty
all-out-effort	heart of gold	painted a grim picture
anybody's guess	heated debate	part and parcel
around the table	high-ranking	picking up the pieces
as sick as a parrot	horror	point in time
at this point in time	how does it feel?	pool of blood
balanced on a knife edge	in a nutshell	pride and joy

beat a hasty retreat

bid (for attempt)

bitter end

bolt from the blue

bombshell

boost

boss

brutal reminder

calm before the storm

calm but tense

cash boost

chequered career

chief

clampdown

crackdown

daylight robbery

deciding factor

desperate attempt/bid

doctors fought

drama

dramatic decision/new
    move

dug in their heels

effortless victory

fell on deaf ears

gave as good as he got

get under way

given the green light

going walkabout

got the message

in due course

in full swing

iron out the problem

jobless youngsters

lashed out at

last but not least

last ditch effort

last minute decision

leading the hunt

leaps and bounds

leave no stone unturned

limped into port

loud and clear

lucky few

luxury liner

major new development/
    project

marked contrast

mercy dash

miracle cure

mindless vandals

mine of information

news leaked out

nipped in the bud

none the worse for wear

not to be outdone

one in the eye

over and above

over the moon

own goal

probe

pull out the stops

put into perspective

quiz (for question)

rushed to the scene

selling like hot cakes

shock

short and sweet

shot himself in the foot

shot in the arm

show of force

sitting on a goldmine

sitting on the fence

$64,000 question

square peg in a round
    hole

still anybody's guess

stuck to his/her guns

sweeping changes

up in arms

up in the air

vanished into thin air

vast amount

virtual standstill

voiced his approval

weighty matter

what of the future?

whole new ball game

wreak havoc

writing on the wall

No doubt you will have your own favourites to add to the list. It may soon be possible to program into a computer an elaborate lexicon of clichés, enter the type of story, say, *murder*; key in details such as the name of the victim, and within a matter of seconds, we could be reading printouts of cliché-ridden news copy.

JOURNALESE

The cliché owes much to journalese. It is the language of the label and instant metaphor, drawing its inspiration from space-starved newspaper headlines.

Every cub reporter . . . knows that fires rage out of control, minor mischief is perpetrated by Vandals (never Visigoths, Franks or a single Vandal working alone) and key labour accords are hammered out by weary negotiators in marathon, round-the-clock bargaining sessions, thus narrowly averting threatened walkouts.

John Leo[2]

Clichés and journalese are usually used when inspiration runs dry (!), especially as a deadline approaches.

HYPERBOLE

Definition of hype

Exaggerated statement not meant to be taken literally.

Concise Oxford Dictionary

Headlines twice the size of the events.

John Galsworthy

Another blood relation of journalese is hype. Hype can be found scattered throughout the media, and in especially large concentrations wherever advertising copywriters gather. And many journalists readily call on hype's assistance to lend support to a flaccid story on a quiet news day.

> Children's lives could be at risk if they swallow quantities of a lethal drug which has gone missing in Cape Town.

Translated: Somebody dropped their sleeping tablets on their way home from the shops. *If* they are found by someone, and *if* that person is a child, and *if* they swallow *all* of them, they *may* die.

> A man's being hunted in Perth after an appalling and unprovoked sex attack on a defenceless three-year-old girl.

But: All sex attacks are appalling:

NO three-year-old girl is likely to provoke such an attack.

ALL small girls are defenceless.

Hype of this order is unpleasant, distasteful and unnecessary. If the story can't stand up without it, it should not be run.

ADJECTIVES

How many adjectives you use will depend on your house style and whether the station's image is 'quality' or 'popular'. Contrast the versions below:

Firemen with oxy-acetylene cutters took three hours to free the body from the wreckage. They said it was one of the worst crashes they'd seen.

Firemen with oxy-acetylene cutters struggled for three hours to free the mangled body from the shattered cab. They said the horrific crash was one of the worst they'd seen.

Did they really 'struggle', or was it just a long job that they were well trained to do? Most stations would think twice about the tasteless 'mangled'. Adjectives add colour but too many make the piece sound like an extract from a lurid novel. Remove them all and the item can sound dull or bland. Handle with care.

QUOTATIONS

A choice quotation can add considerably to the flavour of a report, but there are hazards in using quotes in broadcasting. In print a quote is immediately obvious because of the quotation marks, but it's less easy to show a broadcast audience when a quote begins and ends, so they should be kept short and clearly attributed:

The Prime Minister rounded on the protesters, accusing them of 'behaving like a bunch of anarchists'.

The newsreader can help with the signposting, by pausing for a fraction of a second before reading the quote.

ATTRIBUTION

Information should be attributed clearly to leave the audience in no doubt about who is speaking – remember, listeners can never refer back. This said, attribution can be overdone and badly clutter a piece of copy:

The honourable Peter Threeple, Junior Minister in the Department of Health, said today that an injection of 2 billion pounds would be made available to improve wages in the National Health Service.

Not exactly an attention grabber! So the information should be turned around, and possibly divided between two more-manageable sentences. Then put the facts before the attribution, and shorten the attribution to be still accurate, but much more manageable:

A cash injection of 20 million pounds is to be made available to improve wages in the Health Service.

Health Minister Peter Threeple told the Commons today that the money . . . etc.

The message is often more important than the messenger. In this case the news of the funding is more important than the name of the minister, so the information should be run before the attribution.

Stories should begin with a person's name only when that name is widely known, or as we said in Chapter 8, where immediate context is needed for the quotation that follows. If the audience cannot immediately identify the person, there can be a point of confusion at the start of a story. In fact if you ever find yourself starting a news story with the name of a person/their title, or a company/department, then it is worth considering whether it is the wrong angle: 'The city's police say a man has been found dead on the beach at Fort William . . .' In this case, the discovery of the body is the story, not who has said it. Indeed many things announced by the police or a government department can be attributed in the second line. 'More money is coming to pay for IT networks in our schools. The education department made the announcement . . .'

To avoid cluttering an introduction it is sometimes necessary to choose between giving a person's name or title in the first line. If their name is better known than their job or organisation, then the name should be given before the title, and vice versa.

> The Director General of the CBI, Richard Lambert, has called on the Bank of England to hold down interest rates.

This might work satisfactorily in print, but spoken out loud the first line becomes cluttered and the title CBI may not be universally understood. The attribution should be spread over two sentences and some clear signposting provided:

> The leader of Britain's employers is calling on the Bank of England to hold down interest rates. Richard Lambert, Director General of the Confederation of British Industry, wants the Bank to . . . etc.

The art is to attribute a statement clearly without letting the attribution get in the way. Television has a major advantage over radio – interviewees can appear without a verbal introduction because their names and titles can be displayed on the screen over the pictures.

CONTENTIOUS STATEMENTS

When statements are controversial or contentious the attribution has to be made clearly and cannot be held back until the second sentence:

> 'America's unemployed are a shiftless, lazy bunch of spongers, who should be forced to sweep the streets until they find a decent job.' So said Governor Richman at a news conference today . . .

This first sentence has turned a highly debatable assertion into a statement of fact, and the danger is that the audience may miss the attribution that follows and identify the opinion with the newsreader. The station could lose a large section of its audience – the unemployed. Maintain impartiality by keeping a safe distance from such statements.

This problem is avoided by giving the attribution in the same sentence and signposting that this is a matter of opinion and not fact:

> Governor Richman launched a scathing attack on America's unemployed today . . . calling them a shiftless, lazy bunch of spongers. And, speaking at a news conference, he said they should be forced to sweep the streets until they could get themselves decent jobs.

This gets the broadcaster off the hook and leaves Governor Richman dangling firmly *on* it. (In this case you are leading with the person's name, because it is what they have said which is the story.)

Careful attribution is crucial where facts are being asserted which have yet to be proven true. It is not uncommon with war reporting to find both sides claiming substantial victories over each other at the same time. Unless the facts can be confirmed from independent sources, such statements should never be given without qualification:

> Cornish and Devonian forces are both claiming significant victories today. The Cornish airforce say they shot down 14 Devonian bombers with no losses of their own and the Devonian airforce is claiming to have destroyed every Cornish airfield. Both sides now say they have total air superiority and in official statements today each side alleges the other is lying.

Say, claim and *allege* are useful qualifications for suspect information and distance the newsreader enough to avoid sounding like a propaganda mouthpiece. *Claim* and *allege* should be avoided where no doubt is meant to be implied, and repetition of the word *'said'* can be avoided by using phrases like 'he added' or 'she pointed out'.

IMMEDIACY

One of the great strengths of broadcast news is its immediacy. It has wiped the floor with newspapers when it comes to reacting quickly to changing events. The Cuban missile crisis in 1962, when the world stood on the brink of nuclear war, has been accredited as the catalyst which caused the switch from papers to TV as the prime source of news[3] although newspapers are now retaliating by using their web pages to distribute information faster than their printing machines can roll, and using social media such as Twitter to promote those pages. And all media uses instant messaging to distribute news, such as Twitter and Periscope.

Broadcasters are able to follow events as they unfold. Broadcasters understandably play to their strengths, and most newsrooms heighten the sense of immediacy in their copy by using the present or perfect tenses. While tomorrow's newspaper will tell us:

> Victory celebrations took place yesterday in both India and Pakistan over the agreement to end the fighting in Kashmir. (Past tense)

Today's bulletin might say:

> India and Pakistan have both claimed victory over the agreement to end the fighting in Kashmir. (Perfect tense)

To use either of these backward-looking tenses is to retreat from the immediacy of the action. The present tense is even more up to the minute:

> Thousands of Angolans are fleeing into Zambia to escape fighting which is erupting again in Angola's eastern province.

The word 'yesterday' is taboo in broadcasting. Nothing sounds more incongruous than a station with hourly bulletins giving a time reference that harks back 24 hours. If 'yesterday' or 'last night' have to be used, they should be kept out of the opening sentence and buried further down the story.

Similarly, phrases such as 'this morning', 'this afternoon' or 'this evening' can date copy. So, for inclusion in the 6 o'clock news, the following story would have to be rewritten:

> The chief prosecutor for the Rwandan genocide tribunal pledged this morning to re-arrest a key suspect if he is released . . .

The phrase *'pledged this morning'*, which would stand out like a sore thumb by the evening, would be replaced with the words *'has pledged'*. Some news editors object to prolific use of the word 'today' arguing that all broadcasting is about what happened today, so the word is redundant and can be omitted. Similarly, exact times such as *'at seven minutes past twelve'* should be rounded off to *'just after midday'*, and specific times should be used only if they are essential to the story or heighten the immediacy of the coverage:

> News just in . . . the President of Sri Lanka has been assassinated in a suicide bomb attack. The bomber struck within the past few minutes at the head of the Mayday parade in Colombo . . .

For those listening in the small hours of the morning, references to events *'last night'* can be confusing, and should be replaced with *'overnight'* or *'during the night'*.

Time references have to be handled even more carefully when a station is broadcasting over several time zones. Canada, for example, spans seven such zones. To avoid confusion over their copy, news agencies that file stories over a wide area usually include the day of the week in brackets.

ACTIVE

News is about movement, change and action. Yet too often newswriting is reduced to the passive voice – instead of actions that produce change, we hear of changes that have occurred as a result of actions. 'The car smashed into the brick wall' becomes the limp and soft-centred 'the brick wall was smashed into by the car'.

Hickory Dickory Dock	Hickory Dickory Dock
The clock was run up by the mouse	The mouse ran up the clock
One o'clock was struck	The clock struck one
Down the mouse ran	The mouse ran down
Hickory Dickory Dock	Hickory Dickory Dock

The passive version on the left could be said to be lacking something of the snap of the original. The active voice is tighter, crisper and more concrete.

POSITIVE

Three ways to write a stronger lead: 1. Don't start with 'there is', a dead phrase; 2. Place the emphatic word(s) of a sentence at the end (thank you, Strunk and White); 3. When you find 'after' in your lead, what comes after 'after' should usually go before 'after'. (We hear stories that start something like this: 'Mayor Filch imposed a 9 p.m. curfew on teens after students burned down Jones High School.' The big news is that the kids burned down a school, so what comes after 'after' should go before 'after': 'Students burned down Jones High School today, and Mayor Filch imposed a 9 p.m. curfew on the city's teens.)

Mervin Block, broadcast newswriting coach, author of *Writing Broadcast News –Shorter, Sharper, Stronger* (mervinblock.com)

News is about what is happening, so even what is *not* happening should be expressed in an active, positive way. 'He did not succeed' becomes 'he failed'; 'He was asked to move, but didn't' becomes 'he refused to move'; 'Plans for the hospital would not go ahead for the time being' becomes 'Plans for the hospital have been shelved'.

Double negatives should be unravelled: 'Doctors say it is improbable that the illness will not prove terminal' becomes 'Doctors admit the patient will probably die'.

REDUNDANCIES

Redundancies are words that serve only to clutter up the copy. They should be ruthlessly eliminated:

Check *out*

End result

Eye witness

Period of a week, etc.

One of the worst offenders is the little word '*that*', which can straddle the middle of a sentence like a roadblock:

Rugby, and New Zealand's All Blacks say that they are set to trounce arch-rivals Fiji in the World Sevens Series.

Dump 'that' and contract 'they are'. It slips off the tongue much more smoothly: 'The All-Blacks say they're set to trounce . . .'

Like *that, the* can also be a pain. To be extreme about them both:

> When asked about **the** possible strike action, **the** dockers' leaders said **that** they hoped **that** would not be necessary.

Now read the sentence again and leave out the words in bold.

Every word should earn its place in the copy. Newswriting is too streamlined to carry any passengers. Modifiers such as 'very', 'quite' and 'almost' are excess baggage and should invariably be dumped.

REPETITION

The obvious is better than the obvious avoidance of it.

Fowler's Modern English Usage

Unnecessary repetition of words can jar the ear and should be avoided, but if no alternative can be found, and if it *sounds* right, then don't be afraid to repeat. No one has yet come up with a way of avoiding saying 'fire' in a story about a . . . well, a conflagration, without sounding absurd. Common practice is to alternate the words 'fire' and 'blaze' (if indeed it is big enough to be a 'blaze'!).

Where a *proposal* is involved, alternatives such as *scheme*, *plan*, *project* or *programme* may be used.

Avoid making the newsreader's task more difficult by repeating the same syllables, or consonants.

Your newsreader might stumble over 'In India' or 'The sixth thing' or 'British soldiers'.
Queensland University of Technology Journalism Guide

HOMONYMS

Homonyms are words that sound like others with different meanings:

Bare	and	Bear
Blight	and	Plight
Might	and	Might
Ate	and	Eight
Billion	and	Million
Fatal	and	Facial

Mishearing 'facial injuries' for 'fatal injuries' in a story about an accident could cause increased and unnecessary concern for relatives. Usually the context will make the meaning of the word clear, but beware of baffling the listener.

SINGULAR OR PLURAL?

Should it be the Government *says* or the Government *say*? Opinions differ and many newsrooms settle the issue by writing whatever sounds right to the ear. The trouble starts when inconsistencies creep into the copy:

> The Conservative party says its policies will defend Britain's position in Europe. The Tories want an end to what they describe as 'European meddling' in Britain's affairs.

'The Conservative party says', and 'Tories say' may both sound right individually, but they do not sound right together. Journalists must make up their own mind (although the authors' rule of thumb is, consider whether you are talking about a single body – 'the fire service *is* warning . . .' – or a group of people who make it up – 'fire-fighters *are* warning . . .')

PRONOUNS

Using pronouns in broadcasting requires a special discipline to get round the problem of muddling the listener who can't go back over what has been said:

> Film star Richard Cruise was involved in an ugly scene with fellow actor Tom Gere outside a Hollywood restaurant today. Cruise called Gere a has-been, and Gere responded by casting doubt on Cruise's parentage. He said he would sue.

Is Gere suing Cruise or is Cruise suing Gere? The way around this is to swap the pronoun for a name:

> Cruise said he would sue.

PUNCTUATION

Writing for broadcast is writing to be read aloud. Sentences should be broken into groups of meaning and these should be separated by a visible pause. Semicolons and colons do not work well because they are visually too similar to the full stop (period) or comma.

Pauses that are intended to be longer than a comma can be indicated by the dash – hyphen - ellipsis . . . or slash /. The ellipsis or dash (double hyphen) is perhaps the most effective indicators of pauses because they create more physical space between words than other forms of punctuation. Each new idea should be separated by a longer pause, and the best way to indicate this is to begin a new paragraph.

Capital letters can be used for names or to create emphasis, but if the story is written entirely in capitals, as is often the case (sic), the emphasis and visual signal at the start of the sentence is lost.

SPELLING

> If you're in doubt about how a foreign name is pronounced – just say it with supreme confidence – then no-one will dare correct you!
>
> Linda Wray, newsreader, BBC Northern Ireland

Some people say spelling is irrelevant in broadcasting, but that is not strictly true. The listener may not know if the wurds are speld gud, but misspelled words can act like banana skins beneath unwary newsreaders and cause them to stumble or trip. And of course many scripts are also published on the station's website.

Foreign or unfamiliar names can also be a problem. The solution is to spell them *fon-et-ik-lee* (phonetically) – as they sound. It is also a good idea to warn newsreaders of a pronunciation trap by marking the top of the page. They can then rehearse the troublesome word.

ABBREVIATIONS

Abbreviations generally make sense to the eye, but not to the ear. All but the most common, such as Mr and Mrs and USA, should be avoided.

Names of organisations should be spelled out unless they are commonly known by their initials, such as the BBC. Never use abbreviations that the newsreader would have to translate, such as C-in-C for Commander in Chief. The newsreader may be thrown for a second or get them wrong.

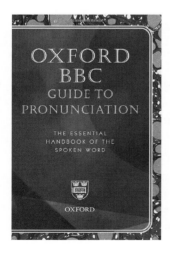

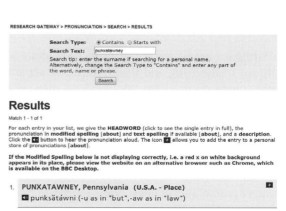

FIGURE 11.4   **FIGURE 11.5**   **FIGURE 11.6**

The BBC publishes its preferred pronunciations in printed form, and you can listen to suggested pronunciations on its internal website.

Some stations require abbreviations to be hyphenated, for example P-T-A, A-N-C, unless they form recognisable words (acronyms), when they should be left intact, for example NATO or AIDS.

NUMBERS

Nothing clutters copy quicker or confuses the ear more than a collection of figures. Even a short figure on a piece of paper can take a surprisingly long time to read aloud.

A single story should contain as few figures as possible, and within the bounds of accuracy numbers should always by rounded up or down to make them easier to take in: for 246,326, write 'almost 250,000', 'almost 250-thousand' or, even better, 'nearly a quarter of a million.'

Broadcast stations vary in their approach to figures, but whatever the house style, clarity is the aim, for the sake of the newsreader as well as the listener. (Resist the temptation to use 'a million' instead of 'one million', as listeners could easily confuse it for 8 million. 'Billion' should also be avoided as this means different things in different countries. Refer to so many thousands of millions instead.) Write out symbols (such as $, £, #) as the words 'dollar' and 'pounds' and 'hashtag'.

PROOF READING

Copy should always be read out loud, to check for the sense and make sure no traps lie in wait for the unwary newsreader. Never leave it to the reader to check the copy through. A sudden rush before the bulletin could leave no time to prepare. The acid test of good copy is whether someone else could read it out loud, having never before clapped eyes on it, and get through without tripping over their tongue.

Below are some examples of hastily written copy which were actually submitted to be read on air:

> Health officers throughout the country are being put on the alert for typyoid cases . . . After six people returning from a Greek holiday were found to have the disease takes twenty one days to incubate and it's thought more cases could develop in the next few days.

> TWO SECURITY GUARDS ARE RECOVERING AFTER THEY WERE SHOT OUTSIDE A CONCERT IN BIRMINGHAM BY THE AMERICAN RAP STAR KANYE WEST. SHOTS WERE FIRED AFTER A GROUP TRIED TO GET INSIDE

> THE N.E.C. ARENA WITHOUT TICKETS. POLICE HAVE ARRESTED A MANAND A WOMAN.

Apart from the spelling mistakes, these stories may look feasible at first glance. Only when they are read through do the problems become obvious.

Even the most innocent words and phrases can sometimes conspire to trap you. Find another way of saying it *before* you go on air:

> Avon's ambulamencement . . . Avon's ambulaments . . . Avon's ambulen . . . Avon's ambewlamence . . . (Pause. Deep breath) The ambulancemen of Avon . . .
>
> British TV

AMBIGUITY

Ambiguity offers the audience a rich source of humour at the newsreader's expense. Howlers can range from the simple snigger:

> Orchestra musicians at the Royal Opera House are threatening to strike next week, if the management turn down a 10 per cent no-strings pay rise.

to the cringingly embarrassing:

> . . . the batsman's Holding . . . the bowler's Willey . . .

Here are some other examples which might have been caught in time if the writer had troubled to read them through:

> Teams of traditional dancers from various parts of Kenya exposed themselves to world scouts delegates in a grand performance.

> About 50 students broke into the college, smashing glass and chanting, 'No cuts, no cuts'. A porter had his hand injured . . .

> During evidence PC John Wilkinson said that John Depledge had given him a violent blow to the testicles. They both fell to the ground . . .

THE HEADLINES

- Avoid clichés like the plague.

- Think before, during and after you write. Is what you have said accurate and fair? Can it be made clearer? Are there too many words?

- Think as you write: is this right?

QUESTIONS FOR YOU

1. The following story needs rewriting to clarify it, tidy up the attribution, simplify the figures and generally knock it into shape. Have a go.

> Flagham Council leader and Housing Chairman, Councillor Fred Bunter MA, has dismissed opposition plans to cut council rents as 'absurd'. Rent cuts of up to 19 per cent had been suggested to help out the 6883 tenants who had fallen badly

into arears. Councillor Bunter said the rent cuts would penalise the council's other 63,722 tenants who had managed to keep up with their rent. The cut price rents scheme was proposed by opposition spokesman on Housing, Councillor Bob Taylor, who said, 'Many of these tenants have no way of paying their rent. They are in severe difficulties, often through no fault of their own, and must be helped.

2. Rewrite the following headlines into a more immediate, direct and active broadcast style:

- In connection with the Security Holdings armed robbery in Parkerville last month, four men appeared briefly in court today. An adjournment was granted for a week.
- The search for twelve fishermen from a Danish trawler in the North Sea ended when they were found safe and well drifting on the sea in a small boat.
- Three schoolchildren died after their school bus was hit by a car on the M1. Other vehicles were not involved.

3. The following story is a complete mess. Whoever wrote it should fear for his/her job. The angle needs pointing up, it has unnecessary repetition, redundancies, convolution, singular/plural problems, hopeless punctuation and too many adjectives. Hammer it into shape and rewrite it to broadcast style.

The Police Department is urgently calling for eye-witnesses following a tragic and fatal fire at hospital in Brunton. The fire broke out in the third floor laundry room at the modern 300-bed General Hospital in Brunton and quickly spread to the casualty ward. Frightened patients in the casualty ward hastily raised the alarm and worried doctors and nurses had to evacuate them from the ward along with all the other patients in the rest of the hospital who later heard the distressing news that an ancilliary worker in the laundry room where the fire began was overcome by the fumes and sadly died in the horrific fire which is still burning fiercely as firemen continue bravely to fight the flames which are still lighting up the night sky. The police say that they think that the fire may have been started on purpose. The flames have badly damaged about half of the hospital. No other patient or member of staff was injured in the fire.

OTHER RESOURCES

- 'Chicago News Producer Hunts Down Clichés' – an article about a Chicago TV station, WLS-TV, that's cracking down on the use of a batch of bad words. 'Not nasty words, but clichés, bromides, redundancies and words that are otherwise objectionable': http://bit.ly/BJCliche.

- 'It's Been Said Before: A Guide to the Use and Abuse of Cliches' – available on Amazon etc.

- Various style guides: the BBC (http://bit.ly/BJBBCStyle); *Associated Press Broadcast News Handbook: A Manual of Techniques and Practices* and *The Canadian Press Stylebook* (Amazon etc.); and for contrast, the style guide for broadcast media in Rwanda (http://bit.ly/BJRwanda).

TUTOR NOTES

A video instructional series on writing and reporting for college and high school classrooms and adult learners; 15 half-hour video programmes and coordinated books, many free: http://bit.ly/BJVideoWriting and more resources from the BBC on writing tuition here: http://bit.ly/BJBBCWriting.

NOTES

1 *Newsman's English*, Heinemann, 1972; George Orwell, *Politics and the English Language*, Routledge, 1940.
2 'Journalese for the Lay Reader', *Time*, 18 March 1985.
3 Anthony Davis, *Television: Here is the news*, Independent Books Ltd, 1976, p. 23.

CHAPTER 12

Putting the Show Together

> The finger that turns the dial rules the air.
>
> Will Durant, US historian (1885–1981)

ITEM SELECTION AND ORDER

In the world of the media, the consumer is king. Greater choice and greater ease of making that choice have taken their toll on audience tolerance. Selection and comparison between broadcast news is now as easy as pressing a button. More to the point, you can get the news you want, when you want it from the Internet and mobile phone, websites, Twitter and various news aggregators. So more than ever the success of a programme depends on the producer's ability to select the stories the audience wants to see or hear – 'news sense' – and their skill in assembling those items into a popular programme.

The producer's first task is to match the coverage to the style and length of the programme. A two-minute headline summary may cover the current top eight stories, providing a sketched outline of events. A half-hour programme may go over substantially the same ground, but in more depth.

What newsgatherers regard as news is usually a matter of considering what's of importance, significance, relevance, immediacy, proximity, human interest and novelty.

'A FAIR PICTURE . . .'

From the millions of words a day that squirt into computers in newsrooms such as the BBC World Service, programme makers have to select and boil down just enough to fill their programmes. In the case of a three-minute bulletin, that may amount to little more than 500 words. But within these limitations the aim is to provide an objective picture of the day's main news.

In a sense we put a telephoto lens to the world. We only show in close-up the things that are news-worthy, and they tend to be sad things. It is a fact of life that a lot of what goes into the news is gloomy and disastrous and sad . . . News judgement . . . is not a very precise science but it is the way in which journalists are trained to say this is an interesting story, it is relevant, we ought to tell the audience this.

Ron Neil, former BBC Director of News and Current Affairs

Media feeds off media. Journalists as a breed are fiercely competitive. They scrutinise one another's programmes, grinding their teeth if someone's angle is better or their pictures are sharper, and if a rival comes up with a new story, then wolf-like (or lemming-like) they charge in packs towards it.

ITN's Channel 4 News has different priorities to most other British news programmes. Its brief is to look in more detail at neglected areas such as medicine, science and the arts and to extend British television coverage of foreign affairs to the oft ignored and usually overlooked developing nations. It has a pace of its own too. Normally the first and second item can be quite long and there may be a third item, and then the 'newsbelt' to pick up the pace. After the break the programme looks at other subjects which are not part of the day's news.

On good days, where hard news abounds, media rivals will often run the same lead story. On quieter days, which produce fewer obvious headlines, it can look as though rival stations in the same city are reporting from different countries on different days of the week.

FIGURE 12.1
News producers simply choose which news clips they want for their bulletin, and download them from a central site. Credit *107.8 Radio Jackie.*

ITEM ORDER

The process of sniffing out and sorting out the news can at first seem bewildering. It is different from day to day and hour to hour, depending on what other stories are in the 'mix' and what stories you have broadcast recently. For experienced journalists such 'news judgement' ceases to be the complex equation it was when they started. The myriad of baffling decisions and bewildering juxtapositions are resolved in a moment, thanks to a mixture of pure instinct and experience.

They do not so much *decide* what makes one story more important than the others, or which stories to run and in what order, they just *know*.

Hard news could be *information of importance to the listener*. Soft news is anything that is *interesting, entertaining* or just plain *juicy*. The more juices a story stirs up and the harder it hits a news editor in the gut, heart or wallet, the higher it's slotted in the bulletin.

> Three subject areas listeners and viewers always respond to are stories about health, heart and pocketbook. You work for WIFM – 'what's in it for me?' and the 'me' means your listeners.
> Valerie Geller, author, *Creating Powerful Radio* (creatingpowerfulradio.com; gellermedia.com)

News selection does become a matter of instinct over time: learned by practice and observation and through newsroom socialisation. Over time, journalists learn the newsroom feel for what is considered news and what is not. This always involves judgement and also bias.

Academics cannot resist the temptation to reduce the decision-making process to a formula, but formulae work best with subjects less complex than the human mind, and belong in the sterile conditions of the laboratory, rather than the creative chaos of the newsroom.

> Anyone who says you can make a journalistic judgement in a sort of sterile bath is talking bunkum, twaddle. You make a judgement because of your empirical knowledge store; you make it because of your family, because of the society in which we live.
> Peter Sissons, former BBC newsreader

The key factors in item selection are the story's significance, its impact on a given audience, its interest, topicality and immediacy. Most of these are related with a good deal of overlap between them.

1. The Significance of the Story

How important is this story in global or national terms? In what measure does it reflect our changing times, and to what degree does the story speak of political change or upheaval?

2. The Material Impact of the Story

Does the story materially affect *our* audience in terms of their earnings, spending power, standard of living or lifestyles? Relevance is incorporated into this notion of significance and impact.

3. Audience Reaction (The Human Interest Factor)

Does the story tug at the heartstrings of the listener or viewer, cause them to suck in their breath, to swear or to smile?

More objectively, what strength of feeling is this story likely to provoke? It may not change the audience's way of life, but for it to be of human interest it should upset, anger, amuse intrigue or appal them, or be about people who have a similar effect.

The *Wow!* factor comes in here, with stories about the biggest, smallest, fastest, most-expensive etc., which are intended to surprise or astound the hearer.

4. The Topicality of the Story

Has the story been in the public eye lately? If so, how largely has it figured? Linked to that is the immediacy factor.

5. The Immediacy Factor (The Yawn Factor)

Is it 'news just in'? Is it a brand new story that has broken, or a new angle on one that is still running? Conversely, has it been running for long enough to reach the point of boredom?

If a story is getting stale, then by definition, it is no longer news. On the other hand a new item may breeze into the bulletin like a breath of fresh air. Its position may then be dictated by its freshness, especially when linked to topicality. In other words, if the bulletin is full of the latest hijacking, then news of a hostage release is a fair bet for lead story.

Some news stations producing regular bulletins concentrate on providing a new-look programme every hour, in the hope that the variety will persuade the audience to tune-in for longer. Others argue that listeners don't stay tuned for long enough to get bored with the same bulletin. They prefer to let the lead story run and run, albeit freshened up and with a change of clothes, until it is replaced by something of equal significance. Again we see a mix of entertainment values and news values in operation.

Where bulletins are revised substantially every hour, there can be a loss of continuity and stories of real substance are likely to be knocked down simply because they are regarded as old. Some stations attempt to strike a balance by running extended news summaries at key points in the day, such as 1.00 p.m. when the current stories are shelved and the day's major items are dusted off and re-run according to their significance that day.

6. Sport/Specialisms

Some might say: 'Sports results? – Bung 'em at the back of the bulletin.' If the practice is to separate the sports news or other speciality like financial news into a section of its own, then each story within that section will be prioritised individually and run together in order of priority. The exception is speciality stories that are significant enough to earn a place in the general run of news. (When is sports news, *news* news?)

7. Linking Items

Frequently items have linked themes or offer different angles on the same story. Splitting them up would be a mistake. They should be rewritten to run together.

8. Actuality/Pictures

Some stories are illustrated. The addition of actuality or footage and its length and quality may be extra factors in deciding where to place each item in the bulletin. It might be policy to spread illustrations throughout, to always lead with a story that has actuality, or to run no more than one phone-quality item.

9. 'And Finally . . .'

> Got a tickler here about some kid who tried to hold up a bank with a water pistol . . .

With items that are bright, frivolous, trivial and can guarantee a smirk if not a belly laugh, common practice would be to save them for the end of the bulletin.

LOCAL CONSIDERATIONS

> For listeners, it is the quality, relevance, timeliness and accuracy of the news that matters, not where it is read from . . . Any individual station should have procedures in place to be able to react to and report on local news events in a timely manner. (Localness is) the feel for an area a listener should get by tuning in to a particular station, coupled with confidence that matters of importance, relevance or interest to the target audience in the area will be accessible on air.
>
> *Localness on Local Commercial Radio Stations*, Ofcom.org.uk

Local consideration could feature highly in positioning items in the bulletin. What might be of interest nationally is unlikely by itself to satisfy a local audience, so the relative weight given to national and local news has to be carefully considered.

Audiences and their needs can change throughout the day. First thing in the morning, all viewers or listeners might want to know is: 'Is the world the same as it was when I went to bed; will I get wet when I leave home; will I be able to get to work on time; and will I be able to contribute to my colleagues' conversation at the coffee machine when I get there?'

How local is *local*? News editors may find the strongest news coming regularly from one location, but may have to consciously drop good stories for weaker ones from elsewhere to try to give an even spread of coverage.

FOREIGN COVERAGE

Central to the question of relevance is proximity. 'Is this story about me or about things happening on my doorstep . . . or is it about strangers 2,000 miles away who I never knew existed?'

Western news values are often insular and unfavourable to foreign stories unless they are about 'people like us'. The judgement can only be what are the most relevant stories around in Britain today.

All things considered, item selection and running orders will often be settled on nothing more objective than the gut reaction of journalists about the gut reactions they expect their stories to produce from their audience. In other words – impact.

But impact without awareness has about as much educational value as being flattened by a runaway truck. If foreign coverage is to do anything more than leave us relieved that it's happening *there* and not *here*, it will need to be accompanied by analysis.

PRODUCING A RUNNING ORDER

PM [23/03/2015 17:00]

Page	Story Slug	Details	Free Text 2	MOS Obj Slug	Actual	Cume	Story Prod	Pre	Tear Appr	-ina Appr	MOS User	MOS Status
	TIME				0:00	0:00						
001	OPENING	ED - Afzal Amin + Theresa May	EX S32 + EX VCS	OPENING Amin OPENING may OPENING richard vox	1:09	1:09		x	x		0:09 0:07 0:11	
	NEWS	Jane Steel	lv ex S32		0:00	1:09						
#	Q Dudley VP	JS - Alex Forsyth	EX S32 + EX VCS	DUDLEY FORSYTH VP	0:54	2:03			✓		0:35	
	Q Extremism	JS - Danny Shaw	EX S32 + EX VCS	EXTREMISM SHAW VP	1:00	3:03			✓		0:36	
	Q Miliband	JS - Alex Salmond	EX S32 + EX VCS	LABOUR MILIBAND ACT	0:40	3:43			✓		0:18	
	Claudia	JS - Read	EX S32		0:11	3:54			✓			
	Q Fox	JS - Tom Symonds	EX S32 + EX VCS	Fox/Symonds vp	0:43	4:37			✓		0:32	
	Horse	JS - Read	EX S32		0:22	4:59			✓			
	Richard III	JS - Read	EX S32		0:15	5:14			✓			
	BULLETIN ENDS	soft post 05:00			0:00	5:14						
100	DUDLEY	Afzal Amin (Today) into SHAUN LEY	EX S32 + EX VCS	AFZAL Amin from Today	4:20	9:34	MS	x	x	✓	0:15	
101		ED - Les Jones	EX S32 + EX FACETIME		4:30	14:0		x	x	✓		
	TIME	soft post 15:00			0:00	14:0						
100	QUARTER PAST HEAD	Jane Steel	EX S32		0:30	14:3			✓			
	TIME				0:00	14:3						
020	EXTREMISM	EM - x3 May clips: Problem + Sharia + Banning Orders grps + places and Yvette clip	EX S32 + EX VCS	EXTREMISM May Tea clip EXTREMISM May Sharia clip EXTREMISM may banning EXTREMISM cooper clip	2:30	17:0 4	JS	x	x	✓	0:20 0:34 0:24 0:17	
021		EM - AFZAL ASHRAF	EX S32 + EX FACETIME		5:15	22:1		x	x	✓		
	TIME				0:00	22:1						
030	CLAUDIA	EM - PHIL BODMER	EX S32 + EX RP41		2:50	25:0	JS	x	x	✓		
	TIME				0:00	25:0						

FIGURE 12.2
A script, cue, questions and background in a briefing sheet.

You never go into the programme with a running order that stays the same throughout the show – ever. Always there are changes; sometimes the whole thing is rewritten.

You're given a running order but you basically throw it away and just wing it throughout the morning.
John Humphrys, Presenter on *Today*, BBC Radio 4

Many newcasters hold the bulletin running order in their heads – especially radio newsreaders who are operating their own studio equipment. Where a technical assistant drives the desk for the newsreader, he or she will have an on-screen running order listing the items and giving their durations, in-words and out-words.

Stations producing longer programmes sometimes combine running order with format. An on-screen log shows what kind of stories should go where, and approximately how long each should be. Using this modular approach, features are plugged in and replaced where necessary, but for items to be fully interchangeable they will usually have to be of a fixed length. The producer's job is to organise the coverage so suitable items of the right length are brought in, and then make sure the programme goes out to plan.

A completed running order can be an elaborate document, giving precise details of items, durations, ins and outs, or it could be a rough guide to what the producers and directors expect and hope for in the next half-hour. TV news has more than one running order to work with. With the list of programme items, which may be constantly changing, will be a list of the visuals that go with those items. TV directors driving programmes which rely on sophisticated production techniques and make increasing use of live reports will frequently have to 'busk' the order, working with a schedule that changes so often, it may never be produced in final form on paper.

FIGURE 12.3

The production area and the studio for BBC Radio 4's *Today* programme.

FIGURE 12.4

The camera's perspective as the newsreader makes a last-minute check before going live. Credit: Katherine Adams/BBC.

Every producer's aim is to find a winning format and stick with it, in the hope that the audience will do the same. But the familiarity factor can work against them. Even belated improvements to a programme that has been creaking with age will usually produce an audience backlash and – initially, at least – lose a number of viewers who were very happy with the product as it was. The art of maintaining audience loyalty is to find what the customers want, and give it to them – consistently.

THE OPENERS

The first few seconds of a programme are all-important. During these moments the audience can be gained or lost. In television news, the openers are usually the most complicated and closely produced part of the programme. They will probably comprise a signature tune and title sequence, featuring sophisticated computer graphics and a tightly edited montage of still and moving pictures. This might be followed by headlines or teasers – tersely worded five-second phrases written to intrigue – perhaps each illustrated with a snatch of footage showing the most gripping moments of action to come.

The openers, demanding quick-fire operation and split-second timing, might be the only part of a news programme, barring the individual items, to be pre-recorded. This is likely to be done during the rehearsal shortly before transmission.

Radio news, which is spared the demanding dimension of pictures, has an easier task. The programme might begin with a signature tune, voiced-over by an announcer, which is faded down beneath the voice of the newsreader, who may give the headlines in turn, each supported by a colourful or intriguing snatch from an interview or report to be featured in the programme. This list of coming attractions is known as the *menu*.

KEEPING AN AUDIENCE – HEADLINES AND PROMOTIONS

Movie-makers realised years ago that not even a blockbuster of a film can sell itself. For a film to do well at the box office, it has to be promoted. Trailers have to be produced capturing the liveliest action and the snappiest dialogue to show the audience the thrills in store. News producers use similar techniques.

Headlines achieve two important functions: at the middle and end of a programme they remind the audience of the main stories and help reinforce that information. Reinforcement aids recall, and an audience that can remember what it has heard is more likely to be satisfied. At the beginning, the headlines, or sometimes teasers, hook the audience in the same way as the cinema trailer, and later serve to encourage them to bear with an item that may be less appealing because they know something better is on the way. During the programme, forward trails, such as 'Coming up, Spot the singing Dalmatian, but first news of the economic crisis', do much the same job.

If a news programme is broken by a commercial break, the audience for the next part of the programme must never be taken for granted. Each segment is likely to end on what are known as *pre-commercials* – a cluster of headlines designed to keep the audience.

> The pre-commercial is one of the best opportunities to bridge viewers to your show. More people will see the pre-commercial than will see the top of your news. Use your very best video and sound from your show. This is your best chance to prove to the audience that your show is worth losing sleep over. Craft your pre-commercial with great care. Better that you neglect the lead story than neglect the pre-commercial. It is that important.
>
> Graeme Newell, Television and Digital Media Training Company (602communications.com)

Good stories alone are no guarantee of an audience. Having the stories and persuading the audience to wait for them is the way to keep them.

ACTUALITY

> Members of your staff – they could be called BBC Reporters . . . should be held in readiness . . . to cover unexpected news of the day . . . a big fire, strikes, civil commotion, railway accidents . . . It would be his job . . . to secure an eye-witness . . . to give a short account of the part he or she played that day. In this way . . . the news could be presented in a gripping manner and, at the same time, remain authentic . . . Such a news bulletin would in itself be a type of actuality programme.
>
> Richard Dimbleby, outlining his proposals to the BBC's Chief News Editor, 1936

Actuality – interview extracts and on-the-spot reports – has for decades been a central feature of TV and radio news reporting world-wide. It's used to transport the audience to the scene, to hear the words as they were said, and to see or hear the news as it is actually happening – hence the term *actuality*. This is where broadcasting scores heavily above newspapers. If a single picture is worth a thousand words, what must be the value of moving pictures – and sound?

Combine audio and video, stills and text, archives and background information and you have of course, the station's website.

> Make your interviewees earn their quotes. It's no good quoting a lot of dull gibberish. Try to keep on interviewing them until they give you something memorable . . .
>
> Martina Purdy, former Politics Correspondent, BBC Northern Ireland

PICTURES

The supremacy of TV news suggests that moving pictures hold the greatest audience appeal, but the enduring attraction of radio must be due in no small part to the way in which radio stimulates the imagination of its audience. It makes radio listening a more active experience than the passive, attention-consuming pastime of watching TV.

FIGURE 12.5

'The Hub' where pictures come in from remote studios, the satellite truck or New Broadcasting House in London.

Developments in TV news have had less to do with changing formats or presentation styles than the availability of faster and better pictures. Television is undergoing a continuing revolution. When TV news began, newsreel film, which could be weeks out of date, was superseded by film reports made the same day. Now there is faster newsgathering using more portable and cheaper digital recorders and live transmission of pictures from the scene.

Good pictures don't just illustrate the news – they are the news. TV broadcasts rely on the strength of the pictures. Their availability determines whether a story is run or dropped, and the strength of those pictures will often settle a story's position in a bulletin.

GRAPHICS

Study after study shows, viewers love maps and graphics. They are typically the most loved part of a newscast. Their greatest power – simplification. Great graphics can make the most complicated story easy to understand. Plain old talking just doesn't cut it anymore. Viewers want to experience a story that entices all of their senses.

Graeme Newell, Television and Digital Media Training Company (602communications.com)

TV graphics can do much to overcome the broadcaster's bête noir – the difficulty most listeners have in absorbing and retaining background information while continuing to take in a steady stream of facts. The context of the story can be explained by displaying and holding key points or quotes on the screen. Without this advantage, radio news has to resort to the old adage of KISS – *keep it simple, stupid!*

Radio producers will try to run an even spread of copy stories, illustrated items and voice reports, and may juggle the position of stories in the programme to try to achieve a pleasing variety. TV producers play the same game with live and recorded reports, stills, graphics and to-camera pieces, working hard not to load the programme with too many static items or on-the-spot reports.

PROGRAMME BALANCE – BEING ALL THINGS TO ALL PEOPLE

Producers will never please all of the people all of the time, but they do their best to please some of them some of the time and leave everybody satisfied.

Groupings and Variety

It's the programme editor who decides on the order of the stories, which is most important, which to put first, what we call 'the lead story' or simply 'the lead'. The stories that follow are ranked in terms of interest to the audience. We aim for a good mix of stories – it's the mix that makes a good bulletin. Further down the running order the stories can often be of similar significance and what you can do there is to group stories together to help the audience through a mass of information. A 'news round up' is always a good way of getting more stories into the running order and it also varies the pace. And finally, some editors also try to put a lighter story maybe a funny story at the end of the bulletin.

Huw Edwards, BBC News presenter

'*Programme feel*' is a key to the success or failure of a show. That feel is down to the rhythm, pace and variety of the programme as well as the substance of its reports, and that feel is enhanced by the way items are grouped together.

Perhaps the ultimate grouping of stories happens very occasionally, when you have two strong stories vying to be the lead at the start of the programme. A news editor and programme producer may be split about which should lead as each item carries significant weight of 'newsworthiness'. Every story has various factors which together suggest their place in the running order, but how do you decide the lead between:

- A pull-together report on 700 local job losses, or a breaking story of a fire in an (empty) church?

- A man stabbed to death in a night time street brawl, or two teenagers killed in a road crash?

- The light plane that crashed killing five people on board, or the fact that another five people were killed when that plane crashed into their house?

What story (or angle) goes first, and how do you signify to the audience that there's another also very important story straight after?

That's why sometimes a news programme may have a 'double barrel lead', with a cue along these lines:

- In a moment more facts and reaction on the day's big story about the 700 job losses at the steelworks, but first let's take you live to the scene of the fire . . .

- Triple tragedy in Blankstown today – with three young people losing their lives. A man's died from stab injuries in Canada Place, and two teenagers have lost their lives after their car seemingly careered out of control on the notorious Michaeltown Bends . . .

- Ten people have been killed after a light plane crashed into a home in St Peter's. Five people on board and another five on the ground have lost their lives. We have two reports tonight: in a moment we will go to the aerodrome from where the plane took off . . . but first Joe Soap is in St Peter's at the scene of the crash. Joe . . .?

Elsewhere in the show, sport and other special interest features are often segmented together, and even world news or local news, if these are thought to hold only a secondary appeal, may be grouped in segments short enough to hold those in the audience who have tuned in primarily to hear something else.

Story groupings may be broken down further by location or comparative weight. Some US radio stations operating an hourly cycle of news will divide the national and local news into major and secondary items and run the secondaries in slots of their own at fixed points in the cycle. These groupings of minor items will be kept short, with brief stories, and used almost as fillers to vary the pace between weightier or more interesting segments.

Segmenting can be counterproductive. Running all the crime stories together would lose impact and might give the impression that the area is a hotbed of robberies and murders. It *might* be better to group them at intervals in the programme. Likewise, film reports or actuality with a similar theme, such as coverage of a riot and a noisy demonstration, are often best kept apart. Too many talking heads (dry, expert opinion) may also bore the audience.

Research for the former British Independent Broadcasting Authority discovered that an audience is more likely to forget an item when stories are grouped together. Researchers also identified a 'meltdown' factor, when similar stories ran together in the audience's mind. They placed a Mafia trial story in the middle of four foreign news items and then among four from the UK. Recall among the British audience was 20 per cent higher when the Mafia story was placed in the unusual context of UK news – normally it would be kept separate (*UK Press Gazette*, 21 July 1986).

Beside all these considerations is one of taste. It may seem good for variety to follow a triple killing with Mimi the dancing dingbat, but the audience wouldn't thank you for it. It would make light of a serious and tragic story. Juxtaposition requires a good deal of care, and to keep the audience informed about where the programme is going, transitions should be clearly signposted:

International news now . . .

Meanwhile, back home . . .

But there is some good news for residents of . . .

Industrial news . . .

On the stock market . . .

Transitions, timechecks, thoughtful linking and headlines help to create programme feel and establish identity. They can be overdone, as *Times* newspaper
humourist Miles Kington observes:

> One example comes from a presenter who was linking a murder thriller to
> a programme about cheese making: 'And from something blood-curdling to
> something rather more milk-curdling . . .'

Indoor and outdoor reports can be mixed, and extra variety added by using male
and female co-presenters. Alternating stories between the two can lift a programme,
and research suggests it helps viewers remember the items. But on a short programme, too many voices can have a confusing effect if each presenter doesn't have
enough time to establish an identity.

The idea is to give a spread of light and heavy, fast and slow, busy and static, to get
the most variety and interest from the material.

> When you are planning a news programme you have to keep things strong right the way through,
> rather than do what happens in a news bulletin, where you start with the most important and finish
> with the most trivial. It's got to have a strong beginning, to hold itself up in the middle and have a
> good end. I want a piece that people can remember.
>
> Rod Mckenzie, former News Editor BBC Radio 1 Newsbeat, XTRA TX

Rhythm and Pace

Rhythm and pace are as crucial to programme feel as the choice of items. The style
of writing, speed of reading, pace of editing and length of each item determine
whether the programme surges ahead or drags.

Individual reports should run to just the right length to hold interest, and leave
the audience wanting more rather than wishing for less. The programme should
be rhythmic, though with enough variety to stimulate interest. Aim for a standard
length for items, with none cut so short as to feel truncated or abrupt, or allowed
to run on to the point of boredom.

Where short news items are used, the overall rhythm of the programme can be
maintained by grouping them in segments that are about the same length as a
standard item, or by inserting them into the programme at regular intervals.

Where an item is less likely to be of prime interest to an audience, it will usually be
trimmed shorter than the others, and positioned between stories which are thought
to be popular and have been promoted as such. The aim is to tempt an audience to
stay tuned for as long as possible and preferably longer than intended.

The importance of rhythm is even more closely observed in radio where news programmes belong in the context of a music show. The audience is used to the rhythm
of the three-minute song, so any single news item over that duration might feel as
though it were dragging. Many news bulletins on such stations are three minutes

long. Stations that pump out fast music to a young audience will often want their news to be the same – bright, youthful and moving along at a cracking pace, for example Radio 1's Newsbeat on the BBC. The brisker the pace of the programme, the shorter the items should be, and interviews with people who are ponderous in their delivery should be cut even shorter to avoid dragging the pace.

AND NOW THE GOOD NEWS?

With stories of global warming, recession, war and crime swamping the airwaves even hardened news presenters have wondered about reconsidering an agenda that equates doom and gloom with news values.

In 1993 BBC presenter Martyn Lewis famously accused TV of consigning viewers to 'a relentless culture of negativity'.

> We should be more prepared than we have been in the past to weigh the positive stories . . . The main criteria for including stories should not be the degree of violence, death, conflict, failure or disaster they encompass, but the extent to which those stories have the potential to shape or change the world in which we live . . . Pressure from the top traps large areas of journalism into a whirlpool of negativity.

Presenter Peter Sissons rebuked, 'it is not our job to go in for social engineering to make people feel better', adding for good measure that the BBC's job was to report the news 'the way it is, even if people slit their wrists'.

MAKING THE PROGRAMME FIT

Many programme makers will share the same bad dream – their show is either five minutes too short and grinds to a halt early, leaving a gaping hole before the next item, or it develops a will of its own, gathering momentum until it becomes an unstoppable juggernaut, overrunning hopelessly and throwing out the programme schedule for the entire network.

It's a nightmare that can (usually) be prevented with a little forward planning and flexibility.

Fortunately, programme templates on a computer deal with the awkward things such as working out timings (even calculating when an item will end, and how much time in hand that will leave), and laying out segments so a producer is not starting from scratch every morning.

Of course there are certain 'constants' in place when piecing together the show. In commercial broadcasts, the starting point is the advertising breaks and other 'furniture items' such as sport and weather around which the other elements must fit. What is left over after all of the constants are accounted for is sometimes called the 'news hole' to be filled with anchor readers, expert commentators on set, field reports, live shots and so on.

But of course there are also times when the format is tossed out in response to a breaking story of major proportions. There are times when a newscast will expand and commercials will be dropped entirely. Programming may be dropped to make room for a major story . . . and this could include a weather story.

CUTTING

Where a programme is in danger of over-running and has to be cut, the incision can be made in a number of ways. The most drastic is to drop an item completely. Another way of saving time is to replace a longer item with a shorter one. Where only a small saving is required, trimming an item on air usually does the job.

The easiest way to do this is to cut something that is live. If you are conducting a live interview, you will be told when to wind-up by your producer, who will also tell you the time you have remaining for the interview, and will count you down during the final moments. If you have 15 seconds left and still want to pursue another point you can put their question in a way that makes your interviewee aware time is running out, such as 'Finally, and briefly . . .'

FIGURE 12.6
Always up against the clock.

Programme makers often include live material towards the end of a programme as a flexible buffer, which can be compressed or expanded to fill in time. Where all the items are recorded and all are to be run producers can be faced with the unenviable task of having to cut an item on air so it appears quite naturally to have come to an end.

This can be made far less fraught with a little help from the reporter. Before you finish editing an item, make a note of a place at which your story can be brought to an early end, along with the words that run up to that point and the duration of the item up to that point. This is known as *pot-point*, and it will give your producer the flexibility to run the item in either its shorter or longer version.

> From New Delhi, our correspondent Simon French reports . . .
>
> POT: 'turning a blind eye to the attacks'
>
> DUR: (Duration) 56"
>
> OUT: (Final words) 'nationalism has turned into a kind of idol worship.'
>
> DUR: 1'06"

In radio the process of cutting or filling is perhaps the simplest of all. Assuming a five-minute bulletin has a sequence of sport, an 'and finally' and weather at the end, the newsreader works out the combined duration of those items and deducts this from the total length of the bulletin. If they come to a minute and a half, then the reader has three and a half minutes remaining for the main part of the bulletin. If the programme started at two o'clock the newsreader knows that he or she has to begin the end sequence by three and a half minutes past two. The reader then aims to come out of the main material as near to that time as possible, and any other stories that have not been read by then will have to be discarded (see also Backtiming, below).

Writing the weather or sport to flexible lengths, with paragraphs that can be kept in or cut, allows the newsreader to make final adjustments so the bulletin can come out exactly on time. This way, late news can be slotted in without throwing the programme timing.

FILLING

Filling is a more serious problem than having to cut, because it implies the programme is short of good material and the producer has been failing in his or her job. Items should never be run simply as makeweights – every story should deserve its airtime. It is up to the news producer to make sure that on even the quietest news day there is enough good material to run, even if it means switching to softer stories.

Many newsrooms compensate for the ebb and flow of news by sending out reporters on slow days to produce timeless features that can be kept on the shelf and run whenever necessary ('evergreens'). In theory, the day should never come when a gap appears in the programme, but if holes do appear, they should never be filled by running a story for longer than it deserves. Nor should they be plugged by second-rate items and limp ad-libs.

Where the programme is slightly short of material, say when a feature has been dropped to make way for a late item, the filling is best carried out in the same way as the cutting – with live material. More short stories may be inserted into the programme, but in TV, even this requires forward planning to line up the relevant stills or graphics to accompany them. The easiest place to pad is in the live to-camera items such as the weather or sport. Scripts for these should incorporate a number of *out-points* where the presenter can finish early, as well as extra paragraphs which give interesting additional information but which will not sound like padding on the air.

Another way to take up slack at the end of the programme is to promote items coming up in the next edition – but stand by for complaints if the station then fails to deliver the goods for example because of breaking news.

The last few seconds are usually filled with the goodbyes or *outs*. It is easy at this stage to be lulled into a false sense of security and to think the programme is over. Don't be fooled, many good programmes are ruined by ending badly. The most important 30 seconds of a show are at the beginning. Next come those at the end. The audience's lasting impressions will be gained in those moments. The start should persuade them to pay attention; the ending will persuade them to tune in tomorrow – or try the other channel.

Don't rely on inspiration to provide ad-libs. The art is to make scripted comments sound spontaneous, and many broadcasters who may appear to be masters of spontaneity will probably have scripted every pause, stumble, word and comma. Few things sound more forced and banal than the artificial exchange of unfelt pleasantries between presenters to pad out the final few seconds of a programme.

FIGURE 12.7

The production gallery. Lights are down but concentration is high as producers and directors prepare for transmission. Credit Katherine Adams/BBC.

If desperate measures are called for, then the radio producer may use music as a flexible bridge before the next item. Television's equivalent is to linger for an uncomfortable length of time on the parting shot of the weather forecast. Music during a programme can often be lengthened or shortened without it showing – especially when there are no vocals – but the problem at the end of a programme is getting the music to end exactly on time and on a definite note.

BACKTIMING

The way to achieve a neat and definite ending is to backtime the music. Producers need to know the duration of the music – usually an instrumental signature tune – and they count back from the second the programme is due to end to find the exact time the music should begin. At that moment, regardless of whatever else is going on in the programme, the music is started, but with the volume off. (This means the audience cannot hear the music but the technical operator can.) As the presenter ends the programme, the music is faded up under them, and fills the gap from the moment they finish speaking, to end exactly when the programme is scheduled to stop.

The golden rule is that the audience should never be aware that the programme before them is anything but the polished and completely professional product the producer intends. Never pad with second-rate material, never cut raggedly and plan ahead so you never have cause to panic.

SECOND THOUGHTS

After a programme most news organisations hold a debrief to discuss what worked well and not so well, and what can be done to prevent mistakes recurring. Introspection can be useful in small doses, but too much criticism from above can stultify creativity, crush initiative and instil a tendency to produce safe, but predictable material.

FIGURE 12.8
The show has to begin and end exactly on time. So the timing of every item is checked at every stage of the programme. Credit: Andrew Boyd.

THE HEADLINES

- What makes a story, a story? Elements such as its significance, impact, human interest, topicality, locality, immediacy and whether you have variety and actuality. But every mix of stories is different from hour-to-hour and day-to-day: remove two stories from a list of ten and those that remain may not stay in the same order in a programme.

- Most stories are about people 'like us' or will affect us.

- Don't simply broadcast from your ivory tower and expect people to turn on. You have to use every trick to seduce them: your audio and video, your turn of phrase, the story selection and order, the hosts, theme tune, presentation style . . .

- There should be a variety of items with different paces, but without being jarring. Promote what is coming up, without giving the impression that the best material is always 'out of reach'. Lead your audience through the programme with phrases such as 'back home' or 'still with crime' . . .

QUESTIONS FOR YOU

1. If you have access to a rip and read service take ten stories from the printer and select seven to make up a bulletin. (If you cannot get at any rip and read, cut the stories from a newspaper.) Then discuss how you chose the three to drop. If the seven remaining stories are too long for broadcast or are written in a newspaper style, rewrite them for broadcast to a maximum of sixty words each. Then working purely on instinct, rank those stories in order to compile a bulletin. If you are in a class, switch your stories with those of a classmate and compare running orders. Now discuss your similarities and differences and see if you can agree an order between you.

2. Now listen to a five-minute radio bulletin and assess the running order. In what order would *you* have run the items and why?

OTHER RESOURCES

- See one of the daily running orders for the BBC Radio 4 *Today* news programme, here: http://bit.ly/BJR4Today.

- What's it like to work on Radio 4's flagship news programme, *Today*? http://bit.ly/BJTodayProd.

- *TV News Story Segmentation based on Semantic Coherence and Content Similarity:* http://bit.ly/BJSegmentation.

- A satirical look at how to put together a TV news feature (strong language): http://bit.ly/BJBrooker; and another on producing a financial report (scroll to 11:40): http://bit.ly/BJBrooker2.

TUTOR NOTES

Set up a half-hour news programme from scratch. Choose a target audience (family, young people, business people, community cross-section, etc.) and consider the kind of programme you want to produce. Students can think about the contents, pace, length of items and programme feel and draw up a brief setting out your plans.

Using the rip-and-read or copy from newspapers, find enough ideas for stories to fill your programme. Remember that length is a crucial factor. Decide the duration of your reports, then assemble those stories into a running order.

Students can write the cues to the stories in a style that is appropriate to the programme you have in mind and decide whether their writing should be terse and emphatic, in a hard news style, or chatty and relaxed, to suit a more discursive feature style.

Think about the overall balance of the programme. Does it have a good blend of light and shade, serious and offbeat? Should you be running special interest items such as sport? Are the stories positioned to hold interest throughout? Is the first half overloaded with heavyweight items?

Now work on the headlines and linking. Students should set it up properly with headlines at the start and a summary at the end; perhaps use full-length headlines or short teasers. Does the programme have a commercial break? If so some pre-comms need to be written. If not, they need to produce a menu in the middle saying what is coming up. Revise the cues where necessary to provide better links between stories. Consider whether back announcements would be beneficial.

In a class situation, groups can discuss their work with another group when they have finished and swap ideas and criticisms.

Why did the world focus on the January 2015 Paris terror attacks, which left 17 dead, but pay little attention to a Boko Haram assault that may have left as many as 2,000 civilians dead in the north-eastern state of Borno? Lead a class discussion on what makes one news story more newsworthy than another. Here are some resources you may wish to use: http://bit.ly/BJHebdo, http://bit.ly/BJGirl, http://bit.ly/BJCleveland.

The website of the Channel 4 (UK) Newsday with schools has some interesting resources: http://bit.ly/BJC4Newsday and http://bit.ly/BJC4Newsday2 (including dozens of worksheets for tutors, although they do date from 2005), as does the site School Video News: http://bit.ly/BJSVN.

CHAPTER 13

News Anchors and Presenters

> Unattractive broadcasters don't make it as newsreaders. There is still an element of the beauty parade about it.
>
> Conor Dignam, editor of industry newspaper *Broadcast*

Audience loyalty is important. Even where rival news programmes are broadcast at the same time and there is little to choose between their coverage, sections of the audience will have their favourite and will probably stick with it. They might like the style, pace and rhythm of the programme, or the way the sport, traffic and weather are put over. Or it could be the special features that match their own interests, such as fishing or business news. It might be that one programme offers more audience participation – phone-ins, or discussions. Or the audience may simply feel more comfortable with the presenters. Meanwhile, the rival station could pick up viewers for precisely the opposite reason – the audience preferring their more formal, authoritative style.

To a family at home, the presenters are like friends or acquaintances that join them in their front room for half an hour or more each day – longer perhaps than most real friends. Small wonder the choice of presenters is viewed with such importance.

THE TALENT

In showbusiness, actors and performers are known as the 'talent' – a label that has been transferred to the newsreaders and anchors of TV and radio stations.

Despite the hard work of the reporters, producers and other members of the news team, a station's reputation will stand or fall on the performance of these few front line people. A good anchor can boost a station's ratings while a bad one will send them crashing. Little wonder the top ones attract top salaries, and the headhunters are always out looking for the most talented and charismatic newscasters.

Presentation styles differ between general programming and news. The more a programme aims to entertain, the warmer, friendlier and more relaxed its style will usually be, while news presenters tend to adopt a tone that is serious and more formal, in keeping with the weightier material of a bulletin.

Despite convention, the two approaches are moving closer together. Broadcast news is gradually becoming more personal and newsreaders more approachable and friendly.

Viewers look for knowledge, believability and professionalism in their ideal presenter.
OFCOM Report 2002

The term 'anchorman' originated in America with Walter Cronkite. In the UK 'newsreader' or 'newscaster' is preferred, showing something of the difference in presentation style either side of the Atlantic – styles which are emulated around the world.

Put simply, British newsreaders are seen as serious and slightly remote authority figures who would never allow their personalities to colour a news story, while US anchors are serious but friendly authority figures who comment on as well as present the news.

The term 'anchor' suggests personal strength and authority, as though the bearer of that title, through a combination of experience, personality and charisma, is holding the programme together and somehow grounding it in reality. 'Newsreader' has fewer personal connotations. The focus is off the individual and on to the news.

QUALITIES OF A NEWSCASTER

On Radio 4 what we try to do is make sure that the professional voices . . . the announcers and the newsreaders . . . above all else speak with informed authority, and that means they must have credibility as far as the listener's concerned.
Jim Black, Presentation Editor, BBC Radio 4

The ideal qualities for a newscaster or anchor have been variously listed as:

- Authority
- Personality
- Credibility
- Professionalism
- Clarity
- Good voice
- Warmth
- Good looks.

The degree of warmth and personality will depend on how far station style has moved towards the 'friendly' approach.

In double-headed presentation, newsreaders or anchors take it in turn to introduce the stories. Many programme makers believe a good combination is to put male and female presenters together.

> Some time ago, it shifted from the emphasis on male anchors to a news team consisting of an older, distinguished-looking man and a younger, attractive woman, creating a sense of family, with the sports and weather reporters being the 'playful kids'.
>
> Lance Strate, Professor of Communication and Media Studies,
> Fordham University, New York, *International Business Times* 2012

MORE THAN JUST A NEWSREADER . . .

> If it's done well it looks very simple. If it's done badly everyone can tell.
>
> Michael Cole, former BBC correspondent

A TV news presenter is usually more than just a pretty face, and the popular misconception that an anchor simply walks into the studio ten minutes before a programme, picks up a script and reads it into a camera could not be further from the truth.

TV newsreaders will usually be seasoned journalists, who have graduated from newspapers and radio and had their baptism of fire as a TV reporter. Their move to presentation will usually have been as much for their proven news sense as for their on-screen presence.

Like most journalists, newsreaders are expected to be on top of the day's events and understand their background so live interviews on current issues will pose no problem. As the day progresses newsreaders follow the material as it comes in and may offer their own suggestions for coverage. Where stations run several news programmes a day, newsreaders work with teams to update their show and help establish its own clear identity. Part of that process will involve rewriting stories to suit their individual style.

In radio, what scores is a clear voice that conveys authority. Radio news presenters can have a variety of different tasks, depending on the size and location of the station. In smaller outfits in Australia and the US, radio news supplied by an agency is often read by music presenters, who have to undergo an instant personality change from purveyor of pumped-up ten-second links, to confident, well-informed bearer of tidings of significance. To cap that, they may have to act as an engineer or technical assistant.

Some bigger stations hire presenters simply for their news reading abilities; others look for journalists who read well on air and can double as roving reporters after their show is over.

Most radio stations expect their news presenters to be able to rewrite agency copy and more besides. British radio usually insists that broadcasters are experienced journalists who can turn their hands to a variety of tasks, including live interviews. In the words of Jenni Murray, presenter of BBC Radio 4's *Woman's Hour*: 'You're not a broadcaster if you don't write your own words.'

FIGURE 13.1

FIGURE 13.2
What the camera sees of the presenters, and what the presenters see of the cameras.
Credit: John Kessler and Barbara Rodgers, CBS 5 San Francisco – courtesy Stephanie John.

PROFESSIONALISM

> Authority isn't a tone of voice that you can copy. It isn't sounding loud or deep or fast or ponderous. Authority is *knowing what you are talking about,* and having the confidence to explain it to the viewer or listener.
>
> Jenni Mills, broadcast voice trainer and author of *The Broadcast Voice* (Focal Press)

Credibility and authority – qualities every newsreader needs – are derived largely from personal confidence. That the newsreader knows what he or she is talking about should never be in question. Consistent credibility and a flawless delivery are minimum requirements for a person whose performance has such a direct bearing on programme ratings – and profits.

FIGURE 13.3

FIGURE 13.4
What the radio presenter sees of the production gallery, and what the producers see of the studio.

Professionalism comes from having a cool head and plenty of experience. But it means more than remaining unruffled.

Professionals hang up their personal life with their coat when they arrive for work and only take it up again when their work is over and they head for home. Along with their troubles, professionals hang up their bias, their background, their politics and their prejudices.

No one can be truly free from bias, but a professional has a duty to see his work is as free from prejudice as is humanly possible. This can only be done by recognizing where personal preferences, opinions and prejudices lie and compensating for them by being scrupulously fair to the opposite viewpoints whenever they appear in the news.

Radio newsreaders have to purge any trace of bias from the voice. The TV newsreader's task is more difficult: the face, which could betray an opinion at the speed of thought, must remain objective throughout.

VOICE

Adverts for jobs in radio frequently call for a newsreader with a 'good microphone voice'. This *usually* means a voice that is reasonably clear, crisp and resonant and free from obvious impediments. Voices that would not *usually* fit the description are those that are piping, reedy, nasal, sibilant, indistinct or very young sounding.

Minor speech impediments such as weak 'Rrs', or 'THs' that become 'Vs' could be barriers to an otherwise promising career. Professional voice training may sort these problems out, and voices that are thick and nasal can be improved by treatment to the adenoids. With effort, voices can often be lowered to give a greater impression of authority, although in the long run voices tend to sound richer and wiser as their owners get older.

Look at the failure of Katie Couric as a network news anchor. Being 'perky' is fine for a morning show that mixes news and entertainment, and perhaps for a special correspondent, but she lacked the credibility and gravitas we look for in an anchor, and it is important to understand that credibility and gravitas are dramatic qualities, relating to presentation of oneself on the audio-visual medium, a performance attribute that again brings us back to looks and personality, with the need to fit into a certain character type or role . . . Broadcasters favor the baritone to convey seriousness for anchors, reporters, and analysts . . . what counts as 'diversity' on television is not the sound, but the look, because television is a visual medium. And given a visual bias, television favors a diverse set of attractive faces to gain the attention of its audience. There is an interesting subtle message here, though, that there may be differences in the way we look, but that acoustically we are all Americans.

Lance Strate, Professor of Communication and Media Studies,
Fordham University, New York, *International Business Times* 2012

Newsreaders with distinctive accents that are not local to a station might find it difficult to persuade a news editor to take them, on the grounds that their out-of-town intonations might not find favour with a local audience. For a national station, managers might prefer to adopt a 'standard' accent.

Another essential quality in a newsreader is the ability to *sightread*. For some people, the seemingly simple task of reading out loud can prove impossible. Not everyone has the ability to read ahead, which is essential for a smooth delivery, and for them sightreading can mean a staccato stumbling from word to word, losing the flow and sense of the item. It can trouble people who are dyslexic or have to read in a foreign language. Some may have this problem without even realizing, as few people are frequently called on to read out loud.

FIGURE 13.5
Presenting at Free Radio in the UK. Credit Kris Askey – Free Radio/Orion Media.

LOOKS, AGE, GENDER, RACE AND DISABILITY

We have discussed charisma, authority and the voices of those who broadcast; a final quality that may be considered by those hiring staff for television may be looks. People who appear on television tend to be attractive to viewers, and if not attractive, have a distinctive appearance that viewers find appealing in some way. That is more than being well groomed and dressed smartly, it is often (rightly or wrongly) to do with their face, skin and body shape.

Employers will say that looking good is simply an added requirement of the job after other minimum requirements are met. But where double-headed shows are fronted by an older man and a younger woman, (perceived) good looks do put added pressure on women wanting to get on air, or to continue their career past a certain age.

In January 2015, a House of Lords committee report in the UK found a bias against older women in media still existed. Part of its conclusion was because the nature of shifts in a newsroom and it urged broadcasters to offer flexible hours and in-house crèches.

There are simply not enough women in news and current affairs broadcasting. Although on the surface it appears that women are well represented, the facts tell a different story. We heard, for example, that men interviewed as experts outnumber women 4 to 1 on radio and TV.

Despite the fact that women make up just over half the population, they are underrepresented, both as staff and as experts, in news and current affairs broadcasting. And although we recognise the fact that the nature of the sector means that there are additional barriers to women – for example, the fast-paced nature of news which can mean anti-social hours, and freelance work that can make it harder for women with caring responsibilities – the situation is simply not good enough. The fact that news has such a wide-reaching audience means that a special effort must be made by broadcasters – public service broadcasters in particular and especially the BBC because of its special status and its dominance as a provider of news and current affairs. We were also concerned about the evidence we heard suggesting that discrimination against women, particularly older women, still exists in the industry.

We found that there isn't enough data on the representation of women in the sector to fully understand the extent of the problem. We noted, for example, that the majority of journalism students are women, and yet there are so few of them in news and current affairs broadcasting sector. We need a robust, extensive body of data in order to figure out what needs to be done to address the problem.
Lord Best, Chairman of the Committee (http://bit.ly/BJ_LordBest)

Gender figures are hard to come by but the report quoted statistics given by ITV News and Channel 4 News producer ITN that showed that 11 per cent of its female workforce was aged over 50, compared with 26.5 per cent of the total male workforce. And the BBC said that

> nearly half of the BBC's news and current affairs workforce is female with more than a third in leadership positions. While the issues and evidence in the report are based on historical cases, we are always looking at what more we can do and are committed to making further progress.

A 'self-selecting' survey by the NUJ (National Union of Journalists) for the Committee also found examples of an old-boys' network or 'blokeish' atmosphere in newsrooms. Sports journalism was one area particularly identified as a difficult area for women to be taken seriously.

I've been told that I was sent to jobs because I'm attractive (and the people I'm interviewing were told I'm attractive), but then I was told not to go for a new job because emotionally I'm a bit weak.

Women are not allowed to age and are expected to be more than averagely attractive and well presented. The same is not true of men. I have been asked my age, told to spend more of my own money on haircuts or clothes. As an intelligent woman I find it insulting; there is a difference between meeting acceptable professional standards of dress and appearance and being judged by a significantly more demanding set of criteria than men.

nuj.org.uk

Not all responses were negative. One respondent said: 'There are lots of women in broadcasting. The medium can be ageist but, by and large, there's no barrier if you're good.'

In June 2014 the BBC announced that

One in seven BBC presenters and actors is to be black, Asian or minority ethnic within the next three years . . . Lord Hall, the director-general, has promised 15 per cent of on-air BBC staff will be black, Asian or minority ethnic (BAME) by 2017, along with one in ten managers.

(Source: http://bit.ly/BJ_BAME)

Less than a year later in the US, *The Washington Post* stated 'The concept is so unusual as to be almost radical: The leading late TV newscast on the leading news station in Washington will be anchored by two white people'.

The number of presenters of different ages, genders and from diverse heritage backgrounds is gradually creeping up in many parts of the world (the story from Washington is perhaps unusual). But we have yet to see very many disabled presenters: the BBC's Frank Gardner is one (he was shot while war reporting: http://bit.ly/BJ_Gardner), and away from news there is also British TV presenter Warwick Davies (who has a form of dwarfism: http://bit.ly/BJ_Davies).

Managers see the importance of having a representation on screen of the community to which they are broadcasting. For public broadcasters, this is equally as important:

> We believe that having a workforce that looks like Britain looks – on and off screen – is a good thing. The BBC is funded by everyone who pays the licence fee and so we have a duty to reflect all our audiences. The better we can represent the whole of the UK, the more relevant our programmes will be.
>
> Joe Goodwin, BBC, quoted at http://bit.ly/BJ_Disabled

THE HEADLINES

- The ideal qualities for a newscaster or anchor have been variously listed as: Authority, Personality, Credibility, Professionalism, Clarity, Good Voice, Warmth, Good Looks.

- *Authority is* knowing what you are talking about, *and having the confidence to explain it to the viewer or listener.*

QUESTIONS FOR YOU

1. We said earlier 'head-hunters are always out looking for the most talented and charismatic newscasters.' What do you think makes a 'charismatic' news presenter? Why should news presenters in particular be careful about the amount of charisma they have?
2. Make a study of three different newsreaders. Award marks out of ten for *authority, credibility, clarity, warmth, personality, professionalism, good voice*, and for TV, *good looks*. Add the scores and see which newsreader comes top in your estimation. Was

this the newsreader you preferred anyway? Do your scores agree with those of your fellow students? Discuss any differences. What do *you* think are the most important qualities in a newsreader? Why?

3. How would you define *professionalism*, and how would you know if it was missing?

4. Obviously numbers of people from different backgrounds appearing on TV is important, but is it less important on radio if you can't immediately tell someone's age, ethnicity or disability? Discuss.

OTHER RESOURCES

- 'How is it possible that the inane institution of the anchorman has endured for more than 60 years?' – article in *The New Yorker*: http://bit.ly/BJAnchor.

- Women in broadcasting:

  - There are several key sites through which more women are encouraged to get into broadcasting: www.soundwomen.co.uk/, Global Women In News (http://bit.ly/BJAriel) and IWMF (www.iwmf.org/).

  - The International Women's Media Foundation found (2015) that 73 per cent of the top management jobs are occupied by men, compared to 27 per cent occupied by women. Among the ranks of reporters, men hold nearly two-thirds of the jobs, compared to 36 per cent held by women. However, among senior professionals, women are nearing parity with 41 per cent of the news gathering and editing: http://bit.ly/BJIWMFReport.

  - UK Parliamentary reports on 'Women in news and current affairs broadcasting': http://bit.ly/BJParly1, http://bit.ly/BJParly2, http://bit.ly/BJParly3, http://bit.ly/BJParly4.

  - A view of the role of women in the newsroom: http://bit.ly/BJNewsroom.

  - A BBC Radio programme exploring the way women's voices have shaped the sound of British radio: http://bit.ly/BJWVoices.

- In December 2013 Channel 4 TV in the UK launched *Alternative Voices* which saw five people with communication difficulties join the channel's continuity team for ten days to introduce some of its biggest peak time shows. The continuity announcers taking part represent an estimated 2.5 million people in the UK living with communication disorders. Among them were a recovering stammerer, a woman with cerebral palsy, a deaf man and two people with Tourettes: http://bit.ly/BJC4Voices.

- A satirical view of the difference between UK and US news anchors (some strong language): http://bit.ly/BJBrooker3.

■ Speech Word Count: a tool that converts your text in reading time. www.speechwordcount.com/.

TUTOR NOTES

Lead class discussions on the following issues.

Do you think newsreaders should be more or less formal in their styles? How would this affect the credibility of their presentation? What do you think gives a newsreader his/her authority? What effect do you think would be the effect on the ratings of 'middle-aged, craggy-faced' woman newsreaders?

Do you prefer single headed or double headed presentation? Why?

CHAPTER 14

'On Air!'

> Television is an invention that permits you to be entertained in your living room by people you wouldn't have in your home.
>
> David Frost, British broadcast journalist 1939–2013

PERFORMANCE

Newsreading is the point where the business of information and the game of show-business meet. But even among the 'heavy' set of newsreaders most outwardly disdainful of TV's gloss and glamour, the act of being oracle to perhaps millions of viewers will always have something of the ego trip about it . . . however hard they may try to deny it.

TV presenters have to live with fame, but while being a public figure might massage the ego when the public is on your side, that same fickle audience will be as quick to complain as they are to compliment, not only if your performance begins to falter, but if they take offence at the cut of your suit or your hair.

Similarly, presenters' mannerisms can sometimes draw more attention than the stories they are reading. Leaning back or forward, swaying from side to side, scratching the nose, licking the lips, blinking hard or waving the hands about are all tics which the budding anchor may have to iron out by patient practice in front of a mirror, or better still, a video camera, before risking his or her reputation before an audience.

PRESENCE

In the hot seat of the TV studio, with flooding adrenalin and a wildly beating heart, the newsreader might find it difficult to remember that real people are sitting the other side of the screen anxious to hear what he or she has to say.

FIGURE 14.1
Preparing to go live with the lunchtime news. Note the autocue, script and laptop – belt and braces.
Credit: Katherine Adams/BBC.

The camera must cease to be a single staring eye set in a metal face, and become an acquaintance or friend. You would not talk *at* a friend, so you should not talk *at* a camera. Speak *to* it. It *likes* you. It is on your side. But what you say and the way you say it will need charisma and the force of confidence to carry through the lens to the viewer the other side. This is the x-factor that marks out a good newsreader. It is called *presence*.

> Anyone can be trained to read an autocue, but to present a news bulletin you have to know what you're talking about.
>
> Nigel Charters, Managing Editor of BBC TV News

Adrenalin can be a problem – either way. While the first-time presenter might have to fight to bring it under control, the older stager might have to fight to keep it going. One radio newsreader used to deliberately wait until the last moment before hurrying into the studio. Often the show's presenter would have fired the seven-second signature tune into the bulletin before the newsreader even sat down. All this was to keep the adrenalin going. Not recommended. Brinkmanship can, and does, lead to disasters on air. But a steady stream of adrenalin, always under control, could be the mystery ingredient behind that all-important and indefinable commodity – presence.

GETTING THROUGH TO THE AUDIENCE – RAPPORT

One of the simplest tricks to help you sound natural on air is to remind yourself that you are talking to someone: one person at a time. Make it a real person, someone you know and feel comfortable with, and whose intelligence you respect. Think of them as sitting across the desk from you, and tell the story to them.

Jenni Mills, broadcast voice trainer, author of *The Broadcast Voice* (Focal Press)

BBC trainees are told:

Information + Presentation = Communication

Successful communication is largely a matter of presentation, and that depends on the way the copy is written, and the way it is read. Good newsreaders are ones who establish rapport with their audience.

Such rapport defies satisfactory definition. It is a kind of chemistry that exists between newsreaders and their audience. Where it is present, both presenter and audience are satisfied. Where it is absent, the information seems to fall short or fail to connect, and the presenter, cut off behind a barrier of electronic hardware, will usually be aware of the fact.

Trainee newsreaders are encouraged to 'bring the script to life,' to 'lift the words off the paper,' to 'project their personalities,' to 'establish a presence' or to be 'up-front'. What's needed is a kind of focused energy, a summoning up of your vitality and the projection of that energy towards your audience.

But rapport begins with never regarding a mass audience as simply that. Each listener is an individual who has invited you into his or her home. You are a guest, an acquaintance or even a friend, and you have been welcomed in because you have a story to tell. Newsreaders, particularly in radio, can easily forget about the audience. Cocooned within the four walls of the studio, they can begin to sound as though they are talking to themselves. They are going through the motions, their concentration is elsewhere and their newsreading will begin to sound stilted, singsong and insincere.

The solution to strident anonymity or mumbling into the microphone is to remember that you are not reeling off information or reading from a script, but *telling* someone a story.

Radio newsreaders have an added disadvantage. In normal conversation, the person you are talking to will be able to see your face. Your expressions will reflect your story. If it is sad, you will look sad, if it is happy, you will smile. Your hands may do the talking for you, gesticulating and adding emphasis. You may have a tendency to mumble but people will make up with their eyes what is missed by their ears by watching your lips.

Now imagine you are talking to someone who cannot see your lips, your eyes or your hands. That vital part of your communication has gone. This is how it is in radio. This handicap is overcome by working to put into your voice all the expression that would normally go into your face and hands. A word of warning – overdo the intonation and you will sound as though you are talking to a child, and talking down to the audience is something no newsreader will get away with for long.

Another handicap for the radio newsreader in particular is the unassuming nature of most radio sets. Most people regard radio as a background activity. The news trickles out of a tiny speaker from a tinny radio in the kitchen while the audience is washing up. So to encourage attention for your news bulletin you have to reach out across the room with an energy and a tone, which cuts across the distractions.

What helps is that most radio bulletins begin with a news jingle. But to reach out and grab your audience you should picture your single listener some distance from you, summon your energy and focus it on that point.

KNOW YOUR MATERIAL

Confidence comes from experience, from being in command of the bulletin and thoroughly familiar with the material. An inexperienced newsreader should spend as much time as possible reading and re-reading the stories *aloud* so when they go on air they are on familiar ground. This will also highlight phrases which clash and jar, mistakes, unfamiliar names that need practice, poor punctuation and sentences that are impossibly long. All these problems are easily missed by the eye, but are likely to be picked up by the voice. Many newsreaders rewrite their stories extensively to make certain the style suits their voice – the best way to be familiar with a story is to write it yourself.

This may sound like stating the obvious, but make sure you completely understand the story you are reading. If you don't, chances are no one listening to you will either. So don't try to bluff it!
Linda Wray, newsreader, BBC Northern Ireland

AD-LIBS

Few professionals rely on ad-libs to see them through a programme. Back-announcements, comments and seemingly casual links are usually scripted. When the programme is running against the clock, a live guest is settling down in the studio to be interviewed any moment *and* there is a constant stream of chatter in your ear from the control room, even the snappiest quips and witticisms thought up before the show tend to be driven from your mind. The best way to avoid embarrassment is to script *everything* barring the timechecks, and even these should be handled with care.

'It's thirteen minutes to two' is the sort of phrase a presenter can take for granted, but try to glance up at a clock yourself and try to give an immediate and accurate timecheck and you will see how difficult it can be to get right. From the half past onwards, the timecheck can involve a little mental arithmetic.

Always engage your brain before putting your mouth into gear – *think before you speak*.

After newsreaders have rehearsed the bulletin, they should try to insist on a few minutes peace and quiet before the programme to read it through again, though in TV this can be a vain hope.

In the end, performance is everything. What would you prefer to hear – a newsreader stumbling through an unrehearsed bulletin bursting with up-to-the-minute stories and failing to make sense of it, or a smoothly polished delivery of material that may be as much as 10 minutes old but makes complete sense?

FIGURE 14.2
Preparing to go live with the radio news. Credit: Katherine Adams/BBC.

THE GATE

Some newsrooms operate a 'gate' to give readers a chance to compose themselves. This is a bar on new copy being handed to the newsreader later than five or ten minutes before a bulletin. Old hands might scoff at this – they can pick up a pile of scripts and deliver them sight unseen without batting an eyelid, but for the less experienced reader, a gate can make the difference between a smooth performance and wishing the studio floor would open up and swallow you.

MAKING A SWIFT RECOVERY

> Before opening mouth, engage brain. Make sure you understand what you are about to read. If you don't understand it, how can you expect that the listeners or viewers will?
> Jenni Mills, broadcast voice trainer, author of *The Broadcast Voice* (Focal Press)

Be honest with the audience and try not to cover up obvious mistakes. Today's audience is quite sophisticated about how video works, and that technical aspects can go awry, and will be understanding if they are not misled.

At the same time, it is also the case that given how well equipped and familiar news people are with the demands of the job, there really should not be flaws in most news programmes. A high level of professionalism is really the expectation of everyone no matter if they are in front of the camera or behind the scenes.

But when things do go wrong, the anchor or newsreader is expected to stay cool and professional. Whatever the ferment beneath the surface, no cracks must appear in the calm exterior. (The coolest recovery on record was probably that of a wartime BBC announcer who pressed on with his script after a bomb fell on Broadcasting House.) The answer is to immediately and completely dismiss the mistake from your mind and focus your total concentration on the rest of the bulletin.

Most fluffs occur when newsreaders are expecting trouble, like a difficult foreign name, or when they have already fluffed and their mind is side-tracked. The irony is that the difficult name is usually pronounced flawlessly, while the reader stumbles over the simple words before and behind it in the sentence.

Perhaps it is this striving for perfection and quality for merciless self-criticism that turns a broadcaster into a top professional.

The art of the accomplished recovery is to prepare for every contingency.

The worst mistake any presenter can make is to swear on air – *don't even think it*; otherwise you will probably say it.

The commonest problem is the recorded report that fails to appear. The introduction has been read, the presenter is waiting, and – nothing. Next to swearing, the broadcaster's second deadliest sin is *dead air*. Silent airspace is worst on radio. On TV, viewers can watch the embarrassed expression on the presenter's face.

If an item fails to appear the radio presenter should apologise and move smartly on to the next. In TV, presenters will usually be directed what to do by the control room. Up to three seconds of silence is the most that should pass before the newsreader cuts in.

Police are finding it difficult to come up with a solution to the murders . . . the commissioner says the victims are unwilling to co-operate.

US Radio

Well, the blaze is still fierce in many places, and as a result of this fire, two factories have been gutted and one homily left famless.

Australian Radio

Following the warning by the Basque Separatist organisation ETA that it's preparing a bombing campaign in Spanish holiday resorts, British terrorists have been warned to keep on their guard . . . I'm sorry (chuckle) that should be British tourists . . .

UK Radio

The . . . company is recalling a total of 14,000 cans of suspect salmon and fish cutlets. It's believed they're contaminated by poisonous orgasms.

Australian Radio

The President is alive and well and kicking tonight, one day after the assassination attempt, just two and a half months into his pregnancy . . .

US TV

And now here's the latest on the Middle East crisis . . . crisis . . . Lesbian forces today attacked Israel. I beg your pardon, that should be Lesbanese . . . Lebanese. (Laughter)

Anon.

Confusing the audience with technical jargon can compound the problem, like: 'I'm sorry, but that insert seems to have gone down.' Or, 'We don't seem to have that package.' Practise what you are going to say when something goes wrong until it becomes almost a reflex action.

When that report does eventually arrive, the audience will have forgotten what it is about and the presenter should re-introduce it by re-reading or paraphrasing the cue.

Where you stumble over a word or phrase, you should judge quickly whether to repeat it. If the sense of the item has been lost, by saying, for instance, 'Beecham pleaded guilty to the murder', when he pleaded not guilty, then the sentence should be repeated. Avoid the cliché, 'I'm sorry, I'll read that again'– 'I'm sorry' will do. If the mistake is a minor one, let it go. Chances are the audience will quickly forget it, whereas drawing attention to it with an apology might only make it worse.

CORPSING

There are few threats greater to a newsreader's credibility than that of corpsing on air. Corpsing is not a literal occurrence but it can feel pretty much the same. It means to dry up, grind to a halt or, worse, burst out laughing.

These are signs of nervousness and panic. Such laughter is seldom sparked off by genuine humour; it is the psyche's safety valve blowing to release a build up of tension. Anything incongruous or slightly amusing can trigger it off.

The audience doesn't always see the joke, especially when the laughter erupts through a serious or tragic news item. Where professional self-control is in danger of collapsing, the realisation that untimely laughter can bring an equally untimely end to a career, and that a substantial part of the audience may write you off as an idiot unless you pull yourself together, can often have the same salutary effect as a swift sousing with a bucket of icy water.

Self-inflicted pain is a reasonable second line defence. Some presenters bring their mirth under control by resorting to personal torture, such as digging their nails into the palms of their hands or grinding the toes of one foot with the heel of the other. A less painful way to prevent corpsing is to not permit yourself to be panicked and pressurised in the first place.

> Finally, the weather forecast. Many areas will be dry and warm with some sunshine . . . It actually says 'shoeshine' on my script, so with any luck, you might get a nice light tan.
>
> BBC Radio

RELAXATION

The key to the confidence that marks out the top-flight professional is the ability to be in command, and at the same time relaxed. This can be a tall order under deadline pressure and the spotlights of the studio.

Tension can manifest itself in a number of ways, especially in the novice news-reader. The muscles of your neck and throat can tighten to strangle the voice and put it up an octave. Your reading can also speed up. Try stretching the shoulders and arms like a cat before relaxing and breathing deeply. This should reduce this tension. (Note: Do this before you go on air!)

Another problem is that beginners can sometimes – literally – dry up. Tension removes the moisture in the throat and mouth and it can become impossible to articulate. Relaxation helps and a glass of water – sipped slowly to prevent the splutters – will usually be sufficient to moisten the lips, mouth and throat.

A word of warning – drink nothing containing sugar or milk. Hot, sweet coffee is out. Milk and sugar clog the palate and gum up the mouth. Alcohol should be avoided for obvioush reashonsh. The same goes for eating food just before going on air. A bolted sandwich before a bulletin can undermine the coolest demeanour. Stray particles of bread and peanut-butter lodged in the molars are a sure way of turning on the waterworks and leaving the newscaster drooling with excess saliva – and there is always the risk of going into the bulletin with a bout of hiccups.

Tiredness can also ruin otherwise good newsreading. Broadcasters often work shifts and have to cope with irregular sleep patterns and, for early birds, semi-permanent fatigue. Weariness can drag down the muscles of the face, put a sigh in the voice and extinguish any sparkle. Gallons of black coffee – without sugar – may be one answer, limbering up the face by vigorously contorting the lips, cheeks and mouth may be another. But don't let anyone catch you doing that on camera, unless you want to end up on the annual collection of out-takes.

FIGURE 14.3
Nine minutes to air and still an empty chair in this radio news studio . . .

THE HEADLINES

- Information + Presentation = Communication

- Always engage your brain before putting your mouth into gear – *think before you speak.*

- To all intents and purposes, always treat any microphone as 'live'.

QUESTIONS FOR YOU

1. Think back to your study of different newsreaders in the previous chapter. Which had the most presence? Is this the one who scored highest on your list? How do *you* define presence?

How successful were those newsreaders in establishing rapport with their audience? Do you think rapport is conscious or unconscious? How would *you* go about establishing rapport?

If you are in a class, prepare and read a bulletin out loud and get votes out of ten for *presence* and *rapport*. Ask your colleagues to try to define why these factors were present or absent in your reading.

2. Plan what you would say if (a) a recorded report went down on air; (b) the wrong audio/video was played after your cue; (c) the next item went missing.

Practise some impromptu timechecks throughout the day. Glance up at the clock and immediately say the time out loud. Which is easier, before the hour or after the hour? How long does it take for the time to register accurately once you have glanced at the clock? Remember to always allow yourself that much time before starting to give a timecheck.

3. Practise the relaxation exercises outlined in the chapter and see if they help you. If not, develop your own that will.

OTHER RESOURCES

- Voice and presentation skills on video, including articulation, pace and empathy, here: http://bit.ly/BJVoiceVids.

- Ten of the best laughing fits in British broadcasting history: http://bit.ly/ BJCorpse.

TUTOR NOTES

Consider inviting a visiting lecturer to show your students how to 'lift words from the page' (maybe someone from a professional acting school), or someone to show relaxation and breathing techniques.

CHAPTER 15

News Reading Mechanics

SPEED

The right reading pace is one which is comfortable for the reader, clear to the listener, and which suits the station's style. That could be anywhere between 140 and 220 words per minute. British radio usually favours three words per second, or 180 wpm, which is a natural and pleasing pace. TV can run a little slower.

Three words per second is also a handy formula for timing a script – a 20-second lead becomes 60 words, a 30-second story is 90 words, and so on.

Pace is less important than clarity, and one of the most helpful aids to clear reading is the pause. The pause is a cunning device with many uses. It divides the copy into sense groups and allows time for an important phrase to sink in. It permits a change of style between stories; can be used to indicate the beginning of a quote . . . and it gives the newsreader time to replenish their oxygen supply!

BREATHING

Newsreaders, like swimmers, have to master the art of breath control. Good breathing brings out the richness and flavour of the voice.

First you have to sit correctly to give your lungs and diaphragm as much room as possible. The upper half of the body should be upright or inclined forward, with the back slightly arched. Your legs should not be crossed.

Air to the newsreader is like oil in an engine. Run out of it and you will seize up. The aim is to open the lungs and throat as widely as possible, so breathing should be deep and from the belly instead of the usual shallow breathing from the top of the lungs. Never run into the studio. Breathless readers will find themselves gasping for air or getting dizzy and feeling faint.

Every newsreader has to know that they are performing. It's like being on stage, you mustn't forget that you are entering people's homes and trying to engage millions of people across the country. So don't shout and don't patronise people or they'll be put off. Pause between each news story so it's clear where one ends and another begins and if you stumble don't worry. Tell the news naturally.

Huw Edwards, BBC News presenter

FIGURE 15.1

The radio newsreader's view of the mike, keyboard, autocue and audio playout system.

A newsreader should take a couple of good breaths before starting and another deep breath between each story. You can top up at full stops (periods) and paragraphs, and, faced with a long sentence, can take shallow breaths where the commas should be. If you have time, rewrite the story and break down those sentences; but failing that, you can insert slash marks to indicate where you can safely pause while still making sense of the copy:

> UNICEF has criticised world governments / for waging an undeclared war on women, children and adolescents. / According to the UN Children's Fund, / more than 600 million children are now living in poverty / – more than at the start of the decade. / The world's poorest survive on less than a dollar a day, / and around a quarter of a billion children aged between 5 and 14 / are sent out to work. / Armed conflict has killed or injured 8 million since 1990. / But the biggest child killer in the developing world is not warfare / but AIDS.

Breathing through the mouth permits faster refuelling than through the nose, but beware of snatching your breath. Avoid gasping by opening your mouth wider and taking the air in shallow draughts.

PROJECTION

There are different schools of thought about whether newsreaders should project their voice or talk naturally. In television a conversational tone is more appropriate to the illusion of eye contact with the audience, and projection matters less because television audiences offer more of their undivided attention than do radio listeners.

Radio presenters have to work harder. They should project just enough to cut through distractions and get attention. Overprojected newsreading makes the listener want to back away from the set or turn down the volume. Under normal circumstances there is no need to bark out the story like a war correspondent under crossfire.

If you can picture yourself at one end of an average sized room with a single person at the other whose attention is divided between chores and listening to what you have to say, then your projection will be about right.

The radio newsreader's voice often has to cut through a lot of background noise before reaching the listener, especially if you are being heard on somebody's car radio or in a living room full of hyperactive two-year-olds. Yelling is not the way to make sure every syllable is heard – clear diction is.

All too often newsreaders can be heard running words together, swallowing the ends of words and leaving sentences trailing in mid-air because their attention has already drifted on to the next story. The newsreader's eyes can't move from the page so neither should their mind. There should be a kind of magnetism between your mind and the script if you are to have any feel for the copy and sound sincere about what you are reading.

EMPHASIS

Copy should be read aloud to establish which words should be given extra emphasis. These are usually the key words and descriptions. For example:

> Canada's FISHERMEN are preparing for the BIGGEST EVER SEAL CULL in their country's history. The government has declared OPEN SEASON on HARP Seals. Up to a QUARTER OF A MILLION are to be SHOT and CLUBBED TO DEATH as they BASK in the sun on the ice floes off NEWFOUNDLAND. The QUOTA for the annual HARVEST has just been INCREASED. Now ANY Canadian citizen, not just FISHERMEN, can JOIN IN the seal hunt.

These words can be capitalised, as shown, or underlined. Some readers favour double underlining to highlight different degrees of emphasis.

Shifting the position of the emphasis in a sentence can completely alter its meaning and tone. This can have a dramatic effect on the story:

> HE said their action had made a walkout inevitable.

Stressing the word *he* might suggest there are others who would disagree with this statement.

> He SAID their action had made a walkout inevitable.

Emphasising the word *said* casts doubt on the truth of the statement, implying there are grounds for disbelieving it.

> He said THEIR action had made a walkout inevitable.

The speaker now sounds as though he is pointing a finger in accusation at another group of people.

> He said their action HAD made a walkout inevitable.

This has an intriguing double-meaning. Does *had* suggest the possibility of a walkout was true earlier, but is no longer the case, or is the stress on *had* a rebuttal, as though denying a suggestion that the action would not lead to a walkout? Think about it. The answer would probably become obvious from the context, but it highlights the importance of having a clear understanding of the item before attempting to read it on air.

A common failing of untrained newsreaders is to imagine that due stress and emphasis means banging out every fifth word of a story and ramming the point home by pounding the last word of each sentence. Another increasingly common phenomenon is to stress unimportant words that simply link a sentence together, rather than the words which do the 'heavy lifting' and help explain the story. Read that last sentence out loud, and you should have given slightly more emphasis to the words, here in upper case:

> ANOTHER increasingly COMMON phenomenon is to stress
> UNIMPORTANT words that simply link a sentence together, rather than
> the words which do the 'HEAVY LIFTING' and HELP EXPLAIN the STORY.

But untrained readers can have a 'robotic' presentation style, seemingly stressing words at random:

> Another increasingly common phenomenon is TO stress unimportant
> WORDS that SIMPLY link a sentence together, RATHER than the WORDS
> which DO the 'heavy lifting' and help explain the STORY.

It makes the reader sound foolish, as though they don't understand what they are saying, and is about as elegant as tap-dancing in jackboots. Each sentence must establish its own rhythm without having a false one stamped upon it. Stress exists not to make the copy punchier, but to bring out its meaning. And to get the meaning over to someone else, you have to know it yourself first.

PITCH

As well as having rhythm, the voice also goes up and down. This is called *modulation* or pitch, and some readers who are new at their business or have been doing it for too long can sound as though they are singing the news. The voice goes up and down a lot, but in all the wrong places. You will be familiar with this style from airline cabin crew and those on the tannoy at your local supermarket. Modulation can add interest to the voice and variety to an item, but random modulation coupled with universal stress can make an audience grateful for the commercial break.

Sentences usually begin on an upward note, rise in the middle, and end on a downward note. These are known as uppers and downers. But what happens to the downers when the last word belongs to a question?

Read that sentence to yourself to find out.

These uppers and downers are signposts to the listener. They subconsciously confirm and reinforce the way the sentence is developing and help convey its meaning.

MICROPHONE TECHNIQUE

Next to swearing on air, the important things to avoid with microphones are *popping* and *paper rustle*. Popping occurs when the mouth is too close to the mike and plosive sounds, such as Ps in particular, produce distortion. The radio newsreader can tell this is happening by listening on headphones, and can prevent it by backing away or turning the mike slightly to one side.

Incidentally, the best way to tell your sound levels are set correctly is to always use headphones, and to have them turned up high enough to drown out your normal speaking voice. Anything too loud will cross the threshold of pain and soon have you reaching for the volume control.

Different microphone effects are possible. The closer the mike is to the mouth, the more of the voice's natural resonance it will pick up. Late night radio presenters use the close-mike technique to make their voices sound as sexy and intimate as someone whispering sweet nothings into your ear. Where a voice is naturally lacking in richness, close mike work can sometimes help compensate.

Conversely, standing away from the mike and raising the voice can make it sound as though the presenter is speaking live on location – useful for giving a lift to studio commentary over outdoor scenes or sound effects.

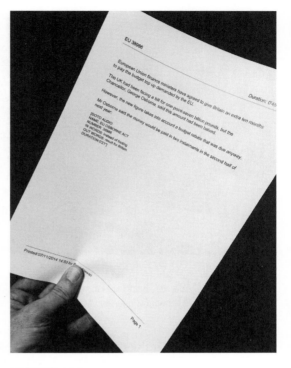

FIGURE 15.2

Preventing paper rustle. If you brace the script between your thumb and fingers the page will be held in tension.

Most directional mikes give their best results about 15 cm from the mouth.

The microphone, being closer to the script than the reader's ears, will pick up every rustle and scrape of the page, unless great care is taken in moving the paper. Use thick paper that does not crinkle, or small pages, which are less prone to bending.

The best way to avoid paper rustle is to carefully lift each sheet, holding it in tension to prevent it bending, and place it to one side. To cut any noise that even this might make, lift the page while it is still being read and place it down *after* you begin reading the next item. The sound of your voice will drown out any paper rustle. This advice, though, is becoming increasingly irrelevant as even radio news presenters read off an autocue screen.

USING THE PROMPTER

Bad spelling and bad grammar can easily confuse the newsreader . . . a comma in the wrong place can even change the meaning of a sentence. Good grammar is not a luxury, it's essential.

Huw Edwards, BBC News presenter

FIGURE 15.3

Half the battle in TV news is being able to read the autocue . . . clearly and confidently. Credit: Stephanie John, Allen Martin, CBS 5 San Francisco.

Most TV stations use devices to project the script on to glass in front of the camera so presenters can give the impression of eye contact with the viewer as they read the news. The intention is to make it appear that they know their material off by heart and are simply telling the story to the audience. What frequently spoils the illusion is the way some newsreaders stare woodenly into the camera, as though trying to make out a spot on the end of the viewer's nose. Worse still is when they screw up their eyes to peer at some mistyped or corrected word on the prompter.

How often do you see junior newsreaders with their faces frozen in a permanent scowl of concentration, eyebrows never moving, as though permanently glued in an ingratiating arch across the forehead? If the camera is the newsreader's best friend, then the prompter has to be seen as the smile on your best friend's face, and responded to as such.

But newsreaders cannot afford to relax too much – they might destroy another of TV's illusions. TV stations often display computer pictures or stills in a box or window to one side of the newsreader. To the viewer the box appears to be behind the reader, but often the reverse is true and readers who are prone to fidget are liable to disappear behind the window.

NOISE, NOISE, NOISE

One blight the TV newsreader has to live with is the constant babble of noise injected directly into the ear through the earpiece, which keeps them in touch with the control room. Into the ear comes not only her countdown but everything said to the camera crews, videotape operators, graphics operators, caption operators, etc. Putting it mildly, it can be a distraction.

BRINGING THE STORY TO LIFE

Once a script has been written and handed to the newsreader it becomes hers alone. The reader must identify with the story and transform it from being mere words on a page. The copy has to be lifted off the paper, carried through the microphone, transported over the airwaves and planted firmly in the listener's imagination. And that is done by *telling* a story.

The test of whether communication has taken place is audience reaction. A new story should produce a response of pleasure or pain. If you were to tell a friend about a family illness, you would expect her to react. If she listened to you with a deadpan expression and turned away unmoved, you would wonder whether she had heard you right.

News should be the same. The audience will respond to you as they would to an actor on stage. As actors strive to give life to their lines, your task is to bring your copy to life. Newsreaders' talents lie in perfectly matching their tone to the story-line. Skilfully done, this makes the story more accessible by signalling its meaning, significance, importance and relevance – the emotions in the voice reflecting in part the emotional response that the story should produce in the hearer. For most experienced newsreaders this process is automatic, but for many new to the business it is a skill that has to be learned.

The skill lies in the subtlety of the storytelling. If newsreaders were painters, they would use watercolours and washes, never lurid oils. Histrionics over the airwaves will result in the listener diving for the off-switch. Only a ham goes over the top and a poor actor fails to do justice to the script. So this is the task of the newsreader – to do justice to the script.

A simple tip – when you are happy, you smile, so when you smile, you sound happy. If a story is light-hearted, then crack your face and smile. But if the news is grave, then the newsreader could do little worse than to sound as though the unfortunate victim has just won the lottery. Hearing 'Four people have died in a pit disaster' read by someone with a broad grin is not only embarrassing, it is insulting. If you want to convey gravity, then frown. If the story is sad, then look sad.

> Take care of the sense and the sounds will take care of themselves.
> The Duchess to Alice in *Alice In Wonderland* by Lewis Carroll

THE HEADLINES

- Don't shout and don't patronise people or they'll be put off. Tell the news naturally.

- Yelling is not the way to make sure every syllable is heard – clear diction is.

- Understand the story to bring it to life. It's called 'communication'.

QUESTIONS FOR YOU

1. Practise sitting correctly to read some copy. Make sure you take plenty of air, but not so much that you have to strain to hold it. Now read the copy into a recorder and hear how you sound. Try different postures to see which gives you the most air and feels the most comfortable.

- Go through that copy again, marking it for breaths and then read it to see if that helps you.

2. Ask someone to time you reading an item of copy that is more than 230 words long. Get them to stop you after exactly a minute and work out your reading speed by counting how many words you have read.
3. Record yourself reading again and practise removing scripts that have been read without making a sound. Also try different amounts of projection to see which sounds best and underline difficult stories for emphasis to see if this helps you.
4. If you have access to a TV studio with a prompter, practise reading to camera. Avoid staring at it and practise animating your features while still keeping a natural expression. (You can download a teleprompter app for your smartphone to help.)

OTHER RESOURCES

- 'Why Did Old-Time Announcers Talk That Way?': http://bit.ly/BJAnnouncers.

- This is called the *Announcer's Test.* It originated at Radio Central New York in the early 1940s as a cold-reading test given to prospective radio talent to demonstrate their speaking ability. The prospect would read the script for clarity, enunciation, diction, tonality and expressiveness. Read sentence 1, then 1 and 2, then 1, 2 and 3 and so on . . . (http://bit.ly/BJRCNY0 or a similar one for those more familiar with classical music (http://bit.ly/BJClassical).

TUTOR NOTES

Copy and distribute to your students this exam, created for radio announcers in New York in 1948: http://bit.ly/BJExam.

PART

Radio

FIGURE 16.1
The studio at the UK's national classical music station, Classic FM. Credit: Ryan Phillips
(www.ryanphillipsphotography.co.uk)

CHAPTER 16

Story Treatment

In July 2003, Microsoft banned Internet chat rooms. This story, as covered in the ITN 5.45 p.m. bulletin, is family-based. It includes issues like the threat of 'grooming', paedophilia, and so on. The same story at 10.45 p.m. has a 'business' treatment – that is, Microsoft quit chat rooms to avoid the predicted stream of expensive legal actions against them.

Robert Beers and Paul Egglestone, quoted on ukjournalism.co.uk

There are many different ways to present a news story for radio from the simple copy story to the full-blown documentary. Television and radio techniques differ because of the use of visuals, but in many respects are similar in the way they package information as news. This chapter explores the different treatments (ways of covering a story) radio gives to news.

What follows is a storyline that represents what *could* happen at a mythical radio station when a big news event happens. In practice of course it's unlikely that a station would follow every single treatment that is outlined below. That's because much depends on the station's 'format' (the overall content and style of a station such as the type and amount of music and/or speech it produces; see: http://bit.ly/BJ_Format) and target demographic (such as age, sex, occupation and income profile; see: http://bit.ly/BJ_Demo), as well as other issues such as budget, equipment and staff availability.

It is a quarter past two on a quiet summer afternoon in Guildford, Surrey, England. The only news worth reporting is that it is hot. The phone rings. Three hands grab for it but only the news editor's practised reaction connects. Relief is at hand. News has broken. News editor Ian Hinds is grilling the caller with all the zeal of the Spanish Inquisition:

When did this happen? Just now? How many dead!? Are you sure?
Where . . .? Outside Guildford station!!?

Fuelled by adrenalin, the news machine leaps into life. A story that develops quickly with new information coming in is known as *breaking news*, or a *running story*. Below is what may happen at a fictitious radio station covering a train crash.

BREAKING NEWS (BULLETIN US)

News editor Ian Hinds lingers on the phone for only as long as it takes to check the details with the police media officer on the phone, then bashes out a few lines on his keyboard. Another reporter is putting in calls to the fire service, while a third is grabbing a recorder and the keys to the radio car.

The story is flashed to 'wires', the internal message system, which will alert the main London newsroom as well as other stations around the country. This will cause an initial wave of calls from other reporters at 'network' wanting to know more about what's happened, but it may also lead to additional staff being deployed to the scene to help in the newsgathering process.

Staff are requisitioned from other parts of the building to help in making and taking calls. One or more is put with the producer of the on-air programme to deal with the influx of calls from concerned listeners. Other producers, presenters and managers put in calls to check the information and gather new facts.

Hinds strides across to the studio, moving quickly, but not so fast as to become breathless, and glancing to check the on-air light is off, he opens the soundproof double doors, informs the presenter he has breaking news (the term 'newsflash' is something of an over-used cliché) and parks himself in the chair in front of the guest microphone.

As soon as Hinds is in place, the presenter Jenny James dips the music she is playing, and says, 'And now over to our news editor Ian Hinds with some breaking news', before firing an five-second news headlines jingle (sounder) and opening the microphone for Hinds:

> Two trains have collided just outside Guildford station. It's thought at least three people have been killed and several others injured or trapped in the wreckage. The accident, which happened in the past half-hour, involved the delayed 1.51 from Guildford and the 1.18 from Waterloo. The names of the casualties and the cause of the accident are not yet known. An emergency number for relatives is being set up. We'll be bringing you that number as soon as it's announced.
>
> That story again . . . Two trains have collided outside Guildford station, killing three, and leaving others trapped and injured. More news on that crash as we get it, here on Surrey Radio.

Jenny fires another instrumental jingle, thanks Hinds on air and plays another song from the computerised playout system, this time something more downbeat in keeping with the sombre news.

Such a 'breaking news' bulletin is news at its most immediate, and highlights the task that radio does supremely well – getting news on air almost as quickly as it happens, and sometimes while it is still happening.

In the script Hinds took care to give the accurate departure times for the trains to limit needless worry from friends or relatives. At the end he repeated the information for those who may have missed or misheard it, at the same time seizing the opportunity to promote his station's news output. Listeners are left in no doubt that if they want to catch the latest on the crash first they should stay tuned.

Now Hinds has to make sure he and his team can deliver that promise.

He's already back in the newsroom badgering the rail company for that emergency number, while those in the phone-in/programme production area are getting calls from anxious friends and relatives of passengers. Holding on for Surrey & Hampshire Trains, whose press office is permanently engaged, Hinds barks out instructions to his team of reporters, which has been galvanised into action. One is on to the police; another is alternating between the fire brigade and the local hospital.

Just then the Surrey & Hampshire Trains' emergency number comes through.

Hinds toys with the idea of a second 'breaking news' bulletin, but quickly drops that in favour of extending the headlines on the half-hour which is now less than three minutes away.

A reporter is making their way to the scene of the crash and it's hoped there'll soon be some audio to put on air.

HEADLINE

The story makes the lead in the headlines on the half-hour. A headline is usually a brief summary of the main points of the story, and is seldom longer than four lines, 48 words . . . or 15 seconds. In the case of the train crash, Hinds dispenses with convention and gives a fuller version.

> A train crash at Guildford has killed three people and injured four others. Several more are feared trapped in the wreckage. Rescue workers are now at the scene, about a mile north of Guildford station.
>
> Both trains were travelling on the northbound line and collided head-on. They were the London-bound 1.51 from Guildford and the 1.18 from Waterloo. The names of the casualties are not yet known. An emergency phone number has been set up for relatives to call for details. The number is 01483 000 000. That number again . . . 01483 000 000.
>
> Train services between Guildford and London are suspended until the track can be cleared. More news on the rail crash as it comes in.

Headlines (or *highlights*) are often read at the start of a major bulletin or news programme to signpost the news and encourage the audience to keep listening. They may be given again at the end to recap on the major stories, or, as in the case above, be read on the half past or quarter hour in lieu of a longer bulletin.

COPY STORY

This is an amplified version of the four-line headline, giving the story in more detail, but without an accompanying interview (actuality). Copy stories are usually short – about 20 seconds, depending on house style. Hinds' 'headline' on the train crash was really a copy story.

Normally on a major story a *voice report* (a 'voicer') or extract from an interview (a 'clip') would be used, but the briefer copy-only form comes into its own when:

- The story is breaking and no interview or fuller account is yet available.

- There is not enough time in the bulletin for a more detailed report.

- A fuller account or interview has already been used, and a shorter version is required to keep the story running without it sounding stale.

VOICER OR VOICE REPORT

Reporter Julian Alleck is driving to the scene in a radio station staff car. The days of radio cars, fitted with broadcasting equipment and a giant mast, are gone. It's due to modern technology: BBC local radio stations each have a small van with a satellite dish on the roof, so they can send audio back quickly. Plus, the mobile phone means a journalist can report from almost anywhere and with one of a number of apps for broadcasters, the signal will sound even clearer and semi-studio quality.

The reporter may have been able to take with them a producer or other colleague to carry equipment, find out information and set up the interviews, but there is some doubt whether they'll be there in time for the three o'clock news. The other reporters back at base are on to the police, fire service and Surrey & Hampshire Trains to get information and try where possible to record interviews on the telephone.

FIGURE 16.2

The script for the train crash voice piece

A station with more journalists will certainly be 'phone-bashing' but will also be able to send out staff either to the scene of the crash or gather audio from other locations (perhaps at the station, the hospital to where the injured will be taken and so on).

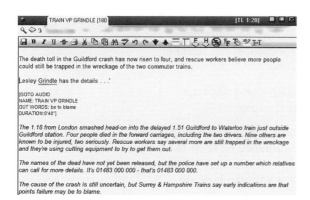

Phone clips are hugely important. The quality of lines is increasingly good, without the crackles and pops of years gone by. That makes them easier to listen to on the radio. Indeed using phone clips gives a greater impression of speed and reaction than a 'quality' recording. Many stations have telephone headsets at journalists' desks so they can record calls immediately, without having to divert them to a studio.

With more information coming in, Hinds is not prepared to settle for a repeat of the copy story at three o'clock, so he asks a reporter to draw the facts together and turn it into a voice report.

Voicers are usually used when there is more information than can be used in a copy story, but where no actuality is yet available (or may never be, for example, a court case). They would usually run for about 30 seconds, excluding the cue, and longer in the case of a major breaking story.

Voice reports are very useful but can be rather dull. They can convey a lot of information on a complicated story, and their inclusion means there is a different voice telling the news, not just that of the newsreader. But they're often over-long and recorded in a studio with no atmosphere. It would be misleading to play sound effects under a 'voicer' such as this, but many stations record them in the car park or out on the street to lift them with a little bit of atmosphere.

Instead bulletins often include live reports, or a live 'two-way' with the bulletin reader interviewing a colleague (either in the studio or out on location) about a story. This lifts the bulletin much more, and can be particularly effective in heightening interest in breaking news.

As soon as the voicer is recorded, it is filed to network for inclusion in the national news feed to client stations for them to include in their *home mix* of national and international news. (That is, they may take some of the individual stories sent by their national news supplier, and then combine them with their local stories to create a bulletin. Alternatively stations may take a feed of the national news bulletin live to air, and then follow it with their own locally produced bulletin.)

Most stories that use a clip (or 'cut') of audio (from an interview) or voice report require a *cue* or *lead-in*, to introduce the speaker.

Above and below the cue is a set of information about the story. This is the *marking-up*. Individual stations have their own ideas about how this should be done, but usually includes information such as the name of the report ('TRAIN VP GRINDLE'), its duration and out cue (the last words spoken). The audio file and the cue sheet share the same name so they are easily paired up. This avoids a newsreader introducing the wrong report on air.

What Hinds wants most of all for the bulletin is the live report from the scene, but in case this is not produced in time, the voicer will provide *holding* material, which can be used as a fall-back or substitute. Holding material can take the form of a copy story, voicer or interview. Good holding material has prevented many a last-minute crisis and loss of face.

TEASER OR TASTER

It is now five seconds to three and Hinds is seated in the *newsbooth* to read his five-minute bulletin, a mixture of local and national news. As the news jingle is playing, he is hoping that one of the other interviews planned will come up trumps in time for this bulletin.

He begins with a teaser:

A train crash at Guildford claims four lives . . . passengers are still trapped.
That's our top story on Surrey Radio at 3 . . . good afternoon I'm Ian Hinds.

Urgent, present tense and brief, the teaser is an enigmatic abbreviated headline used at the start of a bulletin or news programme to act as a lure by giving a taste of the story to come and teasing the audience into listening on to find out more.

A collection of three or four teasers is called a menu. It serves the same purpose as the menu in a restaurant – to whet the appetite. Hinds would usually tease several other stories at the start of a bulletin (*'Inflation is up again and in sport, Big Bobby quits The Flames for retirement'*) but it's going to seem anachronistic to include other stories in an hour with such a strong local lead.

VOICE REPORT FROM THE SCENE

It is now 3.02. Less than five minutes ago, the radio station's car pulled up as close as it could to the crash, and reporter Julian Alleck has got even closer to the action on foot, with his mobile phone in hand.

Alleck's brief is to go live into the news with a minute-long report. After snatching a few words with a Surrey & Hampshire Trains official and a fire officer, Alleck phones the newsroom and says he is in position. In as few words as possible, Lesley Grindle gives him the latest information from calls made back at base, and Alleck stands by to go live. Through his headphones he can hear the station output. Hinds has begun reading the bulletin, and the voicer by Grindle is going out on air.

A few seconds later he can hear Hinds beginning the cue:

So the latest we have on that crash: four people have died, and the number of injured is now up to twelve. More passengers are still believed to be trapped in the wreckage of the two trains, which collided head-on on the northbound line just outside Guildford station. Julian Alleck is there now and joins us live . . . Julian, describe the scene . . .

The picture here a mile up the line from Guildford is one of devastation. The two trains are twisted together beside the track and firemen and rescue workers are cutting open the wreckage to free any passengers who are still trapped.

It seems both trains were on the northbound line when they hit head-on. Their front carriages were torn from the rails by the impact, and are now lying locked together. Both drivers were killed in the crash. It's known that two passengers have also died, both on the London train, where firemen with cutting equipment are now working.

The remaining five carriages of that train have also overturned and are on their sides, while all four coaches of the Guildford train have concertinaed together in a zigzag off the track, but are, remarkably, still on their wheels.

Ambulance crews say they've taken twelve other passengers to the Surrey County Hospital where they're being treated for injuries, and are now standing by while rescue workers continue to cut open the wrecked carriages, to search for any others who may still be on board.

Surrey & Hampshire Trains officials are inspecting the damage, and though they won't say for sure, early indications suggest that points failure might be to blame.

Julian Alleck, Surrey Radio News at the Guildford train crash.

Back at the radio station Hinds picks up from him:

And there's more news from the scene of that rail crash as soon as we get it.

Alleck's voice report, hastily set up with precious little time for preparation, concentrated on describing the scene for the listener. He has placed himself close enough to the action to pick up the sounds of the rescue operation, yet not so close as to interfere with the work of rescuers. His live report has stimulated the imagination by adding colour and description to the more factual studio voicer that was broadcast earlier in the bulletin.

Look back at the report above and Alleck's choice of the words: *devastation, twisted together, cutting open, torn from the rails, locked together, concertinaed, zigzag.*

How do you practise coming up with good descriptive turns of phrase? Reading lots. Listening lots. Looking lots. In other words immerse yourself in words by reading good quality books and publications and listening to good quality broadcasters. If you consciously listen (rather than just 'hear') what they say, and how, and why, some of that will rub off on you. Then try it out for yourself (see the exercises below for ideas).

The live voicer from the scene gives more opportunity for descriptive, accurate and up-to-date reports than is possible with a studio voicer. You have to 'paint a picture' for a radio audience as they can't see what you can: you have to be their eyes. So think about the sounds, colours and even smells and how they can make the story come alive.

Given time, Alleck would have liked to include live or pre-recorded 'actuality', such as an interview with a survivor or rescue worker. His next task will be to gather more facts and get hold of the chief fire officer or a spokesperson for Surrey & Hampshire Trains. He could either interview them live, or record interviews to be played into his live report.

The main difficulty with location interviews is that it might not be possible to edit them, so there is little leeway for mistakes. Increasingly, journalists are going out into the field with laptop computers with sound-editing programmes. This allows them to edit on location and file the story back to base, by FTP. Alternatively reporters have mobile phones with inbuilt MP3 recorders, editing apps and wireless email: they can record audio, do a basic edit, then attach it to an email and send it back to the station.

Note that Alleck ended his report with an SOC, a *standard outcue (payoff)*. This is more than simply a neat way to round off a report and an obvious phrase for the pick up off, it also promotes the fact that the radio station has a reporter live at the scene and heightens the impression of the station's news power.

In this case, the newsreader, Hinds, follows the live report with a *back announcement* (back anno). This is a further piece of signposting and promotion, letting the audience know that if they stay tuned they will hear more on the story.

If Alleck had had more time to take in the situation, Hinds could have conducted a *Q & A* (question and answer, or a 'two-way') session with him, interviewing him live about the story to get more details. To make sure he is not caught out by a question for which he does not have the answer, the reporter will usually provide the list of questions for the presenter to ask. This helps the flow without detracting from the impression of spontaneity.

The role of a reporter in this situation has grown over recent years. As well as proving audio for their local station, they may also be asked to provide audio for their parent company, possibly in the form of a Q&A two-ways with other presenters.

But what if that parent company is a multi-media broadcaster and requires some video? That's another job for the radio reporter at the scene: to take and send some moving pictures of what's going on. The video and the audio can also be used online, but those teams may also request some still pictures be sent, as well as the spellings of the names and exact titles of those who have been interviewed.

And don't forget social media: integrated apps make it quite straightforward for a reporter to take video and post it on, say, Twitter together with a short headline . . . but that's another thing to do.

And all the while, the local and the national news desk are phoning the reporter asking for updates, wanting to know whether that interview's been done yet and if they can 'go live at the top of the hour . . .'

Not only can all these demands add to the pressure on the reporter, they also have to consider where their priorities lie: what platform (TV, radio or online) do they serve first? The national news machine is arguably most important, but should they be serving their local audience first – after all, the story affects them more. By informing the national desk of what's happening, will that encourage more demands from them? And calls coming in on the mobile phone will interrupt an audio or video recording. If a reporter takes video of any interview, the audio can be stripped out for radio, and stills can be taken of the moving pictures . . . but that video will be taken on a non-professional mobile,

FIGURE 16.3

Using 'Luci' to broadcast live from the scene of an incident using a tablet.

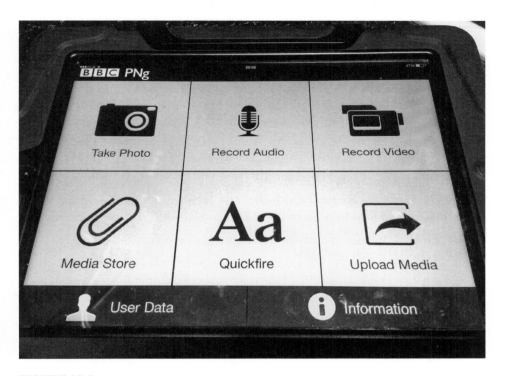

FIGURE 16.4
The BBC's Portable Newsgathering app allows reporters to send content back to the newsroom.

from a distance that works well for pictures and less well for audio. And if you have a handheld mic attached to the phone, how do you hold both in a media scrum . . .? And when do you post updates to social media? And are they text, audio, video, pictures . . .? Oh and Periscope, anyone?

INTERVIEW

Radio stations frequently interrupt their schedules to provide on-the-spot coverage of major breaking news, and Alleck is asked to give his next live report as soon as he has enough information.

By 3.15 his gopher, a student who is getting work experience/internship in the newsroom and hoping to break into radio, has come up with a witness to the crash. The woman was out walking her dog along a footpath less than 300 metres from the collision. She is shaken, but seems almost relieved to be interviewed and unburden herself of the things she has seen.

Alleck weighs up whether she is too unsteady to be interviewed live, but she is intelligent and articulate, and he thinks with careful handling she will cope. He decides to take a chance. Contacting the studio he tells the producer of the afternoon programme to stand by.

A station is likely to have gone 'open ended' with this story by now, especially if the presenter on air has a journalistic background. Music, competitions and many other features will have been dropped to have continuing coverage of the story. The presenter will be helped by having a co-presenter in the studio, who will be another voice for the increasing amount of information to be read out. 'Double heading' also makes it easier for the producer of a show such as this: they can give directions or information to one presenter while the other is speaking, and vice versa. This information will either be via the off-air intercom system (talk-back) or on a TV screen in the studio ('visual talkback').

What's included in this new format could be:

- Calls from eyewitnesses (which could be edited and soundbites from it then re-broadcast in news bulletins).

- Continual updates and recaps of what's happened and the emergency number.

- Extra travel news (not only of the train services through the region but also the potential knock-on effect on the roads near the crash scene)

- Rail experts – perhaps surmising on how this crash could have happened, the layout of the tracks at this junction, the type of trains and their safety record

- Live reports from the reporter at the scene, another at the hospital and so on.

'User-generated content' (or 'eye-witness media') is the name given to the material that is submitted to radio and TV stations by the listeners and viewers. Traditionally the media went and sought the views of those who consumed its fare. Then radio was revolutionised with the phone-in programme and suddenly almost anyone who had something to say could say it (even if it wasn't that interesting!). Now the public submits feedback and photos, texts, emails and video to stations via websites or straight to the on-air studio.

There's still some processing of the material that needs to take place. Some stations have employed an 'audience editor' to trawl the flow of information for nuggets which could make news, and then check the material is accurate and suitable for broadcast.

In this scenario, listeners including some of the train's passengers have sent in still and moving pictures taken on their mobile phones. Once checked these can be put online in a gallery for others to see, and the best ones sent to the 'parent' TV newsroom for possible inclusion in an on-air broadcast. (We wrote about how to verify material submitted by the public earlier in the book.)

The latest information gathered from his colleagues in the newsroom has just been texted to Alleck's mobile phone. He incorporates this into a cue which he bangs out on his notebook PC and sends it back to the newsroom computer, again via the mobile. As soon as it appears on the screen in the studio, the producer tells him to stand by to go live, and moments later, the presenter is reading the cue for his second report.

> More news on the Guildford train crash now. Two trains have collided just outside Guildford station on the London line, killing four passengers and injuring others.

> Our reporter Julian Alleck is at the trackside now. Julian . . .

JA: Thank you. With me is Petra Cavanagh from Guildford, who saw the crash when she was out walking her dog near the railway line . . . What did you see?

PC: I was walking Lucy, my Dalmatian, along the footpath, quite close to the track really, when I saw the London train coming, some way in the distance. At the same time I could hear another train behind me. I didn't think anything of it because the railway line has two tracks at this point, and . . . and one just assumes, of course, that the trains are on different lines.
Then the northbound train passed where I was standing and gave a terrific blast on its hooter; then there was a frantic squealing of brakes and I . . . I suppose I realised then, just . . . before they hit, that they were both on the same line. It was really quite appalling. One could do nothing to stop it.

JA: What happened when they collided?

PC: Well, you understand, I . . . could only see the back of the Guildford train, but there was a simply dreadful noise, like a . . . like a shotgun going off by one's ear, then the train seemed to lift for a moment, and, very slowly it seemed, the carriages began to come off the track, one to the left and one to the right, until they came to rest. One was just rooted to the spot. I mean, one couldn't believe one's eyes.

JA: What did you do next?

PC: Well, I . . . I suppose one should have called for an ambulance, but, er, the extraordinary thing . . . that, er, that didn't enter my mind. I ran to the train, and when I got there I realised how much more badly damaged the other train . . . er, the southbound train, that is . . . was, if you follow me.

JA: What did you see?

PC: It was really rather too horrible. The, er, the two front coaches were crushed together, very badly; I pity anyone who was inside. The other coaches were on their sides. From further back passengers were opening the doors and starting to clamber out. The side of the train had become the roof, as it were. They were having to jump down on to the track from quite a height. Some of them were quite badly hurt. It's a wonder nobody was electrocuted.

> I must confess, I'd been standing there feeling quite sick, and when the people started to come out, I remembered myself, tied Lucy up so she wouldn't wander on to the track, and set to helping the people down.

JA: How long was it before the ambulances arrived?

PC: I really can't say. We were all so busy just helping people out. Others had come by then, from the homes nearby, and I sent one of them back to fetch blankets and another to get some ladders. I can't say I noticed the ambulances arrive.

JA: Thank you. Petra Cavanagh who organised the rescue from the trains until the emergency services could arrive.

The death toll from the crash currently stands at four, with twelve people seriously injured. If the same accident had happened in the evening rush hour when those carriages were more densely packed, the figures could have been far higher.

As I speak, rescue workers are checking the wreckage of the forward coaches to see if anyone is still trapped. It looks as though the line will be out of action for quite some time.

Julian Alleck, Surrey Radio News at the Guildford train crash.

Thank you Julian. And we'll be going back to the scene of that crash, later in the programme.

Julian's next live report comes at twenty to four. By then two more passengers have been freed from the wreckage, both seriously injured. Work is going on to clear the line.

The newsroom contacts Alleck to tell him the Surrey & Hampshire Trains press office in London is now investigating the possibility that a points failure was to blame for routing the southbound train on to the northbound line. But at this stage, the company will not be interviewed about it. The news editor wants Alleck to get hold of a rail official at the scene and put the question to him live. This Alleck does, but the official is, understandably, not very forthcoming.

The interview adds more depth, permits a further exploration of a story and gives an opportunity for informed comment. Standard radio news interviews vary in length depending on house style. Between 90 seconds and about three minutes is almost standard, though those on extended news programmes may run a little longer. Live interviews, which are seldom as concise as edited ones, may also be longer although the 'rule of thumb' is to keep speech-inserts only as long as the average song . . . about three minutes.

NEWSCLIP

The most newsworthy part of an interview is usually edited from it to provide a short sound-bite to 'illustrate' (if we can use a visual term!) the story in a later bulletin. This would usually be a little shorter than a voicer – some 15–20 seconds – and is known as a *clip, cut or insert or sound-bite*. Clip or cut because it is an extract cut from an interview, and insert, because it is inserted into the bulletin. The cue will give the facts of the story, and the insert will develop them with explanation or comment, providing added authenticity to the radio report.

Surrey Radio's four o'clock news is due on air shortly, and Hinds is extending the bulletin to make way for another full report from the scene. Bulletins are a good place to summarise the latest information and use the best bits of the interviews gathered so far. (In fact bulletins are sometimes referred to as 'summaries'.)

Alleck's report will incorporate clips from the interviews with the witness and railway official. These are being edited by journalists in the newsroom from recordings of the two live interviews. These are known as *ROTs* (recording of/off transmission). The edited clips will be played in from the studio.

In addition, Alleck is asked to do a short live interview with a rescue worker. The report is complicated by playing in items from two separate locations and the timing is crucial.

PACKAGE

The four o'clock programme begins with a menu headed by the following teaser:

> The Guildford train crash . . . Four die, fourteen are injured . . . Surrey
> & Hampshire Trains say points failure could be to blame . . . a witness
> describes the crash . . .

After the rest of the menu, perhaps on one other top story and a short weather forecast, Hinds begins the lead story:

> Rescue teams are working to free passengers trapped in the wreckage of
> two trains which have collided outside Guildford station. Four people are
> dead and fourteen injured after the 1.18 from Waterloo collided head-on
> with the London-bound 12.55 from Portsmouth Harbour minutes after it left
> Guildford station. Both trains had been routed on to the same line. Surrey
> & Hampshire Trains say a points failure may be to blame.
>
> For the past hour and a half rescue teams have been working to free
> passengers trapped in the wreckage and efforts are now being made to
> clear the line. Our reporter Julian Alleck is at the scene of the crash . . .

(Live)

> The combined speed of the two trains was thought to be in excess of 70
> miles an hour. The impact twisted together the front carriages of each,
> killing the drivers instantly. Firemen with cutting tools are still trying
> to separate the trains. In all, six passengers were trapped in the front
> compartment of the London train. Two were killed in the crash and the
> other four were pulled out injured, but alive.
>
> Petra Cavanagh from Guildford saw the crash happen:

(Recorded)

> *The northbound train passed where I was standing and gave a terrific
> blast on its hooter; there was a frantic squealing of brakes and I . . . It was
> really quite appalling. One could do nothing to stop it. There was a simply
> dreadful noise, like a shotgun going off by one's ear, then the train seemed*

to lift for a moment, and, very slowly it seemed, the carriages began to come off the track, one to the left and one to the right, until they came to rest. One was just rooted to the spot. I mean, one couldn't believe one's eyes.

It was really rather too horrible. The two front coaches were crushed together, very badly; I pity anyone who was inside. The other coaches were on their sides. From farther back passengers were opening the doors and starting to clamber out. The side of the train had become the roof, as it were. They were having to jump down on to the track from quite a height. Some of them were quite badly hurt. It's a wonder nobody was electrocuted.

(Live)

In charge of the rescue operation is chief fire officer Tony Stims, who's with me now. Tony, how badly injured are the trapped passengers?

Several of them were quite seriously hurt. Lucky to be alive I would say. I'm surprised only two passengers died in the impact and more weren't badly injured.

Was it a difficult operation, freeing them?

More delicate than difficult, OK, obviously we had to take a lot of care with the cutters that we didn't injure anyone further.

You're trying to separate the trains now and clear the track. How do you plan to do that?

Well, we've had lifting gear standing by for the past forty minutes, but we couldn't use it until we were sure everybody was out of the train. The first thing we want to do is haul them off the track, so the railway boys can get the trains running again.

How long will that take?

Half an hour. Maybe more, maybe less. Difficult to say.

Thank you. Chief Fire Officer Tony Stims. Surrey & Hampshire Trains is launching an inquiry into this accident, but says first indications are that points failure may be to blame. This was confirmed earlier by the spokesman here at the scene, John Turbot:

(Recorded)

Obviously we're investigating; it could only really be points failure, beyond that I can't say at this stage.

You mean a faulty points operation directed the London train on to the wrong track?

It's still too soon to be sure but that appears to be correct, yes.

How could that happen?

Well that's what we've got to find out. It's really a matter for an inquiry.

Do you suspect an equipment failure or an operator error?

I'm sorry but as I've already said, that's a matter for an inquiry.

Has the problem now been rectified?

Yes.

Then you must know what caused it.

We've got a good idea, yes, but as I told you, it's for the inquiry to make the final decision.

Four people have lost their lives this afternoon. If you're planning to open the line again today, what assurances can you give commuters that the problem had been solved and won't happen again?

Well let me correct you. We intend to get the trains running but on adjacent tracks which were not damaged in the accident.

(Live)

Surrey & Hampshire Trains' spokesman John Turbot, thank you. Services between Guildford and London are expected to resume within the next hour.

Julian Alleck, Surrey Radio News at the Guildford train crash.

(Back in the studio)

And a phone line has opened for anyone who may have had a friend or relative on either of those trains. It is . . . etc.

As soon as the bulletin is over, Alleck checks on the talkback that the package was successfully recorded back at the station, then files again his last paragraph substituting a network outcue for the Surrey Radio tag. The station will switch the outcues and then send the package via the network's internal messaging system to the London newsroom. It will be Surrey Radio's fourth item on the crash to be sent 'down the line'. Alleck has given the train's correct origin as Portsmouth Harbour to broaden the information for a wider audience.

From its London base, the network newsroom will redistribute the audio to the other local stations in the network.

Alleck's piece with its three inserts is more sophisticated than the basic package, which usually comprises a cue and a couple of short interviews. These are wrapped up in the reporter's own words, which are grouped before the first interview, between the interviews and usually after the last interview. These are known as *links*.

Packaging is useful for presenting a balanced account of two sides of an argument and for permitting the use of more elaborate production techniques to include sound effects or music.

Unlike the standard interview, where the focus is on the interviewee, the package sets up the reporter as raconteur and guide. The cue presents an overview of the story and the reporter's first link adds flesh to that and provides an introduction to the first interviewee. The middle link allows the reporter to summarise any important points that have been left out, and to tie what has just been said to the second interview, which he then introduces. The final link is used for summing up the two arguments, adding important details and pointing the way forward for the story, in this case by referring to the time it will take to restore train services.

Although using packages is in decline, their strength is that you can use extracts of interviews that have been boiled down to their essential information. Contrast the edited interview with Petra Cavanagh with the original live version with her. The edits have been made to focus on the description of the collision and to eliminate unnecessary information and verbal tics.

Stepping away from this scenario for a moment, creating packages on regular news stories can be pretty time consuming: perhaps you record interviews with a total of three people at two different locations, together with wildtrack (background noise). Back at your desk, you take clips from each of them, write a script that links it all together and then mix your sound underneath. All that could take several hours.

But if you prepare better, you'll save time! Pre-interview the guests on the phone to know what they will say and develop your angle from that so you better understand the story you want to tell before you set out. Then you only ask the questions that elicit the responses that you have already heard. And if you gather your interviewees at the same location, you can not only put each of their questions to them consecutively, but also record your own links between them at the same time. Using mic technique and the settings on the recorder to mix the sound 'live' will also save you time back at the studio. So here's how all that might work:

> (*Reporter holds microphone near rushing water for a few seconds and then moves it to their mouth*)

REPORTER: The sound of water . . . running away now, but yesterday was a different story. With me is Sandy Shaw whose home was flooded when this storm drain got blocked. What's the damage Sandy?

SANDY: (*Who has been told that this is the question she will be asked, together with the requested duration of her answer*) All through my downstairs. It was terrible. It just rose and rose . . . I was watching it and all I could do was keep putting things on higher shelves and take stuff upstairs. But the carpet's ruined, and the furniture . . . and the water is disgustingly dirty. I dread to think what's in it.

REPORTER: Well let's find out. Robyn Tumbridge, you're from the university and you've taken some water samples to analyse. What did you discover?

ROBYN: It's not pleasant I'm afraid. As you might imagine, this is water that's run off the roadway so we've certainly got traces of oil in there as well as decaying matter that's probably from a dead bird or another animal. But the drains here backed up from the sewers so unfortunately there's also quite a bit of human faeces that's been identified and the various other bacteria that results from that – so nasty stuff.

(The reporter sees the look on Sandy's face so holds the microphone to her again as a way of prompting a verbal reaction and cutting the need for a link.)

SANDY: Oh oh my god . . . that is so disgusting. I've only been in there a year this last Christmas and . . . The thought of my kids playing on that floor at any time in the future . . . I . . . I . . .

REPORTER: Well the water is flowing now, with a little help from the pumps of the fire service . . . but what went wrong? It's the council's job to make sure there are no blockages of the drains at street level, and the councillor in charge of highways is Terri Brown.

(Terri is expecting this question and speaks with no further prompt as soon as the microphone is pointed in her direction.)

TERRI: Quite simply it's a matter of costs. The local referendum last year made it quite clear that people wouldn't pay a higher tax for the services that were offered and chose instead for a cut. Well a cut in taxes means a cut in services too and that meant that drains on streets like this are now only checked and cleared half as often as they once were. Of course I'm sorry that Mrs Shaw was affected in this way but there is no bottomless pit of cash.

The reporter asks no more questions but turns down the recording level on their machine to create a fade on the atmosphere that's being recorded. (If the councillor had been at another location, a manual fade out could have been done earlier together with a manual fade in at the councillor's office and the subsequent question and answer.) The package has been recorded and mixed at the scene.

MINI-WRAP OR BULLETIN WRAP

Back at the crash site and while Alleck is filing his report, the network intake editor is on to the newsroom asking for an update on the story. He wants a shorter version for the bulletin, preferably wrapped (packaged) and with a maximum duration of 30 seconds, which coming from network with its appetite for news fast and furious is quite a concession.

No sooner has Alleck finished filing his package than reporter Phil Needle is on the talkback passing on the network's request. Alleck decides to give it the full treatment, and solicits the help of Needle to further edit down the interview clips to cram something of all three into the report. In vain, Needle protests about squeezing quarts into pint pots, but Alleck will have nothing of it.

Ten minutes later Needle is on the talkback again offering 50 seconds, and after two more hatchet attempts, they manage between them to concoct the following report:

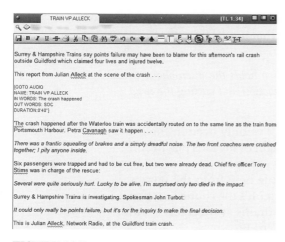

FIGURE 16.5

The bulletin wrap.

All reference to the track being cleared has deliberately been left out, as the position by five o'clock could well be different. Up-to-date facts can be added nearer the time and included in the form of a back announcement.

The wrap works out at nearer 35 seconds to 30, and to boil it down that far has required some 'creative' editing to cut the actuality while still making sense of the narrative. A further two seconds have been shaved off by digitally speeding it up. Any more and Mrs Cavanagh will sound like she's on narcotics.

The piece is already slightly breathless and disjointed, and with time creeping up towards the bulletin, they decide to call it a day and give the duration as 30 seconds, hoping nobody in network notices the deception.

Sometimes reporters can be too clever with mini-wraps, and when Needle plays the edited version down the talkback Alleck is forced to concede that perhaps it does sound a little garbled in places. But his satisfaction at having crammed three pieces of actuality into 30 seconds (or so) overrules his other sensibilities, and anyway, there's no time now to mess around with a remake.

Meanwhile, back in the newsroom, Hinds has just listened to a recording of the opposition 4.30 bulletin and is having convulsions. They have got actuality with one of the survivors from the hospital . . .

In the corner another phone is ringing. It is the network intake editor. His tone is sarcastic. 'About that mini-wrap. Great, if you can follow it. Any chance of a remake? And could you cut it down a bit?'

Out on the railway line at Guildford, somebody's ears are burning . . .

> You can be working on three or four major stories a day with little research backup. You go in and you do your three and a half minute interview, pick out your twenty seconds of actuality, do a voice piece, and at the end of the day you've got to say well, actually, I've just skimmed over a number of issues.
> Richard Bestic, Sky News Reporter

The pressure is certainly on for a broadcast journalist in a breaking news situation. It's down to the speed of the newsgathering process which is made easier by digital technology . . . but more demanding by the need to constantly feed other outputs including the 24-hour rolling news machines. And while the reporter is feeding the news machine, how can they gather information and eye-witnesses . . .?

Now Hinds and his team have to think ahead to the next morning for 'take-on angles'. The story will need to be reflected in the peak-time bulletins but with new lines, perhaps reaction from the area's MP, maybe a union official, the latest on the enquiry and condition checks on those injured. For a speech-based station it would also be necessary to get a journalist live at the scene the next morning to paint a picture of the crash scene now it's been cleared and get the reaction from early morning commuters.

Just as the Surrey Radio newsteam prepare to call it a night and gather in the local pub, someone makes a worrying discovery. None of the potentially award-winning broadcasts were recorded as the 'auto-rot' ('automatic recording off transmission' logger) was not working. Dejected, the hard-working journalists decide instead to go straight home.

Digitisation has given us speed and some simplification of newsgathering ('top and tail' non-destructive editing of a sound wave is faster and easier than splicing tape), but has also increased the pressure to 'turn things around' faster. Speed and pressure can produce a heady cocktail of adrenalin and creativity. But they can also make a near-deadly mix of legal or editorial mistakes . . . and physical or mental breakdowns.

THE HEADLINES

- Don't get too excited and exuberant when a story such as this breaks. It is your job to tell the facts as you know them in a clear and calm manner.

- Be wary of portraying rumours or eye-witness accounts as 'facts'.

- Always remember that there will be some people listening who may be concerned for a relative who could be caught up in the incident which you are describing . . . and then re-consider your tone, pace and language.

QUESTIONS FOR YOU

1. Look at our comment earlier about practising descriptive writing. Now put your new-found experience to the test! Go somewhere new (the docks, an airport lounge, a shopping mall . . .) with a notepad and pen and write a script describing what you see (and hear and smell . . .) If you can, watch the opening minute or so of the Hitchcock movie *Psycho*. Note how the producer moves from a long-range view of the city to zoom into a street, building, room and person. Think of that as you do the exercise suggested above: describe the overview of the scene, and then focus in on two or three specifics. And when you do so, use specific words: the exact colour ('fawn' rather than 'brown'), the sound ('piercing' not just 'loud'), the smell ('sweetly Oriental' rather than 'foreign'). Oh and listen lots to www.bbc.co.uk/podcasts/series/fooc.

2. Go back to Alleck's live interview with Mrs Cavanagh. Without looking at the edited version, show how you would cut it to reduce it to a 35-second newsclip. Type out the quotes you would leave in.

   - What good material do you feel you have had to cut out to get it down to length?
   - Now do the same with the Turbot interview.

3. Take a news story from a newspaper and produce from it a *teaser, headline, copy story* and *voicer*.

   ▪ If you are in a class, all work on the same story and then compare your different versions. Have you all agreed about what to leave in and what to take out? Discuss your differences and see if you can come to some agreement.

4. Now take a newspaper story which quotes two sides of an argument and write it up as though you were doing the script for a package. Include cues and links, and extracts from the interviews. Keep the whole package down to 2 minutes 30 seconds (at three words per second).

   ▪ Now cut the package to 1 minute 30 seconds.
   ▪ Do you find it difficult working out what to leave out?
   ▪ Now turn it into a mini-wrap of just 40 seconds (120 words).
   ▪ What do you think of mini-wraps? Do you find them slick and professional or do you think they can sometimes be too clever? Do they tell you more or less than you would find out from a voicer or newsclip?

5. 'Editing distorts what people say by focusing in on only what the journalist wants them to say. To be fair, people's comments should not be edited.' Discuss.

   ▪ How can you avoid distorting what someone says when you edit their interview?

OTHER RESOURCES

▪ Mobile reporting:

   ▪ lots of mobile journalism resources here: https://tvvj.wordpress.com/, http://iphonereporting.com/, www.robbmontgomery.com/ and www.newsshooter.com/.

▪ Mobile radio/audio:

   ▪ This BBC journalist gives background details of the technical equipment he used to broadcast reports on the January 2015 'Charlie Hebdo' shootings in Paris. The article includes several other links: http://nickgarnett.co.uk/project/paris/.

   ▪ Integrated mobile phone broadcasting equipment via www.glensound.co.uk/, www.luci.eu/ and www.tieline.com/.

   ▪ Use https://audioboom.com/ or https://soundcloud.com/ to record interviews, then embed a soundbite in a tweet or directly to a website. Use www.spreaker.com/ to stream live audio from your location.

   ▪ Voice Record Pro shows levels and exports to various formats: www.bejbej.info/app/voicerecordpro.

- MultiTrack DAW lets you record and mix music and speech if you want to produce a package while on location: www.harmonicdog.com/.

- TwistedWaveEditor is a basic editor: https://twistedwave.com/.

- Mobile video:

  - Universal smartphone camera-mount that securely holds your phone and enables professional picture-taking and filmmaking: www.shoulderpod.com.

  - An external light for filming on an iPhone, Android or Windows: http://iblazr.com/.

  - You can set your phone up as an autocue screen with Promptware Plus app. If you need a bit of practice reading autocue, then this could be a great app for you to have a look at. (Via your phone's app store.)

  - Broadcast live from virtually anywhere, record video for later broadcast, or import and upload edited video files to designated servers when traditional broadcast equipment is not at the scene: www.periscope. tv/, http://meerkatapp.co/, http://bambuser.com/, www.ustream.tv/; and www.stringwire.com/ and www.dejero.com are both specifically designed for journalists.

  - FiLMiC Pro lets you control the ISO, aperture and frame rate, and you easily trim and create sub-clips: www.filmicpro.com/.

  - Switcher Studio can connect three other devices together to allow you to edit different angles: http://switcherstudio.com/en/.

  - Hyperlapse is Instagram's timelapse app, which lets you produce stable tracking shots: https://hyperlapse.instagram.com/.

- Mobile photography:

  - What they call the 'ultimate' guide to iPhone photography: http://bit.ly/BJPics and another similar site of advice: http://iphonephotographyschool.com/iphoneography/.

  - Camera+ gives you in-app editing: http://campl.us/.

  - LapseIt is a great timelapse app (www.lapseit.com/) and 360 Panorama creates panoramic shots (http://occipital.com/360/app).

  - Diptic makes collages of pictures so you can send several images in one go: www.dipticapp.com/.

  - Quick lets you put a caption on a picture before you send it (another way to send more information): www.overquick.com/.

  - Find a Photo is a search engine for 100 per cent free stock images: http://finda.photo/.

- Other useful apps:

  - Tape-A-Call is an app for recording phone interviews on your mobile/cellphone: www.tapeacall.com/.

  - JamSnap allows your photos to come to life with sound. Snap a photo and add your own voice to give a short commentary, add some music that fits the mood, capture the sound of your surroundings: www.jamsnap.com/.

  - This platform allows you to personalise your YouTube videos with a logo or brand, plus performance tracking metrics, such as impressions, number of completed plays, and top referrers: www.reembed.com/.

  - WriteRack: the easiest way to blog on Twitter. You write what you want, as long as you want, and paste it into the WriteRack box. The site will automatically format it into a series of tweets and post them one after the other: http://writerack.com/.

TUTOR NOTES

Surprise your students with an exercise revolving around breaking news. This could be similar to the train crash mentioned above or another incident (say, a shooting in a shopping mall, a large factory fire or a river breaking its banks). What will they do first? And then . . .? And then? Who will they call to confirm? Who will they despatch and where will they go and who will they want to talk with? What other considerations should there be such as health and safety, food, equipment? Then change the scenario so there are developments such as street disturbances in protest at the shooting, a body found in the fire, the flood threatening an old people's home. What do your students do now? How do they develop the story?

1. In the immediate aftermath, news outlets will get it wrong.
2. Don't trust anonymous sources.
3. Don't trust stories that cite another news outlet as the source of the information.
4. There's almost never a second shooter.
5. Pay attention to the language the media uses.
6. Look for news outlets close to the incident.
7. Compare multiple sources.
8. Big news brings out the fakers. And Photoshoppers.
9. Beware reflexive retweeting. Some of this is on you.

Breaking News Consumer's Handbook (http://bit.ly/BJBreaking)

CHAPTER 17

Recording

> In my opinion, the most dangerous machine of them all is the microphone.
>
> Esther Rantzen, British TV presenter

The recording business has come a long way since 1898 when Valdemar Poulsen first captured sound on piano wire fixed to a hand-turned drum. Today, digital recordings of sparkling quality can be made and edited directly on computers of all shapes and sizes, be they dressed up as camcorders, flash-card recorders or mobile phones.

Miniaturisation has made it possible for today's reporters to move unhampered to the forefront of breaking stories and send back live, studio-quality reports via satellite link, mobile phone and wi-fi to be played straight to air or put onto a website. You can go straight to air with SoundCloud and Periscope apps.

Computer editing packages allow you to access your recordings at any point, doing away with the need to spool recordings back and forth to find the part you want to edit. You can trim recordings to within thousandths of a second, time them automatically, speed them up or slow them down digitally, sweeten them by adding bass or treble, and even loop them to run endlessly (especially useful for sound effects). News actuality cuts can be stored directly in the station computer to be played on air at the touch of a button. But it is always worth seeing where we came from before we get carried away.

PRINCIPLES OF RECORDING

Sound

Sound is created by vibrations in the air. The faster the air vibrates, the higher the sound will seem to the hearer. The speed of these vibrations is known as their *frequency*, and frequencies are measured in *hertz*. One thousand hertz is a *kilohertz*. Human speech spans a range between around 50 Hz and 6 kHz. The deeper the voice, the lower the frequency. The human ear can hear sounds from about 16 Hz to 18 kHz.

As well as being high or low, sounds are loud or quiet. Their loudness, or *sound pressure level* (SPL), is measured in decibels. The higher the number of decibels, the louder the sound. Speech rises to about 70 db. A gunshot would approach 130 db and would cross the listener's threshold of pain.

How Recordings Are Made

Microphones convert sound into an electrical signal that varies in relation to the sounds picked up by the mike. The signal is then boosted by an amplifier and passed to the recorder.

Digital recording does not suffer from the hiss and distortion inherent in older analogue tape recorders. You no longer hear the tape, just the signal. That signal is converted into pulses of binary code. Once encoded, the original sound is locked in and cannot deteriorate, even after playing many times. Unlike a conventional (*analogue*) recording, this code cannot become corrupted by hiss, hash, distortion or wow and flutter (alterations in tape speed).

On playback, the binary code is decoded and turned back into a signal. As long as the code can be read the playback will be as close to the original as the equipment will allow. Digital techniques mean the machinery, and not the recording medium, has become the limiting factor in the quest for audio perfection. Copy after copy can be made without any significant loss in quality.

Ribbon mics with their figure-of-eight pattern are used for interviews conducted at a table either side of the mike. Omni-directional mikes suffer the least from handling noise, but because they pick up all round they can draw in unwanted background sounds.

Digital recordings are stored on computer, which hold a radio station's entire playlist of music or many hours of programming. Audio can be edited on computer and items programmed to be played on air in any order.

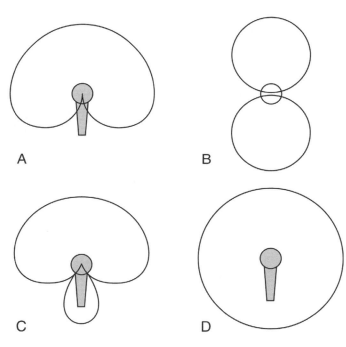

FIGURE 17.1

Microphones are sensitive to sounds coming from a specific area around them. This is known as their 'directivity pattern', which varies according to mic type:

A Cardioid
B Figure-of-eight (top view)
C Hyper-cardioid
D Omni-directional

Types of Microphones

There are three main types of microphones: *ribbon, moving coil* and *capacitor*.

The ribbon type, which is one of the most expensive, has a *diaphragm* of thin aluminium foil that is vibrated by the sounds around it like your eardrum. It moves within a magnetic field to create a signal.

The moving coil, or *dynamic* type, has a wire coil attached to a diaphragm that also vibrates in a magnetic field.

In the *capacitor*, or *condenser* type of microphone, the diaphragm is replaced with the plate of an electrically charged capacitor. These microphones require an electric current, supplied by a battery or the recorder itself.

Ribbon mikes are *bi-directional*. They respond in a figure of eight, picking up voices on both sides. They are often used to record studio interviews or discussions and are placed on a stand or suspended from the ceiling. Most varieties cannot be used out of doors, as any wind will blow against the ribbon creating a whooshing noise.

A specialised version of ribbon mike is the *lip mike* used by commentators. These respond to nearby sounds only and are held against the mouth.

There are two types of moving coil microphone. Some pick up sounds all round. These are *omni-directional*. Others pick up from in front of the microphone only. These are *uni-directional*. Their pick-up pattern is described as *cardioid* (heart shaped).

Traditionally, radio reporters used hand-held microphones of either type. Some mikes are unsuitable because they pick up movements made by the hand. This *handling noise* is kept to a minimum in broadcast-standard mikes.

Stand-mounted uni-directional microphones are usually favoured by newsreaders. Capacitor mikes vary in their response pattern. These are commonly used in television clipped to a tie or lapel.

By using two tie-clip mikes with a stereo recorder you can avoid having to wave a microphone under your subject's nose. This is useful for longer interviews or where the interviewee needs to be put at ease.

USING PORTABLE SOUND RECORDERS

Digital Recorders

Tens of hours of recorded audio can be compressed onto a single computer card; often an LCD screen allows you to edit in the field, saving valuable studio time; sometimes a special interface permits

FIGURE 17.2

A portable 'FlashMic' recorder.

reports to be transmitted directly to air in studio quality along a special digital phone line. Digital technology means no moving parts to wear out, no motors to add weight and no tape to deteriorate and flash cards can be re-recorded on hundreds of thousands of times.

BEFORE THE INTERVIEW

The way you hold a microphone, even the way you sit or stand to conduct an interview, can have a crucial effect on the quality of your final recording. As can the background noise and ambience of your surroundings.

Setting up the Room

Not all rooms are ideal for interviewing. Bare walls and wooden surfaces can produce a bathroom-type echo. This can sound worse on the recording than it did to you at the time, because the brain compensates for its surroundings. If the room is likely to echo, ask to do the interview somewhere else. Failing that, close the curtains and both stand to do the interview facing into them, to help dampen down reflected sound. If there are no curtains, standing and facing a corner of the room will cut the echo a little, and close-mike operation will help some more. You could even drape coats over the backs of chairs to provide a screen to help to dampen reverberations.

Never record across a table. You will have to stretch too far with the microphone and risk one of you being off-mike; the polished surface will reflect sound back in the form of echo. Perhaps just as important is the fact that if you are stretched out in supplication across your subject's executive desk you can hardly be seen to be in control of the interview! You will need to winkle your high-powered interviewee out from behind her desk and sit next to her.

Dealing with Distractions

Phones should be taken off the hook to prevent them ringing, and mobile phones need to be turned off rather than merely switched to 'mute': the radio frequency used will interfere with your recording. If there is noisy air conditioning find out if that can be turned off during the interview.

The mike is more conscious of distracting noises than you will be. While you are concentrating on your interview, the mike will be getting on with its job, which is to pick up any sounds in the room. So if your interviewee has beads that rattle or a coat that rustles, ask them to take them off. The same goes for papers that flap or a clipboard that gets between the person and the mike. Few interviewees ever complain about being asked to disrobe (within reason!) if they are politely but clearly told why. Make a joke of it if it helps.

Much of your work will be done for you if you choose the right microphone for the job. For example a highly-directional mic for picking up interview in a noisy environment, or an omni-directional mic in crowd situations to get the 'just like being there' feel.

Lining Up the 'Victim'

Next, arrange both you and your guest in a sensible recording position. One problem with the hand-held mike is that the user needs to invade the other person's physical space to get a decent signal. In body language terms, this invasion of space only takes place normally when people are fighting or being intimate, so expect some natural apprehension on the part of the interviewee and to feel uncomfortable yourself at first. At this point, plenty of confidence, a little charm, a ready smile, well-brushed teeth and a good deodorant are the reporter's most valuable assets.

A comfortable distance for normal conversation is with faces around a metre apart. To record an interview without having to keep moving your mike arm, you will have to shorten that gap. Arrange your chairs in a 'L' shaped pattern, so when you sit down your knees are almost touching. If you are right-handed, have the interviewee on your right hand side, so you can support your arm holding the mike on the arm of the chair. Other than standing up to conduct the interview, this is the most effective arrangement for the use of a hand-held microphone.

Mike Handling

Seemingly inexplicable clicks and bumps on a recording can often be traced to handling noise from the microphone.

Hand-held mikes should be gripped firmly but not tightly and fingers should be kept still, as any movement can often be picked up as handling noise. So if you have a ring on your microphone hand, remove it before the interview, as mikes are particularly susceptible to the small scraping sounds that a ring might make. Also remove any bracelets.

Take up any excess slack in the mike cable by looping it around your hand. This prevents loose cable bumping against the floor or furniture, which can cause clicks. It is important *not* to stretch the cable so tightly that you tug at the connection into the recorder or the point where the cable enters the mike. These two electrical connections form the weakest part of the cable. It is easy to cause an electrical click on the recording or damage the connection by pulling at the lead.

Reporters' microphones typically work most effectively about 25 cm, or about a foot, away from the mouth. Don't worry, you don't have to lug a ruler around with you! Beware of stuffing the microphone under the interviewee's nose. If it is that close she is likely to go cross-eyed, and an out of focus microphone windshield looks remarkably like a balled fist and has about the same effect on composure. Tuck the mike under her chin and out of direct line of vision.

The Level Check

Next, you need to take your levels. Make sure you are both sitting or standing as you will be during the interview and that your interviewee is comfortable. Now check you are holding the mike at an equal distance between yourself and your interviewee, unless one of you has a louder voice. If so, you will need to move the mike until the levels are balanced.

Then get both your voices 'on the record'. Ask your interviewee something so that they can respond and you can check the recorder is working. It is useful to ask them to state their name and title 'for the record' (and any unusual spellings), as then you not only have a level-check, but you have their correct details alongside the interview, and you can use this statement in your final report as a way of them introducing themselves.

As you take the sound check and adjust the levels you can monitor the recording on your headphones, or immediately listen back to it on headphones or the recorder's inbuilt speaker. A flickering meter is not always proof that a recording is being made! Having set your levels you shouldn't need to adjust them any more on your recorder. Instead, compensate for small changes in volume by moving your mike. This takes practice and it can help to wear discreet headphones while you are recording so you can monitor what's actually being recorded.

If your interviewee leans backwards or forwards, gently reposition your hand-held mike, or if it's a recording feel free to break off the interview and politely explain that she must sit as she was when the level check was made, or volunteer to retake the level with her sitting in her new position. Never nod instructions or gesticulate at interviewees, it only confuses and worries them. Stop and explain the problem (unless you are live!).

Automatic Level Control Versus Manual

But why bother with level checks at all? Most recorders will set them for you automatically. It works like this: recordings made at too high a level (volume) can distort. Automatic systems keep signals below distortion point, and when they fall too low they cut in and boost the signal upwards.

Adjusting the recording levels manually gives you more control and creative freedom. You can use your professional judgement to choose settings to perfectly match different circumstances, instead of passing control to the machine, whose systems were designed to cope with ideal conditions.

Another drawback to some ALC systems is the problem of surge, or *pumping*, which can happen when there is a pause in speech and the ALC hunts for sound to boost the levels. If there is a lot of background noise, such as traffic, or clattering in a noisy canteen, the ALC will surge this forward whenever the person speaking into the microphone pauses for more than a moment. Sometimes it is also possible to hear an ALC system stepping in to hold back the volume of a recording, because the level will dip momentarily.

None of these problems can occur with a manual recording that is correctly monitored, but having to monitor levels means your attention is divided between the recorder and your interviewee. Using ALC means you can save your concentration for the most critical element of the interview – the questions. If you must use ALC do so under perfectly quiet conditions. A better solution is to set the levels manually and monitor them by listening on headphones.

And Finally . . .

After the interview, always remember to check the recording has come out before leaving your interviewee. A quick retake there and then can save a lot of embarrassing explanations later.

FIGURE 17.3
Before the days of digital editing this was the workhorse of a radio newsroom: note the editing block and razor blade!

THE HEADLINES

- Levels, levels, levels. You can boost recorded audio to make it louder, but if someone is off-mic, or too close to it, there is little chance of it being salvageable.

- Don't be like a rapper. Mics are sensitive and so are people: don't thrust one into their face.

- Computers don't have ears! Don't presume that the waveform is king, or always edit where the blocks of colour suggest you should. When you have completed an awkward edit, look away from the waveform on the screen as you listen back to what you have done. That way you can better judge if the edit works and whether the voice 'sounds right'.

QUESTIONS FOR YOU

1. Find a willing partner and practise your microphone technique. Move gradually towards your partner into your normal interviewing position and ask him/her to tell you exactly when you begin to get too close for normal comfort. Did you also start to feel uncomfortable at that point? Practise your technique and ask your partner to suggest ways you could make this invasion of privacy less intimidating.
2. Decide on a subject to interview your partner about and ask him/her to play the part of the inexperienced and awkward interviewee, by shuffling, moving around and

coughing, etc. For your part, attempt to keep control in as pleasant a way as possible. Then, without comment, swap round and repeat the exercise. Then discuss what you learnt and advise one another on how you could have best dealt with that situation. Did you keep up the eye contact?

OTHER RESOURCES

- If you have only grown up with digital editing, see what analogue editing was all about in this short video: http://bit.ly/BJAnalogue.

- Here's a detailed video explanation of what cartridge machines are (they would have news clips or radio station jingles recorded on them) http://bit.ly/BJCarts1 and here are some in action: http://bit.ly/BJCarts2.

TUTOR NOTES

Show your students an old cassette player and let them explore how it works and how sound was recorded. Make a recording, play it back and hear how it sounds. Then take that same cassette and stand it on a loudspeaker for a few minutes before playing it back. Get the students to identify why it sounds different.

CHAPTER 18

Editing

Interviewees should know if their contribution is to be edited. Care should be taken that interviews are fairly edited, and the interviewee has to answer the main points raised.

BBC Guidelines

Few raw interviews appear on air without some form of editing – live interviews are the obvious exception. But where an interview has been pre-recorded, and time permits, the reporter will usually want to tighten it up and trim it to the required length. Just as important is editing out irrelevant questions and statements to throw into focus comments that are newsworthy. You may also want to alter the sequence of questions and answers to point up a strong angle that emerged during the interview.

Finally, recordings are usually fine edited to give them polish by removing mistakes, hesitation, repetition and intrusive background noise, such as a passing lorry or a ringing phone.

Editing has four main functions:

- Reduce length.

- Remove unwanted material.

- Alter the sequence of recorded material.

- Permit creative treatment.

If your brief is to produce a three-minute interview with a Maori leader about his claim to land-rights and you return with seven minutes, then, unless the material is stunningly good, four minutes will just have to go.

The best part of the interview might be at the beginning, so the last four minutes can be chopped. Or the best parts could be the answers to the first, third, fifth and seventh questions, so the others will need to be edited out. On second thoughts, those questions/answers might sound better in a different order, so the unwanted sections should be cut out and the rest edited into a different sequence.

Lastly, you may want to add a creative touch by beginning the item with a piece of Maori tribal music. This will have to be blended in afterwards to fade under the opening words of the tribesman. This is known as a *cross-fade*. But it still has to be included in that overall three minutes.

'YOU CAN'T SEE THE JOIN'

The principle of editing is simple, but the practice takes longer to master. The art is to leave the finished recording sounding completely natural, as though nobody had come within a mile of it. A good edit should be like a good wig: the join should be invisible.

The first rule of editing is that the finished product must make sense. Hacking sentences in half and joining non-sequiturs is not so much editing as butchering. Second, the editing must be in sympathy with the subject's speech patterns. A good edit will never leave the voice dangling on a rising note, as the sentence will sound unfinished and unnatural. Instead the edit should be made during a pause and following a natural downturn in the voice. Commas, full stops and other punctuation points form natural pauses and are usually the best places to make the cut.

Where exactly the edit is made within that pause is also important. The pause will end with an intake of breath before the next sentence. The edit should be made *after* that breath, but in the split second before the speaker starts to utter the next

FIGURE 18.1
Basic on-screen editing: highlighting the section that is to be edited, altered or saved.

word. That breath will then sound as though it belongs to the word after the edit. You won't be able to hear the join.

Obviously the final word on the recording should not be followed by a pause and a breath, as this would sound as though the speaker had been cut off in full flow!

The following shows how a reporter would edit a section to produce a clip for a news bulletin. The words in capitals are the ones the reporter will keep, while the rest are edited out. Read the whole passage though, then just read the words in capitals.

Editing a 30-Second Bulletin Clip

Reporter: OK. So what we need now is for you to explain that again so I can record it. So . . . we're recording – what will you be telling the council?

Councillor: Well, when we get together tonight, what I'll be wanting to know is/ WHY WEREN'T RESIDENTS TOLD THEIR HOMES WERE LIKELY TO FLOOD AT HIGH TIDE?/I mean, nobody had any idea this would happen,/WHY DID THE PLANNERS LET THIS DEVELOPMENT GO AHEAD IN THE FIRST PLACE, FOR GOODNESS SAKE?/I mean, this is what we pay them for isn't it?/WHY WEREN'T THE NECESSARY CHECKS MADE – AND/who is going to pay for it?

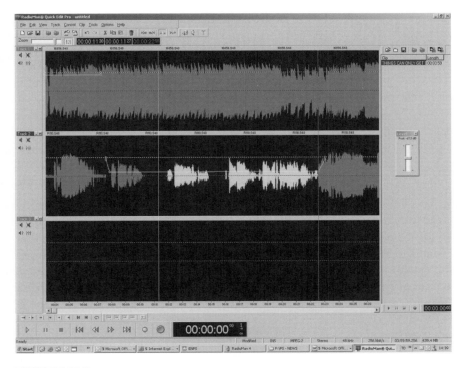

FIGURE 18.2

Introducing a second track so music can be dipped under speech.

– That's the important one,/JUST WHO IS GOING TO PAY FOR THE DAMAGE? ONE THING'S FOR SURE, IT SHOULDN'T BE THE RESIDENTS, AND THEY'RE THE ONES WHO ARE HAVING TO PAY RIGHT NOW./The . . .

Reporter: Have you . . .? Sorry . . .

Councillor: No, go on.

Reporter: What I wanted to ask was/HAVE YOU ANY IDEA HOW MUCH THE FLOOD DAMAGE WILL COST TO PUT RIGHT?

Councillor: THOUSANDS. HUNDREDS AND THOUSANDS OF POUNDS. CARPETS, WALLPAPER, FURNITURE, WHOLE HOMES ARE RUINED, AND ALL BECAUSE SOME FEATHERBRAIN DIDN'T STOP TO THINK ABOUT THE HIGH TIDES. IT'S NEGLIGENCE, AND SOMEBODY SHOULD BE SACKED.

UNETHICAL EDITING

Care must be taken with editing not to distort the meaning of what has been said. Selective, careless or unscrupulous editing can make someone appear to be saying something completely different, and the easiest way to fall into that trap is to take a qualified statement and to harden it up into something stronger than the speaker said or meant.

Reporter: Are you in favour of the death penalty?

Interviewee: 'That's very difficult to say / YES . . . / I suppose so, under certain circumstances, but it's an awful thing to take a life, whatever that person has done. When you're dealing with /MURDERERS AND RAPISTS WHO WILL PROBABLY KILL AND RAPE ALL OVER AGAIN AS SOON AS THEY'RE RELEASED . . . / I don't know, maybe / THEY SHOULD BE EXECUTED. /But there are always those who are genuinely sorry for what they've done and are serving their time – while there's life there's hope. They might change. But it's the others, / THE MANIACS AND FANATICS WHO CAN'T STOP KILLING – THEY'RE A MENACE TO US ALL, / but, on the other hand, that's what prisons are for, isn't it?

If you read only the words in capitals the statement becomes a strong and unqualified call for the death penalty. But taking the answer as a whole, it is apparent that is not what the interviewee was saying. This kind of selective editing that distorts a person's arguments is never ethical, and could never be justified. But reporters are often faced with having to shed some of the context and qualifications to get the audio down to length, and the decisions about what to cut are usually made against the clock.

Where this happens, the story should be explained more fully in the cue or accompanying narrative. Your reporting skills will often mean your explanation will be more concise and economical than that of your interviewee, but the intention should always be to give a fair, accurate and complete picture of what has been said.

BASIC PRODUCTION

Think of audio editing as word-processing – with the spoken word. Unwanted phrases can be cut out, pauses tightened, glitches removed and the order of the interview can be turned on its head by a simple cut and paste process to point up the strongest, most newsworthy sound-bites.

Next, background sound can be added – the hubbub of an airport terminal or engines revving up at the racetrack. Individual sound effects can be brought in – an airport announcement or a squeal of tyres. Then appropriate music can be introduced to illustrate the theme and faded down beneath the first interview.

Just as with editing speech, there are ethical considerations to be made when including music and effects in your production. Most newsrooms would have a strict prohibition against adding sound that is not from the *scene* of the original recording. So, it would be wrong to interview someone at an airport and then to post-produce the interview with terminal noises recorded at another location on another day (perhaps effects from an online library of sounds).

However, recording the airport manager in amongst the hubbub of the departure gate presents additional issues when editing: if you want to use a soundbite from the start and another from the end of the interview, the background noise (announcements, conversations of passers-by, mobility buggies, horns and so on) will 'jump' in the edit. The interview will be accurate but will sound disjointed.

The issue could be exacerbated if you wanted to (ethically) re-order the clips: the buggy in the background would appear to pass before it has approached. Or, if you intend to use the entire interview without moving elements around within it . . . what if the guest makes a verbal slip while answering? You may be forced to make an edit for accuracy and you'd still have the background noise jumping in the edit.

Your editor may consider airing such an interview the ethically correct thing to do: it's an authentic representation of what happened and listeners should know exactly where edits have been made. (After all, TV edits are now more likely to be done across a fade than a cut-away partly for this reason.)

Alternatively you *may* consider the following work-around: record the interview in a quiet corner of the terminal. Then record the hubbub separately but crucially with the recorder at the same level as you had for the interview (so you don't make this 'wildtrack' appear louder than it would have been had they been recorded at the same time). Then you can edit the speech and lay the other effects underneath.

Sound alters our perceptions of a story and journalists should remember that news is not a Hollywood movie. The reporter should be giving an accurate report of what happened at the scene. If sirens are roaring that's fine to include. But it would be considered an ethical breach to get sound effects of sirens from an outside audio source and add them into the report.

But when does 'news' turn into a 'feature'? In other words, when is the subject matter light enough to engage in more 'creative' production which would be more ethically acceptable? If one adds music to an edit, does that help tell the story or is it misleading? Or is that a convention that most listeners would understand and accept?

The *piéce de résistance* of editing is to be able to turn around two different versions of the radio piece for different programmes, plus a couple of sound-bites for the news, while still retaining the same sparkling quality of the original, and then to shrink or stretch each item to exactly the desired length – to the second – without altering the pitch of the voice or music.

Many editing programs ape conventional radio studios by displaying the image of a mixing desk on screen. The mixing desk allows you to blend various sounds together. You can click on the sliding volume controls with your mouse and raise or lower them. Familiar peak-level meters show you how loud or quiet your recording will be. Another window might display conventional tape controls: play, record, pause, fast-forward, rewind, cue and review.

Cut and Paste

The sound is digitised – converted into computer code – by sampling each sound up to 48,000 times per second. Your recording is displayed in a track or band on the screen, depicted as a waveform. The peaks represent loud sounds and the troughs indicate silence. You can also zoom in so that each peak can be picked out individually to make tricky edits easier.

To cut out a sentence, click on to the breath space before that sentence begins and then to the trough after it finishes, which highlights the phrase. Then click on the edit button (often a picture of a pair of scissors, or simply use CONTROL X on the keyboard) and it is deleted. If you want to keep that sentence but move it to another part of the recording, then the process is as simple as the cut and paste on your word processor.

Digital editing is *non-destructive*. You need never edit your original, only a copy of it. The missing portion can be restored in a moment, just by pressing the undo key on your keyboard. If you make a slip you can cancel the offending edit and pick up where you left off. And if you make a complete mess of the whole thing and need to start again, you can simply make a fresh copy of your original, which has been stored in all its pristine perfection on hard disk.

Because each digital copy is a perfect clone of the original, the sound quality will never deteriorate, no matter how many times you reproduce it. And while you are using the raw interview to produce bulletin clips, a colleague can be using the same material to start cutting a package.

MULTI-TRACKING

Overlaying sounds on top of one another to make a cross-fade is also simplicity itself.

Most sound editing software displays the recordings as tracks. Let's say the top track is your interview and you want to quietly fade up music under your interview to reach full volume as soon as the talking ends. You paste your recorded music onto the empty track below the interview and shuffle it around until it is in the right position. Then you draw in your fade with your mouse. At any stage, you can listen back to the portion you are working on to hear how it sounds. When you are happy with the blend you save the result.

To construct an elaborate report, you can build it up section by section, layer by layer, or you can programme the overlay points into the computer and set it to compile the item automatically. Sophisticated edit programs use a time code, like television, to guarantee the timing of each edit will be spot-on to the fraction of a second.

With digital editing you can be as multi-layered as you like. A single operator can combine multiple tracks from a single keyboard – though most news reports seldom call for more than four simultaneous tracks of sound and usually it is only one or two.

Bells and Whistles

An inevitable problem with multi-layered audio packages is one of variation in sound levels. With so many sources, some portions of the final report may be too loud while others are too quiet. With digital recordings, a stroke of the *normalise* key will automatically even out your recording levels.

Similarly, you can adjust the tone of parts of your recording by tweaking the EQ (equalisation). This will change the bass, treble or mid-range tone, or allow other filters to be used for more creative work, such as echo. A *pan* control allows you to send your sounds marching from the left speaker to the right, and making a *loop* will allow you to repeat endlessly background ambience such as hotel lounge hubbub.

The computer can be used to drive entire programmes or news bulletins, with all the interview clips stored on a playlist on the hard disk. The newsreader can choose whether to read the script from the screen or from paper and fires each clip at the click of a button.

As all this technology can be crammed into a notebook computer digital editing can be carried out in the field. The journalist can produce a professionally mixed report and send it back to the radio station along a studio-quality ISDN (Integrated Services Digital Network) line or as an e-mail attachment.

STUDIO MIXING

For more sophisticated productions, one sound source can be mixed with another to achieve a blend. Returning to our interview with the Maori, the tribal song may be blended to fade into the background as he begins to speak and dipped down until it eventually disappears.

To do this in a studio you would need three sound sources. One would have the Maori interview, another the music and the third would record the combination of the two, which would be blended through the mixing desk.

Mixers range from small boxes with a few controls to contraptions with a mind-boggling array of switches, sliders and knobs that look as intimidating to the uninitiated as the flight deck of a jumbo jet. Don't be put off – the idea is basically simple.

A mixer takes two (or more) sounds and allows you to blend them together as you wish. To do this it needs *inputs* to receive the signals, and gain controls to adjust their volumes. Meters display the volume levels, and a main gain sets the final level of the combined signal. When you have balanced the result to your satisfaction the signal is sent through the outputs to another recorder or on to air.

And that is basically it, although sophisticated mixers also have a variety of extra controls for fine adjustments. Larger versions are used as the main *control desks* in radio stations to put programmes on air. Other versions mix and edit television programmes or produce music master tapes.

The volume on a mixer is set by a slider (*fader*) which is usually pushed up to turn the volume up, and pulled down to turn it down.

Setting Levels

The operator of the mixer, control desk or panel rides the levels to maintain a consistent output. The sound should not be allowed to rise so high that it distorts, nor dip too low, or to surge and fall. Some desks have automatic level controls or *compressors* built into them to keep the sound output at an optimum, but running the desk on auto pilot stifles any creativity. It can be a bit like holding every conversation at shouting pitch.

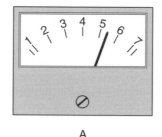 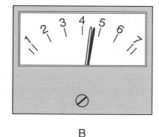 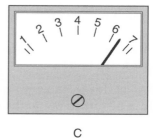

A   B   C

FIGURE 18.3
Setting the levels on the PPMs

A 5½ is the usual peak for speech.
B This stereo meter has two coloured needles to show the different peaks for the left and right channels. Music has a wider dynamic range than speech and sounds louder to the ear, so to avoid blasting the audience levels are usually turned down to peak at 4½.
C Speech over the telephone loses much of its dynamic range. It sounds quieter than normal speech and can be difficult to hear. Levels should be boosted to 6½ to compensate.

Levels are often set on a *PPM* (peak programme meter), which registers the peaks of output but has a dampened action to stop it fluctuating wildly like a VU meter. This makes it easier to use. Alternatively, levels can be displayed as a sequence of green lights that rise and fall with the volume. When they rise beyond a certain point they go red, which means the volume is too high and is beginning to sound distorted.

TYPES OF FADE

Different fades are used to achieve a variety of effects.

Pre-Fade

The fader on a studio desk is essentially the volume control for one particular source – and called this because the sound can fade up or down as you adjust the slider. When you 'pre-fade', you hear the sound source in the studio without putting it on air. This way you can check one item while other audio is being broadcast. In other words the source is heard before (or 'pre') the fader is put up.

An example would be when a local station is opting into the network news. The producer will pre-fade the network to make sure it is being received before crossing over on cue.

The pre-fade buttons on the mixing desk work by sending the sound from the source being monitored to one ear of your headphones, leaving you free to listen with your other ear to what is going out on air.

Cross-Fade

The cross-fade is where one source is faded up as another is faded out, and is commonly used to mix music or sound effects with speech.

Fading Down and Fading Up

This is where the two sounds don't overlap but where one source is faded out and another faded in after a very short pause. This is useful where there are sounds that would jar together if cross-faded, such as two pieces of music in different keys.

Figure 18.4 represents the opening sequence of *Money Talks*. The signature tune (A) dips beneath Note's introduction (B) but does not disappear, bubbling underneath to re-emerge during a pause (C) and dipping again beneath the menu (D). It then cross-fades into a stab (E), which brings the signature sequence to an end. Note introduces the first item (F) which then begins (G).

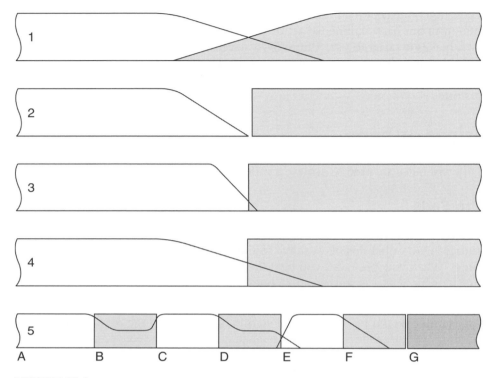

FIGURE 18.4

1. Cross-fade. Where one item is faded out and another is faded in at the same time (e.g. music giving way to sound effects).
2. Fade. The first item fades out completely before the other begins.
3. The first item fades out quickly and the next begins sharply while the first is still dying away.
4. The first item is faded out gradually, continuing to fade while the other one begins (e.g. music under speech).
5. SIGNATURE TUNE: 'It's 4 o'clock and this is *Money Talks* with Penny Note. Good afternoon.' (DIP)

   SIG. (DIP) 'Today new claims of insider dealing on the stock market and the companies that are casing in on the Aids scare.'

   STAB (FADE) 'But first, the budget and the question today that everyone is asking – will he or won't he cut the tax? Etc.' '. . . could push share prices to an all-time high as Peter Lloyd has been finding out in the City.'

   BUDGET / LLOYD 'The market has been in a bullish mood today in anticipation of those tax cuts. Shares have risen and look set to . . . etc.'

Pot-Cut

This means closing the fader rapidly to cut short an item. Care must be taken to 'pull the item out' very quickly and at a natural pause in the speech, otherwise the words will be clipped or trail off. This is made easier by marking *pot-points* on your cue sheet that tell the technical operator where the item can be cut early, and what the last words are before that point.

Fading In and Out

When a sound effect or piece of music is supposed to be bubbling under a recorded item before making its appearance it should be faded in gradually, or it will jar. Ideally, it should blend in so well that the listener will be unaware of its coming in or its going out. Judging the right length for a fade and the precise point at which the audio should be turned up to full volume takes practice. If you are using music, work with the rhythm or bring the song up at the start of a lyric. The fade down should also be smooth and gradual.

THE HEADLINES

- The most important rule – never change the meaning of what the interviewee said.

QUESTIONS FOR YOU

1. Take an interview you have made that could be improved by adding suitable music at the start. Practise using a crossfade to put that music beneath the interview. How long should the music run before being faded out? How loud should it be so it does not drown the interview or disappear too soon? What happens if you crossfade singing under speech?

OTHER RESOURCES

- Guidelines for Ethical Video and Audio Editing from the Radio and Television Digital News Association: http://bit.ly/BJRTDNA.

- Audacity (http://audacity.sourceforge.net/) is a free, open-source audio editing program for Windows, Mac and Linux. Screencast video tutorials are in many places including here: http://bit.ly/BJAudacity1 and http://bit.ly/BJAudacity2.

TUTOR NOTES

Some ready-made examples and ethical questions about editing in this article: 'BBC's Edit of Obama's Inauguration Speech Raises Important Ethical Questions': http://bit.ly/BJObama.

CHAPTER 19

The Studio

While the smallest radio stations can be built into a shack or a shop with little more than a computer and some domestic equipment, most will boast a complex suite of studios, each equipped to perform a different function.

ON-AIR STUDIO

The main event is the main *on-air studio*. This is where the programmes are presented. A radio station worthy of the name would have at least two identical on-air studios in case one develops a fault.

FIGURE 19.1A

FIGURE 19.1B
The same studio, 20 years apart. Note the large desk of faders (in the day when a fader was 'off' when it was up!) and the number of screens, compared with the more compact and tidy layout today.

FIGURE 19.2

And an even more streamlined studio, with equipment based around ViLor technology.

The typical studio is likely to be a hybrid of new and older technology: a computer system coupled with a transmission desk with good old-fashioned faders. Combining manual controls that are pulled up and down with state of the art electronics might seem a strange compromise, but the hybrid system combines the tactile features and intuitive ease of control of a mixing desk with all the flexibility of digital technology.

Standard equipment would include a screen on which the names of songs, jingles, news clips and adverts appear. The presenter uses a keyboard, mouse or touchscreen to play each item on demand. There may be a CD player (to use if the computer playout system crashes); large monitor loudspeakers; telephone and mini-switchboard system; *talkback* (a form of intercom); presenter and guest mikes; and a studio clock with on-air lights.

The studio will be linked to the newsroom via a monitor to receive information such as headlines and the weather. Commercial stations will also have a separate studio complex to make adverts, featuring a mixing desk and mikes so that voice-overs can be recorded.

The BBC's chain of some 40 local (county-wide) radio stations have each functioned technologically separately, using different equipment in their studios, storing audio files locally, and each housing the processors and transmitting equipment to broadcast to their area. The big variation in quality of kit (some of it nearly 30 years old) was considered concerning as local radio stations have a special responsibility to broadcast in times of emergency.

So from 2014 the ViLoR (virtualised local radio) system started to be introduced. That's an IP-based method for uniting the networking and distribution elements of all local BBC radio stations. Increasingly all BBC local radio signal processing, outside sources and transmission routing is being centralised into two large data centres.

Locally, presenters and producers will still have full control over play-out systems and mixing desks, but the actual audio files are stored in 'the cloud' and streamed, mixed and processed in real-time from that remote data centre.

The total number of equipment racks across all BBC local radio stations was 580 – an expensive system to house and maintain. Continuing to use physical kit in local radio stations would see that rise to 760, whereas ViLoR will reduce the number to 290. The aim is to roll out ViLoR across the entire BBC local radio chain by 2017.

BBC press release (http://bit.ly/BJVilor)

TALKS STUDIO

The talks studio is an acoustically treated room for interviews and discussions. Guests sit around a circular or hexagonal table facing individual microphones. There will be visual contact with the main studio through a large glass window.

THE CONTRIBUTIONS STUDIO

The news is typically read from a *news booth* or contributions studio. The control desk is simplified to allow presenters to operate their own audio equipment while they read the news. Scripts are read from a computer screen, with the audio inserts fired off from the same source.

FIGURE 19.3

The view from the gallery into the studio for S33, the studio for BBC Radio 4's flagship news programme, *Today*. Credit: BBC Radio 4, *Today* programme

FIGURE 19.4

FIGURE 19.5

The main studio for the *Today* programme. Note the remote cameras on the wall, which automatically cut to whichever microphone is being used and automatically streams that feed to the website. Radio becomes television . . . Credit: BBC Radio 4, *Today* programme.

The contributions studio is also used to record interviews or reports from journalists at remote studios or on location. These can then be saved to the central hard drive at the station and edited simultaneously by several staff, and then if necessary sent to other stations as a simple MP3 file.

Alternatively, the newsreader may present the bulletin or programme from an on-air studio. National stations might employ technical operators to play in the audio inserts, allowing the newsreader to concentrate on the presentation.

REMOTE STUDIOS

Some radio stations serve large areas where reporters would struggle to cover a story and get back in time for the deadline. Likewise, because of the distance involved, guests might be unwilling or unable to travel to the station to record an interview.

Recording everything by phone is quick and cheap, but at the expense of quality. *Remote studios* are a better solution. These are usually small rooms rented in well-placed larger buildings such as a city hall. They contain a microphone, mixer and possibly a recording deck. The remote studio is connected to the radio station by a broadcast-quality telephone line. Guests can go there to be interviewed and reporters can use them to send back reports.

FIGURE 19.6

FIGURE 19.7

The contributions studio, or pod, in a corridor at New Broadcasting House. It's from here that a guest can do a 'down the line' interview to another station in the network.

RADIO CAR

Radio cars have been essential news gathering tools for on-the-spot coverage of stories such as fires, demonstrations, or live events. The car contains everything you need to send back a studio quality recording from the scene, previously via a UHF or VHF transmitter with a telescopic mast. This has now been replaced with smaller, cheaper, more convenient satellite technology. But the 'kit in the back' remains similar: microphones with hefty windshields and plenty of cable (or radio mikes), often a sound mixer, a talkback system to base.

OUTSIDE BROADCAST VEHICLE

A development of the radio car is the outside broadcast (OB) vehicle, which has sophisticated equipment to mix complete programmes on location and send them out live. These are used for roadshows, large scale OBs or live concerts.

MOBILE PHONES

These have transformed radio coverage, not only in their basic use of a reporter phoning in a story, but also because with the latest gadgetry they can send reports from anywhere in near broadcast quality. And that does away with the need for a radio car, OB vehicle or even a studio.

There are other advantages. More breaking news can be covered live; editors can keep in touch with journalists on the spot without waiting for them to call in; phones can be linked to recorders so interviews can be sent back from remote areas, and sports commentators are no longer rooted to the press box but can broadcast from around the ground.

Instead of dictating a cue, the reporter can hook up his computer to the phone and send the script back almost instantly.

With a little practice it is possible to incorporate a recorded interview into a live report made on the phone. Interview extracts and linking narrative can be edited back at the station and played on air well before you have returned.

If you are in a studio and your interviewee is on the end of a phone you need to find a way of recording your voice in studio quality. The answer is at hand in the form of a *telephone balance unit*, which allows you to use a microphone instead of the telephone handset and lets you adjust the levels to avoid sounding louder than your interviewee.

Phone Levels

Recording levels for telephone reports need to be boosted slightly to compensate for the poor quality telephone line. The phone is unable to convey the full tonal range of the human voice so the ear will perceive the thin-sounding recording as being quieter than normal and listeners will have to strain to hear unless the levels are adjusted.

OBSCENITY BUTTON

Telephones are used for *phone-in* discussions where listeners call in with their questions and comments. Here there is an even greater hazard than the faint phone line – the probability that sooner or later a listener will swear, blaspheme or utter a libel on the airwaves. The presenter's last line of defence is the *obscenity*, or *profanity, button*. As soon as a caller says anything seriously offensive, the presenter presses the obscenity button, and the offending comment never reaches the airwaves – even on a live programme.

FIGURE 19.8

When a studio clock displays more than merely the time

It works by previously putting the whole programme into *delay*. The show is recorded and played back seven seconds or so later: the presenter will play a short jingle and start talking at the same time, but listeners will hear the jingle *followed* by the presenter. The live show has therefore been 'buffered' before its transmission.

When the presenter presses the obscenity button, the programme is snatched out of delay and put immediately into real time: the profanity has, hopefully, been bottled up in that seven-second segment which never went on air.

THE HEADLINES

- Despite its age, radio keeps developing. It takes on new technology meaning better signals, more speed, adaptability . . . but fewer staff.

QUESTIONS FOR YOU

1. If you have access to a studio and a news booth, prepare a bulletin with inserts and present it first with a technical operator at the control desk, and then entirely by yourself in the booth. Do you prefer to drive the news yourself, or be driven? What are the advantages and disadvantages of each type of operation?
2. As eye contact is so important in interviewing, what difficulties would you expect conducting an interview with a guest who is miles away in a remote studio?

- If you are in a class, simulate those difficulties by devising a scenario and conducting an interview with a classmate *back to back*. Do not forget, he/she will need advice on how to use the microphone, how to sit and how to turn on the equipment.

OTHER RESOURCES

- A good overview of studio design, layout and equipment: http://bit.ly/BJStudioLayout.

- For lots of discussions about the future of radio, watch the website of 'radio futurologist' James Cridland: http://james.cridland.net/.

TUTOR NOTES

Conduct a class interview or maybe ask in some guests (a radio journalist and a presenter) and ask them how they imagine the radio station of tomorrow will look. Are they for or against new technology? Ask them which devices that have yet to be invented would make their jobs easier and more efficient.

How do *your students* see the radio station of tomorrow?

Television

CHAPTER 20

Television Newsroom Production

The TV newsroom used to be *only* about news bulletins at fixed times: morning, middle of day, evening. Big network and global newsrooms still have these fixed bulletins – but there is always a lot of live, because that is what TV newsrooms do best.

So here are some broadcast newsroom constants:

> A clumsy sentence in a script is still confusing or ugly.
>
> Fast, accurate scripting is still needed.
>
> An error in a caption or text is still noticed.
>
> An original thought, script or idea is still appreciated.

And now we add . . .

> Until artificial intelligence takes us over, always regard automation systems and computers as extremely stupid. They will still only do what you tell them to.

Then there is the public – not just as audience. All over the world individuals are playing an increasing role in creating television news rather than just consuming it. Almost anyone has the technical means to publish material widely and almost instantly.

THE TV NEWS STORY

A single news event – on screen, website or mobile access – starts with the story and the hunt for ways to tell the story. Not just sound and pictures but other material such as graphics, maps, script and lives. Then the link for the presenter, which may be written before or after the assembly of a packaged report, or even scribbled in seconds for an ongoing live.

There's also online feedback and debate, and archive. The archive no longer goes into a basement room. It needs to be recalled, often several times a day. Stories that hit the public interest can take on a new life, with the public offering information (which should be checked unless it's just witness descriptions), commenting on their blogs or by email (which is read on air if legally and ethically acceptable) or even offering pictures to the channel. The newsroom journalist has become a sort of gateway and moderator.

TV journalists may need to produce a number of versions of the same picture and sound content to be transmitted over mobile TV, internet TV, standard TV and HD (high-definition). Receiving devices may vary from hand-held to very large screens for the home, or giant screens in public places like rail stations and airports.

The skills of basic, accurate television journalism and good writing have not changed. Great sound and pictures still must be honoured.

The regular scheduled bulletins – news you make an appointment to watch – may still be around for many channels, but for most journalists in a modern newsroom it will be a 24/7 operation.

'Breaking' news dictates everything. Running orders are built for different segments or sequences but there is also a rhythm to a day, with build-ups to primary bulletins at the top of each hour. The journalist does not so much sit at the screen as get plugged into it. He will view all the latest pictures as they arrive in the newsroom. He has access to all the items edited from them, and to a vast selection of digitised library and archive material. He will also be alert to new 'lives' – that means new pictures or guest interviewees available for the programme or sequence within a continuous news rolling channel. View it, check it, edit it, save it for later, message it to a colleague, send it for transmission, re-edit it for later use and keep essential elements for the archive.

The technology has been designed to fit the way TV newsrooms work but with it are new ways of doing things, and new problems. No two newsroom operations are identical, but anyone entering TV journalism will soon find that adaptability is the key. That means understanding the technology as well as the basic skills to be a television journalist. The journalist could work at Sky News or GMTV or the BBC in the UK, or CNN or Fox in the USA, and then go back to Sky News and still find that colleagues have a lot in common. The IT may look similar. The news sources may be the same. Yet the journalists in all TV newsrooms will all gather around a screen in hyper-active groups because of a big breaking story. News is still about people after all.

ADVANTAGES AND DISADVANTAGES

One advantage of all this is speedy TV journalism – on air fast, reports assembled swiftly with fast turnaround and of high-grade audio-visual quality. Another is that raw material in sound and picture can be viewed by everyone and prepared in one version or cut-fast for headlines, promos or trails, and another for a regional bulletin or a tease for 'coming up' or a round-up of events.

One disadvantage can be distraction. If newsroom journalists add basic editing and headline cuts to their responsibilities, critics will say, can they pay attention to things like exercising news judgement and communicating with reporters and other colleagues?

Many channels of course will also see savings in this kind of newsroom production. Jobs have been lost. Operating expenses cut. With a digital workflow, stations can produce more sellable news and improve their bottom line.

Many journalists also mourn the decline of the packaged report – it hasn't gone completely but live and breaking news is now the main currency of TV news.

Just like radio, a television package is like a bag with lots of different things which together make a complete self-contained report: the script, pictures, natural sound, interview clips/witnesses, reporter standing at the scene and possibly graphics such as charts or maps.

IN AND OUT

Like radio, there are two basic functions for television news journalists: those who go and get it, and those who put it together for transmission on any platform: TV, website, phone or anything else coming along next year. The newsroom is mostly the editing/production/assembly operation: where it all comes together to make sense of what's happening at any moment in time. Getting news is sometimes called Input, or Intake or Newsgathering. Putting the news together is sometimes called Output or Production.

On the Getting It side, the stories of the day are still usually selected by the home and foreign assignment desks, which can deploy reporters or video-journalists to cover them. Small TV newsrooms may be affiliates of bigger news operations and

FIGURE 20.1

Television production journalism and technology in partnership. A main production tool is an IT system into which all sound and pictures, packaged reports, agency feeds and archive are placed for instant access on desktop stations. Courtesy Sky News.

share resources. Some of the big international newsrooms have reporters, some staff and some freelance, in many parts of the world.

TELEVISION NEWSROOM TECHNOLOGY

In an ideal day the journalist used to take his pile of rushes (raw unedited pictures) to the editor and together they put it together in a way that applies the grammar of television storytelling. Even better, the journalist might have any archive needed, and graphics, and arrive at an edit suite with them all. In reality that rarely happened: new pictures came in half-way through the edit, the archive he wanted isn't available because someone else is using it or it cannot be found and the graphics needed are not ready, or he realises that there's a spelling error in a map or chart. The edit suite cost as much as a small house anyway and it's now being tied up for two hours.

Now multi-media newsrooms look more like the HQ of a James Bond villain aiming at world domination. There are architects who specialise in broadcast newsrooms.

The aim of the all-digital workflow is to get rid of old costly bottlenecks and delays, although new bottlenecks can appear to replace others. Certainly the new systems came with their own problems and with so many things in all aspects of life, the problems often have to happen before they can be fixed.

So now the journalist can browse pictures on the desktop, select pictures and sound and find material from archive or library. A basic simple edit can be done then and there, a script can be written for the presenter, the entire story sent to a senior editor and then transmission. Many versions of the same story can be prepared for different outlets which may have different needs.

The newsroom journalist is now challenged by the modern curse of Too Much Choice. There's so much material available in the newsroom now that it's often hard to know where to begin. It may seem obvious to just grab the most recent pictures. The most recent pictures are the most in demand in a 24/7 operation when a live story is changing or moving in new directions. But for a self-contained report/package that summarises what has been happening it's a blunt instrument to think that the most recent material is always the best way to explain a story to the viewer.

FIGURE 20.2
News to go. Technology like Enterprise sQ is designed to power a newsroom, dealing with fast turnaround production to put material on air. Courtesy Quantel.

What matters in the sharing newsroom is the simple need for direct communication within a team – what are these pictures and where in all this data can I find them?

ORDER FROM CHAOS – THE JOURNALIST'S MOST BASIC NEED-TO-KNOW

There's nothing very random about what is transmitted and when. While 24/7 news channels have lots of flexibility and can be fleet-of-foot with that all-embracing expression 'some breaking news just in' there is still the need for a programme structure: the running order – like radio – is what goes where and when and the order in which things happen on screen.

In either a stand-alone bulletin of television news or a 24/7 endless rolling channel some kind of order of events ensures everyone in the process knows what is happening.

In a television newsroom each story always has to have a name, or a main name and sub-name if one story is so big it has many different elements. What is vital is to be consistent – so if a running order says the story is called 'Israel Clashes', then there could be chaos if the journalist then calls it 'Jerusalem Clashes' or leaves out a single letter in either word. To a running order these are totally different things and if it was confusing enough with people communicating verbally and quickly able to make sense of an error, then imagine how badly it's now going to go wrong with computers in the system.

Bigger newsrooms, with shifts, regular staff turnover and freelances need newcomers to understand and comply unfailingly with a system which leaves no room for error.

In the understandable haste which accompanies live news and any approaching deadline, it is all too easy to go wrong when no one is entirely sure whether the item entitled 'Washington' in the running order is the same as the one headed 'President' on the script or whether it is the same as the 'Election Interview' item.

What is needed is a formula, a drop-down name for a story that everyone can understand and keep the endless eating machine of news functioning. This name is a bit like titles in a traditional library – the kind that has books. The shelves have names for types of books to guide

FIGURE 20.3

In the TV newsroom one priority for the journalist is ensuring that a story title tells everyone what an item actually is. It can also be called a 'slug' or 'catch' or 'catchline' or 'clipname' or just 'title'. Credit: Dalet Digital Media Systems.

the visitor. There are titles like 'Fiction' or 'Sport' or 'Politics' and inside these titles and on the shelves are many different aspects of those single titles, from science fiction to cycling and local government.

The *name* is about publishing and labelling each item. The result of failing to do this is simple – it is lost. It vanishes – temporarily but inconveniently – into a sort of mush of bytes.

The computer system is there to help, so long as you remember WYSIWYG (whizzy-wig) or What You See Is What You Get. The same meaning as Garbage In, Garbage Out.

Ultimately this simple but vital way of controlling newsroom production ensures that the journalist gets his or her material on air at the right time in the right place and without any confusion. It's a critical part of the teamwork that makes the modern newsroom sometimes have the mood of a military operation.

LIVE – THE 24/7 NEWSROOM

The easiest way to do live TV news is to have a single shot of an event. A shot that is always available at any time so a channel can dip in and out of it when needed. It needs very little production effort. It might be a static shot of a transport accident, local traffic chaos, a rocket launch, an eclipse, a big state event or just a building where some international agreement is about to be signed. During and around this shot various reporters talk to the presenter and the presenter talks to experts brought in to explain or comment on what's happening.

Live news can certainly impose a tyranny on the journalist only because everyone in the journalism business is hungry for changing developments. Indeed, it is the moments when a big rolling story *goes quiet* that problems can occur, the most common being a 'development' which is 'unconfirmed' or an 'update' which turns out to be not an update at all.

As with all live TV news – being first is what counts. The global common call from the newsrooms is: first is first and second is nowhere, and variations of that.

A senior producer at the BBC News channel always faces the question – *What are we doing next?*

> This is the very essence of what we do: we devise the perfect running order and then throw it away when something more interesting happens. This could be anything from an explosion to a verdict in a major trial. I expect this to happen several times while I'm in the gallery, and I am rarely disappointed. I've frequently known three stories to break at the same time, so that while one presenter is telling viewers about the first, I'm briefing the other presenter about the next. Important court verdicts are usually rung straight to my phone in the gallery by the producer on the ground, and repeated by me sentence-by-sentence into the presenter's ear.

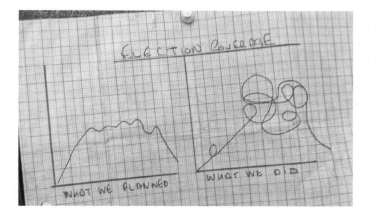

FIGURE 20.4
This scribbled assessment of newsroom planning was pinned on a notice board, probably by someone in a state of grief. But everyone will get over it, and start all over again. Planning in some industries applies prediction of certain events and human behaviour. In broadcast journalism events are by nature unpredictable.

> We get news on air in literally seconds. I emerge from the gallery buzzing but drained. A short debrief with the editors and the presenters, a quick lunch and then it's back on the desk.

Continuous news on a routine day operates a structure like a clock face, usually with fixed slots at fixed times for sport, weather, business and programme trails or promotions. The news tends to fit around these slots in response to news events, mixing traditional packages and background reports with as much live news as possible.

But when the big story happens, this routine is dropped.

The new broadcast journalist will probably then be assigned a specific job to concentrate on.

Any specific task in a TV newsroom could be:

- Monitoring and logging incoming pictures and sound
- Helping a presenter/reporter/correspondent
- Contacting potential guests/experts – people for a presenter to talk to
- Preparing graphics/maps or displays
- Logging and assessing social media (there will be some hoaxes)
- Looking at any stills coming in (there will be some fakes)
- Checking emails/blogs from the public (there will be some liars)
- Logging video offered by the public and checking if they want money or are happy just to have their name mentioned, or not
- Writing scripts but probably only about one aspect of the story
- Writing the updates that scroll on screen
- Monitoring messages from emergency services

. . . and, checking news events that have nothing whatsoever to do with what's going on in case some cunning PR person in the government decides it is a good moment to Bury Bad News.

ORGANISING MATERIAL FROM USER GENERATED CONTENT (UGC) AND CITIZEN JOURNALISM

People sent pictures to television newsrooms long before mobile technology. Pictures might also come from security cameras or public utility and road cameras and many news organisations will have arrangements in place in advance (especially with the police) to re-transmit public camera shots during a civil emergency.

Modern technology has put relatively high-resolution cameras into the hands of millions of people and given newsrooms powerful images. Early content broadcast by television news included the shocking impact of the Asian tsunami and the progress of a confused whale up a river. Quite simply, phone pictures can relay events before the arrival of professional camera crews and reporters.

Large news organisations have full-time staff who will monitor and file public images and make sure they are available to different sequences, the website and news slots.

Journalists must still treat offered UGC in the same way as a traditional phone tip-off – with caution. Some people will go to a lot of trouble just to carry out a hoax. The old maxim remains – if something looks too good to be true, then maybe it isn't.

TYPES OF CITIZEN JOURNALISM IN TELEVISION NEWS

These can be witness accounts and stills or video. TV newsrooms will use the pictures and people will email them in their thousands. Picture and sound formats are usually specified. The 'citizen' must provide his/her name, although many TV channels allow a 'nickname' if the real name is not to be used in any credit.

If you witness a news event, the ABC wants to hear from you. We would like you to send us your newsworthy photos, videos, audio clips or even written eyewitness accounts for consideration for use on ABC News.

ABC News Australia

Originally radio phone-ins did the same job as blogs in news coverage. Now the integration of public opinion in blogs can find its way into breaking TV news so long as it isn't legally dubious, tasteless or suspect.

Another type of citizen reportage is news broken on the web. Sometimes bloggers genuinely uncover something new. News organisations need to verify it – but if true, it's as reportable as anything else.

The argument against UGC is that not enough stories are visual enough to justify the use of what is in effect still amateur video which will come into a newsroom on just about any event at all and, in effect, waste a lot of time on something that needs professional coverage.

One of the problems newsrooms face when receiving UGC is copyright – in other words, who really owns the pictures being sent. It is not uncommon for members of the public to send in pictures which have actually been lifted from a website. They may be pictures owned by a news agency and that presents a newsroom with a whole new set of problems and a reluctant call to the programme lawyers. A few years ago arrangements for handling such material became more formal. Most news organisations present citizen journalists with an online form to fill in, stating clearly what is being offered and what it is to be used for and who has the right to use it, and when and where.

Another consideration is safety. Professional news crews covering fires, public disorder or explosions have been through a lot of training on how to avoid danger. Members of the public might not be as aware of the risks and journalists need to be aware that if a member of the public says they are going to collect material with the aim of sending it to a news service, then they should not put themselves in any danger.

THE HEADLINES

- Computers and automated production systems mean labelling or identifying material and sources has become essential to maintain speed and accuracy.

- In a television newsroom each story always has to have a name, or a main name and sub-name if one story is so big it has many different elements.

- When a big story happens a new broadcast journalist will probably be assigned a specific job to concentrate on – these include monitoring incoming pictures and sound, preparing graphics or displays, getting guests or assessing social media.

QUESTIONS FOR YOU

1. Can you talk your way into a local TV newsroom for perhaps a half-a-day? Explain who you are and why you would like to visit. *Do this on what seems to be a quiet news day.* Try to get the editor's name. Then you could write to or call the editor's office – you may not get the editor, but someone might help. If you get the invitation someone in the newsroom might even show you around for a while but you may then be asked to just sit-in at various places. Make some notes. Do not take pictures. Turn off or mute your phone.

2. Go to the website and find out what kind of news material your local TV newsroom is interested in. Always watch out for anything unusual, or even amusing, that you could film and that might interest them, even stills. Extreme weather is always in demand. Do not do anything hazardous. Do not invade privacy.

OTHER RESOURCES

- *TV News Careers. Who Works in a Television Newsroom?* Dawn Rosenberg McKay: http://careerplanning.about.com/od/exploringoccupations/tp/tv-news-careers.htm.

- Journalist Nick Higham takes a short tour of the BBC television newsroom at Broadcasting House in central London: http://www.bbc.co.uk/news/uk-21830951.

TUTOR NOTES

Organise a TV newsroom morning meeting for a 24/7 news channel. Write one page (A4/foolscap) of news prospects for the day – local, national or global, or all three. Maybe ten stories. One or two short sentences on each story. Print a copy for everyone and one for yourself. Tell them they have a three-hour segment to fill from 1400–1700. What stories are going in and, in detail, how will they be covered, who should be interviewed, are live reporters needed for some of them and where will these reporters be? Do any stories need graphics, charts and maps? Encourage argument.

You could show some clips from films or fictional TV series (or even soaps) about television newsrooms. How much does the fiction waver from the reality? Do any of the situations in fictional programmes actually have some credibility based on real situations? Discuss.

Offer your group a big breaking story – real or imaginary. All TV running orders have been dumped. Live pictures are coming in. What tasks will be assigned to each person or a team? How do they carry out those tasks? What can work well in the newsroom? What can go wrong? Discuss and argue.

CHAPTER 21

Writing Television News

Television news writing is not radio with pictures. It has its own techniques. Apart from the skill of writing to pictures and sound, TV scripts are also laid out differently from those in radio. They have to carry more information. As well as the story, the TV script has to give details of what we see and/or what we hear and the duration of shots or sound/video events. A script written directly into a newsroom computer system will also carry vital information for an item to be automatically transmitted as well as captions and graphics.

- The first thought is not – how do I tell this story? It is – how do I *show* it?

- The language of television scripting is all about cherishing the pictures and sound and adding to them with the words. That is storytelling. Find the pictures and the sound. Pick the most relevant, interesting or informative. Or just plain riveting, humane, thoughtful or emotional. Then get the words.

- It's about simple but clear communication rather than hammering the viewer with masses of wordy detail.

- It's about shutting up when the viewer sees and hears something that fixes him or her to a screen. Do not distract viewers when they are having an interesting experience.

That could all be a summary of what you do. But now we need to learn some techniques.

The television writer works in time – minutes and seconds, with a formula that three words of English (or any European language) takes on average one second to read aloud on the air. Despite word counts and duration calculations in a computer, this simple three-words-per-second guide provides the basis of all writing to pictures in television. This takes into account not only the slight variations in pace between presenters or reporters, but also the different lengths of words used in normal, spoken language.

TV stations lay out their scripts according to a house style, but, for the sake of clarity, visual and narrative information was always traditionally separated into two columns – visual on the left and script on the right. This can be as simple as a reporter in a hotel room with pen and paper or a laptop, placing his words on one side and a note about the visuals on the other. It just helps the brain get around the structure of the script.

In a newsroom, systems which automatically play an item to the audience also require a carefully inserted list of instructions from a dropdown menu.

HEADLINES

Just like radio and webpages, the headlines are the shop-window for a single bulletin or part of an all-news channel. The instructions ensure that what happens on screen fits with the script. Editorially however, headline shots or very short clips of interview still offer a promise of what's to come, or they can tease the viewer.

This is a generic style to show what we hear the presenter say, and what the viewer sees and hears.

HEADLINES

(PRESENTER IN VISION)

(HEADLINE ONE)

Flood waters are still threatening Yorkshire, Lincolnshire and the Midlands. Engineers are battling to stop a flood wall from bursting.

(PICTURES OF FLOODING APPEAR ON SCREEN)

This is the scene there now – hundreds of people have been moved from their homes after cracks appeared overnight. Large sections of two motorways are closed.

(HEADLINE TWO)

(PICTURES OF POLITICIAN AND NURSES)

The political tweet that backfired and caused a mass protest by hospital staff.

(HEADLINE THREE)

(PICTURES OF BOY HOLDING A SWORD)

. . . and the 12-year-old treasure hunter's find that has shocked historians.

(MUSIC STING / OPENING TITLES)

These layouts and the words in the (transmission instructions) vary from station to station throughout the world but they do follow a common pattern. Words written by the journalist go with instructions about what the viewer sees. If the journalist edits the pictures of flooding, then it must be named clearly with the same word used on both the script, and in the computer. The word might be 'floods' but it might be 'river' or 'flood wall' so whatever the name of the story is, it must remain the same through the newsroom process.

Out Of Vision Live Script (Also Called Underlay or Overlay)

These are labels that mean *live script to pictures* – which is usually the presenter talking while pictures and sound are being transmitted. It can start with the presenter in vision, then the presenter is no longer in vision and the screen shows only pictures and sound, but the presenter voice continues.

(PRESENTER IN VISION)

Rescuers are trying to re-float about a hundred stranded pilot whales on a beach on New Zealand's South Island.

(PICTURES. DURATION: 18 secs)

Many of the mammals had already been guided into deeper water, only for them to again run aground at Golden Bay. Scientists don't know what causes groups of whales to beach themselves. (11 seconds of script)

In this case the duration of the words should not be more than the duration of the pictures, otherwise the presenter might pop back into view too early, or the pictures will just stop and freeze at the end.

This script will be technically fine. Since we measure the words at three-words-per-second, here we have a duration of words against the pictures which takes about 11 seconds to be spoken by the presenter. We have 18 seconds of pictures – but that is how it should be.

What is vital is that the pictures do not last on screen for less time than it takes to speak the words. To be safe we should have at least 16–18 seconds of pictures – a few seconds longer than it takes to speak those words. It also lets the pictures breathe a little so the viewer can absorb what is going on.

In this story we see a beach like any other beach, except there are a lot of whales on it and a lot of people trying to help them. So the script usefully adds something we cannot see or hear.

Presenter Plus Stills or Graphics

A still is a single picture. A graphic shows information, with a chart, a graph, text, numbers or maybe a map. Sometimes all of these. This adds visual content and information to a link or presenter intro, in this case before a live interview.

We start with the presenter in vision and then we show a still image and some statistics on a chart.

(PRESENTER)

Old wives' tale or ancient wisdom?

(STILL APPEARS BEHIND PRESENTER – NAME: ECHINACEA)

The herbal remedy Echinacea has been used for centuries to ward off infection. Now it seems it really does work.

The plant was first used by

(GRAPHIC APPEARS BEHIND PRESENTER. SHOWS PLANT IN BACKGROUND)

native Americans. A new university study says it can reduce the chance of catching a cold by

(FIGURES APPEAR THAT SAY: Colds Risk Down by 58%)

58 per cent. And the length of colds was reduced

(MORE FIGURES APPEAR)

by an average of around a day and a half.

(PRESENTER NOW BACK IN VISION)

Professor Ron Eccles who's the director of the Common Cold Centre joins us from the University of Cardiff. Thanks for joining us.

(LIVE INTERVIEW NOW)

(DURATION 1.20)

The use of stills and graphics in this link makes it just possible to use a story where video footage is not available. The graphic showing numbers helps the viewer get basic information. The duration shown for the live interview is just a guide time.

WRITING TO SOUND

Adjectives that describe what can clearly be heard on the screen are best avoided. Cliché phrases like 'screeched to a halt' and 'deafening blast' are unnecessary. If the screech of tyres and roar of the blast can be heard on air, then viewers will already know about it. Anyway, they should decide for themselves whether it is 'deafening' and if the sound isn't there the viewer will suspect the reporter of sensationalism.

The secret of writing to sound is . . . don't.

If there's a sound-bite or some natural sound, then shut up. For a second at least, perhaps longer. A pause will be indicated by a break in the script.

Links need to hold hands with what the viewer sees.

Script links, or presenter intros, need to fit what the viewer sees or hears next.

But the president said he wasn't about to change his mind. Here's our Washington reporter Alison Bell . . .

But as the report starts it is not Alison Bell we see next. It's the president. Even worse – he is a close-up shot.

A solution would be:

As our Washington reporter Alison Bell explains, the President said he wasn't about to change his mind . . .

You might end a presenter intro with the simple:

Alison Bell reports from Washington.

This is usually fine, but if it starts with a long (8–10 seconds) segment of strong sound and pictures then that intro sounds like a mistake.

This problem can be solved by ending an intro with a reference to what we will see and hear – and not end with the name of the reporter. You can put the name of the reporter at the beginning of the sentence – 'As our Ireland correspondent Denis Murray reports . . .' – and then continue the sentence with some reference to what happens as the report begins – 'tense confrontation involving the security forces.' This particular report then started with sound and pictures of riot squads in full body armour and helmets, running out of helicopters and into a field in Northern Ireland.

The reporter did not speak immediately. When all these opening images had been absorbed, he started a famous and thoughtful script: 'A quiet, rural corner of the United Kingdom at the end of the twentieth century.'

Another danger in TV scripting is placing a name caption for the reporter over somebody else. So we have a brief clip of the president in vision right at the start of the report and he is saying:

In the end, that's what this election is about. Do we participate in a politics of cynicism or a politics of hope?

And right across his chest appear the words: *Alison Bell/Washington Reporter.*

This has happened. A story once had a reporter's name and title across a head and shoulder shot of the Queen.

Detail

Print and online journalists tend to pack stories with as much detail as possible. Try that with television and you would lose viewers before the end of the second paragraph. If the information is to sink in, the focus of the story has to be as concise as possible.

The BBC News correspondent Fergal Keane says television news should be 'spare and underwritten' and focus on the critical detail, not losing people in 'a welter of detail and wall-to wall-commentary.'

Canadian journalist, James Bamber, says: 'Only when you've absorbed what you've just heard are you ready for new information.'

Cut any unnecessary detail that would overload the listener. Data, statistics, numbers, titles, places and geographical relationships can be dealt with by captions and graphics. The visual bits are to illustrate and clarify a report rather than add to the general clutter. A picture has to contain just enough information to get its message across in a few seconds.

Television is a medium of impression and mood as much as news. Just enough should be said and shown to leave the viewer with a strong general impression of the story. Too much detail swamps the images and saturates the senses. For the audience to retain what it sees then simplicity is needed, otherwise the load of sound, pictures and words will only cause confusion.

To engage your viewers, tell stories on television the way you tell them in person. Use strong, chronological narratives whenever possible. Studies have found that narrative stories are remembered substantially better than stories told in the old 'inverted pyramid' style. Whatever structure you choose, don't make viewers search their memories in order to understand your story. Give them the information they need when they need it, so they can follow each part of the story. Use words which connect the pieces of the story to each other, and which make the chronology of events clear.

At WCPO-TV in Cincinnati, former news director Stuart Zanger encouraged his staff to do exactly that. He even has a term for it: using 'handrails' to help viewers follow complicated stories. 'When we tell them something important we make sure they got it,' he says, by reinforcing or repeating essential information.

The Seven Habits of Highly Effective Storytellers, Deborah Potter and Annie Lang. This is extracted from an article originally published by *RTNDA Communicator* magazine (http://bit.ly/1P5M54S)

THE TELEVISION NEWS PACKAGE

The word 'package' is used in both radio and television. It is a stand-alone report which is pre-recorded. The link/intro script into the package will also contain its duration and the In Words and the Out Words and any live name/place captions and the time into the package when they must appear on screen.

It is like a bag with many things tossed into it. In television it mixes script/interview clips/graphics/maps/reporter talking to camera/natural sound. It can be some or all of these. Some newsrooms use a package if it is part of a sequence which includes live reports. Sometimes the reporter starts live, then links into her own package that she recorded earlier, then we go back to her for an update. Most of the time it just tells us a story, with no live sections at all.

Until a few years ago the package was the most common currency of TV News, using the power of the medium to condense the essentials of a story or event or process.

The package is still used and is the polished end of the TV reporting skill. Looking at the history of the package we realise that the way the journalist communicates has not changed much, even though the technology has made packaging faster and more creative. More than 30 years ago an editor at BBC Television News, Alan Protheroe, sent a note to his staff and there's nothing dated about this advice:

> What we are trying to do is to ensure that any given report encapsulates the whole story; that it is told coherently and well, in words and pictures, so that the viewer is shown what has happened, where it happened, if possible how it happened, why it happened and what is likely to happen next.

If the viewer is asking 'What was that about?' then the report has failed and the viewer will decide the channel is boring.

The endless quest for TV news is strong image. But most images are not that – most are quite dull, or illustrate whatever point the writer is making at that moment, or may be archive/library (also known in North America as File Tape). The crude way of packaging is to write a script and then just slap in any pictures that seem to fit whatever point you are making – what some TV journalists call: See Dog, Say Dog.

A more professional approach is not to tell the viewer we are looking at a dog. We will tell the viewer what kind of dog it is . . . or why we are looking at the dog. In general good packaging means that pictures show What and words say Why.

This example of scripting to pictures seems flat and dull simply because the pictures don't seem to have any work to do.

	(We see and hear: Minister gets into a blue car)
Reporter says:	After the agreement the minister got into his dark blue official car and drove straight into an embarrassing encounter. He'd just agreed to the car emissions restrictions but his . . .
	(We see and hear: Car is stopped/Protesters climb onto car/Wave posters)
Reporter continues:	. . . car was then surrounded by dozens of protesters who climbed onto the bonnet and roof and waved posters.

If that section of script tells you exactly what you can see, then it failed.

We can probably see that his car is blue (or dark blue) and anyway, the colour is hardly relevant unless the car colour has some significance. We can certainly see people around his car and they might look as if they are making a protest and we can see posters or banners.

The problem with scripting like this is quite simple – it makes sense when you read it, yet it should not. The paradox of good packaging is that a script read in isolation should not make total sense in words because that means the sound and pictures have no work to do. They become irrelevant, and therefore not television journalism.

The other problem with that script is that the sentences are too long. A good script will contain one single thought in each sentence. You can also use present tense.

> (We see and hear: Minister gets into a blue car)
>
> Reporter says: He's reached an agreement on emissions after five hours of talking – but the minister doesn't get far . . .
>
> (We see and hear: Sound UP – shouting/Car is stopped/Protesters climb onto car/ Wave posters)
>
> Reporter says: Students from the college next door are waiting quietly on a side-road . . . (reporter pauses for a second) . . . and they don't miss a chance to make their anger clear . . .

Not perfect, but better. It adds to what we can see and hear and gives us a few seconds of sound to absorb what is going on. The use of the present tense is also a powerful tool in television scripting. We see it now, so tell us now.

> Think of pictures as visual proofs. To do that we need to think visually. Don't say: I'm writing this – what will illustrate my words? Say: What pictures will tell this story with a minimum of words?
>
> Neil Everton, Reuters Foundation
>
> I have seen countless television reports in different countries that are essentially radio reports with pictures slapped on top. General pictures, used to cover an essay from a reporter, are known in broadcast jargon as 'wallpaper' because the picture editor is asked by the journalist to 'cover that with some pictures'. This is a dreadful technique. It dates back to the days of news being covered on film, by people who had been trained in the film industry and teamed with journalists who had learned their profession in newspapers and radio.
>
> Rick Thompson, *Writing For Broadcast Journalism*

Always seek out pictures and sound that tell your story most effectively. This means look through your raw material for:

- Faces
- One big wide shot
- Close up shots
- Action and reaction
- Emotion
- And above all . . . moments that tell you not to say anything.

Also try to use static shots for news packages – pans and zooms are awful to edit and are best left to longer features.

Packaged TV news benefits from having the first and last scenes run a little longer to give the opening pictures time to establish and to let the closing shots leave an impression.

Another good reason for leaving a couple of seconds at the start of the report before beginning the commentary is in case the report is put on air slightly late. The convention is to have the opening shots last two seconds longer than the commentary and to avoid starting the commentary at the exact moment the pictures begin.

In a sequence as part of a package about a parachute jump you have a twelve-second shot of the parachute tangled in a high tree and the teenager doing the jump has released himself thinking he can climb down. Now he is also tangled in branches. Rescuers are telling him to stay.

It would be excessive to write:

> It wasn't exactly the kind of red letter thrill day he had in mind. He jumped from three-thousand feet and narrowly missed a church steeple before a massive poplar tree got in the way. (Words: 12 seconds)

Too long. We have twelve seconds on pictures and sound so you have too many words. A single frame on social media could be the teenager in branches with the parachute – and now you are talking all over the drama and getting in the way.

One way to retain all that information would be to let us see what's going on . . . say something to explain . . . then shut up. You could start the script after maybe three seconds and stop it three seconds before the end of the pictures.

> No way to end a three-thousand feet jump . . . he'd just missed a church steeple. And then this . . . (Words: 6 seconds)

Now we can see and hear what is going on and just a few words can add new information. Then you can start a new section of script for the next sequence. Remember – do not distract viewers when they are having an interesting experience.

USING ARCHIVE

Some newsrooms use words like archive and library (or file tape) as interchangeable.

Simply, archive is very old stuff that you may have to pay for. Library pictures are just used to fill a need in a report. Archive includes scenes of past wars or an assassination or the first Moon landing.

Library means pictures of an airliner that's crashed two hours ago, except it's *not that* particular one that crashed – just pictures of the same airliner (and make sure it is) that you had in the library database and possibly provided originally by the manufacturer.

Most TV stations have their own libraries. The library will keep valuable pictures, sound and stills to illustrate and enhance reports. Library and archive material is now digitised and can be made available straight onto the journalist's desktop.

Library searches can be time consuming unless you know exactly what you want and use search logic. If you are writing a story about the early days of the Beatles then you might do a search for 'Beatles' (not 'Beetles') and find that there's a mass of archive available. So try to be specific in the same way you'd hunt for something in a search engine. If the script is about, for example, a music museum now on the site of a famous concert, then you should be looking for archive of that specific event. And a reminder – do you pay for it?

In the script it might be obvious that this is archive of a specific place, or event, because that's what the script is about anyway. Library archive shouldn't just pop up in a report for no reason. Scripts sometimes include phrases such as 'It was back in 1966] . . .' or 'It was 50 years ago today . . .' or 'When it all started . . .' These may be tiresome if overused but can do the job of preparing the viewer for a bit of history or something that helps drive the narrative along.

Before digitisation, archive was often retrieved by a *verbal* request by calling the library extension number. There was plenty of scope for misunderstanding. A request for pictures about the end of a legal case involving euthanasia (say it!) resulted in a pile of pictures about a student protest in China. Those pictures were filed as *Youth In Asia*. Or you could end up with pictures of a former President called George Bush when what you wanted was George W. Bush.

Research aside, the library database plays an important part of the storytelling.

Television news has been around homes for so long that several generations have grown up with it. Archive pictures should not be an afterthought and yet because of the nostalgic desires of some viewers they can add a thoughtful ingredient to any routine story which has a past. The database should also be able to tell you about any restrictions on the pictures – such as who can use them and/or who owns them and should be paid.

The library also provides more routine pictures of people, places and buildings and these may be needed just to support the script. Many will be bland or dull, but still useful. Aware of this some big news organisations will invest time in shooting material just for library purposes. It can provide better quality shots of buildings such as The White House or the British Parliament.

Archive and library pitfalls for the writer include:

- pictures of a building in sunshine or surrounded by trees in full leaf when today is in deep mid-winter, or vice versa

- a sports personality in the wrong shirt – he moved to another team last year

- a foreign building with the wrong flag

- places with the same name. Is that Birmingham, England, or Birmingham, Alabama?

- pictures of identifiable elderly people taken last year – a grim thought, but are all those people still with us?

- birds, trains and locomotives, classic cars, ships, flora and fauna in general – you can use them, but do be careful because the world is full of experts on something. Is that really the Greater Spotted? Or is it the Lesser Spotted? Is that a Mark One or a Mark Three? Get it wrong and you'll end up with an over-loaded inbox and all over social media.

Stills are often used in TV news when they have added value, such as a spectacular single frame of a sporting moment. But a reminder – always check if you have permission to use the image, or whether you have to pay (see Chapter 2).

WHAT YOU SEE – WHAT I SAY

There is one thing unique to television news scripting that every journalist must be wary of – always ask: *what do we see when I say this?*

Remember that, like radio, talking on air is publishing. What the journalist writes is spoken and in law is a published statement. So beware the juxtaposition of script and images. What meaning could an ordinary person attach to certain words and images together? Always ask – what am I telling the viewer at this moment? Could what I say and what we see imply wrong-doing by association?

A channel once carried a short simple story about three businessmen in another country being investigated over a building project crime – but what viewers saw were three different people who happened to be in the news that day from the same country and those pictures had arrived on the same global news feed. So then there had to be a brief apology. Another programme had a script which said that there was a risk of terrorists being among airline ground staff – and showed some library pictures of . . . airline ground staff. So this had to be followed up with a presenter saying – apologies, we didn't mean those people.

One set of pictures combined with a script can have a meaning which the journalist may not have intended:

(We see – The 'Super-Crème' Chocolate Factory)

Reporter says: Pleasantville. Normally a quiet backwater famous for its chocolate has become a haven for big-city drug dealers now moving into rural areas . . .

So what we see at this point is a close up shot of some harmless company or small factory.

Always ask yourself – are we seeing someone's home? Somebody's car? Or a building that can be identified and therefore the people who work in it? Are they drug-dealers? Well unless you can actually prove it – then they just make chocolate bars.

Be careful about what you say if it creates a new meaning because of what we see.

THE HEADLINES

- Television news scripting is about simple, concise but clear communication rather than hammering the viewer with masses of wordy detail. It's about stopping the commentary when the viewer sees and hears something that fixes him or her to a screen. Do not distract viewers when they are having an interesting experience.

- Let stories breathe a little – pause the script and offer a few months of sound/image.

- Think – what pictures will tell this story with a minimum of words?

- Just like radio and webpages, the headlines are the shop-window for a single bulletin or part of an all-news channel.

- Data, statistics, numbers, titles, places and geographical relationships can be dealt with by captions and graphics.

QUESTIONS FOR YOU

1. Record about 15 minutes of a news channel and find a packaged report. It would probably be about two minutes long. Work out how many seconds the reporter is talking for – that is, how much of the report is the reporter? If the reporter is talking for a combined total 30 seconds of the two minutes then the sound and pictures must be doing something useful. Then can you find a packaged report in which the reporter is talking a lot? Compare them.
2. Can you pick a day when you can concentrate on one single big news event – then try to see how the same story is written on the BBC, ITV, Sky News, CNN, Fox News, Al Jazeera? Did they all use similar writing styles – even if they had the same pictures?
3. Can you give your TV scripting some style and substance by studying word-power? There are of course plenty of online resources for this. But go to a second-hand book shop and get yourself a dictionary of famous quotations and a thesaurus. Sit down and look through them. Read poetry.

OTHER RESOURCES

- NewsLab – 'In today's multimedia world, journalists need more than the basics. They need new ways of finding and telling stories that will engage and inform the communities they serve, while staying true to the fundamental principles of accurate, fair and independent journalism': www.newslab.org/

- Top tips on writing television news – Advancing the Story: www.advancingthestory.com/

TUTOR NOTES

You could arrange some shot-listing and scripting to sound and pictures which can keep people busy for a whole day or even several.

It means getting *about* 40 seconds of *already edited* pictures on a news story, preferably with lots of movement or a variety of shots. A simple local event is fine. Stories about politics and diplomatic talks do not work for this very well; forest fires, local emergencies, floods or a local exhibition or carnival are better. It can be an old story – it does not need to be a story that day.

Remove any trace of a reporter track. This means either sourcing any online new feeds without track, or recording from output and muting any track.

Get raw copy on the story – more than they really need. Print and handout to everyone.

Get the group, together, to watch the material twice. Then a third time to write a shot-list measured in seconds.

For example:

> 0 sound and pictures start
> 5 a wide shot
> 10 something in medium close-up is seen
> 20 another wide shot
> 25 people
> 35 ends with a wide shot
> 40 pix end

Show it through once more.

Tell them:

> Write a short presenter intro to the story and straight into . . .
>
> . . . a script to the pictures. Each second is on average three words.
>
> You cannot re-edit this – you must write the words to fit the pictures as they are.

Give them a deadline – this could be 30, 45 or 60 minutes. Only the tutor can judge.

They each put their name at the top.

When everyone is finished (or if anyone says 'almost' that will have to do) tell them to print and collect their scripts.

Ask them to swop scripts around, so they do not have their own.

Line up the material again at the start. You will end up doing this for every one of the group.

Each person reads the presenter link they have been given.

Start the pictures and say 'Cue' – each person delivers the script in their 'best broadcasting voice' please. If anyone stumbles, it is OK to start again.

By giving each script to a person who did not write it, the person who did write it can watch the screen and see the result.

Feedback each time.

This kind of exercise can fill an entire day.

After doing this for a 40 second report you can move on later in the week with a 1.20 minute item making them write into and out of a clip of someone talking.

CHAPTER 22

Gathering Television News: Reporting and Video Journalism

Through the 1980s and 1990s the main way to get television news was through a bundle of processes and technology called ENG (Electronic News Gathering). Film – the rolls of pictures in cans – went to media museums. Digital formats then pushed ENG aside in much the same way as ENG pushed film away and even the same arguments could be heard about quality and craft skills in the face of increasing digital newsgathering.

But it soon became clear that the digital format had big advantages over analogue videotape. Picture quality was higher and the cameras could store the images in a form that could not easily be corrupted, even after generations of copying. Once the pictures were downloaded into an edit computer, they could be compiled in any sequence, and that order could easily be changed. Extra shots could be inserted in the middle of a report without having to remake everything that followed. With analogue recordings the report was built up shot by shot onto videotape. So if you want to make a change in the middle of a report you had to redo all the sequences which followed. Of course these are just evolving tools of the trade.

Most television newsgathering is still a reporter and a single cameraman, or woman. But getting the news also has other categories:

- A Crew: the camera and sound crew with a reporter is rare in most routine daily news stories but new broadcast journalists need to be aware of what happens. This gives quality results and lets the journalist concentrate on the story and interviews. Also safer in dangerous situations such as civil disturbance or war zones. Also for current affairs, features, backgrounders and specials such as strands of perhaps four or five films on one subject or investigations. Anything that takes time and money but is felt to be worth it. A full crew, including lighting, would certainly be used for an interview with a head of state or head of government or a rare interview with a normally reclusive major player in global business.

- VJ (Video Journalist): a journalist with a camera, who will not be used for an interview with a head of state or government. Useful for getting close to a subject. Good for discreet filming when a full crew might be cumbersome or intimidating for sensitive matters. Also for fast reaction to a run and grab news event that is safe to cover. Many district journalists for local channels are VJs as they can move fast and work independently.

- Pocket News and mobile devices: phone pictures and video, webcams, public offerings and mini-cams. May also be for secret filming with buttonhole-sized cameras. Newsrooms may accept lower quality if a memorable shot of an event or story has big audience value. A substantial amount of video from phones gets into newsrooms: political and social unrest, natural disasters, serious accidents, wild weather, terror attacks or sometimes just local incidents that fit into the strange, unusual or amusing.

CREW/CAMERAMAN/CAMERAWOMAN

Despite the falling cost, and size, of filming equipment there is still a need for someone who only films. These are also the kind of reports that will be put together with a craft editor and there may be a separate sound recordist if the item is particularly hazardous or complex or if sound is a vital component, or problem.

The cameraman's main tool is likely to be a high-end (high-grade) professional camera which shoots in widescreen format and may be High Definition. Sound and pictures are stored on disc or a memory card. Filming is direct and to the point – and this applies no matter what equipment is being used.

What the picture editor or journalist needs from the cameraman is a sensible selection of angles and sequences of long shot, medium shot and close-up. He wants well composed, in focus, rock-steady pictures held for a minimum of ten seconds, preferably 20. For news, think static. Static shots are the best currency for continuous and daily news – moving pans and zooms are for travelogue and documentary and are guaranteed to give an editor problems when it comes to assembling a news report. How do you cut into a pan or a zoom? How do you follow a shot looking up an interviewee's left nostril?

A reporter and a cameraman work as a team and both have ideas to contribute about which shots to use in the report. Some friendly rivalry usually exists: 'I'll get the best pictures. You get the best words.' You can usually spot the difference at one of those big international conferences – the journalists pick up the local newspapers to see the story text while the cameraman is also looking at the pictures to see what frames the photographers got.

SOUND RECORDIST

The recordist packs a wide selection of microphones. Most mikes are susceptible to wind noise, when even a slight gust across the top can be transformed into a roaring hurricane. Outdoor camera mikes will be protected by a windshield of acoustic foam covered by a fluffy fur-fabric muff. This stops wind blowing across the microphone but does not stop the wanted sound getting to the microphone within.

A directional rifle mike is standard kit for location recordings. The recordist can stand or kneel out of vision and the mike will pick up sound from the direction it is pointed across a narrow angle. It can even isolate individuals within a group. The recordist's aim has to be good. A couple of degrees out and the gun mike will pick up the wrong person or background noise instead.

Another drawback with the gun mike is that with its cover off it can look a little too much like its namesake, so it is best avoided in battle zones unless the recordist wants to become a target. The alternative for interviews out of doors is for the reporter to hold a stick mike with a foam windshield, similar to those used in radio.

Indoors, where wind noise will not be present, a pair of tie clip or clip-on mikes is usually favoured. The disadvantages are that they can pick up clothing rustle, and because they work on the condenser principle, they can draw in spurious background noise, such as the rumble of traffic or air-conditioning. An alternative is to use a couple of directional desk top mikes.

FIGURE 22.1

A separate sound recordist is likely to be needed for doing longer complex links from a location or if sound is going to be a problem, especially in stories when we go back to the reporter several times. Courtesy UTV News.

Another important part of the kit will be a radio mike.

This frees the reporter from the leash and is useful for situations where lengths of microphone cable would be a handicap, such as in crowds where the reporter might get separated from the recordist, or where it is necessary to film the reporter walking alone without the unnatural accompaniment of trailing cable.

They have to carry a transmitter, which is a small box with a length of dangling wire. This is most conveniently clipped to the back of a belt, away from the camera, or put in a pocket.

LIGHTING

Again we are still within the coverage quota of Full Crew. The issue for the broadcast journalist is whether a story or interview is complex, precious or rare and needs to look just right. Securing an exclusive interview and then discovering that it looks terrible is not career-enhancing. Modern cameras can cope perfectly well with outdoor shots in bright daylight. What they will never do away with is the lighting assistant's creative touch, which can render unflattering subjects more interesting and work wonders with flat or dull images.

The lighting technician's basic kit includes lights for indoor use. These lamps are powered from the mains, and will be fitted with moveable flaps, known as barn doors, to direct the stream of light. The lights model the subject, pick it out from the background and eliminate unwanted shadows.

Also in his equipment, the lighting technician will have one or two small hand-held battery-powered lamps for occasions where larger, tripod-mounted lights would be inappropriate, such as in a moving crowd. For extra flexibility, an array of smaller lamps may be included, with spares, extension leads and sun reflectors for outdoor shooting. Larger scale lighting, to flood an entire hall for example, would usually be supplied by a contract lighting company.

A basic guide to lighting for journalists is included in the Camera Shots chapter.

THE VIDEO JOURNALIST (VJ)

The VJ mission is to do all the shooting and the interviews, shoot his or her own piece to camera if needed, ingest all that into a laptop or desktop, lay an audio track, and then edit the lot and file it back to base.

As the concept graduated over time it became part of a more mixed economy for news channels. It wasn't just a case of a VJ being just one person with a camera and one story. The VJ enabled newsrooms to see all the angles on a story covered with multiple cameras instead of one. That extra camera could bring extra dimensions when VJ shots were edited alongside conventional ones.

Like so many developments in every industry the strengths and weakness had to be identified and lessons were learned. The deployment of the modern VJ evolved in a very simple way – the equipment got lighter. VJ operation is also good for discreet filming when a full crew might be cumbersome or intimidating for sensitive matters, also for fast reaction to a news event that is safe to cover.

VJs are often also trained in editing, but can usually also feed their rushes back to a newsroom so they can get on with another assignment while the newsdesk journalist (or a specialist editor) gets to work on their pictures. Some work from home and others from existing bureaux. They may be used to complement bureau coverage by staying on at a news conference to meet later deadlines. A substantial number of VJ jobs are in places other than broadcast newsrooms. There are VJs providing material for the websites of newspapers, magazines, PR agencies, charities, government departments, trade unions, businesses and health organisations.

THE VIDEO JOURNALIST CHECKLIST

At the top must be – you know what the headline for the story will be. You know who you are going to interview and why and when and where. You know what you will film and what it might look like and sound like and what the light might be like today. You have set yourself a deadline to finish all filming and given yourself time to put it all together.

The VJ then needs a written list to remind him or her to keep all the tools needed in the right place at the right time and to keep them regularly checked:

- Batteries
- Headphones

- Do you need any lights?

- Microphones (wired and radio mics)

- Potential weather problems today?

- Spares for anything vital

- Tripod or other suitable camera support

- Is your phone fully charged?

- Can you park at your location?

The Video Journalist needs to plan for the best way of telling the story. Working alone for sound and video and doing the interviews needs a kind of mental map in the mind of what the final story might look like.

If indoors check the lighting and if outdoors check the weather as well. Think how these will affect how the shoot? The simple guide is:

- wide shots – establish the location/setting

- close ups – to see people and their reactions and lift the sound

- over the shoulder shots – for basic interview cutaways for editing

- natural sound – smooth the edit by recording several minutes of local sound

- safety shots – take some extra wide shots before you leave location.

VIDEO JOURNALIST: BASHAR SHARAF

Bashar Sharaf is a Jordanian journalist and a trainer who has worked in more than 13 Arabic countries, in addition to the UK and Turkey, mainly training on video journalism and multimedia.

Bashar is also a radio roving reporter for BBC Xtra Arabic.

He also produces audio visual content for the web as a video/solo journalist. In 2013 one of his radio packages on BBC Xtra was chosen as the pick of the year.

He is known to be one of the first video journalists in his region, yet he likes to call himself a Digital Storyteller. He aims to use the VJ storytelling digital technique to break down stereotypes.

He says: 'One of the virtues claimed by supporters of the VJ method in Britain and America is that it can bring out stories over a period of time that larger crews would have a problem with, or would just be too expensive.'

Bashar managed many projects, such as establishing audio visual production units at refugee camps in Jordan, to help document stories of refugees. He also led the BBC Media Action team in Libya to produce the Libyan version of the BBC *Question Time* debate programme. More recently he was a member of the twofour54 media team that worked on the re-launch of the Abu Dhabi TV main news programme.

The main advice he gives to his trainees is:

You lead the camera; don't let the camera lead you.

Shoot what you need before shooting what you want.

You are a story teller who tells the story in pictures first. Then words come to add, not to describe.

FIGURE 22.2

Bashar Sharaf: 'Shoot what you need before shooting what you want.'

POCKET NEWS

This includes phone pictures, mini-cams, buttonhole cameras and the camera inside a Formula One car that gives a driver's eye view. Lower quality is often accepted if an event has big audience appreciation, but quality is improving all the time.

Simply pointing the phone camera at what is happening and hoping for the best is not entirely intuitive and just guessing that you might get useful material is not an option. Also, film more material than you think you need. You can never have too much. But you might regret having too little.

Phones can get sound and pictures at a fraction of the cost of a crew or professional camera operation. This is a television method frequently also used by many newspapers to enhance coverage on their websites. But to know how to get pictures, sound or stills of useful quality for a big audience needs both training and practice. A phone is too lightweight to give a shot any kind of stability. One way to reduce (though probably not totally avoid) the wobble-vision problem is to prop yourself against a wall, post or tree while shooting. Gathering material like this in a hazardous situation, like a protest, is not advised. You may also have to edit some of the material yourself and then send it from what could be a remote location.

For undercover work a camera can also be look just like a button, a technique used by a TV reporter to investigate hygiene in a hospital. In that case the reporter got a job as a cleaner and was able to gather evidence after complaints from patients and visitors.

Cameras have been put in just about every imaginable place: cars, toys or in furniture. Television documentary teams have embedded cameras in snow and even inside a lump of elephant dung (to get close up shots of wildlife) and although

FIGURE 22.3

A mobile satellite dish is also sometimes called a Fly-Away system which can be moved between locations at short notice. They have been used everywhere from Everest to the heat of a desert. Courtesy Channel NewsAsia.

FIGURE 22.4

Getting news means getting access to where important events are happening or often just getting close to the action. Courtesy ITN.

such tricks are less common in news, someone is coming up with similar ideas all the time. There are even cameras that can be swallowed, to enable doctors to have a look inside a body, and their very existence will inspire news producers to come up with ideas for stories.

For a journalist it raises plenty of moral issues of course, but the most important reason for secret filming with a hidden camera is public interest justification – that is, that there have been complaints from the public to a broadcaster about an incident or a place.

That can justify the use of such cameras within the editorial guidelines of either the channel or a state regulator. Simply using tiny cameras on a speculative fishing expedition, to find out if there's any mischief worth reporting on, is legally and ethically ill-advised.

FIGURE 22.5

News links vehicles tend to hunt in packs wherever the news is happening. From these vehicles reports and lives can be sent back to newsrooms. Raw material is also sent so that newsrooms can arrange or package them in different ways for headlines and the website.

THE JOURNALIST AS ADVANCE GUARD – A RECCE

It's a military term of course, derived from reconnaissance. It is done quite regularly for events that will have a team of hundreds, but is rare in daily news with the exception of programme specials. A recce is something that a journalist may have to do for such special occasions as national elections and big outside broadcasts. It means going in advance into the place where filming is happening and ensuring there are no surprises on the day.

If you get a chance to recce a location before the shoot then you can act as the eyes and ears of the outside broadcast (OB) team. You may even be the producer in charge so you don't want to make a fool of yourself before coverage even starts. You don't have to be of a technical personality to do a recce, but you do need to be aware of what is needed to get a story on air – and this usually mean live news. If you get the recce right – then your colleagues will sing your praises for years and you might find yourself assigned to some very exciting stories.

So here's what is absolutely vital for large OBs and events.

- The full postal address of the location and that also means the post code or zip code. Get a weather forecast.

- Name of any contact at the location and his or her numbers.

- Maps – and get several of them. Paper maps are often faster and clearer to access than relying only on a phone app.

- Parking – can the crew and/or the OB vehicles park nearby and if so, where can they park and for how long and is there easy in and out access?

- WiFi – can you get access here for your laptop?

- Do you need special permits in advance? Is photographic ID needed?

- When is sunrise and sunset? Day or night shoot? Or both?

- Facilities – toilets, food, drink, accommodation. Are hotel rooms needed and where are they and how do we get to them?

- Power – if it's indoors are there plenty of sockets and do you need to talk to a local house electrician?

- Number of people to be filmed. Is it a big 1+1 interview or a boardroom discussion or a cast of hundreds? Are children or animals involved in this?

- Will other crews be there? Where might they be located? Have you got the best location? If you are doing a recce first then grab the best spots before competitors do.

A modern TV journalist in the field usually also has to do radio and online too, so you will need to understand the full range of options when it comes to recording, editing and sending large files back to your base, wherever it is in the world.

In the BBC, we have an app which sends video material, complete with metadata, straight into our 'Jupiter' content management system. We also have an intranet site which facilitates the uploading of audio. But sometimes you find yourself using hotel WiFi or some other connection that just doesn't get on with Jupiter's protocols, and then you need another option. There are services you can sign up for on-the-fly, such as WeSendIt and WeTransfer which will allow you to upload files, and your colleagues at base will be able to download them at their end. And sometimes you will still have to book an old-fashioned satellite provider to feed it.

In Libya (in 2013) internet speeds were running at just 100 kbps, which is barely enough to send an ordinary email. No amount of fancy tech solutions could get round this, so a good knowledge of reliable local satellite providers was invaluable. It all comes back to the traditional question for which producers must always have an answer: what will you do if it all goes wrong?

Nick Tarry, Field Producer, Global News, BBC

GLOBAL NEWS EVENTS

Evolving technology brings evolving problems. Although some global stories are predictable and some are not, careful planning, mass deployment and big investment can be disrupted because someone has lost a one-inch connector. Like emergency services everywhere, there are people in large news operations who spend their time planning for a bomb attack or natural disaster that has not actually happened yet.

For events we know are happening, or certain to happen, planning can be based on prediction, experience and backup. These can be anything from a local carnival or festival to major world conferences or peace talks. Newsrooms have national election coverage planned well in advance.

Nelson Mandela died at the age of ninety-five after suffering from a respiratory infection. Although this was not unexpected he spent the last months of his life in hospital and no one knew when the end would come. International media had spent years preparing for this.

A senior journalist explains the problems, and the lessons.

The demise of the world's best loved and most respected statesman was always going to be a massive global TV event – and the long ten days of mourning leading up to his actual funeral presented major challenges for international broadcasters who had been preparing their coverage plans for many years.

These best-laid plans would be challenged to breaking point by two major factors. First, no one had any sense of when Mr Mandela would finally pass away, and second, the actual government plans for the ten days of mourning were a closely guarded state secret. In African culture there is a strong sense that it is taboo to talk about someone's death while they are alive and the government, the Mandela family and the ruling African National Congress were extremely reluctant to discuss their plans. So broadcasters had expensive and elaborate coverage plans in place but they didn't know when they would activate them and they didn't know if their best guesses would actually be part of the final plan.

Several broadcasters hired roof-top spaces that were never used, others even rented houses in Mr Mandela's village which was declared out of bounds and never actually used during the event.

The key was to stay flexible and not to stick rigidly to your original plan. Even if that plan has been in place for years when the news breaks anything can happen. Broadcasters had been advised by the government that they would be given an hour's advance warning of Mr Mandela's demise to enable them to activate their live positions before it was formally announced by President Zuma. Many meetings and rehearsals were held by all the major media on how we would best use this hour to organise their teams. Editorial policy advisers issued guidelines on what to do if the news broke first on Twitter or from family sources. In the end we all got about less than two minutes warning and it was largely luck that the world audience managed to scramble across a live TV feed to broadcast the President's announcement.

Likewise our live coverage of the National Mourning Service only came together at the last minute. On the day itself some kit ordered by our Special Events team failed to arrive on site – The Special programme couldn't go on air and with minutes to spare our News team presented by George Alagiah had to pick up a baton with no script or autocue and go live without warning for the next four hours. That is the kind of surprise that would give many a producer a heart attack but in the finest traditions of news reporting the team delivered an excellent programme which worked smoothly. Remember the audience only sees what appears on the screen. They don't know what didn't happen that you'd planned to put on air.

The lesson is that even a set piece event which was as highly planned as the Mandela coverage is ultimately unpredictable – anything can go wrong and will go wrong. The key to success is be prepared for that. Don't get wedded to Plan A to the point where you have no alternatives up your sleeve. Always have a Plan B, C and D in the back of your mind because you'll probably end up using one of them anyway.

The Mandela funeral stretched over ten days and that in itself was a major challenge – how to keep the audience engaged over such a long period. We were fortunate that it was a multi-locational event and we were able to spread our teams across eight or nine locations across South Africa which kept the coverage fresh and original. That required careful planning and a big investment if we were to reflect the scale of the event. We knew in the first instance we needed to be at Mr Mandela's residence in Johannesburg to see dignitaries paying their respects to the family, and we knew we had to be at his old home in Soweto where large crowds of mourners would gather. After that first phase we needed to be in Pretoria for the Laying-In-State, FNB stadium for the National Service, Robben Island where he'd been imprisoned for 27 years, Waterkloof airbase from where he began his final journey home to the Eastern Cape. We needed to be in Mthatha as the plane and the coffin arrived and finally we needed to be in Mr Mandela's home village of Qunu for the actual funeral.

Qunu provided major challenges – it is a remote rural area with no hotels, no shops and few facilities. Our teams had to bring their own food and their own electricity and live in camper vans. This was compounded by several days of non-stop rain which turned the field they were staying in into a quagmire. Kit failed, equipment got drenched and it was only the ingenuity of our engineers which made everything work on the day. For all these locations to get on air smoothly it was important that each location had a dedicated team leader who could troubleshoot and solve production crises on the ground while other team members were live on air at other locations. There is no substitute for boots on the ground – and a producer in a wet field in Qunu will always be able to make better informed decisions than a manager in a suit sitting in London.

It is important to have a united team who share the same objective. All our teams around the country wanted to give Nelson Mandela a dignified and respectful send-off which all our audiences around the world would feel wasn't just professional but was also a beautiful tribute to Mr Mandela. This enabled all our teams to deliver distinctive material but with a common theme of respect running through it.

For all that the biggest lesson I take away from the Nelson Mandela event was the importance of traditional journalists' skills.

Our much missed late colleague Komla Dumor scooped the world by getting himself invited into the Mandela household during the mourning period where he interviewed five of Mr Mandela's family. Other broadcasters including the BBC had been bidding for the family for months and months with limited success – when the moment came Komla secured the interviews not through door-stepping or hounding the family but simply because they'd seen him on TV and thought him to be an honest and respectful journalist they could trust.

The lesson for all young journalists is that, in the finest traditions of Nelson Mandela himself, nice guys with lots of integrity and humanity can win the day.

                    Peter Burdin, BBC World Affairs Unit Editor, BBC Africa Bureaux Chief 2009–2014

FIGURE 22.6

Newsgathering is time-critical and the Broadband Global Area Network (BGAN) has shrunk the world. It enables journalists to broadcast within minutes of arriving at the scene of a story in a remote area. The crew can use a small terminal and dish about the size of a laptop to link to commercial communications satellites run by Inmarsat, the International Marine Satellite organisation that was originally set up to allow ships at sea to stay in contact with base. When opened, turned on and pointed the terminal finds out where it is in the world as it locates the best signal from a geo-stationary satellite, rather like the satnav in a car. Courtesy Inmarsat.

THE HEADLINES

- Sound and pictures can come from a full crew, a video journalist or pocket and mobile devices. But news needs static shots, properly framed and suitable for editing.

- Shoot what you *need* before shooting what you *want*. Get your vital shots and sounds. Then if you have the time, get what is Nice to Have as a bonus.

- In major news events – predicted or not – stay flexible and do not feel a need to stick to an original plan. Even if that plan has been in place for years, when the news breaks anything can happen.

QUESTIONS FOR YOU

1. Can you start some practical TV newsgathering with your phone? Some birds and bees in your local park might be enough. Lean against something and see if it improves the stability of your shots.
2. Is there a broadcasting exhibition coming to your area? Most of them are free to visit if you register. You can see the latest newsgathering equipment, talk to the people behind it, find out how it all works and even get some hands-on experience. Any decent sales person will regard you as a future customer.

OTHER RESOURCES

- Typhoon Haiyan hit the Philippines in November 2013, killing more than 5,000 people. Alex Thomson of Channel 4 News reported about a tweet he received – 'a random speculative tweet from a total stranger . . . a man called Christian.' This single tweet led to an example of a TV news package that takes the viewer on a journey: http://bit.ly/1DQwphh.

- Practical tips from those experienced in mobile reporting as well as their recommended apps and techniques for producing video on smartphones: http://bit.ly/1ykMVpC.

- VSATs and satellite trucks provide the links that feed pictures and packages and get correspondents live on air. BBC senior producer Ann Sedivy, Danny Savage and colleagues explain how VSATs work – from sending pictures and editing to booking lines: http://bbc.in/1NkKeei

TUTOR NOTES

Get your students to do a detailed plan for coverage of a big event coming up in your city or country. Go online to scout the venue, locations and routes. Where will they position cameras and reporters? What can be prepared in advance? What subjects might be worth some short background films that can be dropped into the live coverage? What can go wrong? Go to resource and facility-house websites to check broadcast equipment hire costs and do a budget for your OB equipment.

Everyone could do a TV news broadcast recce of your site – as if a big rolling all-day live news event is happening there soon. Just needs pen and notebook. Go out and about and make notes about several good live camera positions, great backgrounds for live reporters and places to do interviews. Are there any hazards – are there live positions that are high up and how can they be made safe?

CHAPTER 23

Getting the Shots

If you can't sell your pictures, then you weren't close enough.

Traditional. Freelance news cameraman

Just as there is a grammar to language, there is a grammar to camera shots. A journalist with a lens attached to any kind of technology needs to know these and a journalist working with a cameraman (or woman) or a crew needs to know how to communicate.

There are many shot styles but still two basic conventions: the camera is either static, or it moves. Trends change of course and some programmes can have a house-style of fast moving camera shots, sometimes with the shot whipping all over the place. News tends to work best with static.

You do not just point the lens at the subject or the action. TV news shots are about composing and framing. The camera is only an impersonator of the human eye, but with one important advantage – it can zoom in and out of a scene.

Three shots form the basis of most news camerawork – the long shot, medium shot and close up. These expand into more different shots in everyday use, showing a person for example.

- VLS/Very Long shot/Wide Shot. This gives the viewer a big establishing shot of the scene.

- LS/Long shot. The complete body is in shot. Remember to give foot-room as well as head room. This shot allows the viewer to see the background and so establishes where the subject is.

- MLS/Medium Long Shot. Sometimes called the three quarter shot. The bottom of the frame cuts at the knees.

- MS/Mid Shot. The bottom of the frame cuts off near the waist whether the person is standing or sitting. Can be used for the more relaxed interview or for introducing a guest or presenter.

- MCU/Medium Close Up. The bottom of the frame is cut off at the breast area. This is the most common standard interview shot for news.

- CU/Close Up. Usually cuts off at the neckline. The face and not much else.

- BCU/Big Close Up. This shot cuts off the top of the head but eyes and mouth are usually in shot. It is a very intimidating shot and sometimes used when someone is either under interrogation or talking about an emotional subject. It's in your face.

FIGURE 23.1
Very long shot/wide shot

FIGURE 23.2
Long shot

FIGURE 23.3
Medium long shot

FIGURE 23.4
Mid shot

FIGURE 23.5
Medium close up

FIGURE 23.6
Close up

In all TV news production these shots refer to the distance the subject is from the camera, and therefore how much of that subject fills the screen – long shots show the subject a long way off, while close ups by definition draw them nearer the viewer.

On location, where the camera is also taking in the surroundings, the long shot would give a view of the whole picture or location: a whole room or corridor, tanks rolling on a hillside, the burning building with the fire-fighters in front.

The medium shot reveals more detail: is the subject doing something or holding something; the tank commander perched in his turret; a jet of water swallowed up by flames billowing from a top floor window.

FIGURE 23.7
Big close up

The close up focuses in on the action: the tank commander's face; the nozzle of the fire hose with spray bursting out.

A shot commonly used for establishing locations is the general view (GV) or very long shot (VLS) which gives a panorama of the entire scene. Local TV stations keep a stock of GVs showing buildings such as hospitals or courts which feature regularly in the news. You can choose your camera shots by running the sequence through in your mind's eye and deciding which shots would go best together.

FIGURE 23.8
The cameraman's precarious work to get this panoramic shot will certainly be used for a wide variety of news stories. It would be used for a story that day but since he can over-shoot the scene the shots can be kept in the library file. Courtesy UTV.

HOLD THE SHOTS

Shots should be held for far longer than you might think. Edited TV reports often cut from shot to shot every five seconds, but to give the picture editor or newsroom journalist five seconds of pictures worth using the cameraperson will need to record at least twice that much. Every shot should be held for a count of ten or even 20. Some documentary editors prefer to work with a minute per shot.

There's a good reason for this apparent over-production. From the raw video an editor will want to find five perfectly-framed, in-focus, correctly exposed and lively seconds that will add interest to the report. The cameraman's job is to provide enough material for the newsroom to work with.

For daily news, pans and zooms can be a problem simply because of the length of time they can take.

Static shots always work best. They are simple and don't give the viewer too much of a jolt.

But in longer form features however a pan or a zoom can add interest. We could use a zoom if the image we are zooming into is becoming more important in the script, or we might move away from a subject if the picture *around* that subject becomes important – for example we start on a man standing in a field, apparently alone, but when we zoom out we see that he's in the middle of a vast area of burned down forest because the story is about forest fires.

A pan or a zoom should be taken in three parts. It should establish itself, move and then settle down. Hold the start. Do the pan. Hold the end.

FIGURE 23.9
Start of a zoom in. If this shot is held for about ten seconds it can also be used as a static shot.

FIGURE 23.10
The zoom in has started . . .

FIGURE 23.11
Zoom ends and the shot should be held for ten seconds. At the edit stage, the story has the option of the zoom, or the static shots at each end.

The shot should begin with the camera steady, then pan or zoom and rest at the end of the movement. The opening and closing shots should be held for ten or more seconds, giving the camera operator three shots in one. Cutting from a zoom to a zoom, or a pan to a zoom, or vice versa, can make the viewer feel ill.

GRAB ACTION SHOTS FIRST

In a city suburb the roof of a junior school has collapsed during a storm. A teacher and her young students are trapped. The storm has passed. Within the first 15 minutes a cameraman and a reporter arrive. The emergency services: fire-fighters, police and ambulance are already at work. And of course, there are anxious parents.

On any fast moving story the cameraman becomes the hunter; his task is to 'shoot it quick before it moves', to capture the moment before it disappears.

In a story like this, a reporter is going to go live from any position that the police will allow, but a reporter with a cameraman may also have to think about the visual and sound elements that tell the story for a full TV pre-recorded report that will be needed later.

After establishing that the children and the teacher cannot be filmed, the cameraman quickly grabs a long shot of fire-fighters and police.

These sorts of shots can never be repeated; they have to be grabbed while they are available. The interview with the rescue chief, close ups of his team and scenes of the school can wait. The temporary shots – shots that will go away – are filmed first.

SHOOT FOR IMPACT

News is often about action and change, so the camera should be looking for things that are moving or are in the process of change – a new airliner on its first flight or a decisive final few seconds in a sporting event.

Pictures which have the greatest impact are those that capture the action at its height. The sports photographer will try to snap the ball going through the posts; the news photographer will go for the champagne smashing against the side of the hull, or the ribbon parting the moment it is cut. TV is the same, but the moving picture sequence takes the viewer up to the point of action and follows it through.

SHOOT IN SEQUENCES

But there is a critical difference between the work of the cameraman and the photojournalist who uses a stills camera. In news reportage both are looking for that crucial moment, but the photojournalist just has to freeze a fraction of a second in time. The cameraman has to capture enough footage to show what is happening.

In a news report, few shots are held for longer than several seconds. But this should never be regarded as a rule – a shot is as long as it needs to be if it shows something that tells the story. A single element of the story could take 25 seconds to tell. This means that not one, but several shots are required, enough to give the edit stage plenty of choice. And those shots should represent a range of images from wide shots to close up; from the big picture to points of detail.

The sequence could begin with a long shot taking in the entire scene of the schoolroom where the roof has fallen in, also showing the street with the emergency services. There may be members of the public – and certainly parents – unless the police have decided to impose an exclusion zone.

Next comes a close up on a section of the school where the children are trapped and then a shot of a fire-fighter's face. This kind of sequence also needs to ensure it does not deceive or mislead. It has to follow events in a way that is honest and yet not entirely literal. The reaction shot of a person might actually be a minute later but it should still be relevant to the visual storytelling. The editing of these shots is to compress time and not to distort what happens.

As filming takes place think about the editing. A particular shot may make a good ending or opening and then you will hope it looks useful when viewed back. Have action shots, the reaction shots, activity and people.

CONTEXT

There is more to most news stories than high drama and fast-moving action. Just as important are the reasons behind the drama; the consequences of it; its effect on people.

A major criticism of TV news is that by featuring the short scuffle with police or single ugly scene during a three-hour demonstration viewers are left with the distorted impression that the whole protest was violent or unruly.

This is where it becomes vital for the reporter to explain the context of what has been shown and to screen other shots offering a clearer, more normal representation of the event.

The journalist has to bear in mind how to construct the report from the shots available at the time.

With the school there are five phases: the opening scene itself; the work of the emergency services; attempts to free the children and the teacher; public reaction or activity; the eventual rescue of the children and the teacher.

Shots should be picked to tell the story, to illustrate each of its phases and the main points within each phase.

One obvious other point – do not get in the way and if a police officer tells you to move, you do it.

SOUND

The sound of the story adds to the viewer's sense of being there. At the school that means sounds of shouting and instructions, sirens approaching and anxious parents are all essential to the story, and the reporter's script should pause to let them come through.

The microphone has an infuriating habit of amplifying stray sounds that the human ear would filter out. The trouble is, when those sounds are played back, the ear becomes almost perversely aware of them. It can be frustrating for the viewer, who can spend more time trying to work out where that mysterious mechanical sound (a generator perhaps?) is coming from rather than concentrating on the report.

There are three ways around this: turn off whatever is making the sound (and that's only rarely possible), do your shooting elsewhere or show where the noise is coming from. A little background noise (such as a busy street), when relevant to the story, adds atmosphere.

INTERVIEWEE CLIPS

Even more important are the short snatches of interview, also called grabs or clips or sound-bites. With TV's emphasis on pictures, these are likely to be shorter than those used in radio. The sound-bite should encapsulate the main point of the argument; the strongest opinion or reaction. Again there is a danger of distortion by over-emphasising the already emphatic and polarising a point of view, and this danger can only be eliminated by carefully explaining the context in which the remarks were made.

To cover the school story, the reporter will want to interview a senior police or fire officer, parents and any witnesses. The camera will usually be set up to feature the interviewee in three-quarters profile, looking to one side and slightly towards the camera, as he answers the reporter's questions.

CUTAWAYS AND BRIDGE SHOTS

Back at the school the reporter has just got the police chief to explain what's happening. He says they have managed to talk to the teacher – the children are safe but a few have some cuts and bruises; there are 22 children in there and they are aged nine or ten; the doors and windows are blocked by collapsed rubble.

The police officer says two important things: that the children are safe if a little bruised and he also says that rescue workers can now see into the classroom. But in between these statements the police officer takes a message. The reporter wants to run both statements together, but decides to cut out the message interruption because it was garbled and largely irrelevant.

The difficulty here is that the police chief was standing in a different position when he made his second statement. If the two answers were edited together there would be an unsightly jump (jump-cut) on the report. The officer cannot do this interview again because he gets another message and he is called away. The reporter has no choice. She has to go with what she's got. What she needs now is a cutaway shot to bridge the two statements.

In a radio interview the first and last sentences can be edited together, while the rest is discarded. Providing the editing is carried out professionally, no one will spot the join. But in TV, the join would be all too obvious. The sound might flow smoothly across the two sentences, but the picture would leap about the screen as the subject jerked in an instant from one position to another.

It might also look as if the interview was being dishonestly manipulated but in reality it is not.

To cover the join, the original pictures either side of the edit have to be replaced with a different sequence. The pictures shown should be of a related scene, such as an illustration of the speaker's remarks, which could be a shot of a fire-fighter close to the rubble of the collapsed roof. The original soundtrack of the answers is retained, but the jump in the policeman's face is covered by the alternative pictures.

Cutaways are necessary where the shots of the subject are similar. However, it might be possible to do without them when the cut is from a medium shot to a close up, as the switch to a different type of shot could cover the jump.

THE LINE

For very simple cutaways the cameraman will position the reporter so she seems to be looking at the interviewee. If they both appeared on screen looking say, to the left, it would seem as though they were talking to a third person and not to one another. TV people would say the camera had 'crossed the line', an expression which causes great confusion to journalists new to TV reporting.

The line is like an imaginary piece of string between two people. Providing the camera doesn't cross it, it can move anywhere and the two will appear to be facing each other in conversation. As soon as the line is crossed, the two will face the same way and the illusion will be broken. The line has to be observed with action shots as well.

Returning to the earlier example of the advancing tanks, if the cameraman shoots them from one side, then crosses the column to shoot the other, the sequence will show the tanks advancing first in one direction and then turning and retreating.

Crossing the line seems bizarre to the viewer because it is as though the observer of the scene has shifted rapidly from one viewpoint to another. Where you have to cross the line, the switch in direction can be disguised with a buffer shot. The camera can stand in front of the moving object and show it coming towards it, or pan to show the object approaching and then passing.

FIGURE 23.12
The line

1. Cameras are positioned to shoot across one another, showing each speaker in three-quarters profile. Providing neither camera crosses the line, when the speakers appear alternately on the TV screen they will be seen facing one another in conversation.

2. If a camera does cross the line the speakers will be shown facing the same way, as though talking to someone else off-camera. The impression of conversation will be broken. *(Usually you have only one camera but this is for illustration purposes only.)*

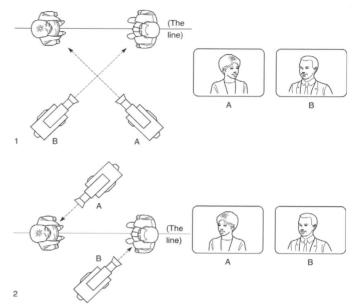

CONTINUITY

Edited reports have a way of telescoping time that can play tricks on the unwary reporter. Someone might be filmed in a long shot wearing a hat and again three minutes later in close up – without it. During that brief interlude he might also have loosened his tie, removed his jacket, put on his reading glasses and held his phone to his ear. Was it his right ear or his left anyway?

Cut those two shots together and the effect would be interesting, if not weird. At the very least it would distract from what he was saying. Always keep an eye on continuity. Common continuity problems in television journalism are:

- glasses on the face in one shot and taken off in the next

- clocks in the background that change

- ties or scarves appearing or disappearing

- curtains open and then closed

- jackets on or off

- holding an object in one hand and then the other

- levels of liquids in transparent glasses or cups moving up and down.

FIGURE 23.13
One moment the glass is nearly full. This appears in a shot.

FIGURE 23.14
A second later it's down but the viewer did not see anyone drink from it.

BUILDINGS

Many news editors declare with prejudice that buildings are boring and often even dictate that a news report should never start with an image of a building – unless the building itself is the subject of the story.

They mean stories about diplomacy or politics that often have little to show except Talking Heads. So the reporter has little extra except another shot of Westminster, the White House, the Elysée Palace, cars arriving and leaving and sometimes a flag. Shots that we've seen a thousand times before and appear to be lazy TV reporting.

What can help is to look at a building from a point-of-view that is different from the aspect of an adult of average height. That means getting a shot from the ground looking upwards, or some detail in the architecture, or art or the skilled work of a mason, or framing the building through trees or fencing. Anything that makes it look different from the normal eye-line.

PIECE TO CAMERA (PTC) ALSO KNOWN AS STAND UPPERS

Most reporters like to enhance their reports by appearing on camera from time to time. This is not the same as live reporting in vision. These shots, known as pieces to camera (but also called stand-ups or stand-uppers), usually feature the reporter standing in front of the scene in question, or hopefully something relevant to the story. If this is a carnival with lots of colour and movement, there is no excuse for the kind of stand-upper which has a blank wall in the background. It is also worthwhile for the reporters to be seen at the location – especially if the channel has paid a lot of money sending them there.

FIGURE 23.15
The background adds variety and shows audiences that the TV station goes where the news is and that its reporters are out and about. It is useful to rehearse, at least once. Recorded PTCs and Stand-uppers are usually short – two or three short, simple, concise sentences is the easiest way. Take care with big numbers and today/yesterday/tomorrow time references. Courtesy UTV.

For a PTC you will almost always have a cameraman. Tell him what you are going to do. It only takes a moment to talk about the framing and what the viewer will see around you. For a more complex PTC you may even want to suggest a zoom towards you, or away.

The action should be used as the backdrop. It adds variety and shows audiences that the TV station goes where the news is and that its reporters are out and about. The piece to camera can be used at the beginning of an item to set the scene, in the middle to act as a bridge linking two threads of the story or at the end as the reporter's way of signing-off; TV's equivalent of radio's standard out-cue. PTCs and Stand-uppers are usually short – their static nature can slow down the action and the reporter's memory might not be very good.

For court cases, where quotations need to be accurate, or stories involving statistics or numbers, then a notebook is not only accepted but may well enhance the PTC. After all, if you are quoting the judge or providing statistics and you look at your notebook, then the viewer is more likely to believe you.

SPECIAL FILM EQUIPMENT

There are lots of different ways to get interesting shots with equipment that can be cheap and simple to the most elaborate and expensive. Which one you choose will depend on a whole host of things, such as time and location and, above all, budget and the kind of story or programme you work on.

This is a Useful To Know section. Journalists in general do not actually operate special film equipment, such as a drone. Larger broadcasters have their own specialists. Smaller channels will hire in.

The extent of anything that resembles special equipment may be a tripod, which is vital for steady simple shots and static lives, and if there's any lighting needed it may be one or two simple lights combined with some creative use of reflections.

This section deals with both simple and more sophisticated ways of getting your shots. It's not equipment that is in routine standard use – but the journalist can greatly enhance his or her work by understanding what is available or how to improvise. If you are working on a longer form report some of this can be worth the investment.

Special equipment could be used for background features, special reports or if you are working on a strand of features – such as five items over a week looking at different aspects of a story. Remember to over-shoot. If you are paying for something special then get more than you need for your report so then you have leftovers to file as library and to use for several years.

Basic Lighting

The modern DV camera will provide high quality pictures when your subject is correctly lit. The cameras, with the inbuilt pop-out or pop-up monitors, give a reasonable impression of whether the light is going to cause trouble. Poorly lit areas and very bright sunny conditions both pose problems for the camera operator.

The camera is capable of producing pictures in very low light conditions. To be able to do this the picture signal is automatically boosted, which results in grainy pictures. To prevent this loss in picture quality you need to find some way of increasing the light hitting your subject.

VJs will usually have some training in use of light but this is a just a very basic list of tips for the journalist to be aware of – and remember that single frames as well as moving pictures will be needed for the website. So you might want single frames that look good.

Ask yourself whether it is essential to do this interview indoors or can it be done outside in daylight?

Ask if there is another room you could use which is better lit.

Place the subject near to available light sources.

Don't be afraid to re arrange furniture or lamps to ensure your subject is lit. Spotlights – such as the Anglepoise type – can be particularly useful. Put things back when you are finished.

Put your subject beside or facing a window to use the natural light coming into the room.

Tripod and Tall Legs

The tripod is the most basic support, from thin light styles for small DV to heavier 'legs' for larger cameras. The modern lightweight tripod for DV cameras is quick to set up, but should be treated gently. The screws/levers that allow the legs to telescope up and down for folding or framing need only be finger tight. But do keep your fingers away from moving parts – a sudden drop in the telescoped legs can cause nasty injuries. Tall Legs is a tripod with much longer than usual legs or more extensions to enable the camera to shoot from a higher angle than usual.

FIGURE 23.16
Every street corner should have one. The cameraman had actually just unclipped the camera from the tripod for a moment to get a different shot. A colleague is watching the equipment. It may look just like a pile of metal, but it is not cheap.

Vehicle Mounts

You can clamp cameras to many parts of a car – inside or out – but be careful that they don't cause obstructions or you might find yourself in legal trouble. A suction pad can be stuck to the bonnet and you can film forwards or backwards into the car. A door mount is a frame that looks like a roof rack and hooks over the door.

Small Cameras/Minicams

The most basic minicam is about 8–10 cms long. There are smaller cameras but this is the most commonly used size because it provides acceptable quality shots. It can fit into places where a full-size camera just cannot be used such as the inside or outside of cars, bicycles or helicopters.

Action cameras such as GoPro™ can be put onto a pole and film in places which would be impossible for a conventional camera. You are limited only by your imagination.

TV journalist and film-maker Iain Webster assembled his own equipment combination to show the audience what happens when people get into trouble at sea.

The equipment used to get a lifeboatman's eye view of rescues for UTV's Portrush Sea Rescue involved a 'lipstick' camera tied to a Royal National Lifeboat Institute (RNLI) helmet. A small microphone was wrapped in felt and a 'Marigold' rubber glove finger was cut to provide waterproofing. Self-amalgamating tape sealed all the cables. The camera lens and microphone were cabled back to a small waterproof Peli case which contained a small Canon HDV (tape) camcorder with an AV input. The Lifeboat person put the camcorder into record mode and wore the case on the back of a diver's webbing belt. As they started the camera I helped launch their D class lifeboat! The kit cost around £800, plus hours refining the set up. This set up wasn't available then as an off the shelf item. I needed great quality shots and sound. The RNLI said the equipment captured the best viewpoint of a rescue they had ever seen. For action shots I now use two GoPro Hero cameras which do the same job, with better image quality and mounting options, at half the price. The latest model, the Hero 4, shoots up to 4k resolution, slo-mo and can be controlled by an iPhone.

Journalists can hire GoPro cameras but they're easily affordable and you can film yourself for YouTube capers! Today, the GoPro takes seconds to mount – is waterproof to 40+ metres – and the live pictures can be streamed to your iphone via built in WiFi and Bluetooth to allow you to position the shot and replay the footage once the action's been captured on its Micro SD card. I have a variety of mounts for cars and bikes, helmets and clothing. Plus a 'selfie pole' to allow presenters to film themselves.

Iain Webster, Network Media

FIGURE 23.17

Mini-camera attached to a helmet. Tiny cameras can be used for television journalism to get shots that earn their place by providing a point of view that surprises, informs and holds attention. Courtesy Iain Webster, Network Media (NI).

Splash Bag

All cameras should have a basic rain cover but this is one stage up. The camera is normally sealed into the bag, making it suitable for conditions of extreme wet such as filming on a speeding boat. The disadvantage is that the camera is difficult to operate as the controls are hard to get at.

Wheels

These need a smooth surface. For pre-planned features or current affairs programmes you could get a professional base which is really a camera mount on wheels. But use your initiative when filming and see if there's anything around you with wheels – cameras can go into a supermarket trolley or onto a chair with wheels. Even children's toys have been used.

FIGURE 23.18

A drone fitted with a camera is now common for getting shots that would be difficult or impossible to film from the ground. The drone removes the need for a full-sized helicopter and the equipment that a helicopter needs. Courtesy Channel NewsAsia.

Drones

Small remote-controlled camera flying drones have been around for years and were mostly used by the military and hobbyists. They are even being used to shepherd sheep.

The issue for the journalist – about to ask the editor for permission to use a drone – is to think about when and where these kind of shots would be useful. Aviation authorities have strict rules, permissions and safety standards about using a drone and it should never be flown beyond the line of sight of the operator.

Operating a drone illegally can carry serious penalties. If the journalist sees a useful tool for broadcasting, what security forces and police might see is a potential attack. Or what a celebrity lying on a beach regards as a breach of privacy. Safety managers are also aware that there is a risk that a drone might malfunction and fall on someone.

Using a drone near places like the White House, a parliament building, a prison, a security or police headquarters, an airport or any sensitive site is not advised. Swiss police questioned three TV journalists for using a drone in a high-security no-fly zone at the World Economic Forum in Davos.

FIGURE 23.19

It is not by chance that the reporter is holding the microphone in her left hand. If it was in her right hand then her arm and the microphone might cut across our guest and the trophy, which is obviously what the lens and viewer needs to see. Courtesy UTV News.

FIGURE 23.20

When filming in a room or office always try to put a Filming in Progress sign on the door, or Take Care – Filming in Progress. It does not need to be as grand as this one – this was for a big shoot in public with a team of about 20 people. For news, just write on a sheet of paper and stick it to the door or any other location where people need to be warned.

TELEVISION MICROPHONE TECHNIQUES FOR REPORTERS

Viewers are used to seeing microphones, but if you have placed it a bit too far into or across the subject's face then you will feel the cameraman tapping your arm down a little. This is when the microphone is in danger of contaminating the shot.

In addition to the basics for radio use, for television do not:

- Wave it or shake it about like a wand.
- Move it as if prodding at the subject.
- Hold it close to yourself all the time – or forget that we need to hear the subject as well as your questions.

Do:

- Hold it steady.
- Move it gently with your arm rather than flip it with your hand.
- Keep it dry.

THE HEADLINES

- Shots have names. These include the long shot, medium shot, close up, big close up.

- For news, static shots always work best. They are simple, direct and don't give the viewer too much of a jolt. They are also easier to edit.

- You do not just point the lens at the subject or the action. TV news shots are about composing and framing.

- News is often about action and change, so the camera should be looking for things that are moving in front of a static camera shot.

- Think of the editing as you film. A particular shot may make a good ending or opening and then you will hope it looks useful when viewed back. Have action shots, reaction shots, activity and people.

QUESTIONS FOR YOU

1. Go out with your camera or phone. Take both still and/or video shots of buildings, streets, landscapes . . . anything that interests you really. But as you do this think of shot names – long shot, mid-shot . . . close ups. For video, notice if your shots wobble a lot and seem unusable.
2. Try leaning against a wall, tree or post to get the shot and notice the difference.
3. Watch drama and movies the way a news cameraman would. Do you notice which shots stand out, how they are composed and where the camera is positioned?

OTHER RESOURCES

- Film maker Christina Fox (UrbanFox.tv) has a wide range of examples and detail about camera and sound work for TV journalists: www.urbanfox.tv/index.htm.

- More shot sizes from Daniel Chandler ('The 'Grammar' of Television and Film') at http://bit.ly/19Bmeku.

TUTOR NOTES

Get your group into small teams with cameras/phones. Send them to a local park for an hour, as if the park is relevant to a news story. Get half the teams to do endless pans and zooms. Get the other half to do nothing but static shots. Compare and contrast.

Exercise – What's Going On? Some of the team will be using the cameras or take turns as the actor/subject. Get the 'actor' to do something with head and hands – it could just be at the keyboard.

They need to get:

- A wide shot of the subject

- A close shot of what the subject is doing (hands / keyboard)

- A close shot of the subject's face

- A medium shot from behind the subject but we still see what the subject is doing

and . . . something else. It could be a ground shot of the subject's feet, or a big close shot of the keyboard or a shot of the subject taken from the door of the room or from the outside through a window. Up to them.

It could be made more interesting or varied with other props – such as the subject cutting carrots or apples, reading, using a pen or playing with Lego.

CHAPTER 24

Editing the Pictures and Sound

Writing the script is only part of the story. Once the shots and sound have been collected they have to be edited. This is how the grammar of television news is applied. The report may also need library pictures, archive or graphics. Editing is usually done in conjunction with the scriptwriting. Some journalists prefer to write words to pictures, others match pictures to words. But in practice, the process often takes place simultaneously.

The raw material out of the camera is often still described using traditional terms – rushes, or even footage.

This section deals with editing the material and compiling a report – either a short news item or a longer feature or package. It deals with the most vital principles of editing rather than the technology which is updated constantly or with the way editing is organised by a broadcaster. Some have craft editors plus shoot-edit crews and/or VJs/reporter-editors or a combination of all of that. Many basic news items are both scripted and edited by the journalist inside a newsroom. But everyone needs to know the principles in the same way as everyone needs to understand the shots.

There are some basic principles for news:

- Do not fake real continuity. Do not take shots from one location or time and pretend they happened in another.

- Do not join a zoom to a zoom. It looks at least inelegant, at worst shocking.

- Do not join a pan to a pan. The viewer loses track of where they are.

- Avoid cutting while the shot is moving. Cutting before movement begins and waiting for the movement to end looks and feels more natural.

- Keep continuity between shots. If someone is standing up in one shot then cutting to them sitting down in the next looks ridiculous. If you don't have a shot of the person sitting then you will need a cut away to give the person a chance to sit while out of vision.

- Do not cut between similar shots. If two shots are too similar then the edit will look like a mistake.

- Use sound at every opportunity: the sounds of people, streets, action, machines or nature.

- Try to ensure you have used the best shot available. If you are in a hurry it can be very easy to use a poor shot when a better one exists somewhere else within the images. If you see two or more similar zooms or pans on the rushes, the last take will often be the best.

SEQUENCE OF SHOTS

Editing is an extension of the shooting process. The editor is building on the work of the sounds and pictures that have been acquired from the location. Camera shots will often be out of sequence – the last thing in the raw material may be the first thing needed for the report. The editor's job is to select the best shots, put them in order and trim them to length. One of the advantages of a shoot-edit professional and for a VJ who also edits is that he or she will know already what is available.

Edited shots should cut from one to another smoothly and logically and follow a train of thought. If this rule is broken, the images that result are likely to be jerky, unrelated, confusing and detract from the story. Every change of scene or sequence should be properly set up to register with the viewers. General views (GVs) or long shots are often used as openers or establishing shots to set the scene, although that may not always be the case.

There's a political demonstration at a global summit conference . . . they just want to make their views known and hand in a petition.

We see the demonstration advancing and get an idea of the scale of protest. As we begin to wonder who is involved, a medium shot cuts in to reveal the organisers striding ahead and perhaps there's a brief interview with one of the leaders, walking and talking at the same time. But what was supposed to be a peaceful protest has turned sour. Perhaps we have no idea why at this stage. We then have a close-up of a man burning a banner or a flag.

Rearrange the sequence of these shots and you may remove the context and offer the viewer more questions than answers. Begin with the close-up and you have no idea of the scale of the protest – is it ten people or a thousand? Cut then to the long shot and the action appears to be moving backwards. Unless you cut progressively and smoothly – like the human eye – the logic of the sequence will be destroyed. It is easier to follow the action if you bridge the close-ups and long shots with medium shots.

SHOT LENGTH

Every shot should say something and stir up interest. It's useful to think of a shot as an event – then it's there for a reason. The moment a shot has delivered its message and its appeal begins to wane, it could be cut and then joined to the next shot. Action and movement within a static shot generally holds interest.

How long you should hold a shot depends on a number of different factors:

- The instinctive decision by the editor about what the shot is 'worth'. There should never be rules about how long a shot should be, even in news. In general four seconds could capture the action. Three seconds may 'feel' right, slipping into the overall rhythm of the item, or the shot could be cut to deliberately vary that rhythm and change the pace.

- Shot length may be determined by the length of a clip of a person talking, or sound-bite. Here, a long quote need not dictate using the same visual of the speaker throughout. If visual interest wanes the editor can switch to another relevant picture, while the clip continues to run beneath. This could be a simple reversal, showing the reporter and interviewee together, or a visual chosen to illustrate the subject being talked about.

- Where visuals are being matched to the script, the shot will be cut to fit the section of narrative.

- Where the shot contains so much detail that it becomes impossible to take in at a glance, the editor may hold the picture for a while to let the scene register or give viewers time to read words on banners or placards.

- Shots can be held to allow them to be dissolved into one another, as the extra length creates space for the overlap.

The most obvious place for a change of shot is at the beginning of a new sentence or paragraph. This has a certain logic but can soon become stale and repetitious. You can provide welcome relief by illustrating a single sentence with a number of different shots.

Long sequences can be broken up with general views of related subjects. A long-ish commentary on a space project could be relieved by adding shots of the space centre, technicians working and employees walking, over the soundtrack of the commentary.

The action can be brought closer to the viewer by using insert shots. These are the close-ups of walking, marching feet, protest banners. When it comes to editing, shots like these are called overlays because they are laid over the existing soundtrack.

TELESCOPING THE ACTION

Things we see on camera can appear to take a long time – a static shot of a person walking along a corridor may last ten seconds but seems to take longer. This is fine for a documentary. But there's no room in news for the boredom of waiting around for something to happen. So to telescope time and drive the action forward you can use a technique known as intercutting.

A motorcade carrying the president is approaching in the distance. The camera follows the arrival of the president and entourage for 45 seconds until it reaches the steps of a building, then continues the shot as they go inside. In all, we may have a total of three minutes of footage. This is more than would be required for the report, so to telescope the action – to compress time – the editor decides to join the shot of the motorcade approaching in the distance to the last few seconds of the cars pulling up at the venue.

The editor links the two shots with a cutaway taken earlier of a clutch of armed police. You could of course totally ignore all the shots of the cars approaching and just use the moment when they are arriving and stopping. Another that would have worked is an earlier shot of the fenced-off crowds straining to catch sight of the approaching motorcade. These are related to the original scenes and tell us something new about them. The edited sequence telescopes three minutes of action into just maybe 12/15 seconds – and even that is long-winded for news.

DESKTOP EDITING

With old analogue video editing you built up the report on tape shot by shot. If you want to add a fresh scene in the middle – too bad – either you drop it in over an existing shot, or you have to unstitch the rest of the report after the edit and make it all over again.

In the first generation of editing the raw sound and vision was loaded into the computer and digitised into clips. The computer can be programmed to swallow up a straight section of footage, or can capture clips individually or in batches. A still frame from each captured clip is displayed on the screen. The clip can be played simply by pointing the mouse over it and clicking. Then the editor selects the clips he wants and, using the drag and drop technique familiar to all computer users, assembles them in any order.

The clips, with their accompanying soundtracks, are put together on a timeline – as it says, a line on the screen with timings on it. The editor can play the clip from any point on the timeline and can shuttle backwards and forwards to cue and review the sound and pictures.

Most news reports are compiled using straight cuts. These are the kind of simple edits that are also sometimes done by journalists themselves in the newsroom.

As one image ends, the other begins without an overlap. But the point where one image gradually gives way to another is known as a transition – getting from one shot to another without giving the viewer a jolt. There are natural transitions that were filmed at the time (a big lorry crossing the shot) and transitions that come with the software and can be done at the edit stage, like a windscreen wiper with one shot on one side of the wiper while the next one is on the other side.

The most common transition that sometimes does find its way into a news report is called a dissolve – as one image fades out the other fades in. Two tracks are laid down on the timeline one above the other. We'll call them A and B. To dissolve between A and B so the image on track A gradually gives way to the image on track B you drag a transition onto the timeline and place it between them. You stretch the transition to the length you want and make it fade from track A to B or vice versa. Then you preview your transition to check that it works.

Editing video sound is pretty much the same as in radio. You can adjust each element of the soundtrack for volume, add bass, treble or a host of other effects, and crossfade one track beneath another. And if you don't like anything that you've done, then you don't have to bin it and start again from the beginning.

With modern editing you can start at any point and remake your work infinitely. And if you cut out a piece by mistake it doesn't matter, because non-linear editing is non-destructive. Any cuts you make are to a clone of the digital footage (also called the rushes) which remains intact in the computer memory.

THE CRAFT EDITOR

Although the quest by television news organisations at the start of the last decade was for multi-skilling, there are still professionals who work as full-time craft editors. This editor is the television news equivalent of a sub-editor in print journalism. The editor is the journalist's first viewer. Craft editors – also called package editors by some channels – edit longer form reports and packages or anything that is more complex than a basic news report of a few shots and a clip.

If the journalist is working with an editor it is vital to get him or her fully involved and that means first of all – tell them what the story is about. If they look blankly at you then you have just failed to tell the story to your first audience. And, is this an update or new version of an earlier news report? Or is it a new feature report? And how long is it meant to be? Are graphics, archive or maps being dropped in? They also need to know when it is needed – which is often ten minutes ago, but then it might not be needed for another four hours or the next day.

- Don't spring surprises on your editor. Keep him up to date with any changes to the story.

- Plan and structure your story before you start. This may or may not mean writing a draft script – and print it off with plenty of line spacing so you can adjust the words.

- Let the editor view the pictures but also explain where you need to use what in the story. Or where is that vital five-second clip of the witness?

- Know what your closing shots should be – know this before you start. You can change your mind of course but knowing how to end avoids panic and that last shot is vital anyway.

- Don't leave too much too late. Finishing an edit 30 seconds before it goes on air does NOT make it a better story even if you think it makes you seem dynamic.

- Think sequences and events rather than shots. Ideal sequences can tell stories with very few words so they make stories flow and enhance your script greatly.

FIGURE 24.1

Modern editing is now highly portable. Advances in compact hard drive storage mean that the edit – by a video-journalist for example – can be completed on location and then uploaded as a finished item. Many producers also save edit time back at base by doing a preliminary edit before loading the initial cut into an online edit system. This is an Apple Macbook Pro which contains the edit platform, Avid Media Composer. Courtesy Iain Webster, Network Media (NI).

RECORDING THE COMMENTARY (SCRIPT/TRACK)

This can be done either before any editing takes place – which is not usually the best option unless the journalist is very experienced and knows exactly what sound and picture will be needed. It is done better in stages: recording the commentary – also known as the track – up to each clip or natural break in the edited story.

By far the most effective way is to edit all the sound and pictures and only then the journalist can lay down his (carefully timed) track. This ensures the primacy of the pictures and sound. They have been selected first and the journalist is now forced to write a tight and lean script. If the timing is out, the journalist goes back to the start of the last shot and takes it again.

The journalist will be constantly snipping at sentences now to make the length of the script fit with the length of the sound and pictures.

A script which 60 seconds ago was written as 'the president's briefing after the talks was short – a mere five minutes and he admitted he had little more to say . . .' might then become 'he admitted he had little to say . . .' (short clip) 'five minutes later he was off again . . .'

EDITING SHOTS FOR INTERVIEWS

Interviews can either run to full length, depending on news merit, or for a report will need to be edited to select the right clip. You should not cut abruptly between two of the spoken sentences otherwise the viewer gets a jolt.

An example is like this clip with a duration of about 40 seconds:

The interviewee says:

> We learned a lot of lessons after we brought in that law and those lessons mean that we now know what should have really been done in the first place. I think we made mistakes – well, we all do in life don't we and, well, you know, eh . . . it just happens if you don't have the right information to start with and yet you think at that time that you're doing the decent thing. But we've got a better idea now and that's what we are asking everyone to approve. I think in politics you must do what is right at a moment in time even you later find that you could have done it better.

This 40 seconds might be fine for a ten-minute current affairs report, but it is a bit too long for a news report of two minutes. In this case we could lose the bit where she says: 'I think we made mistakes – well, we all do in life don't we and, well, you know, eh . . . it just happens if you don't have the right information to start with and yet you think at that time that you're doing the decent thing.'

Editorially, the point could be made in the script, in particular in the few script words before the clip: 'She admitted that they didn't have the right information . . .'.

So we could condense the clip by taking that out without substantially misleading the viewer or misrepresenting the interviewee.

So if we edit the sound, then the clip would say:

> We learned a lot of lessons after we brought in that law and those lessons mean that we now know what should have really been done in the first place.

> But we've got a better idea now and that's what we are asking everyone to approve. I think in politics you must do what is right at a moment in time, even you later find that you could have done it better.

The original 40 seconds has now gone to about 23 seconds. Remember that we measure European languages at a rate of about three words per second.

This is probably still long for a news report, although it might be an important quotation and therefore earn its duration on editorial merit. The point here is about the editing. We can edit the audio but what does this look like? It looks like a jolt – as if the politician's head had suddenly jerked. We cannot have that because it looks terrible, almost like some technical fault, and also gives an impression of censorship.

So that's why we need to get rid of the (literally) talking head for a second or two to ensure the audio edit blends in with the visual edit. The basic methods to use are the Two shot, Reverse two shot, Interview cutaway and Set up shots.

Two Shot

The camera is pulled back behind the reporter, and the shot is re-framed to include the interviewee and the head and one shoulder of the reporter. The interviewee listens while the reporter talks. Watch for continuity problems; you don't want the interviewee smiling after a serious interview, or removing or replacing spectacles.

Reverse Two Shot

The camera is moved behind the interviewee (or where the interviewee was just located) to frame up on the reporter's face. The reporter looks as if she is listening and may even repeat some questions. Busy politicians, for example, rarely have the time to stay for this, but it can be done after the politician leaves. This shot is hardly original or inspiring but is better than nothing at all. Many years ago they were called 'noddies' – it is best to avoid doing any obvious nodding at all.

Set Up Shots

Sometimes you can use the two shot, especially a wide two shot, to introduce your interviewee. But this only works for very short introductions, of the sort you'd get in a brief news report. Generally it's better to use your imagination and find better shots in the rushes of your subject doing something, anything that is relevant which could be meeting people or chatting at a conference or just a few seconds of their trade, job or activity.

Basic Interview Cutaways

Figures 24.2–24.4 show basic shots for editing interview clips together.

EDITING VOX POPS

Similar to the principles of vox pops in radio, but television has an added problem. Just hope that some people were looking camera left, some looking camera right, so that in the edit you can inter cut effectively (especially if conflicting views are being expressed) between faces in different directions. It looks better and appears much more natural.

USING MUSIC

The use of music in television journalism is a matter for individual newsroom editors. Most news channels ban music completely from news reports while others will allow music on longer feature items and music is often used in channel promotional trails.

FIGURE 24.2
We have an interview with him but we don't want it all. So you use this bit . . .

FIGURE 24.3
Then cut to this shot of the same person to cover an edit. If we do not then the head will jerk suddenly and the viewer gets a jolt. A cut-away of the person carrying out action that is part of the first shot looks neater. Anyway, he is talking about music.

FIGURE 24.4
And then we can cut back to the subject for the rest of the clip.

No editing which includes music should start unless the music is known to everyone involved and it's usually better to put the music into the edit memory before you start cutting the audio and pictures. The images can then be cut to the changing phases of the music.

If you're shooting a musical event, a choir for example, then make sure you run for sound; the camera is not switched on and off between shots, but keeps recording the sound while the shots are framed and re framed. As a VJ you need to do the same.

If you are shooting music as an important element in a longer feature report you will need at least three takes of the same piece of music. One wide shot as a master shot and a complete take of the sound; and two more takes for cutaways: hands, instruments, strings, face, lips and pages of music.

FIGURE 24.5

Basic editing is often on the desktop in an open-plan newsroom and with headphones. Craft editing is best done in a separate room with low lighting to give a clear view of the images and clip names and to avoid sound distractions. Working with an editor is a fruitful learning experience for the new broadcast journalist as she can see what works – and what does not – in building up the elements of a story.

THE HEADLINES

- Some basic simple picture/sound editing can be done by the journalist with desktop software but many newsrooms have editors or package editors for longer stories.

- The editor builds on the work of the sound and pictures that have been acquired from the location. Working with the broadcast journalist, the editor will select the best shots, clean up sound, put the story in order and trim shots to length.

- Explain the story to the editor – and your ideas. Let the editor view the pictures but also say if there is anything you need to use and hopefully where it might be in the rushes. Where is that vital five-second clip you must have?

- Know what your closing shots should be.

QUESTIONS FOR YOU

1. Camera time again – but this time can you shoot for the edit? Go get some wide general view shots – but when you get your close-ups, reverses and cutaway shots think of how they will be used inside the general view to compress time. Have a look back and decide whether your Shots for the Edit will work.

2. You might need to do this alone. Do you have any movies at home with a commentary in any bonus material? Perhaps the director or the editor talking. Watch about 30 minutes of one film with the added commentary. Then watch about 30 minutes of another film *without* the commentary and even start doing your own commentary. You will start the habit of Watching for the Edit.

OTHER RESOURCES

- PC Advisor has a review of free video editing software. 'The question we wanted to answer was whether free software is good enough to fulfil the average home user's video editing requirements': http://bit.ly/1ygm5i0.

- An overview of news and editing conventions. A video with useful commentary that provides a guide: http://bit.ly/1D7Vnau.

- From jump edits to transitions. Short BBC School Report video explains some of the methods in editing sound and pictures: www.bbc.co.uk/schoolreport/21549429.

TUTOR NOTES

Ever since editing in TV news has been going on, editors have been getting ideas from the craft of cinema. Ask everyone to watch a film sometime one week, anything at all. But with a specific aim. Ask them to write down what happens in about ten edits in the film. How the edits look, cutaway and reverse shots, dialogue edits, how do they create a transition or compress time?

It doesn't matter if several of them report back on the same film because they may identify different things.

CHAPTER 25

Live Reporting in Sound and Vision

All reporters are now expected to go live. That means a combination of several things that must be sorted out fast: preparing the known information as quickly as possible is the priority – find out what has happened, where and when and get as many details as possible plus a decent quote from someone at the location that helps to explain the story.

You can get more details later. On a breaking story you may well go live several times.

Also check the location for problems such as the weather or any hazardous interruptions (which includes people, animals or props) and then think about what needs a bit of a performance, such as showing something or moving on location.

You are live, in vision, talking, or sometimes talking and walking at the same time and hopefully having a good reason for doing so.

You might be 'live' for no particular reason other than the fact that it is a journalistic device. You may be a live commentator in news or sport, or as part of a live two-way with the base studio. There are four basic kinds of live in vision reporting, but be aware that the names given to these vary a lot in different newsrooms and in different countries. In some places the live piece is called a Rant or even an Action Rant.

These are generic names.

- The Two-Way, also known as the Down The Line (DTL) when the reporter at the scene responds to some questions from the studio presenter. 'Our reporter Peter Jones is there. Peter? What's been happening?' The presenter in studio then asks Peter a couple of questions. It is very important that the reporter knows this is a two-way and not a monologue.

- The Live Link or Throw means the presenter hands over to the reporter at the scene and the reporter is often linking into a report he or she did earlier and may also do live interviews at the scene. 'Peter Jones is there now . . .' It might also be the link into the live reporter. The reporter then carries the entire story without any presenter intervention. The reporter needs to Hand Back to the studio otherwise nobody will know that he is finished.

- Breaking update/Live Update means the presenter may just link to the reporter on a story just happening and it may be no more than a 40-second live in vision report. The reporter may also step aside from the lens to show the viewer what is happening. The other kind of device is simply to have the reporter in the studio, sitting beside the presenter with the latest news.

- The Video Wall *(also see Data, Graphics and Visuals)* keeps the reporter live in the studio, standing and usually to one side of the presenter. The reporter can use a range of interview clips, graphics and images to explain a complicated story. Unlike a location live, the reporter can have a prompter but then he will have to master that skill as well.

- The graphics montage. Reporters might be expected to be live on location and have graphics added by newsroom to the shot, often appearing one at a time (animating) and adding to the information from the reporter. Communication between newsroom and reporter are vital to make sure the reporter is talking about what we see in the graphic. Memorising numbers accurately is difficult but it's also usually acceptable to have notes if you are using numbers or direct quotations. It means a brief break of eye contact to show that you are reading the figures from a note, which is natural and therefore acceptable. In this case a traditional written note with pen and paper is probably safer than a mobile device which can cause problems with Finger Trouble.

What all of these have in common is that the reporter is supposed to be telling us what is happening at the location the reporter is actually in. Or at least near to it.

What often happens is that reporters are placed in front of empty buildings at 10 pm, in the dark to tell the 'latest from the meeting' when the meeting actually ended at 5 pm. Another situation awkward for the reporter is when he's just arrived somewhere and having been there for ten minutes is asked by the presenter 'what's been the mood like there today?' These are situations which provide plenty of fun for all those comedy programmes which parody the way news is reported.

WHAT WORKS WELL?

Movement, relevant background and something worth saying make the best live reporting. The reporter is at the scene of a story and can move and talk and show the audience something of interest – it might just be a landscape where an historic battle took place or it might be the scene of an overnight fire with smoke drifting about. It's vital to give every live a sense of occasion – give the viewer an interest and show why you are there as well as having your reporting ready.

When you are live and in vision, nothing else can be happening in your life except your story.

FIGURE 25.1
A display of parasols in the garden shop or a hunting pack of live-on-air reporters? Television journalists, crews and engineers have set up a typical pop-up media-village at Westminster in London where politicians, commentators and journalists gather for continuous live reports.

WHAT WORKS LESS WELL?

Being live for no particular reason and having nothing much to say.

Or standing in front of a brick wall. Or standing in front of the story – telling us about the overnight fire that we cannot see because the *reporter is in the way*. Another problem is bad communication between location reporter and the studio or director – such as not being told how long the live should be, or that it is not a two-way but a live link with no presenter questions. The reporter can also make his own life difficult by talking too quickly or using long and complex sub-clauses. This can upset the viewer who might be wondering if the poor man is having breathing problems. It's safer to keep it simple and that, after all, aids the live storytelling anyway.

Then of course, there are the animals and children (they don't know your script!) and the weather, and props that fall apart, and the car alarm that goes off because the reporter touched the car. Then background noise should also be checked – a noisy generator that's not in the shot (heard but not seen) would need to be explained. Even a phrase like 'it's very noisy here' works well because it will help the viewer get the point.

FIGURE 25.2

So why is the reporter standing on what appears to be a ventilation shaft? Sometimes just the smallest elevation will make a big difference to getting the background right. If she was two feet lower the viewer would see her standing on front of a wall that could be anywhere and reporter and cameraman need the viewer to see where she is. The journalist must be prepared for a bit of choreography before going on air. Moving up, down, left, right, at the same time she is concentrating on her words. Everyone will also check that it is safe. Courtesy Channel NewsAsia.

TOP TIPS

Going Live is about staying calm, talking only about what you know, avoiding speculation, avoiding any blur between fact and comment and ensuring good communication with the gallery.

For the reporter on location, that story is the only thing in the world that matters at that moment.

Your tooth hurts? We don't care. You are cold and wet? Well, it's a cold and wet story. You have to take the cat to the vet? Sorry, nothing to do with this incident. You cannot go live and carry it off with hard facts and authority if you're also wondering what to buy your mother for her birthday.

Never assume that other people know an event is live. If you have contributors always ensure they *know* it is live. This happens at big events, like national elections or anything with continuous coverage and a cast of hundreds. The reporter is based on a specific location and may be moving about – she walks up to someone involved and starts doing an interview. Usually these are pre-arranged. But sometimes they can be spontaneous and this can be risky. This needs to start with words from the reporter such as 'Mr Stewart is here now. Mr Stewart we are live on Channel 12 . . . sorry to interrupt you but can you tell us . . .?' so at least Mr Stewart now knows.

Try these:

- Rehearse. Rehearse that first answer or opening sentence. It will help you to organise the basic facts for the rest of the two-way. Rehearse any walking, talking and movements you need to do.

- Get your information organised into simple and short statements. Do not let irrelevant words fill the time available. If there's a vital bit of news don't worry about repeating it.

- Do not believe the studio when they say they're coming to you at a particular time. Assume that will change. Just when you think you have time to nip into that café and grab a coffee the gallery is shouting, 'Coming to you next! Coming to you NOW!'

- Do not try to write it all down and try to memorise every single word – just think of three vital points you want to get across.

- Do not be afraid to use a note for direct quotations or statistics. It is OK to break eye contact with the camera briefly to get a quotation, a number or an accurate statistic. The viewer is also more likely to believe you. Use a small notepad or small prompt cards – not separate sheets of paper that will rattle in a wind.

- In a presenter/reporter two-way, do not try to churn out a long, packed reply to the first question. Leave yourself other things to say if the two-way is going to be as long as two minutes with several questions. Make sure you know whether it IS a two-way with a presenter or just you on your own.

- In a two-way, think out how to deal with questions you cannot possibly answer, in effect when the presenter asks you about something you cannot possibly see or know. You might think that it should not happen, but it does. Just talk about what you know.

- Always tell the cameraman in advance if you are going to turn and gesture at something, or hold up a prop, or in fact anything unconventional at all. This may seem obvious, but anyone new to this does not always remember the need to frame the shot.

- Beware the public. Check your location for any potential problems from passers-by. Most public locations should be fine but a bar full of drunks as a live location is asking for trouble. In many parts of the world a camera crew and reporter arriving is like a space-ship landing and attracts attention. Can you get up higher? Can you hide away yet still show the location? The unexpected of course may not just be something that happens in the news event you are reporting from. There was an incident when a woman asked a reporter who was live at a court building for directions to the bus station.

- Know how you're going to end – which could be a throw forward to what is to happen next, or just a quick final summary of the story so far.

HAVE A STRUCTURE

Collect the facts into a beginning, a middle, and an end.

Work out what you want to say – then say it. Have that logical and simple structure. Use short sentences rather than a mass of sub-clauses.

What can you use in the background to help the story? Is the shot behind you relevant? Are you standing in a place that fits the mood or the facts? Preferably both.

Make sure you're not obscuring any action you might be talking about – get out of the way, but you can keep reporting by voice.

The studio can also trip or hijack the reporter on location, such as this incident when the presenter started a live two-way with a TV reporter at the scene of the Virginia Tech shootings.

Presenter:	NBC television has released new clips of the video they received.
	(clips play)
	(Presenter now crosses to reporter, live at Virginia Tech:)
Presenter:	Good morning – a dramatic new twist in these dreadful events?
Reporter Live at Virginia Tech:	Yes, eh, I've been off campus for a couple of hours. Can you remind me of the massive new twist please?
Presenter:	Just the fact that there are further images being released by NBC. We're getting a sense now of the extent of the material sent to that TV station.
Reporter:	Yes. This is the result of quite a lot of negotiation between NBC and the FBI . . . (reporter continues)

In this case honesty with the audience was the best policy and the reporter just followed all this by telling the audience, quite calmly, about what he knew.

FINALLY, FIT IN

A business suit looks absurd in a muddy field and dress-down and mucky is out of place among politicians. If you need big boots in a field then wear big boots. Political and business lives need more formal styles for both men and women – which usually means dressing in the same way as the people they interview. Male and female sport reporters can get away with a style commonly called Smart-Casual. Health and safety people tell off reporters who fail to wear a hard-hat in a hard-hat building area.

If you are reporting live on the worst monsoon in the history of southern India then your editor might *want* to see you wet. An umbrella is fine for other rain problems (although be warned that it can cause sound difficulties) and if you use an umbrella use either a plain one or one issued with your station brand if required by your publicity people.

The best way to get through a live is to enjoy yourself. Once mastered after a bit of practice, it is a lively and thrilling way to do television journalism.

And remember to rehearse if you have time. Even 20 seconds will do. The more you rehearse – the more spontaneous it can look.

And – another reminder – you are never alone with a microphone. Or a camera. With that microphone on you behave and talk as if anyone, anywhere, can hear what you say and at any time.

THE HEADLINES

- TV news lives can be a two-way, also known as the Down The Line (DTL), when the reporter responds to some questions from the studio presenter.

- Or a basic live link or throw – the studio presenter links to the reporter at the scene. The reporter may just talk – perhaps a live update – or link into a report he did earlier and/or live interviews at the scene.

- Movement, relevant background and something worth saying make the best live reporting. Try to give your live a sense of occasion – give the viewer an interest and show why you are there as well as having your reporting prepared.

- Make sure your cameraman knows what you plan to say and do or if you want to walk and talk and show things. Or even hold up props.

- The more you rehearse – the more spontaneous it can look.

QUESTIONS FOR YOU

1. Can you read to a fixed time and tell a story fluently and neatly? You may want to do this one in private. Find a story today – or indeed anything that interests you. Write three vital points you want to make. Do not write an entire script and try to memorise it. Stand up – perhaps facing a wall – and tell the wall (really) the story in 30 seconds. Time yourself. Do it several times until you get it perfect.
2. If you are a student get a friend on the course to film you doing the same story in voice and vision – perhaps on a phone. Then swop over. Help each other.

   Then try the stories as a two way where you take turns as reporter/presenter.

3. Like to make it more advanced? Do the story while walking and talking at the same time. Start static, move, then stop.

OTHER RESOURCES

- A video with reporter Jon Sopel explaining why it's important to remember that you are part of a team. He says it's vital that you are all thinking along the same lines from the start: http://bbc.in/1jYUM4E.

- 'Organising what you want to say is critical in delivering a smooth live shot. Beginners will try to memorise every word, which is dangerous. Forget one tiny part of information and you'll stumble through the rest of your report . . .': http://media.about.com/od/televisionandradio/a/Live-Shot-Tips-For-Tv-News-Reporters.htm

TUTOR NOTES

This one will take an entire day. Depending on how many video cameras you can get, put your group into live reporting teams of four in each. The teams must research and plan one single news story to be reported on live so all four in each team know all about the same story. It is best done outside. They can take turns on camera, as reporter and two others in the team can be guests to be interviewed 'live' by the reporter. Then they all swop about. Record it all and let everyone have a look. Limit each 'report and interviews' to about two minutes. Do check on how long all this reviewing might take – every live might need ten minutes to view and feedback on. A good start is to pose the question to each one – 'would you do it any differently if you had to do it all over again? Then what?'

Get them to do a written risk and probability assessment about doing a live news report from a specific location. Think of some real places in your area – it could be a recreation area or park, outside a school, a court building or the car park of a supermarket. Get them to think about how to do the live in a safe way, thinking about hazards and what difficulties there might be in particular places.

CHAPTER 26

Data, Graphics and Visuals

Viewers consuming news both on the TV screen and online are accustomed to masses of information on display. They have the studio and presenter in their face. Then the reports and the live reporters at the scene and that endless rolling and zipping scroll of latest news, plus information about what they are looking at now, and next, plus the local time and the weather and the station logo so you know which of 200 news channels you are tuned to.

Business channels like Bloomberg have the screen bombarded with visuals, graphics and text information. But that is what the target audience expects and wants. Channels spend time on marketing research to get the overall look just right.

The term 'visuals' covers a multitude of information methods: stills, slides, captions, computer-generated charts, graphs and stylish images that establish corporate identity and appear to fill the wall behind the newsreader. Virtual reality is part of the storytelling.

Graphics and Astons (a common term for text and data in the lower third of the screen) are used to convey updated information in a clear and concise way. An older word – ticker, from the noise made by telegraphic machines a century ago – came back into use for crawling text.

In all channels these changing bottom-third tickers and other on-screen graphics also enable the journalists to carry on providing the wider headlines whilst focusing on one big or breaking story as and when necessary. Those watching need as many visual clues as possible as they often don't have the sound up.

Most of the viewers to news channels expect this text information on screen. They want it because it aids them in the way they use the channel. In view of this the graphics are increasingly important. You need them to grab the attention of the viewer and draw them to the story. Interactivity and regular headlines are a key part of the tools that a news channel needs to inform its audience. People use the channel to dip in to get the latest headlines.

For the journalist dealing with graphics there are some simple but important rules. Inaccurate maps, for example, will damage credibility. Where is Crete and where is Cyprus? Find out. How do you spell the name of that film star? The newspaper journalist who went for an interview for a television job did not do himself any favours by saying 'at least in TV you don't need to know how to spell'.

You must also know your House Style. CNN, Sky News, the BBC and Al Jazeera all have visuals, but they also have their own style. That can mean anything from colours in charts and maps to the font used and the spelling.

There are plenty of software packages built into newsrooms for the journalists to do their own basic graphics and captions.

Richard Jarrett, who trained hundreds of newsroom journalists on Visualization in Real-Time (Vizrt) graphics, says:

> This is a tool that really helps TV journalists to do their job – to explain things simply and clearly. It's a wonderful tool that enables producers, reporters and correspondents to add their own graphics into their stories. These can go into intros and played in live, or recorded and cut into packages. The joy of the system is that it is template. So journalists only have to choose the template that suits their story and add images and text. The templating means that the graphics match the house style, and the variations within the templates and their animations mean that journalists can produce really quite sophisticated and slick-looking graphics.

More complex graphics come from a graphics designer. The journalist is the proof-reader – not the designer. It is not career enhancing to say: 'That spelling mistake was the fault of the graphics people. That's not my responsibility.'

FIGURE 26.1
Modern weather charts are still the most familiar example of visualising data. The common term, Big Data, also means graphic storytelling about anything from global consumer trends to what model of car people buy in one area. Another challenge is to make visualised data as eye-catching on mobiles as any other screen. Courtesy ChyronHego / Metacast ®.

Have you connected with your artistically minded graphic designer? If you asked for a map of Australia showing 'Darwin' did you mean the main city of the state called Northern Territories or did you mean a map of Australia blended with a still picture of a famous nineteenth-century scientist with a beard?

Try working your visuals like this.

Simple

Avoid on-screen clutter. Keep your visuals or statistics simple, even if they are moving and animated. Percentages are fine for financial news or science but for most viewers the words *10 per cent of drivers have Ford cars* is better expressed as *1 in 10 drive Fords*.

Bullets

Bullet points if needed should be simple blobs or dots or numbers. Take care about using corporate logos as the bullets. It might be rare to find that you are told to pay to use the logo, which may have copyright, but then maybe you are doing a visual which says there have been complaints about their products or any kind of bad publicity.

Colours

Think about any unwanted messages in your colours. Do colours on maps or charts have any political connections that might either offend or cause confusion? Orange and Green have always been problem colours for coverage of Northern Ireland because Orange is perceived as the colour of Unionism and Green as the colour of Nationalism, so broadcasters always avoided both colours and went for alternatives.

Maps

Even though simple maps are created with pre-loaded software, try to use a consistent source in your newsroom as a reference. *The Times Atlas of the World* is a popular source. In Britain the place called the Persian Gulf is the water between Iran the country (or south-west Asia) and the geographical place called the Arabian Peninsula. Some channels elsewhere call it the Gulf. Alaska is sometimes incorrectly visualised as part of Canada rather than a state of the USA. The capital of Australia is not Sydney; it is Canberra. There is a Tripoli in Libya but also a Tripoli in Lebanon.

If an incident happened fifty miles from the capital city, then show and name that capital city as well as the location of the accident. Local news stations may have their own guidelines on who knows where places are.

Getting maps, names or places wrong has lively consequences and plenty of audience reaction. An error on a map is right in the audience's face and keeps the Twitterati busy. More seriously, it can damage the credibility of a channel in an instant and an error on a local channel causes uproar inside and outside the newsroom. Journalists can create simple maps at the desk but for more complex maps with animations or multiple elements a graphic designer would take over. The journalist might scribble a basic line-drawing before starting to create the real map, for example within a few minutes of a report about a train crash.

Direct Quotations

If it says that in the script make sure it says that in the text or graphics. Quoting a politician (and it should be a very newsworthy quotation) by placing that quotation on screen and then using different words in the spoken script does not aid the viewer. It causes confusion.

(A)

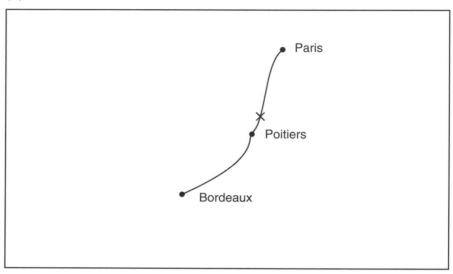

FIGURE 26.2A

A rail crash in France just north of Poitiers. The scribbled newsroom journalist's map idea shows three places and they should be named in the accompanying live script. But this dull map has no reference points. Three blobs and a line and the X-marks-the-spot of the crash don't make a useful map.

(B)

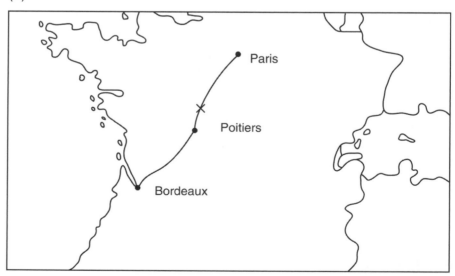

FIGURE 26.2B

This is how a graphic designer might see it. A better map with a visual impact that is more familiar to the viewer, showing a coastline and geographical perspective.

Give Sources for Statistics

Figures should be sourced. Who did the research? A chart for changing house prices should show on the graphic just who did the survey or the calculations. Don't leave the viewer thinking – just who came up with those figures? It's also fair and honest to give the source of the work you are using to create a graphic.

Scrolling Text/Crawling Text

These are usually words at the bottom of the screen. They are simply written news updates/breaking news that crawl continuously. They can be a big hazard for new broadcast journalists because of finger trouble (also known as spelling trouble) and attract ridicule. One channel produced a rolling news banner stating that it was 'Obama' – not 'Osama' – who was dead.

Face/Name Captions

Avoid placing a name caption over shots of a different face. The opening of a report by Joe Black may have a caption:

JOE BLACK

Washington

But are we looking at the face of the President at that opening moment of the report? Has Joe been elected? We might take the correct spelling of a name for granted but also beware of name variations and never make assumptions. The name Ian could be Iain. Smith could be Smyth. Cathy could be Kathy. Check.

STILL PICTURES AND FRAME GRABS

While TV may be about moving pictures and sound, a good still picture captures a moment in time. It takes viewers into the story. It can freeze an event or action and – if held on screen long enough – allow the reader to see every nuance and often revealing things you do not notice in video.

It can be helped by a script that might say: 'the window where the killer is believed to have fired from can just be seen in the top right' or 'the woman is to the left, in red, running . . .'

While most channels pride themselves on getting first with pictures of a breaking story, they won't always succeed. News agencies with more troops on the ground will sometimes beat them to it. Agencies send out hundreds of still photographs daily that are saved directly into a picture store. Digital pictures can be reduced, enlarged or cropped on screen. Most TV stations will have a stock of freeze frames or grabs of leading politicians and personalities – a frame grab is a single frame taken from video, in effect a still picture.

Stills appearing in the middle of a TV report are common now and still images are still used by many stations as insets – a generic term for a picture behind the news presenter. A big TV library could have up to a million transparencies in a digital store.

But take care with copyright. Who owns that picture? Is it NASA, Disney, a museum or archive or from a member of the public who was just passing and got lucky? The new journalist should check.

WRITING TO STILL PICTURES AND SCREEN INSETS

Always beware double-meaning with stills and words together. A judge may end a trial and say to the convicted man: 'You are a cruel and evil man and you will go to prison for life . . .' and a caption may carry a picture of the judge who said those words rather than the criminal. But to place the words 'cruel and evil' under a picture of the judge who *said it* may have a different message for viewers. Visualise this by closing your eyes, imagine a picture of yourself and put the words 'evil mass murderer' beneath it.

A straightforward personality still picture should be on the screen for a minimum of five seconds. That's no more than 15 words of script. The maximum time depends very much on the subject. A fairly busy action shot of casualties being carried by stretcher away from a crash needs longer to register than the library still of a well-known politician. What matters in the script is that it fits the image at the moment it is on screen.

> 'Referring to the . . .
>
> (Introduce still of Governor)
>
> . . . latest freeze in interest rates, the Governor of the Bank said . . .

Bringing in the still a few words later makes a difference:

> Referring to the latest freeze in interest rates . . .
>
> (Introduce still of Governor)
>
> . . . the Governor of the Bank said . . .

Choosing the right moment at which to return to the reader in vision is just as important. It is not acceptable to whisk the picture from under the viewer's nose without good reason. Much better to wait until the end of a sentence.

Where events call for a sequence of pictures, it is important to maintain the rhythm by keeping each on the screen for approximately the same duration.

Six, five and seven seconds would probably be reasonable for three successive stills referring to the same subject. Five, twenty and eight would not. The temptation to go back to the reader on camera for a few seconds between stills should be avoided, otherwise continuity is broken. In this context, a brief shot of the reader becomes another but unrelated picture, interrupting the flow. If returning to the reader during a sequence is unavoidable, it is far better to make the link a deliberately long one.

OVERLAYS/CHROMAKEY/CSO

Chromakey is an electronic means of displaying still or moving pictures behind a reporter or presenter. It is also known as Colour Separation Overlay (CSO) or Colour Keying. It works by eliminating one colour from the screen and replacing it with a picture or graphic. Blue was the most commonly used colour but now green has become the most suitable colour. The presenter stands in front of the coloured screen. An onlooker in the studio will see only the presenter standing in front of the brightly coloured back wall of the set. Only the viewers at home will see the presenter and image combined.

Unseen by the viewer, the back of the set is the coloured backdrop. This colour is switched out automatically by the vision mixer and replaced with a picture or visual from another source which could be video, another camera or graphics.

With better imaging and hardware, many companies are avoiding the confusion often experienced by weather presenters, who must otherwise watch themselves on a monitor to see the image shown behind them, by lightly projecting a copy of the background image onto the blue/green screen. This allows the presenter to accurately point and look at the map without referring to monitors.

The only problem is when the presenter wears the same colour as the one switched out by the chromakey. If the presenter's tie is a matching shade, that too will disappear, leaving what appears to be a hole punched right through him to the photograph or scene behind.

BIG SCREEN VIDEO WALL

This is a visual technique which has names such as Video Wall, Big Screen or a hybrid of both like Video Screen or Big Wall. It enables the presenter or reporter to stand beside or in front of changing clips of interview, stills or graphics to explain a story. A typical wall has about 200 LED tiles that can transmit different images for a presenter or reporter to stand in front of and explain the story.

Sometimes it is pre-recorded but is often live, with the presenter handing over to a reporter who stands on the other side of the studio. The reporter is framed to the right or left of changing images and the method is often used to explain complicated issues which require only clips of people talking and/or statistic graphics showing trends or evidence or research.

If the reporter is linking in and out of interview clips then it's important that the person talking in the clip is framed to look towards the reporter and not away, hence the importance of the reporter's place on camera. If the position of the reporter means that the person talking is framed to look away from the reporter it will look very odd. The reporter needs to sometimes turn and gesture towards the video wall in a natural way – this assures the viewer that the reporter knows what is going on and that the viewer and reporter are, in effect, sharing an experience.

This technique can be enormously effective in using a range of pictures, interviews and graphics to explain complicated issues. But the correspondent must come across in delivery and body language as though he or she were quite naturally talking to someone, and yet at the same time reading from an autocue and all the time aware of when they should look or motion towards the graphics and video next to them . . . Your style must be conversational.

Vin Ray, *The Television News Handbook*

FIGURE 26.3

The video wall/big screen is now a common storytelling tool in studios. This can show changing images, including graphics, stills and charts, for a presenter or reporter to guide the viewer and explain the story. Courtesy Sky News.

ACRONYMS IN VISUALS

Acronyms were mentioned in an earlier chapter but using acronyms and abbreviations in visuals needs just a pause to ask – does everyone know what this means if I show it? Is this a familiar acronym, or is it rare? The important distinction to make is between acronyms that *most* viewers will understand and those they may not.

Familiars?

AA
NASA
NATO
UN

Less familiar?

QUANGO
ATM
MADD
D & V

It should make sense that Familiars are well known, although AA could be either Automobile Association or Alcoholics Anonymous, but then it should be clear from the story anyway. NATO and UN hardly need to be spelt out in a graphic or visual if you are reporting on military or international issues. NASA should not need to be defined in a story about space.

The others present more of a problem for the journalist working on a graphic simply because they are less familiar and may need explanation, although that depends on whether it is for general news or a specialist programme or sequence. ATM (Automatic Teller Machine – the thing you get your cash from) is well known to people in banking while others might call it a cash dispenser or just cash machine. MADD (Mothers Against Drunk Driving) is better known in America than in Europe. D & V (diarrhoea and vomiting) is known to hospital nurses but would be a mystery to the average viewer. A QUANGO is a Quasi-Autonomous Non-Governmental Organisation.

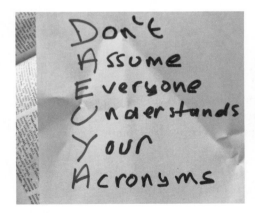

FIGURE 26.4
The rolled up piece of paper tossed to a TV journalist by an editor. Doesn't everyone know what DAEUYA is? Check your visuals for acronyms that might make your audience wonder what you're on about.

FIGURE 26.5
Technology makes information look better but the way the brain processes it or receives it on different screens is more complex. For statistically rich graphics to tell a story the journalist's script needs to reference what we see. Here, it could mention '35 yards' and explain the relevance, as well as anything else illustrated or highlighted in the image. Courtesy ChyronHego.

THE HEADLINES

- Visuals can be: stills, slides, captions, computer-generated charts, graphs, big screens, animated info-graphics, maps and charts.

- Check that a script matches what the viewer sees in a graphic, image or caption.

- Check that a script and image of a person *when combined* do not create a message you did not intend.

- Double-check spellings – and locations for maps and charts.

QUESTIONS FOR YOU

1. Can you find a duration for a graphic to be on screen? Look at factual magazines (or their websites) and find some graphics, charts or maps. Pick a few and decide how long you need to look at each one until you understand it. If you need to look at even a simple graphic for 60 seconds then think about what would happen if that were in a TV news report. Print and online factual graphics can be more complex because people can look at them as long as they wish.

2. Find any story about an incident in a country you know little or nothing about. Using an atlas, trace an outline of the country and then mark the relevant places mentioned in the story. Can you also write a short 20-30 second TV news script about the incident? Ensure that whatever is shown in your map matches the script.

3. Try writing tickers – the crawling text at the bottom of a screen. Find any story and write four or five single, simple sentences: how it started and what happened then? Each sentence should be one single new thing that happened.

OTHER RESOURCES

- 'NPR's Robert Krulwich and medical animator David Bolinsky explain how a flu virus can trick a single cell into making a million more viruses.' Short and well-designed graphic animation and script that explains a complex idea in three minutes: http://bit.ly/1sEBxyy.

- Channel 4 News has a selection of graphics, infographics, maps, charts and animation explainers: www.channel4.com/news/graphics.

- More about data journalism in newsrooms: www.journalism.co.uk/news/recalculating-the-newsroom-the-rise-of-the-journo-coder-/s2/a555646/.

TUTOR NOTES

Give them all a news story with a lot of numbers and statistics. Ask them to write a TV news script for the story (about 40 seconds) to be spoken alongside a graphic showing no more than four of the statistics. Each statistic or number should have a name, for example:

Sales of:

> White paint – down 8%
> Wallpaper – up 4%

They can write the text for the graphic inside the text for the story – for example in bold while the spoken text is not bold. The four statistics can appear (be animated) one after the other until all four are revealed and preferably held for the last five seconds. Do the animated statistics match the script? Can some sentences in the script add information to the statistics?

Ask the group to each use MS Office SmartArt to display statistics as well as any quotations or charts. They can experiment with shapes, fonts, charts and design. A pie-chart of a recent election result for example. They can discuss what seems over-complex for explaining data in a news story – or what works well.

Tutorial: http://bit.ly/1FKIcQl.

CHAPTER 27

Presenting Television News

Certainly, presenters are in the front line. They get all the plaudits when it goes right and all the brickbats when it goes wrong. It's tough when others lose the scripts, the Autocue goes down, the researchers have got the wrong interview, your information is incorrect and the lighting explodes in the studio, but you still have to plough on holding the show together.

Janet Trewin, journalist and TV presenter. From: *Presenting On TV and Radio*

Presentation styles differ in television between general programming and news. The more a programme aims to entertain, the warmer, friendlier and more relaxed its style will usually be, while news presenters tend to adopt a tone that is serious and more formal, in keeping with the weightier material of a bulletin.

The term 'anchor' originated in America with Walter Cronkite who presented the CBS Evening News for almost 30 years. He was often described in viewer polls as The Most Trusted Man in America. In Britain 'newsreader' or 'news presenter' is more common, showing something of the difference in presentation styles either side of the Atlantic – styles which are emulated around the world.

QUALITIES OF THE TELEVISION NEWS PRESENTER

One of the great myths is that the only quality needed is to look good. It needs much more than that – some American stations used to audition by only listening to the candidates and not even looking at them. If those making the decision didn't like the voice then they didn't even look at them. You can do a lot with a person's appearance but if the voice is distracting or irritating then the executives would be taking a risk.

The ideal qualities for a presenter for television news certainly overlap those for radio – authority, credibility, clarity, professionalism and then looking as if you actually know what you are talking about.

TV newsreaders will usually be experienced journalists who have worked as reporters. They're supposed to understand where news comes from. If a presenter on a 24/7 news channel is doing a two-way with a reporter then the presenter is

FIGURE 27.1

The laptops are not there as props. They enable the presenters to see news updates. But they will take their guidance in their ear from the editor/producer in the news transmission gallery, which is usually next door or just above the studio. Courtesy Channel NewsAsia.

supposed at least to know what it's like *to be* at the story as well as understanding the story itself.

Like most journalists, newsreaders are expected to be news addicts, steeping themselves in news events throughout the day. They are required to be on top of the day's stories and understand their background so live interviews on current issues will pose no problem.

As the day progresses newsreaders follow the material as it comes in and may offer their own suggestions for coverage.

THE LOOK

Simple is always best. For news television recommended clothing includes solid light pastel colours or dark serious colours. It depends on the kind of programme. Fabrics which are blends (such as wool and polyester) seem to hang on screen much better than all-natural fabrics.

Avoid wearing a lot of white, black or a vivid red. Cameras may have difficulty responding to those colours. Black and white together can be particularly distracting but 'off-white' colours are fine. These come with various names chosen by retailing marketing departments – such as beige, champagne, ivory or magnolia. What colours you actually wear depend on many factors: colour of the set, the colour of your eyes or the texture/colour of your skin as well as the context and style of the programme or location.

If you're telling the viewer about some vital news event then the viewer should not be thinking: 'Is that Mickey Mouse on his shirt?'

ACCESSORIES

Journalists should not let these add-on bits distract the viewer. Or attract too much attention from the lens. Fat knots on scarves – especially wool – can bulge and give an illusion of being bigger than the head. Too much jewellery on the upper part of the body is distracting.

It also depends on the kind of programme or the story – jewels and silk don't fit in with reports on poverty or distress. A male presenter doing mainstream news will be expected to wear a tie. A tie can convey authority. The less formal nature of sport, or news aimed at a young audience, can work with a more casual look.

FIGURE 27.2

The best guidance is to dress as if you are reflecting back to the kind of people you might talk to about a story. Politics, business and diplomacy have a style fit with ties, neat scarves and a business-like look for men and women. Rock climbing, farmland and the plight of dolphins usually do not.

COLOURS AND FABRICS

This advice applies to both men and women.

- Avoid clothing patterns such as close small checks, pinstripes or herringbones, especially if there is a sharp contrast in colour. Such contrasting patterns generate a distracting shimmer when viewed on-camera.

- Both men and women should avoid pure black suits and jackets, particularly in combination with pure white shirts which can drain colour from the face. Light pastel shirts are more flattering. For women, go for the unfussy look if you are trying to appear smart and authoritative – bold patterned scarves and loud jewellery can detract attention from what you are actually saying. For jackets and suits, fairly neutral colours tend to work best – deep saturated reds are not usually as successful as middle-reds.

- Try to avoid highly reflective materials or clothes that make noise when you move. Avoid clothes which fold in a way which makes contact between the fabric and a clip-on microphone.

- If you wear jewellery, make sure it is not making any noise. Avoid jewellery which may cause reflections that can be picked up by the camera.

- Glasses. Light frames are less distracting than heavy dark frames. But always avoid tinted glass at all costs or glass that darkens in bright light.

In addition to this there are some specific tips for each gender to convey authority in news programmes.

Women

Avoid:

- Black clothes – unflattering on television and camera dislikes black.
- Frilly and fuzzy knitted fabrics
- Make-up that leads to shiny skin
- Dark roots or any highlights of orange tint
- Hair that falls well below the shoulder
- Brown or orange shades of lipstick.

Prefer:

- For business and serious subjects wear dark medium colours (blue or grey shades for example)
- Crisp and sharp fabrics (wool or cotton mixed with a little synthetic fibre can work well)
- Matt treatment for the hair and skin – avoid anything that emphasises a shine
- Moist lips with any rosy, mid-red or pink shade
- Hair that clears the shoulder line.

Men

Avoid:

- Club blazers with metal buttons
- Club ties
- Loose tie knots or ties that slip to one side
- Ties combined with button down collars – it looks untidy when these are combined
- Ties with small detailed patterns like tiny squares or lines . . . or images of Homer Simpson
- Hair that drifts over the top of the ears.

Prefer:

- For business and serious subjects wear dark colours (dark blue or grey/ gunmetal shades – but avoid black)

- Simple, uncluttered ties; avoid loud patterns

- Hair regularly trimmed on the sides and above the ears

- Button-down collars without a tie are fine for a casual mood, or for sport

- Always have make-up for studio presenting.

PROMPTING SCRIPT TECHNOLOGY

Prompter is a general term usually given to the technology used by presenters in studio and sometimes on location. The script appears directly across the camera lens, but the viewers can't see it – accomplished users give the impression that they're just talking naturally.

You can generally see only four or five lines of your script and it scrolls upwards as you talk. So if you do not know when the sentence is going to end it will interfere with your natural breathing. The prompt operator follows your script and ensures that no matter how fast or slow you're talking, it keeps up with you. But if you don't use it convincingly, your presenting will look flat and stilted. Often there may not be an operator at all and the prompt is operated by the presenter using a foot pedal. This is more common in short news summaries on smaller channels and it takes a bit of practice. Avoid twitching your foot. Voice recognition technology is also becoming more widely used. It aims to follow along with the voice in real-time.

The key is to remain natural and relaxed. Speak in a way which projects the voice – the key to this is to imagine that the one person you are talking to is just behind the camera. You are projecting-talking; not shouting! Like radio, have this voice in your head that says: 'Hey, listen to this!'

Do not exaggerate facial language. It can look awful. If the script has the words 'tragic accident' (aren't they all) then don't put on your Tragic Face. Since you don't want to smile either, then just remain natural.

It all sounds easy, but using these devices needs practice. News presenters need to understand the story to ensure they are not just reading words. They need to cope if the prompter goes down and that means keeping a hardcopy script in front of them with the story at that moment.

The usual moment to break eye-contact and move away from the lens is when the script contains either statistics or a direct quotation; then bring the head

FIGURE 27.3

Presenter view. The prompter is the presenter's friend, but you still need to get to know it. That means practice. The script is projected across the front of the lens so the presenter can continue to make eye-contact with the viewer. Courtesy Sky News.

FIGURE 27.4
An iPad can be turned into a portable teleprompter. It slots into a custom-made mounting plate to hold it below the prompter glass and can be used with an electronic or DV camera. Courtesy Autocue.

back upwards to relocate the next sentence. Suddenly it doesn't sound easy anymore.

'FILL FOR 90 SECONDS!'

So something has gone wrong and the editor or director is giving this dreaded instruction. It means to ad-lib of course. It also means that the presenter should not panic and therefore offer some unwarranted opinion or comment about what's in the news. The most popular way to fill is to refer the viewer to your website. But if there's a serious technical problem it can often be best to be honest with the viewers and just tell them there's a technical problem. If you do that then they might understand why you might be repeating the main points of the news again while someone in another presentation function comes to your rescue.

Two presenters makes it all easier because they can talk to each other, although it should be without comment or opinion on serious news items. In the end it is always useful to have something mentally prepared for that moment which you hope will never come.

NERVES

Dealing with nerves needs a formula.

Try: *Rehearsal means Visualisation = aids Relaxation.*

Visualisation is a method used by some athletes and actors. They talk about seeing themselves crossing the winning line long before they go to the starting position in a race. They imagine a successful first night on stage and everything went perfectly. Picture yourself on air, either walking and talking or being static in a chair. See yourself as calm and confident. These images will be like actual events in your brain. This author used to think this was a bit suspect, but after training so many sports professionals to do TV, and hearing their consistent remarks about visualisation in sport, it started to make sense.

Also get more oxygen. Relax by rotating your head slowly to loosen neck, shoulders and throat for a few seconds. Breathe in, then out very slowly. Perhaps three times is enough to give you a good oxygen feed.

MAKE-UP AND PERCEPTION

You don't usually need make-up for live reporting from a location in a muddy field or the scene of floods. But in a studio, with its intrusive lighting, make-up for both men and women is vital for a professional look. Even more so with high definition.

Large news operations still retain full-time or part-time make-up artists for the presenters but in many places the presenters do their own make-up.

Men need as much advice about make-up as women and while there are plenty of female reporters in the dusty fields of conflict who would hate the idea of having make-up in that situation, there are also men who haven't given make-up a single thought. But in studio, there is nothing unmanly about a male presenter having make-up and it is worth remembering that many politicians would not like to be seen in public without a bit of powder on the face.

Politicians and male news presenters have a precedent for this that goes back many years. The Richard Nixon appearance on television – probably still the most telling make-up incident – is a warning to all men.

In 1960, Richard Nixon was to face his opponent in the US Presidential Elections, John F. Kennedy, in a television debate. Nixon, who had been unwell, arrived looking tired. Kennedy, who was tanned, looked fit and youthful and rested.

There are conflicting versions of this story about whether Kennedy had make-up already, or whether Kennedy just declined to have make-up at the time of arriving at the studio and Nixon felt he had to make the same decision. But Nixon ended up with a problem when television was the primary medium of communication. He did not have the right make-up for television – and this happened in a social period when it was unusual for men to have make-up at all.

> Nixon suffered a handicap that was serious only on television: he has a light, naturally transparent skin. On an ordinary camera that takes pictures by optical projection, this skin photographs well. But a television camera projects electronically, by an 'image-orthicon tube' which has an x-ray effect. This camera penetrates Nixon's transparent skin and brings out (even just after a shave) the tiniest hair growing in the follicles beneath the surface. For the decisive first program Nixon wore a make-up called 'Lazy Shave' which was ineffective under these conditions. He therefore looked haggard and heavy-bearded by contrast to Kennedy, who looked pert and clean-cut.
> Daniel J. Boorstin, *From News Gathering to News Making:*
> *A Flood of Pseudo-Events* (http://bit.ly/1FQeqIm)

Political analysts at the time remarked that the same debate *on radio* gave an impression that Nixon outshone Kennedy on policy, debate and in addressing the issues. Yet the very same debate on television led viewers to call to ask if Nixon was unwell.

Journalists working in television journalism, for either modern high definition television or online platforms, should be aware of the Nixon incident. It is quite simple: have some make-up when you need it, especially in a lighted studio.

'COMING UP . . .'

Like radio, you are never alone with a microphone.

You are never alone with a camera either.

Journalist Kenny Toal had a bad reaction to a cheese pie just as he was going to co-present a programme. He vomited several times into a waste-basket while on air. 'I was sick five or six more times during the programme,' he told *The Guardian*, 'we were forced to improvise so I could throw up off screen.'

A presenter on Minnesota Fox 9 News was doing the weather and discovered he had a metal coat hanger still connected to his jacket.

Emma Baker was waiting to read her morning bulletin on Anglia TV apparently unaware that she was on air and in vision. She was seen grooming her hair and adjusting her microphone.

A viewer told the *Daily Mail*:

> It was much more interesting than the usual local news. It was like a soap opera unfolding. When she put her hand up her shirt it seemed that she was fiddling with her bra. I saw her tummy.
>
> This all went on for about three and a half minutes and she was preening herself and pouting like Madonna, sticking out her boobs. Then somebody obviously told her it was going out live and her face went ashen. It was as if she had been hit by a thunderbolt.
>
> She started reading the news but how she got through it all I will never know. Top marks to her for that.

THE HEADLINES

- The qualities for a presenter for television news overlap those for radio – authority, credibility, clarity, professionalism and then looking and sounding as if you actually know what the story is about.

- Dress as if you are reflecting back to the kind of people you might talk to about a story. Politics, business and diplomacy stories have a style fit with ties, neat scarves and a business-like look for men and women. Presenting environment and farmland need a more casual look.

- For studio reporting or presentation have some basic make-up. It is less important on location.

- You have already been told you are never alone with a microphone – but you are never alone with a camera either.

QUESTIONS FOR YOU

1. Can you do a show reel – enlist a friend to help? Make about three/four minutes with lots of bits doing interviews/basic news, even some filling time/ad libs, the weather. Bear in mind that people who get this may only watch parts of it. Make sure it is well lit.

OTHER RESOURCES

- On 'Journograds' Hannah Gray writes about her day at Sky's Westminster studio shadowing a news presenter for Sky News Tonight: http://journograds.com/2014/12/21/shadowing-a-sky-news-presenter/.

- The image of the broadcast journalist in movies and television (University of Southern California) is a study and video resource about how TV presenters and reporters have been represented in fiction: http://bit.ly/1HLdELD.

TUTOR NOTES

If you have studio access (of any kind of sophistication) get your group to present some basic straight news in vision. Get them to fill time in an imaged 'something gone wrong' situation. If they start saying or doing inappropriate things if it all goes wrong – play it back to them so they appreciate the experience and the moment. They will never forget it and will understand that you are never alone with a camera.

Record a TV news bulletin or channel segment of 30 minutes. Play it back and get the group to concentrate entirely on the presenter – how he or she moves, stands, sits, talks, looks, does live interviews, gestures and does he or she project credibility. What are Credibility and Charisma anyway? How can we define these? Are there different perceptions and judgements about male and female news presenters? Discuss.

CHAPTER 28

The Television News Studio and Gallery

STANDBY FOR TRANSMISSION

When Shakespeare was to be performed for a modern audience it was a television news studio location which helped to update humour written four centuries ago. *Much Ado About Nothing* is a play that relies on misunderstandings and overheard conversations, so where better to set a modern television production of the play than a television news studio – perfect for eavesdropping.

It is also a place of illusion, all in the lights, the tricks of the camera and a vast range of images, backdrops or virtual reality. A plain screen background is switched out

FIGURE 28.1
The set needs to combine dynamic lighting and rigs or pedestals to ensure smooth camera moves. A studio can be like stepping into a cupboard, or a factory. It will either be a fraction of the size it appears to be on screen, or cavernously large. Courtesy Sky News.

and replaced with an image, or the video-wall (sometimes called Big Screen) where a reporter stands and gestures to the changing images, charts and clips behind him as he explains the complexities of a story.

Some sets and backdrops exist only in the memory of a computer. They can be changed at the touch of a key, or tilted, rotated, zoomed into or panned across, all in perfect synch with the foreground. Even the camera operator is being keyed out of existence, thanks to motion sensors that lock on to the presenter and follow him around. Illusion is piling on illusion.

THE SET

The news programme could have its own studio or share a set with the rest of the TV station. The background could be the newsroom, or a picture window that appears to be looking out on a local scene but is in reality an image captured by camera. Behind the desk, the backdrop might be nothing more than a set of painted wooden panels or highly coloured cloth.

Studios can be expensive so several programmes may use the same studio. Sets can be constructed to pull apart in moments; the boards behind, known as flats, may be turned around to reveal a surface of different colour and texture, or the whole studio may be transformed in an instant into some new computer-generated concept of reality.

FIGURE 28.2
A gallery/control room is like mission control and it certainly has less paper flying around than it used to. Courtesy Sky News.

Built into the presenter's desk will usually be a keyboard and a monitor to show what is going out on air. The desk may have a glass island in the centre with the monitors inside it and pointing towards the presenter position. On some desks it might just be a laptop beside the presenter. Plenty of space is left on the desk for scripts.

A virtual reality area in the studio will be able to interact with virtual graphics. More sophisticated technology provides animations, allowing the presenter to move around and even appear to touch things. If the presenter is talking about property prices he can have virtual houses or buildings and can pick them up and move them around. As long as it helps with the telling of the story that is.

CONTROL ROOM/GALLERY

'45 seconds to transmission . . .'

'Standby studio . . .'

'Do we have our lead story?'

'No. We do not have the lead story . . .'

'20 to transmission.'

'On air in 15, 14 . . .'

'. . . we do not have the lead story. We do NOT HAVE the lead story'

'. . . 13, 12, 11 . . .'

'Lead item is ready. It is ready!'

'. . . three, two, one . . . on air. Run titles.'

Maybe you have seen those old submarine movies. The dim red lights, the atmosphere taut with expectancy. Each person at his post, every eye straining at a flickering dial or gauge. To the uninitiated it is a little like that in the TV control room, also known as the gallery.

The director is captain in the gallery. A journalist might decide what to lead with and decide what stories go into a programme, or how a live interview is conducted, but when it's live on air then the director has the responsibility to ensure it all goes smoothly. The director tells the presenter what is happening, what *is not* happening, or what is about to happen, for example a news package and/or a live interview. If a segment or programme is under-running on time the director might use the weather to adjust the duration. Under-running might mean asking the weather person to do a long forecast; over-running means a short one.

When a script has to be altered, the output editor or another journalist will usually update the text within the news production system and then get it to the presenter. Other prime targets for tinkering are repeated headlines (recaps) at the end of the bulletin.

The overall mood and operation of a TV news gallery has not changed much in the past ten years, except that most control is through icons on a monitor screen rather than only switches on a desk. Material is transmitted through the main newsroom IT system. The monitors – plenty of them – also provide a widescreen view and better clarity. The studio floor is likely to have computer-controlled robotic cameras.

The red light for action stations is the red transmission warning. A bank of monitors dominates the wall in front of the director, displaying a more bewildering variety of pictures than most television showrooms. These include all the camera pictures and angles, pre-recorded news reports, reporters standing on location ready to go live, graphics, titles and the presenters. All are fed into the control room gallery to form the director's list of ingredients.

The transmission monitor shows what is currently on air. Beside that the next shot is lined up ready to go. Another monitor will have the script prompter screen. Others show what each camera is looking at in the studio. In a regional gallery another shows what the network is seeing so the director can tell exactly when to opt in and out of network with the regional programme.

Continuous news channels may be less likely to worry about programme junctions or about opting in or out of regional programmes. And to make sure the station is keeping up with the opposition another monitor reveals what is going out on other channels.

The worst thing about being a director:

When you find the presenter has misread a rota and you have to find a new presenter at short notice. Or you run a report and there is no sound and the next item is not ready to run. Or you experience a complete news production system failure, no scripts can be found and your presenter has to use handwritten scripts at the last moment and there is no Autocue. It happened on Newsround many years ago and the presenter ad-libbed the whole programme – ignoring the out of vision reads so we were 2 minutes under!

The best thing about being a director:

Managing to get a programme out in a presentable fashion when there is chaos all around you with breaking news. Or being creative in the studio with camera moves and graphics or being in charge of the gallery team and encouraging them to contribute new ideas to the programme.

Peter Davidson, Senior BBC News Director

BUILDING THE PROGRAMME

With so much material to be co-ordinated from so many sources, the director and team could hardly be expected to rely on their memories to guide them through the programme. As much as possible is scripted, though news programmes are fast moving and likely to change as stories come in.

FIGURE 28.3
Running orders on monitors and the stories they go with. With the running order everyone knows what's happening next. Courtesy Autocue.

Every item will be on a separate row so pieces can be dropped or added as needed. Each segment of script within a 24/7 news channel can include details of camera shots and visuals such as stills and graphics, as well as a duration for the item.

In stand-alone news bulletins ad-libs are discouraged except in an emergency when the presenter has to fill time. Ad-libs are less of an issue in continuous TV news which, in general, is allowed to be a bit rough around the edges occasionally.

The programme might opt out of the network to offer regional news or it could supply national news to the entire network. Either way, split-second timing is essential. In stand-alone programmes an unscheduled five-second delay can feel like eternity, although on a continuous news channel the presenters need be alert enough to fill time and technical gaps.

Like radio, a stand-alone TV news programme at 1300, for example, will have a linear order: Headlines/Titles/Lead/Second Story/Third . . . etc. Often the order will be unfinished and subject to corrections and additions. A new lead might arrive five minutes before the programme is due on air. Stories may be dropped to make way for others, and extra items might have to be included to make up time.

The producer makes decisions about the content of the news programme and the director makes those decisions work on air. With news the problem is seldom one of having to fill: scripts might have to be edited and shortened even while the programme is going out.

The nearest the director may come to rehearsing the show is the pre-recording of the title sequences shortly before the programme begins. That a TV news programme ever gets on air without a mistake seems little short of miraculous to the onlooker. The viewer sees only what is on screen, but behind it all there is much happening apart from the director, the sound and vision engineers – and the news producer talking down the presenter's ear. Newsroom journalists are running about, graphics and maps are being checked or corrected, late changes to scripts are being sent through. Within the same hour there is a train crash, an earthquake, an important political resignation and a local team has just won a world championship.

So much can go wrong: a fast-moving story and the wrong guest is put into the chair beside the presenter; the presenter is given the guest we need, but we have the wrong name; the next item is not ready so we go live to a reporter on location and the reporter is not ready either; the sport sequence presenter cannot be found; someone has broken the rules and brought a drink in and spilled it down a control panel; the robotic cameras keep malfunctioning.

When mistakes do occur, there is always an inquest to find out how and why, to try to prevent them happening again. With the shrinking world's news coming in thicker and faster, that uncomfortable sense of teetering even closer to the brink can only continue. But somehow, it rarely seems to show.

Welcome to the world of the broadcast journalist.

THE HEADLINES

- News channels and news bulletins have a running order of stories – where they appear in the news and how long. Everyone needs to know what will happen next.

- The programme is managed in a control room or sometimes called the gallery. The director is in charge and tells the presenter what is happening or about to happen, for example a news package and/or a live interview. The programme editor has overall control of the journalistic aspects of the programme.

QUESTIONS FOR YOU

1. Can you get into a news gallery at your nearest local TV station? Be honest about your ambitions when you ask. Try to find a name to contact. If they agree, turn up early, well dressed and *do not take a drink* into the gallery. Stand or sit at the back. Make notes. Ask permission if you want to take pictures. Turn your phone off.

OTHER RESOURCES

- The Royal Television Society explains what goes on behind the scenes of Channel 4 News. Find out what the different jobs are: www.rts.org.uk/rts-behind-scenes-channel-4-news.

- The controlled chaos of a production gallery. Two journalism students go to NBC News. In the newsroom – witnessing history by Joe O'Connell: www.northeastern.edu/news/2014/10/nbc-news-coops/.

- Chris Cook, a lead news director at BBC News, explains how code helps him make headline sequences work smoothly at just the touch of a button: http://bbc.in/1HgNG4z.

TUTOR NOTES

The director works out how he can follow the running order, timings and scripts to maintain the smooth running of the programme, gallery and studio.

Remind your group about the different treatments a TV story can have:

A simple read from the presenter.

Presenter talks over a short segment of pictures and sound.

Presenter introduces a packaged report.

Presenter throws to reporter live at a location.

Presenter throws to reporter live in the studio with graphics and/or a video wall.

Presenter interviews a guest or expert live, either beside the presenter in the studio or from a studio in a different location.

Using news events of the day, get everyone to write a running order of their choice with a name for each story, how long they *think it is worth* and which of these treatments would work best.

Restrict their programme segment to perhaps 15 minutes to hit a crucial deadline. Then ask them to do timings. If they add the story durations together do they fill 15 minutes, or under-run or over-run? Do any of their chosen stories have flexibility of duration (cut or expand) to hit the 15 minute deadline?

Useful Twitter Accounts to Follow

Lots of tools and resources:

- Journalism Tools (@journalism2ls)
- Journalist's Toolbox (@journtoolbox)

Schools and training:

- Poynter (@poynter)
- Justin Kings (@newsleader)

News and comment:

- Press Gazette (@pressgazette)
- Columbia Journalism Review (@cjr)
- American Journalism Review (@amjourreview)
- Mediagazer (@mediagazer)

Digital journalism and the future of journalism:

- Nieman Lab (@niemanlab)
- Pew Research Center (@pewresearch)
- Future Journalism (@the_fjp)
- PBS MediaShift (@pbsmediashift)
- Steve Buttry (@stevebuttry)
- James Cridland (@jamescridland)

Investigative journalism:

- Andy Donohue (@add)
- CIR (@cironline)

Individual reporters and media folk:

- Emily Bell (@emilybell)

- Paul Bradshaw (@paulbradshaw)

- Steffen Konrath (@stkonrath)

- Peter Stewart (@TweeterStewart)

- Paul Chantler (@PaulChantler)

Journalism and PR:

- Journalistics (@journalistics)

Journalism podcasts:

- Journalism.co.uk: available on iTunes with a wide variety of reporting information.

- Sree Show: on digital media and technology (www1.play.it/audio/sree-show/).

- It's All Journalism: on iTunes, this is a weekly podcast about the changing state of media.

- Journalism/Works: From the Newseum in Washington, DC, this podcast focuses on 'journalism that matters . . .' (www1.newseum.org/podcast/journalism-works/index.html).

- Columbia Journalism School: This archive podcast on iTunes features panel discussions and lectures by leading journalists in the field.

Journalism newsletters (adapted from www.poynter.com):

- American Press Institute's Need to Know newsletter – 'fresh, useful insights for people advancing quality, innovative and sustainable journalism' (www.americanpressinstitute.org/category/need-to-know/).

- Futures Lab – 'Each week we bring you a video roundup of fresh ideas, techniques and developments to help spark innovation and change in newsrooms across all media platforms.' Via iTunes.

- Journalism.co.uk – vacancies, news leads and training listings (www.journalism.co.uk/).

- NiemanLab – 'Nieman Lab is a project to try to help figure out where the news is headed in the Internet age. Sign up for The Digest, our daily email with all the freshest future-of-journalism news' (www.niemanlab.org/).

- PBS MediaShift's newsletters – MediaShift delivers the best news on media and technology directly to your in-box (www.pbs.org/mediashift/).

- Pew Research Center – daily Briefing on journalism and media (www.journalism.org/).

- Poynter's morning newsletter – from the media and journalism training site (www.poynter.org/).

- The Local Fix – 'Big Ideas for Local Newsrooms: A weekly roundup of news and resources for local journalists. Once a week we will be curating some of the best writing on journalism sustainability and pairing it with concrete advice, tools and resources for people who care about local news.' (http://tinyletter.com/jcstearns).

Notes on the Use of Live Streaming Mobile-Phone Apps for Journalists and News Outlets

OVERVIEW

Periscope, Meerkat, Stringwire (and UStream, Bambuser) are apps which allow you to stream live video directly from your smartphone. Instead of having to record a video and then tweet a link to it, your Twitter followers can actually be watching you live – meaning you can share breaking news or live events *as they happen* to lots of people at the same time, and get their reaction.

Although each service is different, in general people can follow you, just as they do on Twitter, 'like' what they see (on Periscope with a heart icon) and (in most cases) *comment on what you are showing or saying, and interact with you in real time*. Periscope is owned by Twitter and automatically tweets to all your Twitter followers when you start a show. On other services you have to do this manually.

Think of these apps as YouTube without the hassle of uploading: you can immediately be your own live TV station, broadcasting from wherever you are. News and content will never be the same.

Some of the attraction of these services is because of the general ephemeral nature of the streams: Periscopes are available to view for only 24 hours and Meerkats are never archived (although there are workaround hacks that enable you to keep your shows for longer). So there's an exclusivity of watching now, what other people can't see.

Periscope (because of its formal integration with Twitter) is the most used and perhaps the useful at the moment. Of course one of the other apps may be bought and run by, say, Facebook, which will open up lots of possibilities, but until then I'd suggest using Periscope (currently only on iPhones and Windows . . . The Android app is 'coming soon'. STR.EAM and tarsi work on the Android platforms).

For a great walk-through of how to set up Periscope, with lots of screen shots, click here: www.trafficgenerationcafe.com/periscope-tutorial/.

POSSIBLE USES OF LIVE STREAMING

Yes of course there will be lots of people who will (as the initial craze on Periscope showed) simply broadcast the scene of the inside of their fridge, or similar. But on a professional basis, there are lots of potential uses for live streaming for news reporters, community groups, sports clubs, councils, music venues, restaurants, celebrities, small businesses . . . In fact almost anyone.

A key thing is to remember the advantages of such streams: they are 'live' and 'video' and are broadcast to a (potentially) mass audience – so play to those strengths. There's perhaps little point showing things that would have been better if they had been recorded and edited and put online. Or if there's little or no movement or interaction (on Periscope you can see messages your viewers send you right on the screen as you look at the camera, so read those messages during the stream, answer your viewers' questions, thank them for their contributions). Another point to keep in mind is that whatever service you use, people can only watch you if they too have the app (or go to the app's website): the broadcasts aren't actually streamed through Twitter.

Since joining Periscope I have watched a few dozen broadcasts, and read as many blogs and reviews about the service as possible. And I have a background in live broadcasting and have written books on it, and on social media. Now I have come up with pages of ideas to make live-streaming work for people. Here are just a few for journalists whether you are in print, radio or TV . . . whether you are a professional or community reporter:

- Scheduled events

  - News conferences and openings – perhaps the events that the national or regional media won't report. If you are there to get an interview with one of the speakers after the event, why not stream the entire thing to democratise your coverage? Invite your followers to send you questions or observations about what's happening, that you can put to interviewees later.

  - Conferences and trade shows – interview the speakers, the participants and those attending. Get them to give you product demonstrations and answer FAQs sent in by viewers.

- Breaking news

  - En route to a story – if someone else is driving, you can stream your journey to the scene of a breaking event. Your viewers can see you get the latest information and start writing your report, work your way through potential road diversions, talk to police at the scene, set up your professional equipment and find people to interview.

  - At the story – while the camera crew is setting up why not 'rehearse' eye-witnesses by having them appear on your Periscope stream? Show the inside of the sat-truck and how the gear is set up. While you are waiting for your slot on the TV or radio, give your stream-viewers (the station's die-hard fans) the exclusive latest information on what's happened.

- For stories that happen when the 'broadcast' show is off air: reporters for NBC4 Los Angeles used Periscope and Meerkat to show a police car chase. You could even, with a bit of work, produce and present news bulletins on Periscope during the day when your scheduled bulletins are not scheduled. Or for newspapers which don't have bulletins, an intermittent Periscope channel showing different stories and interviews through the day (the *Oxford Mail* live-streamed the bomb squad detonating an old mortar shell).

- For eyewitness journalists at a breaking news event. News-gatherers can verify and collate what is seen at a location where their reporters can't get to. Periscope's geolocation feature – which Meerkat does not currently offer – will be particularly useful for reporters (although this is less specific than it was). Uniquely the Stringwire app – developed by US broadcaster NBC – allows a 'producer' to mix between several shots from different phones to create a 'TV-like' programme of best content, and it is that mixed-feed which is seen by viewers. The founders of Periscope say: 'What if you could see through the eyes of a protester in Ukraine?' Or, more simply, show views of serious weather from around your area through the use of the app by trusted stringers?

- Interviews
  - Most interviews are not live, they are pre-recorded and edited with the very best material used. Sometimes only a ten-second soundbite is taken from a ten-minute interview. Now you can show the full interview as it happens.

  - Showbiz interviews – the big star has come to town. Yes, you the reporter have lots of questions, but maybe your viewers have some great ones too. Stream the interview live and get them to post their questions on the screen for the celeb to answer straightaway. When they look at the camera and address their fan by name and answer their question, a bond is created because of your stream.

  - Private streams – use this facility to only allow certain people to see the stream you broadcast. That way you can run a competition where the winners get to ask the VIP questions and have them answered directly, one to one.

- Behind the scenes
  - So often, reporters get to go to places where the public can't. Now you can show them that view from behind the stage at the concert hall, or the chairman's box at the pitch, or the call centre at the police HQ. Have a walkthrough so your viewers feel as though they are there and

involved. Sky News, one of the broadcasters hosting the Battle for No 10 programme, used Periscope to give a behind-the-scenes look: Joe Tidy livestreamed the view from behind the camera and walked around the 'spin room', where journalists and broadcasters were analysing the night's events. He also used the chat and 'love heart' functions to encourage the 200 viewers to post questions, comments and reactions, keeping them engaged.

- Or maybe you can get somewhere where the public is allowed to go, but rarely does: what is the view from the worst seat in the house at the local theatre? One police force showed what it was like to be in one of their cells and got viewers to direct where the camera-person should go and show.

- Added value

  - Explainers – *The Economist* used Meerkat to explain UK deflation with their economics correspondent answering questions sent in by readers on Twitter, on a live stream.

  - Video-Blogging – You can appear on a live blog post streaming what would normally have been your written content: a live blog post during which people can interact with you asking questions and passing on comments on your reports.

- As a source for news

  - Fed up with not getting their point of view across, or press releases not being reported by the mainstream media, many companies, councils and sports teams may start using Periscope to get their messages out. They will be able to talk directly to people instead of going through a third party. A council could rebut political accusations with a live stream after telling local media to tune in. A sports team could announce their new signing live . . . showing the star being taken around their dressing room and putting their name on the dotted line on the contract. Reporters may have to follow these streams to find out what's going on.

We're always looking to give reporters any tool that will help them tell stories in more immediate and immersive ways. And these apps have encouraged many, and converted some, to become a broadcaster without expensive equipment.

Potential issues:

- Copyright issues – Could streams be banned in certain places? How? Could someone take your phone away from you?

  - Consider sports/football matches: broadcasters have paid for rights, but lower league clubs may welcome the coverage – although a stream video will be distant and poor, without a commentary, and be a drain on battery and data. NBA, NFL and MLB have policies that restrict both reporters and fans from live-streaming game action. The NBA says media are allowed to stream live press conferences and interviews to *their own websites*, but not to third-party platforms like Meerkat or Periscope. Aside from press conferences, the NBA also says that 'Non-Game Action Content' – which includes video taken at practice, interviews in the locker room, etc. – may not be live streamed. The MLB's media credential policy:

any video related to Games, captured within the ballpark, and carried online, must be limited to 120 seconds and cannot be carried live; (c) no live or taped audio or video is permitted to be captured from 45 minutes prior to a scheduled Game time until that Game has concluded; (d) a manager's pre-game interview or other content may not be transmitted live, and audio or video transmissions of such content may be transmitted online for no longer than 120 seconds; (e) a manager's post-game press conference may be captured via video or audio and cannot be carried live or online; and (f) audio or video interviews with players, Club personnel and baseball officials posted online may not be longer than 120 seconds in duration; provided, however, that the Bearer will have the limited, non-exclusive and non-transferable license to use on its own online distribution platform product or site for news coverage of the Game and other editorial purposes up to a total of 120 seconds of the audio and video identified above in subsections (b-f) about each Game.

- Certainly it is illegal to stream a movie as you watch it (although quite who would want to watch 90 minutes of a film out of focus, in portrait rather than landscape and with poor sound . . .?)

- Similarly, live streaming a concert performance potentially infringes the copyrights of multiple parties, including the artist, the label and the publisher. And the same goes for including music in your stream, even if it was incidental. So no 'record reviews' . . . and if you film inside say a shopping centre, and the background piped music is heard, you could get into trouble.

- Oh and be careful about the use of copyrighted logos or artwork too (it's not just music and moving pictures that are copyrighted).

- What if Brand A films a VIP at a red carpet event . . . but that VIP is contracted to appear for Brand B? (There is a precedent: actor Katherine Heigl's lawsuit against a US store which tweeted a picture of her shopping. It was a $6 million claim settled out of court. She said she had a right to know where her image was going to be used (www.adweek.com/prnewser/katherine-heigl-goes-litigious-over-duane-reade-twitpic/90576).

- What about streaming a school play for grandparents? What if the play was written by a teacher rather the script being professionally produced? What if it had been written by students?

- What about use of trademarked names? The Academy Award people strongly protect the use of the word 'Oscars'. Do most people know that?

- Privacy

  - If you're in a public place, like the street, the beach or a conference you have no reasonable expectation of privacy. Someone can take your picture, record or stream video of your activities and movements in public, and you wouldn't have much legal basis to complain about it. But remember what you may think as a public area may be private property: the bus is owned by a private company, an open space may be owned by a farmer, a shopping centre is not the same as a high street. Are you OK to film there?

  - A general view of a beach may be one thing. Showing semi-naked sunbathers, particularly if they are children, is another. The same goes for things like 'upskirting'. Consider whether your stream goes beyond recording to harassing or stalking, invasion of privacy, peeping and so on. Gratuitously showing nakedness, abuse etc. is obviously not allowed on these services.

  - What if you pull a live prank on a member of the public? They have a right not to be humiliated in public . . .

  - . . . and what if that prank goes wrong and the member of the public is physically hurt?

- Security issues

  - Such as people filming during a tour of the White House or Buckingham Palace.

- Defamation and contempt issues

  - Presenters who have no legal awareness, making slanderous remarks about people or products . . . or giving their views about ongoing court cases, or other legal issues such as naming children or sex abuse victims.

- Other issues

  - If companies and groups engage, perhaps they could make money from it? Certainly they'll get more publicity and promotion.

  - There is some spamming going on and offensive comments, but people are easy to block from having their comments appear on future shows.

  - Publicly available WiFi networks that could become more clogged given the data required for streaming.

Glossary of Terms Used in Digital and Multimedia Broadcasting

Many terms vary from country to country and we have tried to be as universal as possible.

Acoustic screen A mobile screen covered in sound-absorbing material which is used to shield a microphone from noise from another part of the studio, or to help 'deaden' a studio's acoustics.

Actuality/act Interviews or sounds recorded on location. In news programmes it is usually someone speaking for around 20 seconds. In features and magazine programmes it often means recorded material that isn't speech. In TV it is called sync.

Ad lib Talking without a script, possibly from bullet points, but in the main improvised.

Affiliate An independent TV or radio station that carries programmes of the network with which it has a contract.

AGC Automatic Gain Control, equipment which equalises the differences in volume, by automatically adjusting the levels to reduce dramatic changes.

Agency copy Story received from a news agency.

Analogue The traditional delivery of radio output, through an aerial. It is prone to interference and lacks the sound quality of digital.

Anchor (US) In North America, a newscaster fronting continuous 24-hour news or a single news programme. Presenter is the usual UK term.

Angle An item of information in a news story that a journalist chooses to emphasise. It may be giving the latest development in a story, or a local angle, emphasising the point of relevance of that story to a local audience.

ARC Aspect Ratio Converter is a device for converting pictures from the old 4 by 3 size and shape to widescreen 16 by 9, or the other direction.

Archive/file Usually a digital storehouse of previously broadcast material, which may be audio, pictures, stills, webpages and text.

Aspect ratio A way of defining the shape of the pictures by width and height. Old TV sets showed pictures which were 4 units wide and 3 units high. Now monitors show a wider image which is usually 16 units wide and 9 units high, making the image much wider. The same ratio applies to digital video cameras. See *Widescreen*.

Assignment   The designation of a story by an editor to a reporter.

Aston   Brand name for a type of caption generator. Words on the screen such as a reporter's name, or a location, or on a clip of a person speaking giving his or her name and sometimes a title.

Atmos   Atmosphere. General background noise like traffic, weather, nature.

Avid   Makers of computer-based digital editing equipment.

Back announcement (B/A, back anno)   A final sentence giving extra information to be read by the anchor or presenter at the end of a recorded item or report.

Backlight   Lamp shone behind interviewee to pick him/her out from background, eliminate shadows and highlight hair. See also *Key*, *Fill*.

Back projection   Where pictures are projected on to a screen behind the newsreader. Also known as CSO (colour separation overlay) and Chromakey.

Back timing   Adding together the durations of several programme elements and subtracting them from the time that they all need to have finished by, thereby working out what time they need to start.

Bed   As in 'music bed'. A piece of music (sometimes other audio such as natural noise) played under speech.

BGAN   Broadband Global Area Network. Satellite communications that can be used by journalists and crews in remote locations to send back sound and picture material from a portable terminal and dish.

Bi-directional mike   A microphone which will pick up sound in front and behind it.

Boom mike   Microphone held on a long telescopic boom manoeuvred by a sound technician.

Breaking news   (Spot Story). Any story that is happening right now.

Briefing sheet   A producer's job is to give the presenter all the information that they will, or might need to carry out the interview. This will be written onto a briefing sheet

Bulletin/update/cut in   News sequence that may be between two and five minutes, but can also be a report that interrupts another programme during breaking news.

Camcorder/digital video camera   Hand-held camera and recorder.

Cans   Slang for headphones.

Capacitor mike   Battery-operated mike, often of the tie-clip variety.

Carrier wave   Frequency wave which is modulated to carry a video or audio signal.

Catchline/slug/clipname   A one or two word name used to identify a story, for example, President/Israel/Floods/Plane Crash.

Character generator   Caption machine.

Charge coupled device   Unit that converts the picture coming through the lens into a television signal. It has individual light-sensitive sensors to make up each part of the picture (pixels).

Check calls   Regular newsroom calls or messages to the emergency services.

Chromakey (colour separation overlay, CSO)   See *Back projection*.

Clean feed   Sending the on-air feed of the programme being broadcast, down a line, for example to a radio car contributor, so they can hear and respond to their verbal cue.

Clickbait   Online content aimed at getting attention and attracting visitors to a particular web page. Particularly for sensational news items.

Clip   See *Newsclip*.

Clock start   A precise timing for an event or occasion – such as joining up with the rest of the network.

CNN   Cable News Network.

Commentary booth   Small booth in which the reporter records the narrative (or track) for a news item.

Contact   Any source of news information.

Convergence   The merging of mass communication outlets (print, television, radio, websites, together with the portable and interactive technologies) allowing stories to be told through a variety of media.

Cool Edit Pro   Software for editing digital audio.

Copy story   News story with no accompanying audio or visuals.

Correspondent or 'corr'   A journalist who is an expert in a particular subject

Coverage   The amount of time and resources given to telling a story.

Crane   A small piece of equipment in a studio or a vehicle on location, comprising a movable arm or boom (generally hydraulic) that moves a camera, or a platform on which are a camera and a crew.

Crawl   The written information, such as news headlines, that runs (crawls) across the bottom of a TV screen

Crossfade   The overlapping of one sound with another.

Crossing the line   A term in television to describe what you have done if you position a camera on either side of a line of action or eye line. If someone is facing in one direction in the first shot they appear to have turned around in the next shot.

Cue   Introduction to a report (also called the link or intro). But also an instruction to a presenter to start and stop speaking. This may be given verbally, by gestures or in writing. See also *In-cue and out-cue*.

Cut   See *Newsclip*.

Cutaway   The insertion of a shot in a picture sequence which is used to mask an edit.

DAB (digital audio broadcasting)   Transmission system offering digital quality audio.

DAT (digital audio tape)   Matchbox-sized digital recording medium.

Dead air   Silence on-air due to equipment malfunction, such as a playout system which has crashed or a fault with the transmitter.

Debrief   The meeting after the programme during which those involved discuss how the programme went, what worked, what didn't work and what to do differently next time.

Decibel (db)   Unit of loudness.

Delay   A recorded delay of several seconds in playing back a 'live' phone-in programme to trap obscene calls.

Digital recording   The storage of sound and/or pictures which have been encoded as a series of numbers. Playback translates those numbers back without the noise or distortion of conventional (analogue) recording.

Digital workflow   End-to-end digital production process. Usually a process from idea and initial capture of material in the field or the studio, through production, post-production, transmission, multiple-platform use and archiving.

Directivity pattern (pickup)   Area over which a microphone will pick up sound.

Disco, short for discussion   The abbreviation for a discussion in the studio.

Dissolve   Edit term where one picture is faded out and another is faded in simultaneously.

DOA   Dead on arrival. Emergency services jargon for a victim who has died either before help could arrive or before the ambulance could reach the hospital.

Donut   In which the presenter in the studio hands over to the reporter on location, who describes the situation and interviews a guest before handing back to the presenter in the studio.

Doco   Pronounced 'docco'. Abbreviation for 'documentary'.

Drive-time   Radio jargon for the period during radio listening when a substantial part of the audience is travelling in cars – early morning, early evening.

Drone   A small remote-controlled aircraft fitted with a camera for getting shots that would be difficult or impossible to film from the ground.

Dub   Simply to copy audio from one source to another, usually, though not always ones of different types. That is possibly from one minidisk to another, but more often from, say, a digital to analogue or vice versa.

Dupe   Short for duplicate, a copy of a radio or TV programme.

DVCam™   A professional version of the DV format developed by Sony.

DVC Pro™   A professional version of the DV format developed by Panasonic.

Earpiece   Device used by presenter to listen to instructions from the studio control room.

Edit controller   The heart of a computerised editing system which is programmed to control the precise location of each edit.

Embargo   'Not to be released until . . .' date on a news release. Device intended to control the publication date of an item of information.

ENPS   Electronic News Production System. Powerful computer network developed by AP to allow any journalist in a news organisation to call up story material on demand. ENPS can also link to other systems.

Equalisation   Improving audio quality by altering the frequency characteristics.

Fade out   1. Where a picture fades out, usually to black or to white. 2. Gradually bringing down the volume of an audio signal until it disappears.

Feature   Usually the pre-recorded, packaged report of voices and other audio that tells a story. Can also be the term to describe a live item in the programme such as a competition, although not 'fixed furniture' such as news and travel.

Feedback   The process that happens when the sound from a speaker is fed through a microphone, which is then heard out of the same speaker.

Field producer   The producer of a news story who is on location (in the field) rather than at the TV station.

Fill lamp   Casting a soft light to fill in shadows. See also *Backlight*, *Key*.

Float   The pictures shown on screen when a presenter is talking or interviewing a guest, which illustrate what is being talked about (they are floated over the voice of the presenter). The sequence is sometimes called an OOV (pron: 'oove'), which is short for *Out Of Vision* or underlay, which is shortened to ulay.

Fly-on-the-wall (Vérite)   Documentary style unmediated by reporter or narrator. The aim is to have the camera watching the action unnoticed, like a fly on the wall.

Futures file   File in which stories and news events which are known to be happening on a certain date are placed, so that coverage may be planned in advance.

FX   Shorthand for sound effects.

General view (GV)   Camera shot showing an entire scene to establish location.

Genny   Slang. Short for 'generator' which provides power backup for a broadcast station or on set.

Glitch   A malfunction of mechanical, electrical, or electronic equipment.

Go   The direction to start an item ('go theme').

Graphics   Sometimes shortened to Gfx: words, diagrams, maps, etc. that appear on screen.

Handling noise   Unwanted clicks and sounds picked up by a microphone as a result of handling and moving it.

Hard news   Newsroom term for story of importance about events of significance.

Hard news formula   A hard news story will cover most of the basic facts by asking the questions, who? what? where? when? why? and how?

Headline   Short summary of a news story given at the start or end of a bulletin or a website, or grouped with other headlines in lieu of a longer bulletin. Also known as highlights or summaries. See also *Teaser*.

High definition (HD)   High quality images of many thousands of pixels in picture capture or transmission. Can also work with computer displays.

Highlight   See *Headline*.

Holding copy   The first version of a story left by a reporter to be run in his/her absence while he/she is out of the newsroom getting further information on that story.

Human interest   A feature about a person or personality with colourful details and emotional appeal.

Ident   Piece of recorded music played to introduce or identify a particular programme, feature or presenter. Also known as stab, jingle, sounder.

In-cue and out-cue   These are instructions to say when a report begins and ends. The in-cue is the first few words of that report, and the out-cue the last few words. The in-cue is a useful check that the right report is being played, and the out-cue tells presenters, directors and technical operators when the report is finishing.

Ingest   Copying media onto a server system. Sometimes also capture or digitise.

Insert   See *Newsclip*.

Intro (Introduction)   1. The first, audience-winning and most important paragraph of a news story, giving the main angle of the story and the central facts. 2. The introduction (cue or lead) to a report or recorded item. Also known as the headline sentence.

In vision (IV)   Instruction on script to indicate presenter should be on camera at that point.

Jingle   See *Ident*.

Join in progress   When a programme starts broadcasting coverage of an event which has already started, for example a live news or sports event.

Jump cut   An edit in a sequence of shots which has the subject jerking from one position to another.

Key words   One or two words which sum up the most important point of a news story.

Kicker   See *Tailpiece*.

Lead   First item in a news programme or the written cue/link/intro to a news item or report.

LED   Light-emitting diode. Low-powered light used for electronic displays (on/off indicators, level meters, etc.).

Level   The volume of a source, such as music or a voice. It must usually peak (depending on the desired effect and the other sources being mixed) between 5 and 6 on the meter.

Lighting grid   Construction suspended from the ceiling of a studio to support the lights.

Links   Narrative linking or bridging interviews in a report, summarising or giving additional information. See also *Package*.

Links vehicle   Mobile vehicle used as a platform for a transmitter.

Lip mic   A noise-excluding mic used when lots of background noise is present, for example during a football match commentary.

Live Real Audio   Internet radio system, making it possible to download radio programmes onto a computer.

Lower third   Caption or super in the lower third of the picture.

Marking-up   Marking a story with important details, such as who wrote it and when and the catchline.

Menu   Collection of tasters at the start of a programme giving forthcoming attractions.

MD (Mini-Disc)   Digital recording medium using miniature compact disc.

Mixer   The main desk in a studio also called a 'desk', 'console' or 'panel'. Various sources arrive at the mixer, each with their own channel (volume control) to allow their sound to be balanced.

Multi-angled story   One which carries a number of different angles on the same story.

Networked   A live programme which is broadcast in several stations in the same group at the same time

News agency   A company which finds, writes and distributes news material to many journalists, such as Reuters, Associated Press (AP) and Agence France Presse (AFP).

News agency wires (or 'the wires')   The latest news stories written by journalists from agencies as they appear on the newsroom computer system.

News belt   A round-up of short news stories, which themselves may be 'nibs' ('news in brief').

Newsbooth   Small studio where bulletins are presented on air.

Newsclip (cut, insert)   Short extract of an interview to illustrate a story.

Newsflash/cut in   Interruption of normal programming to give brief details of an urgent breaking story. Continuous news channels also refer to breaking news.

Newsmix   A news summary comprising a mixture of local and national news.

News release   Publicity handout either from a website or on paper from any organisation or public relations company.

Newsroom conference/meeting/briefing/planner   Journalists gather, sometimes more than once a day, to talk about what stories to run in the news and how they should be covered on all media platforms.

Newsroom diary (prospects)   A list of all the known possible stories and news events that are taking place at a particular moment in time. Also usually has names of who is on shift and when and where.

Noise reduction   The electronic reduction of interference induced by the transmission system.

Non-linear editing   Editing out of sequence, afforded by digital storage of audio and video data. Segments of sound or pictures can be cut and pasted like words in a word-processor. This offers greater flexibility than linear editing, where sounds or pictures once had to be assembled in order.

OB   Outside broadcast.

Obscenity button (profanity button)   Switch used for taking a programme instantly out of delay to prevent an obscene caller from being heard on the air.

OFCOM   The UK regulatory body for all telecommunications, including radio and TV.

Off-mic   The term used when someone deliberately or unintentionally is picked up by a microphone without them speaking directly into it. It has the effect of reducing the volume of that voice and also making it sound thin and hollow

Omni-directional mike   Microphone with circular pickup pattern.

Open-ended   A programme with no specific end time, usually used in the event of breaking news or an emergency

Opt-in and opt-out   1. The process of switching between local and network transmissions. Opting-in occurs when a local station goes over to a live network programme and opting-out takes place when it returns to its own programmes. 2. Opt-out is an early point at which a report may be brought to an end.

Outcue   Prearranged verbal cue to show that a tape or a bulletin has come to an end. A standard outcue is the regular ending to a voice report, such as 'John Smith, New York'.

Out of vision (OOV), also called underlay   A TV news item where the pictures are seen by the viewer and the presenter does the (hopefully) matching script but he or she is out of vision.

Out-takes   Discarded material edited from a report or from raw sound and pictures.

Package   A complete broadcasting news report composed of edited interview clips as well as any combination of natural sound/pictures/graphics/reporter's piece to camera or reporter at the scene – all linked by a reporter script.

Peak programme meter (PPM)   Meter for measuring peak signal level. Its specially damped action prevents flickering and produces a steady reading.

Phono   Report or interview made by telephone. Also a type of lead used to connect one piece of equipment to another.

Photoshop   Image processing software used for print and screen design work.

Piece-to-camera (PTC) or stand-upper; stand-up   Information given by a reporter on location and in vision. Unlike the Live Link the PTC is usually the definition for a pre-recorded reporter piece.

Pixel/pixels   Tiny dots which make up a picture on screens and printouts. Term originates from 'picture element'.

Pre-fade   Listening to an item without playing it on air. Used to check levels, cue music and check the signal.

Question and answer (Q&A); also known as Two-Way   When a reporter is interviewed on air about a story he/she has been covering, often during breaking news.

Reaction shot   A video recording of the response of a person to action or words.

Remote studio Small studio some distance from the station's main building where guests who cannot make it in to the station can be interviewed or join a discussion. It can be linked to the main station by satellite or cable, permitting studio quality sound and pictures.

Rifle mike (gun mike) Directional mike for picking up sound at a distance.

Recording of (off) transmission (ROT) Recording of the output. It can also refer to watching online a programme that has been missed by the listener or viewer, Watch Again/Listen Again.

Rosr (US) 'Radio on-scene report' – a reporter at a news scene.

Running order The planned order of items in a programme.

Running to time The phrase used when a programme or report is on target to finish at a certain time.

Running story/rolling story One that is developing and constantly changing, throwing up new information that requires frequent revision and updates.

Rushes Raw sound and pictures as they come out of the camera and before any editing. The term originates from film production, when the film needed to be processed in a 'rush' so it could be checked before the actors and crew could be sent home.

Scanner 1. Radio which automatically tunes in to broadcasts by the police and emergency services. 2. Outside broadcast vehicle. 3. Caption scanner.

Scoop An exclusive story

Scrambler Device for scrambling satellite TV signals so only authorised viewers equipped with an unscrambler can receive them.

Self-opping When a presenter operates his/her own control desk without technical assistance.

Shoot When a reporter and camera person are out recording a story, they are 'on a shoot'.

Shot sizes Various names or acronyms given to TV news shots. For example: VLS/Very long shot/wide Shot; LS/Long shot; CU/Close up.

Signposting In a news programme, this means comprehensively headlining and forward trailing the programme to keep up audience interest. During a story, it means highlighting the central theme of the story at the start, amplifying that theme in a logical manner, repeating key points where necessary, and pointing the story forward at the end.

Slug See *Catchline*.

Sound-bite (grab) Portion of an interview or snatch of actuality selected for screening.

Sounder (jingle, stab) See *Ident*.

Sound on tape/SOT Even if it's on digital media, it's called SOT, and generally used so a presenter can aim to stop talking in time for the SOT.

Spot story (US) An item of breaking news, such as a fire or an air crash.

Stab (or 'sting') Short, emphatic jingle. See *Ident*.

Standard outcue (payoff)   See *Outcue*.

Standby   A person or item ready to be used as a substitute, usually on an emergency basis. So, 'standby weather' (a script a presenter can read if for some reason a pre-recorded weather report fails) and 'standby guest' (someone available for interview should another person become unavailable).

Stand-upper (stand up)   See *Piece-to-camera*.

Stock footage   Archive shots of common events used to help tell a story e.g. passengers and scenes from a local airport

Stringer   Freelance correspondent.

Summary   1. See *Headline*. 2. News programme or bulletin (Update/Cut In) rounding up the most important news events.

Super (caption)   As in superimpose. Title or caption superimposed or digitally generated on the picture. Also can be called an Aston.

Switching pause   Short pause in transmission before and after the network bulletin to permit local stations to opt-in and out cleanly.

Syndicated material   Recordings sent out to radio stations by PR and advertising agencies to promote a company or product.

Tailpiece/kicker/ . . . and finally   Some channels have a style format which likes a light-hearted story at end of bulletin or newscast.

Teaser, taster   Snappy, one-line headline, usually at start of programme or sequence designed to tease the audience into wanting to find out more. May include a snatch of actuality.

Telephone balance unit (TBU)   Device used in the making of recorded telephone interviews. Permits interviewer to use a studio microphone and balances the levels of the two voices.

Teletext   Process for transmitting written and graphic information on to TV using the spare lines of a TV signal.

Timecode   Numbers, in a series of four. These are recorded on the pictures but not as part of the picture although they are often displayed superimposed over the pictures on a monitor. The numbers, left to right, represent hours, minutes, seconds and frames. The basic function is to help you log pictures and clips, and control the editing process.

Timeline   A representation of the story, in a diagram form, displayed on the editing monitor of a digital edit suite. It shows where sound and pictures have been placed on a specific video or sound track.

Tip-off   Call from a stringer or member of the audience to let the station know that a story is breaking. See also *UGC*.

Toss   A short handover or 'throw' from one news presenter to another. A 'split story toss' is a reading of part of a news report by one person and the rest of the cue by another.

Touchscreen studio   A studio where all the equipment is controlled electronically by touching part of the screen of a computer.

Trail (or promo)   Telling the audience about items which are to follow.

TX   Shorthand for transmission.

UGC   User Generated Content. When members of the public send a station pictures and/or sound of a breaking news event. Sometimes also called citizen journalism or eyewitness news.

Umbrella story   A single story incorporating a number of similar items under one banner. See also *Multi-angled story*.

Uni-directional mike   Microphone which responds mainly to sounds directly in front of it.

Vérite   Actuality programme or feature made without accompanying narrative or commentary.

Video wall/big wall/big screen   Images, including graphics/captions and clips of interviews which are behind and/or beside a presenter or reporter in the studio.

Visuals   The visual element of a TV report that goes beyond moving pictures/sound. Can include video wall, graphics or even objects held by a presenter.

VJ or Video Journalist   Reporter with a digital video camera who shoots, interviews, edits and scripts.

VOD   Video On Demand lets users to select and watch video content over a network as part of an interactive television system.

Voice over   Commentary recorded over pictures by an unseen reader. See also *OOV*.

Voice report (voicer)   Details and explanation of a story by a reporter or correspondent. More expansive than a copy story. Permits a change of voice from the newsreader.

Vox pop   Latin 'vox populi' or 'voice of the people'. Refers to street interviews conducted to poll public opinion. Sometimes just called man in the street interviews.

VU meter   Volume unit meter. Imprecise meter for monitoring recording and playback levels.

Waveform   Digital speech is displayed on a computer in the form of zig-zag waves of sound. These can be edited on-screen.

Widescreen   The size (shape) of many screens, where the ratio of width to height is 16 units wide to 9 units high. It is said to have an aspect ratio of 16 by 9, often written as 16 x 9. It replaced the older 4 by 3 ratio.

Wildtrack   Recording of ambient sound for dubbing later as background to a report.

Wipe   Crossing from one picture to another, giving the impression that one is wiping the other off the screen. A transition from one shot to another without giving the viewer a jolt.

Wire service/wires/agency   News agencies send raw copy and stories out to newsrooms.

Woodshedding   Marking a script to indicate pauses and voice inflections/as with a slash mark for a pause/a double slash for a long pause // an underline for <u>emphasis</u> and a double underline for <u>heavier emphasis</u>.

Index